BRITAIN

IN THE

VOLUME II
1939–1970

EDITED BY
LAWRENCE BUTLER AND
HARRIET JONES

INSTITUTE OF
CONTEMPORARY BRITISH
HISTORY

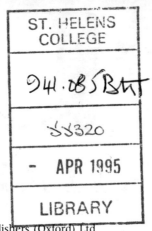
Heinemann Educational
a division of Heinemann Publishers (Oxford) Ltd
Halley Court, Jordan Hill, Oxford OX2 8EJ

OXFORD LONDON EDINBURGH MADRID
ATHENS BOLOGNA PARIS MELBOURNE
SYDNEY AUCKLAND SINGAPORE TOKYO
IBADAN NAIROBI HARARE GABORONE
PORTSMOUTH NH (USA)

© Lawrence Butler and Harriet Jones at The Institute of Contemporary British History

ISBN 0 435 31925 6

Also available in hardback ISBN 0 435 31923 X

First published 1995

98 97 96 95
10 9 8 7 6 5 4 3 2 1

British Library Cataloguing in Publication Data is available from the British Library
on request

Designed by Jim Turner

Cover design by Aricot Vert Design

Front cover: *Friday Night* by Ruskin Spear. CSO Contemporary Art Collection/Mary
Spear

Printed in England by Clays Ltd, St Ives plc

Other titles in the series include:

Britain in the Twentieth Century Vol. I, 1900–1939   ISBN 0 435 31924 8 (softback)
ISBN 0 435 31922 1 (hardback)
ISBN 0 435 31926 4 (3 Pack)

Modern European History 1871–1975   ISBN 0 435 31928 0 (softback)
ISBN 0 435 31929 9 (hardback)
ISBN 0 435 31930 2 (3 Pack)

Contents

Acknowledgements

Grateful acknowledgement is made to the following sources for permission to reproduce material in this book.

DOCUMENTS IN CHAPTER 1

1.1: *Punch*. **1.2** and **1.4**: Crown copyright, reproduced with the permission of the Controller of HMSO. **1.5**: © D. Low, *Evening Standard* / Solo Syndication and Literacy Agency Ltd / Centre for the Study of Cartoons and Caricature, University of Kent at Canterbury. **1.6**: Imperial War Museum, London. **1.7**: Crown copyright is reproduced with the permission of the Controller of HMSO. **1.9**: Reproduced by permission of Hodder & Stoughton Ltd. **1.10–1.12**: Crown copyright, reproduced with the permission of the Controller of HMSO. **1.13**: © Times Newspapers Ltd, 1944. **1.14**: Gladwyn Jebb, *The Memoirs of Lord Gladwyn*, Weidenfeld and Nicolson Ltd, 1972. **1.15**: Crown copyright is reproduced with the permission of the Controller of HMSO. **1.16**: *Documents on Australian Foreign Policy 1937-49, Vol V*. Commonwealth of Australia copyright reproduced by permission. **1.18** and **1.19**: Crown copyright, reproduced with the permission of the Controller of HMSO. **1.20**: Reproduced by permission of Hodder & Stoughton Ltd. **1.21**:Crown copyright is reproduced with the permission of the Controller of HMSO.

DOCUMENTS IN CHAPTER 2

2.1: By permission of Norman Longmate. **2.2**: By permission of the Central Statistical Office. **2.3** and **2.4**: Imperial War Museum, London. **2.5**: Crown copyright is reproduced with the permission of the Controller of HMSO. **2.6**: J.M. Keynes, *How to Pay for the War (Vol XXII, The Complete Writings of John Maynard Keynes)*, 1940, by permission of Macmillan Ltd. **2.7**: Crown copyright is reproduced with the permission of the Controller of HMSO. **2.8**: B. Pimlott (ed.), *The Political Diary of Hugh Dalton, 1918-49, 1945-60*, Cape, 1986. **2.10**: By permission of Lord Halifax. **2.11**: © D. Low / *Evening Standard*, Solo Syndication and Literacy Agency Ltd /

Centre for the Study of Cartoons and Caricature, University of Kent at Canterbury. **2.12**: Sir J. Wheeler-Bennet (ed.), *Action This Day: Working with Churchill*, Macmillan, 1968. **2.13**: The estate of the late Sonia Brownell Orwell and Martin Secker & Warburg. **2.14**: J. B. Priestley, *Postscripts*, William Heinemann Ltd, 1940. **2.15**: By permission of IPC Magazines Ltd. **2.17**: Conservative Political Centre. **2.18**: Reproduced by permission of Hamish Hamilton Ltd. **2.20**: Reprinted by permission of David Higham Associates Ltd. **2.21** and **2.22**: F.W.S. Craig, *British General Election Manifestos, 1900-1974*, 1975, by permission of Macmillan Ltd. **2.23**: © Times Newspapers Ltd, 1945. **2.24**: Reprinted by permission of David Higham Associates Ltd. **2.25**: Conservative Political Centre / Bodleian Library, Oxford. **2.26**: D. Butler and G. Butler (eds), *British Political Facts, 1900-1985*, by permission of Macmillan Ltd, © David Butler 1986.

DOCUMENTS IN CHAPTER 3

3.1: Barbara Castle, *Fighting All The Way*, Macmillan, 1993. **3.2**: Reginald Maudling, *Memoirs*, Sidgwick and Jackson, 1978. **3.3**: Lord Morrison, *Herbert Morrison: An Autobiography*, Odhams Press, 1960. Reprinted by permission of Reed Consumer Books. **3.4**: Clement Attlee, *As It Happened*, William Heinemann Ltd, 1954. **3.5**: © D. Low / *Evening Standard*, Solo Syndication and Literacy Agency Ltd / Centre for the Study of Cartoons and Caricature, University of Kent at Canterbury. **3.7** and **3.9**: Crown copyright, reproduced with the permission of the Controller of HMSO. **3.10**: By permission of the British Iron and Steel Federation. **3.12**: Reproduced by permission of Penguin Books Ltd. **3.13**: Reprinted by permission of the Peters Fraser and Dunlop Group Ltd. **3.14**: Reproduced by permission of Hamish Hamilton Ltd. **3.15**: H. Macmillan, *Tides of Fortune 1945–55*, Macmillan, 1969. **3.16**: *News Chronicle* / Solo Syndication and Literacy Agency Ltd / Centre for the Study of Cartoons and Caricature, University of Kent at Canterbury. **3.17**: © D. Low / *Evening Standard* / Solo Syndication and Literacy Agency

Ltd / Centre for the Study of Cartoons and Caricature, University of Kent at Canterbury. **3.18** and **3.19**: F.W.S. Craig, *British General Election Manifestos, 1900-1974*, 1975, by permission of Macmillan Ltd. **3.20**: Conservative Political Centre / Bodleian Library, Oxford. **3.21**: D. Butler and G. Butler (eds), *British Political Facts, 1900–1985*, by permission of Macmillan Ltd, © David Butler 1986. **3.23** and **3.24**: F.W.S. Craig, *British General Election Manifestos, 1900–1974*, 1975, by permission of Macmillan Ltd. **3.25**: Conservative Political Centre / Bodleian Library, Oxford. **3.26**: D. Butler and G. Butler (eds), *British Political Facts, 1900–1985*, by permission of Macmillan Ltd, © David Butler 1986.

DOCUMENTS IN CHAPTER 4

4.1: Crown copyright is reproduced with the permission of the Controller of HMSO. **4.4**: Reprinted by permission of David Higham Associates Ltd. **4.5–4.8**: Crown copyright, reproduced with the permission of the Controller of HMSO. **4.9**: D. Butler and G. Butler (eds), British Political Facts, 1900–1985, by permission of Macmillan Ltd, © David Butler 1986. **4.11**: Lord Citrine, *Two Careers*, Hutchinson, 1967. **4.13**: © 1989 Edwin Plowden. Reproduced by permission of Curtis Brown Group Ltd, London. **4.15**: D. Butler and G. Butler (eds), *British Political Facts, 1900–1985*, by permission of Macmillan Ltd, © David Butler 1986 / H. Pelling, *A History of British Trade Unionism*, Penguin, 1976. **4.16**: *Punch*. **4.17**: Michael Stewart, *Life and Labour: An Autobiography*, Sidgwick and Jackson, 1980. **4.19**: Crown copyright is reproduced with the permission of the Controller of HMSO. **4.20**: Crown copyright is reproduced with the permission of the Controller of IIMSO.

DOCUMENTS IN CHAPTER 5

5.1 and **5.2**: Crown copyright, reproduced with the permission of the Controller of HMSO. **5.3**: Reproduced with permission of Curtis Brown Ltd, London on behalf of the Estate of Sir Winston S. Churchill. © The Estate of Sir Winston S. Churchill. **5.4– 5.8**: Crown copyright, reproduced with the permission of the Controller of HMSO. **5.9**: Reproduced by permission of the Royal Institute of International Affairs. **5.10–5.14**: Crown copyright, reproduced with the permission of the Controller of HMSO. **5.15**: D. Butler and G. Butler (eds), *British Political Facts, 1900–1985*, by permission of Macmillan Ltd, © David Butler 1986. **5.16**: Crown copyright is reproduced with the permission of the Controller of HMSO.

DOCUMENTS IN CHAPTER 6

6.1 and **6.2**:Crown copyright, reproduced with the permission of the Controller of HMSO. **6.4**: Express Newspapers plc / Centre for the Study of Cartoons and Caricature, University of Kent at Canterbury. **6.5**: D. Butler and G. Butler (eds), *British Political Facts, 1900–1985*, by permission of Macmillan Ltd., © David Butler 1986. **6.7**: Conservative Political Centre. **6.8**: By permission of David Butler. **6.9**: © Times Newspapers Ltd, 1957. **6.10**: C. A. R. Crosland, *The Future of Socialism*, Cape, 1956. **6.11**: By permission of the Labour Party. **6.12**: By permission of *New Left Review*. **6.13**: © Mirror Group Newspapers. **6.14**: Reproduced by permission of Hodder & Stoughton Ltd. **6.16**: By permission of the TUC. **6.17**: By permission of Blackwell Publishers. **6.18**:Crown copyright is reproduced with the permission of the Controller of HMSO. **6.20**: Reproduced by permission of Penguin Books Ltd. **6.21**: Crown copyright is reproduced with the permission of the Controller of HMSO.

DOCUMENTS IN CHAPTER 7

7.1: Reproduced by permission of Hodder & Stoughton Ltd. **7.2**: D. Butler and G. Butler (eds), *British Political Facts, 1900–1985*, by permission of Macmillan Ltd, © David Butler 1986. **7.3**: © *The Observer*. **7.4**: R.R. James, *Anthony Eden*, Weidenfeld and Nicolson Ltd, 1986. **7.5**: *Punch*. **7.6** and **7.7**: Conservative Political Centre. **7.9**: Crown copyright is reproduced with the permission of the Controller of HMSO. **7.11**: Solo Syndication and Literacy Agency Ltd / Centre for the Study of Cartoons and Caricature, University of Kent at Canterbury. **7.12**: Conservative Political Centre. **7.13**: © *The Spectator*. **7.14**: Michael Foot, *Aneurin Bevan: A Biography, Vol II, 1945-1960*, Davis Poynter, an imprint of HarperCollins Publishers Ltd. **7.15**: © *The Economist*, 13 February 1954. **7.16**: Philip M. Williams, *The Diary of Hugh Gaitskell*, Cape, 1981. **7.17**: Reproduced by permission of Hamish Hamilton Ltd. **7.18**: Conservative Political Centre / Bodleian Library, Oxford. **7.19**: Reproduced by permission of Penguin Books Ltd. **7.20** and **7.21**: By permission of the Labour Party. **7.23**: By permission of the House of Commons Library. **7.24**: Crown copyright is reproduced with the permission of the Controller of HMSO. **7.25**: By permission of the Labour Party. **7.26**: Crown copyright is reproduced with the permission of the Controller of HMSO. **7.27**: By permission of David Butler. **7.28**: By permission of *Private Eye*. **7.29**: D. Butler and G. Butler (eds), *British Political Facts, 1900–1985*, by permission of Macmillan Ltd, © David Butler 1986. **7.30**: Crown copyright is reproduced with the permission of the Controller of HMSO. **7.31**: © The *Sunday Telegraph* Ltd, 1962. **7.32**: © Times Newspapers Ltd, 1963. **7.33**: © *The Spectator*. **7.34**: By permission of the Institute of Contemporary British History. **7.35**: By permission of the Labour Party. **7.36**: D. Butler and G. Butler (eds), *British Political Facts, 1900–1985*, by permission of Macmillan Ltd.

DOCUMENTS IN CHAPTER 8

8.1: By permission of Pluto Press. **8.2–8.6**: Crown copyright, reproduced with the permission of the Controller of HMSO. **8.8–8.10**: Crown copyright, reproduced with the permission of the Controller of HMSO. **8.11**: Evelyn Shuckburgh, *Descent to Suez: Diaries 1951-56*, Weidenfeld and Nicolson, 1986. **8.13** and **8.14**: Crown copyright, reproduced with the permission of the Controller of HMSO. **8.15**: K. Kyle, *Suez*, Weidenfeld and Nicolson, 1991. **8.16**: Crown copyright is reproduced with the permission of the Controller of HMSO. **8.17**: © *The New Statesman*.

DOCUMENTS IN CHAPTER 9

9.1: A. Graham and A. Seldon (eds), *Government and Economies in the Postwar World*, Routledge, 1990. **9.3**: © Times Newspapers Ltd, 1964. **9.4**: James Callaghan, *Time and Chance*. By permission of Harper Collins Publishers Ltd. **9.5**: *Punch*. **9.6**: By permission of Susan Crosland. **9.10**: Roy Jenkins, *A Life at the Centre*, Macmillan, 1991. **9.12**: James Callaghan, *Time and Chance*. By permission of Harper Collins Publishers Ltd. **9.16**: Reprinted by permission of David Higham Associates Ltd. **9.19**: Crown copyright is reproduced with the permission of the Controller of HMSO. **9.21**: By permission of the Institute of Contemporary British History.

DOCUMENTS IN CHAPTER 10

10.1: Solo Syndication and Literacy Agency Ltd / Centre for the Study of Cartoons and Caricature, University of Kent at Canterbury. **10.2**: Cecil King, *The Cecil King Diary, 1965-70*, Cape, 1970. **10.3**: Conservative Political Centre. **10.4**: D. Butler and G. Butler (eds), *British Political Facts, 1900–1985*, by permission of Macmillan Ltd, © David Butler 1986. **10.5**: © Tony Benn 1987. Reproduced by permission of Curtis Brown London Ltd on behalf of the author. **10.6**: Reproduced by permission of Hamish Hamilton Ltd. **10.8**: By permission of the Institute of Contemporary British History. **10.11**: © *Daily Sketch* / Solo Syndication and Literacy Agency Ltd. **10.14**: © The *Telegraph*, plc, London, 1969. **10.19**: Reproduced by permission of Hamish Hamilton Ltd. **10.20**: © Times Newspapers Ltd, 1970. **10.21**: Conservative Political Centre / Bodleian Library, Oxford.

DOCUMENTS IN CHAPTER 11

11.2 and **11.3**: By permission of Blackwell Publishers. **11.5**: Mary Evans Picture Library. **11.6**: By permission of the Labour Party. **11.7–11.11**: Crown copyright, reproduced with the permission of the Controller of HMSO. **11.13**: A.N. Porter and A.J. Stockwell, *British Imperial Policy and Decolonisation, 1938-64, Vol. 2: 1951-64*, 1989, by permission of Macmillan Ltd. **11.17**:© The *Telegraph*, plc, London, 1966. **11.18**: Reproduced by permission of Michael Joseph Ltd. **11.19**: Reproduced by permission of Hamish Hamilton Ltd. **11.21**: Reproduced by permission of David Higham Associates Ltd.

Every effort has been made to contact copyright holders. Any omissions or errors will be rectified in subsequent printings if notice is given to the publisher.

Preface

THE Institute of Contemporary British History (ICBH) was founded in 1986 to promote the study of contemporary British history in schools and universities and to disseminate fresh scholarly research into Britain's recent past. We are an educational charity which survives on research grants, sales of publications and corporate sponsorship; we receive no public sector grants. The documentary reader project has been made possible through a major grant from the Leverhulme Trust, and the volume editors would particularly like to thank that organisation for its generous sponsorship. We would also like to thank Blackwell Scientific Publications Ltd and MITAC (UK) Ltd for donating computer software and equipment without which our work would have been far more tedious.

We have also depended upon the goodwill and support of a number of individuals and institutions, without which a project of this magnitude would not have been possible. The invaluable encouragement and advice of both A-level examiners and teachers, in particular Alan Midgley, W.O. Simpson, Michael Wells, R. Peacock, Anthony Seldon and Wayne Birks, has been of great help to us. Dr Sarah Street, and her successor, Martin Maw, at the Conservative Party Archives have helped us to locate much unpublished graphic material. Jane Day, at the University of Kent Cartoon Archive, has helped us with many inquiries. We would also like to thank the staffs of the British Library in Bloomsbury and in Colindale, the University of London Library and the House of Commons Library. The staff of the Public Record Office have helped us immeasurably with their usual efficiency and courtesy. The Photograph and Art Departments of the Imperial War Museum have kindly allowed us to reproduce items from their collections.

We have attempted to keep abreast of new historiographical debates, and we owe a debt of thanks to a number of academic specialists, including Dr Stephen Ashton, John Barnes, Dr Stuart Ball, Dr Kathleen Burk, Dr David Butler, Dr Richard Cockett, Dr Chris Cook, Dr Lewis Johnman, Dr Wolfram Kaiser, Peter Rose and Professor John Young. Professor Peter Hennessy generously made available to us his unparalleled knowledge of official records for this period. Special thanks are due to Anthony Gorst, whose continuing encouragement and guidance have helped to ensure the completion of the project.

Finally, we would like to thank our colleagues here at the Institute for their unflagging support: Dr Peter Catterall, Dr Brian Brivati, Virginia Preston, Matthew Elliot, Michael Kandiah and Paul Nicholson.

Introduction

THE teaching of history has changed considerably in the past decade, as the focus has shifted away from the use of traditional textbooks and towards the use of primary sources. This book, like its earlier companion volume, is intended to meet that need by providing a single comprehensive source of documents on British history between 1939 and 1970. This book differs from other document collections in that we have included a wide range of types of document, in keeping with the broadening definition of historical evidence. In doing so, our aim is to encourage the reader to become more familiar with primary sources and to become more imaginative about the use of evidence in history.

Although the book follows a conventional chronological framework, individual chapters address specific themes. Given the tremendous variety and volume of material available, we have tried to include documents which would not otherwise be available in print. Indeed, many of the sources collected here are published for the first time. In our criteria for selection, we have attempted to strike a reasonable balance between comprehensiveness and variety.

Documentary evidence is the raw material of the historian, whose interpretations of the past are constructed from a careful sifting of many documents of varying kinds: official government records, parliamentary debates, political speeches and election addresses, journalistic accounts and commentaries, diaries and memoirs, private papers and letters, oral testimony and statistics. Increasingly, historians are coming to recognise the value of non-written evidence: political cartoons, party propaganda such as election posters, photographs, advertisements and miscellaneous ephemera.

The teaching of history today is coming increasingly to emphasise the use of primary source material, and students are encouraged to develop their own analytical skills through direct examination of historical documents. When approaching a new piece of evidence, three questions should always be borne in mind. Who wrote or created the document, and for what purpose? When was it written or produced? For what audience was it created? It follows, therefore, that no piece of evidence should ever be accepted at face value, and in this sense documents cannot be trusted to 'speak for themselves'.

Different types of evidence can pose their own special problems, and we will try here to give some examples of possible dangers of which students need to be aware. For example, official documents from the Public Record Office (PRO) have to be understood in terms of their function in the policy-making process. Policy formulation by governments usually involves protracted attempts to reconcile competing interests. Discussion papers circulated in this process, generally written by civil servants, may reflect a particular stance based on economic, political or diplomatic concerns. The balance between such factors may vary; economic considerations may be outweighed, for example, by political expediency. In document 5.8, for example, the Foreign Secretary, Ernest Bevin, explains to his Cabinet colleagues in 1947 why Britain must withdraw from Palestine. To prempt criticism Bevin has to put his case forcefully, pointing out the failure of British policy in the territory, and attempting to portray withdrawal in positive terms.

Equally, when considering extracts from parliamentary debates, the reader ought to be aware that politicians asking questions, supplying answers or making statements are not necessarily aiming to convey factual information. Instead, they may be trying to score party political points, discredit their opponents or disguise embarrassing policy difficulties or reversals. In document 4.10, for example, the prominent Labour minister Herbert Morrison outlines his government's nationalisation programme. In reading this extract, it would be important not only to bear in mind this speech's purpose in portraying public ownership in as politically 'neutral' a light as possible, but also to remember the importance of nationalisation to many of the Labour Party's rank and file, with whom the government was keen to maintain good relations.

When using extracts from the press, the reader needs to consider questions such as the editorial allegiance of the newspaper or journal, normally determined by the political views of its proprietor. While this may be clear enough when considering editorial commentary, straightforward press reporting of events may not always be as objective as it is intended to appear. Such reports may implicitly be coloured by the political bias of the reporter or editor. For example, the way in which sympathetic newspapers, such as *The Times*, promoted the Conservative press conference at the Selsdon Park Hotel in 1970, as illustrated by document 10.20, gave an impression of new life and dynamism to a set of policies which had essentially been in place for a number of years.

The personal accounts of participants – diaries, memoirs and oral testimony – while valuable, cannot be expected to be wholly objective. A diary entry, for example, may be simply the immediate response to a day's events, written from a very personal perspective, not necessarily with full access to the facts. Thus, a diary is not always a fair representation of the opinion of the author, whose views may well moderate as he or she gains more perspective on an issue. On the other hand, diary entries may be written up days or weeks after the events described, or even revised many years later, and it may be difficult to establish when that is the case. Some diarists consciously write for subsequent publication, a factor which may lead them to be selective in their version of events. Document 1.9, for instance, is an extract from the diary of Sir John Colville, private secretary to Winston Churchill during the Second World War, and therefore uniquely placed to provide a 'behind the scenes' insight into policy-making at the highest level. No historian, however, would be content to rely solely on Colville's account in discussing Anglo-Soviet relations during 1941. Other sources, particularly official records, would normally be consulted to arrive at a more balanced view.

The problem of assessing memoirs or oral testimony is rather different. Here, recollections may be affected by the passage of time, the application of hindsight, the need to justify one's own record and possible lapses of memory, commonly leading to the conflation of events. This means that such sources should not be relied upon exclusively, although they can reveal important background influences which may help to explain the position adopted by an individual. It is important to bear in mind, however, that individual recollections of the same event can vary enormously. Document 3.1 provides an all too rare insight into the experiences of a young female politician, Barbara Castle, shortly after her election as an MP. Though written many years after the events recounted, this extract manages to convey some of the excitement created by the 1945 election results. Document 3.2, on the other hand, provides an insight into the perspective of the 'losers' in 1945. Here, the tone is cooler, more sober and analytical.

In several chapters, we have included extracts from 'witness seminars', sponsored by the ICBH in recent years, in which a number of participants in key events are invited to share their recollections. Document 7.34, for example, refers to a gathering of figures from the right wing of the Labour Party, recalling their feelings at the arrival of Harold Wilson as party leader. The unique nature of the witness seminar format enables something of the flavour of debate at the time to come through.

Private papers and correspondence can give glimpses into the true motives or opinions of individuals, which are often unclear from official records. Document 7.6, for example, is a record of a meeting of a small working group of Conservative officials and ministers concerned to discuss electoral strategy in the run-up to the general election of 1955. The frankness which marks the discussion provides an informative and enlightening contrast to published party propaganda in this period. Equally, in the case of correspondence, letters are written to a known and specific individual. The same author may disclose quite different views to other acquaintances.

We have included a good deal of statistical information, presented in the form of graphic charts, which convey important trends and patterns in a more accessible way than raw statistical data. The problem with using statistical evidence is first to find reliable and consistent sources, then to establish why the statistics were collected in the first place and to understand the purposes for which they may have been used. Because the weight of such evidence may appear on the surface to be irrefutable, statistical data can be particularly misleading, and are often employed to lend credence to otherwise questionable assertions. For example, statistics relating to immigration in the 1950s are notoriously difficult for the simple reason that records were not kept on immigrants from New Commonwealth countries for a number of years. The data presented in documents 7.23 and 7.24 are therefore based upon educated guesses by researchers, in this case from the House of Commons Library.

The themes which we have explored above apply equally to visual forms of evidence. The same questions of authorship, intention, date of origin and audience should be used in the interpretation of such documents. Political propaganda, of course, has an obvious audience in the electorate, and its intention is fairly clear. Cartoons can be used to put forward the editorial view of the publication in which they appear in a similar fashion to press reports, and a single dramatic image can often perform that task more powerfully than several column inches of reasoned argument. For example, document 1.5 is a cartoon by David Low which appeared not long after the evacuation of Dunkirk. Hence, Low shows Britain in defiant mood, facing the enemy alone, against all odds. It would be rash, however, to conclude that this image captured a universal feeling, and to overlook its strong morale-raising intention.

One final point, of which we ourselves are well aware, is that while we have attempted to include a fair and broad selection of documents, our choices have inevitably been affected by our interests and experiences. Nevertheless, we hope that this collection, like its earlier companion volume, will provide a useful new source of primary material for students of twentieth-century British history.

CHAPTER ONE

Global War, Strategy and the Grand Alliance, 1939–45

IN 1939 Britain found itself plunged once again into a European war. This war would soon become global in its scope, and was to have even more far-reaching consequences for Britain than the First World War. After a relatively quiet interlude of so-called 'phoney war', Britain was to confront the situation long feared by its military planners: that of facing simultaneously aggressors in Europe, the Mediterranean and the Far East. By 1941 the situation had been transformed, with the entry into the war of the Soviet Union and the United States. The alliance with these two vastly more powerful countries ultimately saved Britain from defeat, but it also demonstrated Britain's relative decline as a world power. Beyond their common desire to defeat Nazi Germany, there remained ample scope for tensions between the three Allies, above all over their differing conceptions of the postwar world order.

The war had important repercussions on Britain's claims to be an imperial power. Important territories in the Far East were conquered by Japan; their recapture remained a key British aim. In other parts of the empire, notably India, an effective contribution to the Allied war effort was complicated by nationalist resistance to British rule. Other components of the empire, notably the Dominions, found that, despite their loyal rallying to Britain, the latter was powerless to defend them effectively from aggression, which led them to regard the United States as their surest source of protection. Indeed, the British empire remained a matter of contention between Britain and the United States for much of the war. While for Britain the preservation of the empire was an obvious and indisputable war aim, for the United States the war provided an opportunity to prise open Britain's closed imperial economy, a practical consideration made potent by its combination with a long tradition of American anti-colonialism. Partly as a consequence of sustained US criticism, Britain devised a new conception of colonial rule, couched in positive, constructive terms, emphasising partnership rather than domination. Britain would be held to these principles after the war.

The degree of co-operation achieved between the three Allies had been impressive. As the war drew to a close, a dominant concern was whether this co-operation could be maintained after the war. It was already clear that the character of the postwar settlement would be determined largely by the United States and the Soviet Union. While at Yalta, early in 1945, agreement appeared to have been reached on potentially divisive questions concerning the future frontiers of Eastern Europe, the seeds of the cold war were arguably already visible.

From the 'Phoney War' to Fighting Alone

Following the German invasion of Poland on 1 September 1939, the British government, in keeping with the guarantee to Poland made in March 1939, sent an ultimatum to Berlin demanding an immediate withdrawal. When no satisfactory response was obtained, Britain declared war on Germany on 3 September. At the outbreak of the war, Britain's prospects were hardly encouraging. Its economy was still suffering the consequences of the depression; France, its only ally, was not militarily strong; the Soviet Union had recently concluded a non-aggression pact with Germany; and there seemed little chance of assistance being provided by the still neutral United States.

The British government hoped throughout the autumn and winter of 1939–40 that a quick resolution of the war was possible before serious fighting began. Its strategy was essentially passive, limited to an economic blockade of Germany, based on an assumption that the German economy could not withstand shortages of raw materials and foreign currency. No military offensive was to be begun until Germany had taken the first steps. The result was the so-called 'phoney war', which lasted until April 1940.

1.1   Anton, 'But apart from this, life is going on just the same as usual', *Punch* cartoon, 13 September 1939.

For Britain, a major obstacle to peace was the nature of the Nazi regime. An important assumption made by the British government was to distinguish between 'moderate' and 'extremist' Germans. The Permanent Secretary at the Foreign Office, Sir Alexander Cadogan, writing in July 1940, captured the sentiment that a prolonged military struggle might threaten Hitler's domestic popularity.

1.2   Sir Alexander Cadogan, minute, 25 July 1940 (PRO FO 800/322).

■ I don't accept the thesis that all Germans are equally wicked, but even assuming it to be true, I maintain – and have always maintained – that it was not very clever to put that in the forefront of our propaganda.

Even if it is a true reflection, it is not a helpful one, because it leads nowhere. It can only point to the necessity for massacring or – on a longer view – sterilising all Germans. And I don't think that is really practical politics.

At the present moment, Hitler is presumably on the crest of a wave. Any attacks that we make on him will not (on the French assumption) appreciably strengthen his position.

But there are elements working against Hitler. There is a rather impressive volume of evidence to show that, in spite of military triumphs, there is no great enthusiasm for the war in Germany. There is a certain lassitude in Germany and if, after all their efforts, the Germans are asked to embark in small boats to land on mined beaches in this country, or to run the gauntlet of our fighters in troop-carrying 'planes, it may be that that will not redound to Hitler's popularity.

It seems to me that what we want to get into the minds of the Germans is that we do not desire that even they shd. be denied the right to live in peace, and even comparative plenty, and that it is only Hitler and his system that stands between them and the exercise of that right …

If Hitler produces a specious plan for a 'New Europe' (and if we have been able to produce no better one), probably our best line of attack wd. be as suggested in a recent telegram to Washington – viz. that this all looks very nice but is of course in reality simply designed to subserve Hitler's end of domination. The economic paradise which he depicts is really only a German playground: the other States of Europe are to supply him with food and raw materials for the manufacture of his munitions (which is Hitler's 'cure' for unemployment) for the domination of the rest of the world and for the denial of freedom to all other peoples …

The removal of Hitler, if that could by one means or another be brought about, must have a profound effect. It is difficult to believe that Goering, his successor designate, or any other of the German leaders could maintain German unity in the way that he does. When people sometimes speak to me of the marvellous efficiency of the Dictatorships, I always remind them that they may be rather deficient in stability and continuity, and offer to review the position with them again 6 months after the death or disappearance of either Hitler or Mussolini.

I submit therefore that our propaganda should concentrate against Hitler and the Nazi system. They may not be so all-powerful as they look, and dissension in Germany would be worth a number of Army Corps. ∎

The German invasion of Poland was completed in less than a month. Hitler and Stalin divided the country between them, after which Hitler made tentative peace moves towards the West, claiming that he had no aggressive intentions towards either Britain or France. These moves struck a responsive chord in some sections of British opinion, including the government. On balance, however, the view held sway that peace could be negotiated only with a 'trustworthy' German government, which Hitler's was not – a view voiced by Prime Minister Neville Chamberlain in the following parliamentary speech.

1.3   Neville Chamberlain, speech to the House of Commons on German peace proposals, 12 October 1939 (*Hansard*, 5th ser., 352: 564–68).

∎ On 1st September Herr Hitler violated the Polish frontier and invaded Poland, beating down by force of arms and machinery the resistance of the Polish nation and army. As attested by neutral observers, Polish towns and villages were bombed and shelled into ruins; and civilians were slaughtered wholesale, in contravention, at any rate in the later stages, of all the undertakings of which Herr Hitler now speaks with pride as though he had fulfilled them.

It is after this wanton act of aggression which has cost so many Polish and German lives, sacrificed to satisfy his own insistence on the use of force, that the German Chancellor now puts forward his proposals. If there existed any expectation that in these proposals would be included some attempt to make amends for this grievous crime against humanity, following so soon upon the violation of the rights of the Czecho-Slovak nation, it has been doomed to disappointment. The Polish State and its leaders are covered with abuse. What the fate of that part of Poland which Herr Hitler describes as the German sphere of interest is to be does not clearly emerge from his speech, but it is evident that he regards it as a matter for the consideration of Germany alone, to be settled solely in accordance with German interests. The final shaping of this territory and the question of the restoration of a Polish State are, in Herr Hitler's view, problems which cannot be settled by war in the West but exclusively by Russia on the one side and Germany on the other.

We must take it, then, that the proposals which the German Chancellor puts forward for the establishment of what he calls 'the certainty of European security' are to be based on recognition of his conquests and of his right to do what he pleases with the conquered.

It would be impossible for Great Britain to accept any such basis without forfeiting her honour and abandoning her claim that international disputes should be settled by discussion and not by force ...

We seek no material advantage for ourselves; we desire nothing from the German people which should offend their self-respect. We are not aiming only at victory, but rather looking beyond it to the laying of a foundation of a better international system which will mean that war is not to be the inevitable lot of every succeeding generation ...

The peace which we are determined to secure, however, must be a real and settled peace, not an uneasy truce interrupted by constant alarms and repeated threats. What stands in the way of such a peace? It is the German Government, and the German Government alone, for it is they who by repeated acts of aggression have robbed all Europe of tranquillity and implanted in the hearts of all their neighbours an ever-present sense of insecurity and fear ...

There is thus a primary condition to be satisfied. Only the German Government can fulfil it. If they will not, there can as yet be no new or better world order of the kind for which all nations yearn.

The issue is, therefore, plain. Either the German Government must give convincing proof of the sincerity of their desire for peace by definite acts and by the provision of effective guarantees of their intention to fulfil their undertakings, or we must persevere in our duty to the end. It is for Germany to make her choice. ■

Dunkirk and the fall of France

Britain's initial strategic calculations were overturned by the events of May and June 1940. In a series of rapid, blitzkrieg campaigns, employing surprise armoured attacks, the Germans invaded Norway, Denmark, the Netherlands, Belgium and France. The British government had assumed that France would be able to hold the line, giving Britain time to mobilise fully. By May 1940 the British Expeditionary Force in France numbered only 10 divisions, none of which was armoured, compared to France's 104. The rapid German advance left the BEF and 30 French divisions trapped close to the French coast. Miraculously, during the evacuation from Dunkirk between 27 May and 4 June, one-third of a million British and French troops were brought across the Channel to safety, although precious equipment had to be left behind. Although this saved most of the BEF, it spelt doom for France, which was quickly overrun by the Germans and sued for peace.

At the height of the crisis in France, the British Cabinet considered requesting peace terms from Germany, but they were convinced by Winston Churchill that this might be counterproductive and that it was essential to convince Hitler that Britain could not be defeated. Like his colleagues, Churchill assumed that the United States would eventually become involved in the war. Meanwhile, the Chiefs of Staff presented a grim picture of the military situation.

1.4 Chiefs of Staff, recommendations to Cabinet, 27 May 1940 (PRO CAB 65/7, WM(40)141st minutes, appendix).

■ (i) We should do our utmost to persuade the United States of America to provide aircraft, particularly fighters, as soon as possible and in large numbers, including those from stocks now held by the United States Army and Navy.

(ii) Measures should be taken to ensure the strictest economy in A.A. ammunition expenditure.

(iii) The most ruthless action should be taken to eliminate any chances of 'Fifth Column' activities. Internment of all enemy aliens and all members of subversive organisations, which latter should be proscribed.

(iv) Alien refugees are a most dangerous source of subversive activity. We recommend that the number of refugees admitted to this country should be cut to the minimum, and that those admitted should be kept under the closest surveillance.

(v) In order to ensure the necessary co-operation between Civil and Military authorities, operational control of all Civil Defence Forces, including county and borough police, &c., should be vested in the Ministry of Home Security and exercised through Regional Commissioners.

(vi) Any evacuation which the Government intends to carry out in emergency should be carried out now. We recommend that a modification of the scheme for reception areas, in view of the dangers of invasion, should be carried out.

(vii) Immediate steps to be taken to obtain destroyers and M[otor].T[orpedo].B[oat].s from the United States of America.

(viii) Every possible measure should be directed to obtaining the active support of Eire, particularly with a view to the immediate use of Berehaven.

(ix) Our intelligence system to be strengthened with a view to getting early warning of German preparations for invasion of this country.

(x) Dispersal of stocks of raw materials to free our West Coast ports to deal with the heavy increase in imports should now be made.

(xi) So far as is practicable, distribution of food reserves throughout the country with a view to meeting the disorganisation of transport which may occur.

(xii) Bunkering facilities and other arrangements necessary to deal with a heavy volume of merchant shipping in West Coast and Irish ports should be organised.

(xiii) All unimportant and luxury imports to be cut out.

(xiv) Finally we consider that the time has come to inform the public of the true dangers that confront us, and to educate them on what they are required to do and what NOT to do if the country is invaded. ■

The fall of France left Britain, together with its empire, to fight the war without allies, a situation unanticipated in September 1939. It also encouraged Hitler to bring forward his planned invasion of the Soviet Union. Moreover, German military successes encouraged both Japan and Italy to enter the war, which increasingly became a world conflict. In the darkest hour of the war for Britain, Churchill replaced Chamberlain as Prime Minister. Britain's chances of survival hinged largely on whether help could be obtained from the United States. President F.D. Roosevelt was sympathetic, but his hands were still tied by an isolationist Congress. David Low's cartoon therefore contains more than an element of bravado.

1.5   **David Low, 'Very well, alone',** *Evening Standard* **cartoon, 18 June 1940.**

From the Battle of Britain to the Bombing Offensive

With France defeated, Hitler's attention turned to Britain. No German invasion attempt could succeed until air superiority over the Channel had been achieved. Therefore, during August 1940 the German Luftwaffe began attacks on RAF airfields in southern England. The resulting aerial battle, 'the Battle of Britain', saw a desperate contest between the Luftwaffe and RAF fighter squadrons. The latter, aided by modern aircraft like the Spitfire, by radar and by knowledge of secret Luftwaffe codes, succeeded in overcoming the numerically superior German forces. A crucial German error, made in response to an RAF raid on Berlin, was to divert effort to air raids on British cities, the Blitz. The practical consequence of the Battle of Britain was that German invasion plans were postponed in October 1940 and put off indefinitely in January 1941.

The RAF's success during the Battle of Britain came at just the right time to revive flagging British civilian morale, and much propaganda value was derived at home, not least by Churchill, from the activities of 'the few'.

1.6 RAF poster, 'Never was so much owed by so many to so few', 1940 (Imperial War Museum).

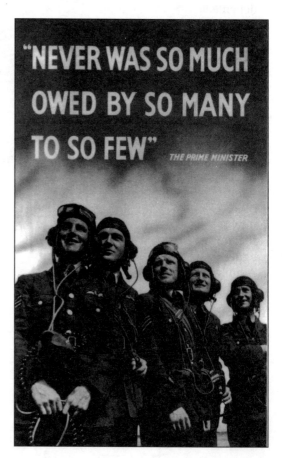

"NEVER WAS SO MUCH OWED BY SO MANY TO SO FEW" *THE PRIME MINISTER*

After the summer of 1940, Britain was forced to rethink its war strategy. Given the sheer scale of economic resources now available to Nazi Germany, it seemed unlikely that the economic blockade could have much effect. In September 1940 Churchill outlined for the Cabinet what he saw as the main strategic issues, explaining that the key to eventual victory was a bombing offensive against Germany.

1.7   Winston Churchill in Cabinet, 3 September 1940 (PRO CAB 66/11, WP(40)352).

■ I venture to submit to my colleagues the following points which suggest themselves to me in reading the deeply interesting survey of the Minister of Supply:–

1. The Navy can lose us the war, but only the Air Force can win it. Therefore our supreme effort must be to gain overwhelming mastery in the Air. The Fighters are our salvation, but the Bombers alone provide the means of victory. We must therefore develop the power to carry an ever-increasing volume of explosives to Germany, so as to pulverise the entire industry and scientific structure on which the war effort and economic life of the enemy depends, while holding him at arm's length in our Island. In no other way at present visible can we hope to overcome the immense military power of Germany, and to nullify the further German victories which may be apprehended as the weight of their force is brought to bear upon African and Oriental theatres. The Air Force and its action on the largest scale must therefore, subject to what is said later, claim the first place over the Navy or the Army.

2. The weapon of blockade has become blunted and rendered, as far as Germany is concerned, less effectual on account of their land conquests and power to rob captive or intimidated peoples for their own benefit. There remain no very important special commodities the denial of which will hamper their war effort. The Navy is at present somewhat pressed in its task of keeping open the communications, but as this condition is removed by new Admiralty measures, by the arrival of the American destroyers, and by the increasing output of anti-U-Boat craft from our own yards, we may expect a marked improvement. It is of the utmost importance that the Admiralty should direct their attention to aggressive schemes of war, and to the bombardment of enemy or enemy-held coasts, particularly in the Mediterranean. The production of anti-U-Boat craft must proceed at the maximum until further orders, each slip being filled as it is vacated. The Naval Programme does not impinge markedly upon the Air, and should cede some of its armourplate to Tank production ...

5. The danger of invasion will not disappear with the coming of winter, and may confront us with novel possibilities in the coming year. The enemy's need to strike down this country will naturally increase as the war progresses, and all kinds of appliances for crossing the seas, that do not now exist, may be devised. Actual invasion must be regarded as perpetually

threatened but unlikely to materialise as long as strong forces stand in this Island. Apart from this, the only major theatre of war which can be foreseen in 1940–41 is the Middle East. Here we must endeavour to bring into action British, Australian and Indian forces, on a scale which should only be limited by sea transport and local maintenance. We must expect to fight in Egypt and the Sudan, in Turkey, Syria or Palestine, and possibly in Iraq and Iran. Fifteen British Divisions, 6 Australasian, and at least 6 Indian Divisions should be prepared for these theatres, these forces not being, however, additional to the 55 Divisions which have been mentioned. One would not imagine that the ammunition expenditure would approach the last War scale. Air power and mechanised troops will be the dominant factors.

6. There remain the possibilities of amphibious aggressive warfare against the enemy or enemy-held territory in Europe or North Africa. But the needs of such operations will be provided by the arms and supplies already mentioned in general terms.

7. Our task, as the Minister of Supply rightly reminds us, is indeed formidable when the gigantic scale of German military and aviation equipment is considered. This war is not, however, a war of masses of men hurling masses of shells at each other. It is by devising new weapons, and above all, by scientific leadership, that we shall best cope with the enemy's superior strength …

8. Apart from a large-scale invasion, which is unlikely, there is no prospect of any large expenditure or wastage of military munitions before the Spring of 1941. Although heavy and decisive fighting may develop at any time in the Middle East, the difficulties of transport, both of reinforcements and of supplies, will restrict numbers and expenditure. We have, therefore, before us, if not interrupted, a period of eight months in which to make an enormous improvement in our output of war-like equipment, and in which steady and rapid accumulations may be hoped for. It is upon this purpose that all our resources of credit, materials, and above all, of skilled labour, must be bent. ■

It took some two years for the RAF's Bomber Command to be built up to the necessary strength. By 1942 it was ready to embark on the controversial campaign of 'mass area terror bombing' on German cities, orchestrated by Air Chief Marshal Sir Arthur 'Bomber' Harris.

The Grand Alliance

Britain's nightmare in 1940 – the prospect of single-handedly confronting Germany, Italy and Japan – receded with the entry into the war of the Soviet Union and the United States in 1941. Britain and the United States had been drawing closing together for many months previously, beginning with the 'destroyers for bases' agreement of September 1940, under which Britain received fifty US destroyers in return for US leases on naval bases in the British West Indies. In March 1941 Roosevelt introduced the Lend-Lease Act, enabling Britain to buy war materials from the USA on credit.

Britain became increasingly dependent on the efforts of its two much stronger partners. Being part of an alliance, while essential, created strains for Britain, which was required to make concessions to its allies and was not always able to defend its own interests. Tensions arose in particular over the respective world roles of Britain and the USA, as the latter had long regarded the British empire with suspicion. Traditional anti-colonial feeling in the USA combined with resentment towards the economic privileges that Britain enjoyed through its empire to produce pressure on Britain to dismantle the system of imperial preferences constructed in the 1930s in favour of freer trade.

In August 1941, still before the United States entered the war, Churchill and Roosevelt, meeting off Newfoundland, had signed a document known as the Atlantic Charter, *a declaration of the postwar aims of the democratic countries. This was subsequently a source of Anglo-American tension, because whereas Roosevelt interpreted the charter as an undertaking by Britain to give its colonies independence, Churchill had understood its provisions to refer to freeing the peoples of Nazi-occupied Europe.*

1.8   *The Atlantic Charter,* **14 August 1941 (London, HMSO, Cmd. 6321 PP VIII, 1940–1, 591).**

■ The President of the United States of America and the Prime Minister, Mr Churchill, representing His Majesty's Government in the United Kingdom, being met together, deem it right to make known certain common principles in the national policies of their respective countries on which they base their hopes for a better future for the world:

First, their countries seek no aggrandisement, territorial or other.

Second, they desire to see no territorial changes that do not accord with the freely expressed wishes of the peoples concerned.

Third, they respect the right of all peoples to choose the form of government under which they will live; and they wish to see sovereign rights and self-government restored to those who have been forcibly deprived of them.

Fourth, they will endeavour, with due respect for their existing obligations, to further the enjoyment by all States, great or small, victor or vanquished, of access, on equal terms, to the trade and to the raw materials of the world which are needed for their economic prosperity.

Fifth, they desire to bring about the fullest collaboration between all nations in the economic field, with the object of securing for all improved labour standards, economic advancement and social security.

Sixth, after the final destruction of the Nazi tyranny, they hoped to see established a peace which will afford to all nations the means of dwelling in safety within their own boundaries, and which will afford assurance that all the [sic] men in all the lands may live out their lives in freedom from fear and want.

Seventh, such a peace should enable all men to traverse the high seas and oceans without hindrance.

Eighth, they believe all of the nations of the world, for realistic as well as spiritual reasons, must come to the abandonment of the use of force. Since no future peace can be maintained if land, sea or air armaments continue to be employed by nations which threaten, or may threaten, aggression outside of their frontiers, they believe, pending the establishment of a wider and permanent system of general security, that the disarmament of such nations is essential. They will likewise aid and encourage all other practicable measures which will lighten for peace-loving peoples the crushing burden of armaments. ∎

The alliance of convenience with the Soviet Union after 1941 did not allay long-standing British suspicions of Moscow, which were intensified by ideological hostility towards Communism. Tensions had increased in November 1939 when Stalin declared war on Finland. Only the collapse of Finland prevented Britain and France sending military aid. However, the German attack on Russia in June 1941, together with Hitler's decision to declare war on the United States in December of that year, probably sealed the fate of Nazi ambitions.

In June 1941 Churchill's wartime private secretary, Sir John Colville, recorded in his diary the announcement of the invasion of Russia. He noted the reactions not only of Churchill and Sir Stafford Cripps, Britain's Ambassador to Moscow, but also of key government ministers, including the Foreign Secretary, Sir Anthony Eden, and the Dominions Secretary, Viscount Cranborne.

1.9   **Sir John Colville, diary entry, 22 June 1941 (in Sir John Colville, *The Fringes of Power: Downing Street Diaries, Vol. One: 1939–October 1941*, London, Sceptre, 1986, pp. 481–2).**

∎ Awoken by the telephone with the news that Germany had attacked Russia. I went a round of the bedrooms breaking the news and produced a smile of satisfaction on the faces of the P.M., Eden and Winant. Winant, however, suspects it all may be a put-up job between Hitler and Stalin (later the P.M. and Cripps laughed this to scorn).

Eden rushed off to the F[oreign] O[ffice] for the day; the P.M. decided to broadcast and actually came down to the Hawtrey room at 11.0 a.m. to prepare it; Sir Stafford and Lady Cripps motored over to discuss the situation and ended by staying to lunch and dine …

At lunch the P.M. trailed his coat for Cripps, castigating Communism and saying that Russians were barbarians. Finally he declared that not even the slenderest thread connected Communists to the very basest type of humanity. Cripps took it all in good part and was amused …

The P.M.'s broadcast was not ready till twenty minutes before he was due to deliver it and it gave me great anxiety, but even more so to Eden who wanted to vet the text and couldn't. But when it was made it impressed us all: it was dramatic and it gave a clear decision of policy – support for Russia.

After the ladies had left the dining-room there ensued a vivacious and witty debate between the P.M., supported in spirit but not much in words by Sir S. Cripps, on the one hand, and Cranborne and Eden on the other … The question at issue was: 'Should there be a debate in the House on Tuesday about Russia?' Eden and Cranborne took the Tory standpoint that if there was it should be confined to the purely military aspect, as politically Russia was as bad as Germany and half the country would object to being associated with her too closely. The P.M.'s view was that Russia was now at war; innocent peasants were being slaughtered; and we should forget about Soviet systems or the Comintern and extend our hand to fellow human beings in distress. The argument was extremely vehement. I have never spent a more enjoyable evening. ■

Britain and the USA: strategy and relations

Among the tensions between Britain and the United States were those surrounding strategy – for example, over the importance to Churchill of re-establishing British control of occupied colonies in South-East Asia. However, at a conference in Washington, DC, in December 1941, Churchill and Roosevelt reached agreement that the defeat of Germany should take precedence over the defeat of Japan.

The fundamental strategic agreement between Churchill and Roosevelt was reflected in the formal decisions on strategic planning taken by the military chiefs of both Britain and the USA in February 1942 – document 1.10 (overleaf). In July of that year the Combined Chiefs of Staff decided to postpone an invasion of Europe and an offensive in the Pacific in favour of landings in North Africa, scheduled for November 1942. 'Operation Torch', as the landings were called, proved successful, and by May 1943 Axis forces had retreated from North Africa. In July 1943 Anglo-American forces landed in Sicily, paving the way for an invasion of Italy, which Churchill regarded as the Axis powers' vulnerable flank.

1.10 **US and British Chiefs of Staff, agreement in principle on strategy, 17 February 1942 (PRO CAB 80/33, COS(42)75, annex I).**

■ I. GRAND STRATEGY

1. At the A[merican]–B[ritish] Staff conversations in February 1941 it was agreed that Germany was the predominant member of the Axis Powers, and, consequently, the Atlantic and European area was considered to be the decisive theatre.

2. Much has happened since February last, but, notwithstanding the entry of Japan into the War, our view remains that Germany is still the prime enemy and her defeat is the key to victory. Once Germany is defeated, the collapse of Italy and the defeat of Japan must follow.

3. In our considered opinion, therefore, it should be a cardinal principle of A–B strategy that only the minimum of force necessary for the safeguarding of vital interests in other theatres should be diverted from operations against Germany.

II. ESSENTIAL FEATURES OF OUR STRATEGY

4. The essential features of the above grand strategy are as follows. Each will be examined in greater detail later in this paper:–

   (a) The realization of the victory programme of armaments, which first and foremost requires the security of the main areas of war industry.

   (b) The maintenance of essential communications.

   (c) Closing and tightening the ring round Germany.

   (d) Wearing down and undermining German resistance by air bombardment, blockade, subversive activities and propaganda.

   (e) The continuous development of offensive action against Germany.

   (f) Maintaining only such positions in the Eastern theatre as will safeguard vital interests ... and deny to Japan access to raw materials vital to her continuous war effort while we are concentrating on the defeat of Germany.

III. STEPS TO BE TAKEN IN 1942 TO PUT INTO EFFECT THE ABOVE GENERAL POLICY

The Security of Areas of War Production

5. In so far as these are likely to be attacked the main areas of war industry are situated in –

   (a) The United Kingdom

(b) Continental United States, particularly the West Coast

(c) Russia

6. *The United Kingdom* – To safeguard the United Kingdom it will be necessary to maintain at all times the minimum forces required to defeat invasion ...

Closing and Tightening the Ring Around Germany

13. This ring may be defined as a line running roughly as follows – Archangel, Black Sea, Anatolia, the Northern Seaboard of the Mediterranean, the Western Seaboard of Europe.

The main object will be to strengthen this ring and close the gaps in it, by sustaining the Russian front, by arming and supporting Turkey, by increasing our strength in the Middle East, and by gaining possession of the whole North African coast.

14. If this ring can be closed, the blockade of Germany and Italy will be complete, and German eruptions, e.g., towards the Persian Gulf or to the Atlantic seaboard of Africa will be prevented. Furthermore, the seizing of the North African coast may open the Mediterranean to convoys, thus enormously shortening the route to the Middle East and saving considerable tonnage now employed in the long haul around the Cape.

The Undermining and Wearing Down of the German Resistance

15. In 1942 the main methods of wearing down Germany's resistance will be:–

(a) Ever-increasing air bombardment by British and American Forces.

(b) Assistance to Russia's offensive by all available means.

(c) The blockade.

(d) The maintenance of the spirit of revolt in the occupied countries, and the organization of subversive movements.

Development of Land Offensives on the Continent

16. It does not seem likely that in 1942 any large-scale land offensive against Germany except on the Russian front will be possible. We must, however, be ready to take advantage of any opening that may result from the wearing down process referred to in paragraph 15 to conduct limited land offensives.

17. In 1943 the way may be clear for a return to the Continent, across the Mediterranean, from Turkey into the Balkans, or by landings in Western Europe. Such operations will be the prelude to the final assault on Germany itself, and the scope of the victory programme should be such as to provide means by which they can be carried out ... ■

Despite the differences between Britain and the United States, Churchill placed great emphasis on the special nature of their relationship and was generally on good terms with Roosevelt. While visiting Washington in May 1943, Churchill, whose mother was American, speculated on the future of this 'special relationship'.

1.11   Winston Churchill, discussions at the British Embassy, Washington, DC, 22 May 1943 (PRO CAB 66/37, WP(43)233).

■ Mr. Churchill said that there was something else in his mind which was complementary to the ideas he had just expressed. The proposals for a world organisation did not exclude special friendships devoid of sinister purposes among others. He could see small hope for the world unless the United States and the British Commonwealth worked together in what he would call fraternal association. He believed that this could take a form which would confer on each advantages without sacrifice. He would like the citizens of each, without losing their present nationality, to be able to come and settle and trade with freedom and equal rights in the territories of the other. There might be a common passport or a special form of passport or visa. There might even be some common form of citizenship, under which citizens of the United States and of the British Commonwealth might enjoy voting privileges after residential qualifications and be eligible for public office in the territories of the other, subject, of course, to the laws and institutions there prevailing.

Then there were bases. He had himself welcomed the Destroyer–Bases deal, not for the sake of the destroyers, useful as these were, but because he felt it was to the advantage of both countries that the United States should have the use of such bases in British territory as she might find necessary to her own defence, for a strong United States was a vital interest of the British Commonwealth and vice versa. He looked forward, therefore, to an extension of the practice of common use of bases for the common defence of common interests. Take the Pacific, where there were countless islands possessed by enemy Powers. There were also British islands and harbours. If he had anything to do with the direction of public affairs after the war, he would certainly advocate that the United States had the use of those that they might require for bases.

■

The war in Europe

Churchill was determined if possible to avoid a repetition of the military carnage of the First World War. This led him to resist pressure, from both the United States and the Soviet Union, for an early invasion of Europe.

The Anglo-American decision to postpone an invasion of France until summer 1944 inevitably led to strained relations with the Soviet Union, and increased Stalin's suspicions of the West, because the delay meant that the greater part of the struggle against the German army had to be shouldered by the Red Army. The delicacy of this issue had already been described by British diplomats in Moscow early in 1942.

1.12 **British Embassy, Moscow, telegram to Foreign Office, 12 February 1942 (PRO FO 371/32876).**

■ . . .

3. Soviet Government are only interested in us as allies to the extent to which they think our activities will assist:

(a) their own victory in the war

(b) their own security after the war.

4. As regards (a) they are disappointed as we have not been able to send forces to the Eastern Front or achieve success elsewhere. Our material aid is important but not decisive. They accept the explanations politely, but they are not interested in the reasons or motives. We move up and down their chart by results alone and at present we are not very high.

5. As regards (b) they are suspicious. They await our decision about their territorial claims aiming at military security. If we do not accept them they may be confirmed in their belief in our utterly innate ill-will, but they will not necessarily become more difficult to deal with, perhaps the contrary. Meanwhile our day to day political relations are reasonably cordial over secondary matters ...

7. For the rest – the Soviet Government are supremely self-centred and so long as they get all they want or all we can give (I do not mean only 'give' material things but collaboration in every field) will give not more than they have to in return. They are no different in this from other people but they are more thorough and consistent in their egotism and they do not realise that generosity is sometimes the best policy. ■

The long-awaited Allied invasion of France, D-Day, finally came on 6 June 1944. This enormous operation involved the landing of US, British and Canadian troops in Normandy, with the US General Eisenhower acting as Supreme Allied Commander. By the second day of 'Operation Overlord', around a quarter of a million Allied troops were ashore. Heavy fighting continued in the area throughout June. Once Allied forces had captured Caen early in July, the way was open for the tanks to penetrate the German defences. Paris was liberated in August, and Eisenhower's forces crossed the prewar German frontier on 12 September.

On the evening of 6 June, King George VI made a radio broadcast to the nation. Clear parallels were drawn between the events of D-Day and the Dunkirk evacuation of 1940.

1.13   **King George VI, radio broadcast, 6 June 1944 (reported in *The Times*, 7 June 1944).**

■ Four years ago, our Nation and Empire stood alone against an overwhelming enemy, with our backs to the wall. Tested as never before in our history, in God's providence we survived that test; the spirit of the people, resolute, dedicated, burned like a bright flame, lit surely from those Unseen Fires which nothing can quench.

Now once more a supreme test has to be faced. This time the challenge is not to fight to survive but to fight to win the final victory for the good cause. Once again what is demanded from us is something more than courage and endurance; we need a revival of spirit, a new unconquerable resolve. After nearly five years of toil and suffering, we must renew that crusading impulse on which we entered the war and met its darkest hour. We and our Allies are sure that our fight is against evil and for a world in which goodness and honour may be the foundation of the life of men in every land.

That we may be worthily matched with this new summons of destiny, I desire solemnly to call my people to prayer and dedication. We are not unmindful of our own shortcomings, past and present. We shall ask not that God may do our will, but that we may be enabled to do the will of God; and we dare to believe that God has used our Nation and Empire as an instrument for fulfilling his high purpose.

I hope that throughout the present crisis of the liberation of Europe there may be offered up earnest, continuous, and widespread prayer. We who remain in this land can most effectively enter into the sufferings of subjugated Europe by prayer, whereby we can fortify the determination of our sailors, soldiers and airmen who go forth to set the captives free ... ■

The British Empire

The alliance with the United States and the Soviet Union inevitably raised questions about Britain's capacity to maintain its world role, particularly through the empire. Although there had been a massive and successful mobilisation of imperial resources on the outbreak of war, military reversals in the Far East – including the humiliating loss of Singapore, Malaya, Hong Kong and Burma to the Japanese early in 1942 – and the apathetic response of the local populations, as well as the apparent vulnerability of India and Australia to Japanese attack, caused grave worry in London. Even more serious, perhaps, was continuing US pressure on Britain to undertake to eliminate the system of imperial preferences, as part of a 'multilateral' or free-trading postwar world economic order. Negotiations on this controversial issue continued throughout the war but were inconclusive because of the reluctance of Churchill and his colleagues to surrender the perceived advantages of the empire. In addition to specific commercial considerations, there was a strong moral element in US anti-colonial rhetoric. Roosevelt periodically advocated the placing of Britain's colonies, particularly those in Asia, under international control, in preparation for their eventual independence. Such notions horrified Churchill, who told the House of Commons in November 1942: 'We mean to hold our own. I have not become the King's First Minister in order to preside over the liquidation of the British empire.'

Churchill's pro-imperial views were broadly shared by the government and senior officials. Within the Foreign Office, Gladwyn Jebb was one of a group of officials given responsibility during 1942–3 for predicting Britain's place in the postwar world. As Jebb later recalled, his colleagues did not seriously envisage Britain's handing over its world responsibilities to the emerging 'superpowers'.

1.14   Gladwyn Jebb, *The Memoirs of Lord Gladwyn*, London, Weidenfeld & Nicolson, 1972, pp. 112–13, 116–17.

■ My first effort at a long-term policy was distributed early in August [1942] in the shape of a memorandum entitled 'Relief Machinery, the Political Background'. It was ... considerably influenced by what we believed to be the working of the American official mind. Its general line was that our whole approach should be influenced by political considerations. Should we, in fact, regard the existing tentative scheme for the administration of post-war relief as capable of extension to other spheres, in other words as a prototype of some new and better League of Nations; or should we regard it as a temporary machine designed to cope with certain restricted and technical problems? There was little doubt that the first conception was that favoured by the US administration who seemed to favour a world organization after the war based on the United Nations as a whole and directed by a small 'policy committee' – probably the four Powers only. There might also, it seemed, be regional organizations each led by one Great Power. 'Colonial resources' would be internationalized and 'technical commissions' could deal on a world-wide scale with communications and transport. The whole rather loose system was clearly designed to be based on immense American sea and air power and (to a secondary degree) on the British Navy and Air Force and on the Russian Army. 'Bases' could be shared, and would serve to represent the power of America in the four continents. By this means there might be constituted a 'concert of the world', which might be expected to keep the peace as it was kept, in Europe, by Britain between the Battle of Waterloo and the beginning of the First World War. In other words we should be approaching the 'American century' or the 'century of the common man' – the terms seemed to be largely identical.

If this should prove to be the American (or New Dealer) Dream, what should be our response? Should we accept it, or try to whittle it down together with the Russians and our European allies, thereby assuring a high measure of autonomy for Western Europe, and for Eastern Europe, under the leadership of Russia? Were we, in any case, to regard the maintenance of the British Empire and Commonwealth as our primary objective? Were we to contemplate the survival of Germany as a Great Power? Were we, finally, bound to restore France and her Empire to the status of a Great Power as well? Whatever the answers to these questions, the four-Power conception, as such, seemed to have much to be said for it, that is, if each Power was regarded as a leader of a certain group of states. Nor would it be inconsistent, however interpreted, with some underlying Anglo-American co-operation. Besides, even if the conception was unacceptable what were the alternatives? They seemed to me to be the following:

(1) A strong and self-sufficient British Empire and Commonwealth capable of pursuing some independent policy of its own. This did not appear to be a tenable thesis. The events of the war had made it inevitable that the Commonwealth should break up as a political entity even if, as we might hope, it retained some value based on mutual goodwill.

(2) An attempt to associate ourselves, if possible in a leading position, with Western Europe and its colonies thus forming some kind of European bloc to act as a counterpoise to America and Russia. There was probably little prospect of achieving this immediately after the war, though certain steps towards it might well be compatible with the 'world system' recommended by the USA. It was just conceivable that some Western European states might agree to our representing them in a World Council.

(3) A revival of the League of Nations, perhaps located in Washington rather than in Geneva. This was unlikely, and probably undesirable. The League of Nations might, it is true, have achieved more if the Council had really embraced *all* the Great Powers. If any successor did this it would not be inconsistent with the general 'Four-Power' idea ...

The final version entitled *The Four Power Plan*, proud product of our collective thought ... The first assumption was that the three Great Powers would after all after the war take account of their world-wide interests and responsibilities and be both able and willing to enter into world-wide commitments in order to prevent any other nation from again troubling the peace. This was followed by a long and frank discussion of whether the UK herself was in fact likely to do anything of the sort. There would be many people who would maintain that it was undesirable, as beyond our powers, and that we ought to 'hand over the torch' to the Americans and the Russians – those over a certain means level tending to favour the first and those under it the second course.

But on the whole it was thought that if we did not 'fulfil our world-wide mission' we would sink to the level of a second-class Power and thus, in the long run, be likely to suffer an agonizing collapse from which we should emerge as a European Soviet state, the penurious outpost of an American pluto-democracy, or a German *Gau*, as forces might dictate ... ■

India and the Dominions

One of the most serious threats within the British empire was unrest in India, orchestrated by a vigorous nationalist movement. Aggrieved at being involved in the war without consultation, the Indian National Congress launched a campaign of non-co-operation with the British, and demanded immediate self-government. Churchill, during the 1930s the focus in Britain for opposition to Indian independence, remained adamant that India's future could not be discussed until after the war. Faced with Japanese proximity to India, Britain desperately needed to win over the Indian population to support the Allied war effort. Moreover, United States criticism of British rule in the Subcontinent was becoming deeply embarrassing to Britain. Early in 1942 the Cabinet decided to send Sir Stafford Cripps, then Lord Privy Seal, to India with offers of modest concessions to the nationalist movement, and a promise of self-government after the war. Congress rejected this offer as inadequate and unleashed the massive 'Quit India' rebellion, the most serious Indian uprising since the Indian Mutiny of 1857. The British authorities responded by banning Congress and detaining its leaders.

On his return from India, Cripps set before the War Cabinet his conclusions on the failure of his mission. The complexities of Indian politics that he described would continue to confound the British authorities until their withdrawal from India in 1947.

1.15   Sir Stafford Cripps, 'Report on mission to India', 6 July 1942 (PRO CAB 66/26, WP(42)283).

■ In retrospect, I do not find it easy to assess with precision either the causes which led to the failure to secure agreement or the width of the gap which lay between the failure and success. From the outset there were powerful influences working against a settlement, the most powerful of which was Mr. Gandhi. The decline in confidence in our prospects of victory due to the Japanese successes in the Far East, and especially our defeats in Malaya and Burma, had also a considerable effect. There is no doubt that there was a wide-spread feeling, especially among Hindus, that if the Japanese were to be victorious it might be better for Indian interests if Indian politicians had taken no overt part in India's defence, and also, especially in Hindu business circles, a feeling that the process of defending India on a national basis would involve disproportionately great material and financial losses which would not be offset by any political gain. On the other hand, there were powerful elements in favour of all-out resistance, which included some of the principal Congress Leaders such as Nehru as well as the Muslims and Sikhs and much Middle and Left-Wing opinion ... But throughout the negotiations Mr. Gandhi exerted his influence against any agreement. His motives are always difficult to discern, but his non-violent doctrine alone made his opposition natural. This would induce him to any course of action which would prevent Congress from being drawn into the active organisation of India for its own defence by violent means. Another factor of importance was Mr. Gandhi's appreciation of the challenge of his own position. Had agreement been reached he must have been superseded in his leadership of Congress by Nehru or some other supporter of violent resistance, and he may well have foreseen that in such circumstances it would have been extremely difficult for him to stage a come-back. He was, therefore, I think, determined to fight against agreement at all costs ...

While none of the minorities are prepared openly to oppose the claim for Indian self-determination, and all of them professedly support that demand, they are none of them ready to abandon the idea that the British Government should in some way interfere in the process of making the constitution of a free India to secure provisions in the constitution for their protection. I hope that my conversations have helped to bring them face to face with the inconsistency of their position, and to a recognition that it is only by Treaty protection that we can, once granted the right of self-determination for India, secure minority rights ...

I feel that, as a result of my visit, India has itself been made to face the practical problem of self-government in a way that it has never had to face it before, and that, although there must be a period of great confusion of thought and difficulty as a result, this is a necessary stage through which we must pass ... ■

The response of the Dominions at the outbreak of war had been, as in 1914, impressive. Yet, as the war unfolded, strains in their relations with London emerged. After the fall of France, for instance, Canada had recognised the importance to its security of friendship with the United States, formalised under the Ogdensburg Agreement of 1940. Similarly, Australia had been concerned about Japanese intentions even before Japan entered the war.

By early 1942 the situation in the Far East seemed desperate. With Japanese forces poised to enter Burma, London frantically urged the Australian government to help in the region's defence. However, as Dominions Secretary Clement Attlee candidly admitted in the following telegram to the Australian Prime Minister, there was little that Britain could do in return to defend Australia, which was encouraged instead to look to the United States.

1.16 Clement Attlee, telegram to John Curtin, 20 February 1942 (Department of Foreign Affairs, *Documents on Australian Foreign Policy 1937–49, Vol. V,* Canberra, Australian Government Publishing Service, 1982, pp. 546–7).

■ Cablegram 233

MOST IMMEDIATE   MOST SECRET

Following for the Prime Minister from the Prime Minister. (Begins): I suppose you realise that your leading division, the head of which is sailing south of Colombo to N[etherlands] E[ast] I[ndies] at this moment in our scanty British and American shipping ..., is the only force that can reach Rangoon in time to prevent its loss and the severance of communication with China. It can begin to disembark at Rangoon about 26th or 27th. There is nothing else in the world that can fill the gap.

2. We are all entirely in favour of all Australian troops returning home to defend their native soil, and we shall help their transportation in every way. But a vital war emergency cannot be ignored, and troops en route to other destinations must be ready to turn aside and take part in a battle. Every effort should be made to relieve this division at the earliest moment and send them on to Australia. I do not endorse the United States' request that you should send your other two divisions to Burma. They will return home as fast as possible but this one is needed now, and is the only one that can possibly save the situation.

3. Pray read again your message No. JOHCU 21 in which you said that the evacuation of Singapore would be an 'inexcusable betrayal'. Agreeably with your point of view we therefore [put] the 18th Division and other important reinforcements into Singapore instead of diverting them to Burma and ordered them to fight it out to the end. They were lost at Singapore and did not save it, whereas they could almost certainly have saved Rangoon. I take full responsibility with my colleagues on the Defence Committee for this decision; but you also bear a heavy share on account of your telegram No. JOHCU 21.

4. Your greatest support in this hour of peril must be drawn from the United States. They alone can bring into Australia the necessary troops and air forces and they appear ready to do so ...

5. I am quite sure that if you refuse to allow your troops to stop this gap who are actually passing and if in consequence the above [evils] affecting the whole course of the war follow, a very grave effect will be produced upon the President and the Washington circle on whom you are so largely dependent ... ■

Colonialism reappraised

International criticism of colonial rule and London's need to retain the loyalty of the colonial populations, together with humanitarian concern, led to major reappraisals of the purpose of British colonial rule during the war.

Emphasis was increasingly placed on the importance of raising colonial living standards through economic development and welfare provision. Although two Colonial Development and Welfare Acts were passed during the war to fund this, practical constraints, such as shortages of materials and personnel, prevented much being achieved in wartime. Nevertheless, colonial rule had been given a new, apparently progressive rationale, as the Colonial Secretary, Oliver Stanley, sought to explain in Parliament in 1943.

1.17   **Oliver Stanley, speech to the House of Commons on colonial policy, 13 July 1943 (*Hansard*, 5th ser., 391: 48–52, 69).**

■ The central purpose of our Colonial administration has often been proclaimed. It has been called the doctrine of trusteeship, although I think some of us feel now that that word 'trustee' is rather too static in its connotation and that we should prefer to combine with the status of trustee the position also of partner. But we are pledged to guide Colonial people along the road to self-government within the framework of the British Empire. We are pledged to build up their economic and social institutions, and we are pledged to develop their natural resources ...

It is the tendency, both here and abroad, for those who criticise, or indeed for those who are interested in Colonial administration, to concentrate on political evolution, and it is by our success in that field, success in advancing these Colonial territories towards self-government, that critics are apt to test both our sincerity and our efficiency. I do not mind being judged by that test if those who use it are aware of and understand the full content of the approach to self-government. But it is dangerous if that test is to be too narrowly interpreted, for hon. Members will all agree that, if self-government is to succeed, it has to have solid, social and economic foundations, and although without them spectacular political advances may draw for the authors the plaudits of the superficial, they will bring to those whom it is designed to benefit nothing but disaster. It is no part of our policy to confer political advances which are unjustified by circumstances, or to grant self-government to those who are not yet trained in its use, but if we are to be true to our pledge, if we really mean as soon as practicable to develop self-government in these territories, it is up to us to see that circumstances as soon as possible justify political advances and to ensure that as quickly as possible people are trained and equipped for eventual self-government. Therefore, to my mind, the real test of the sincerity and success of our Colonial policy is two-fold. It is not only the actual political advances that we make, but it is also, and I think more important, the steps that we are taking, economic and social as well as political, to prepare the people for further and future responsibilities ...

It only remains for me to say that anybody who occupies my position now in time of war must suffer from a slight feeling of impatience. There is so much to do and so much we are prevented from doing by the shortages which are inevitable in war-time – the shortage of expert advice, the shortage of labour and, above all, the shortages of material ... Meanwhile, I have no inclination to apologise for the British Colonial Empire. In the past, as even our critics must admit, we have brought to millions of people security for life and property and an even-handed justice which they have never known before. Now it is our responsibility and pride to help those millions along the road to a full, happy and prosperous share in the world of the future. ■

Planning for Peace

The steadily improving military position after 1943 enabled the Allies to consider the postwar settlement. Many members of the British government were nervous about the future intentions of the Soviet Union. The spectacular successes of the Red Army in Eastern Europe served only to intensify these fears.

Churchill's views on postwar relations with the Soviet Union were not consistent; on occasion, he could be pessimistic, though he also hoped that some form of continuing co-operation between Britain, the United States and the Soviet Union would be possible after the war. In January 1944 he wrote to the Foreign Secretary, Sir Anthony Eden, in optimistic terms.

1.18   Winston Churchill, minute to Anthony Eden, 16 January 1944 (PRO PREM 3/399/6, ff. 81–3).

1. You will remember all the discussions we had at the beginning of 1942 about the future of the Baltic States and the very strong line I took against our committing ourselves to their absorption by Russia at that time. We solved these difficulties for the time being by the 20 Years Treaty ...

2. I ask myself, how do all these matters stand now? Undoubtedly my own feelings have changed in the two years that have passed since the topic was first raised during your first visit to Moscow. The tremendous victories of the Russian armies, the deep-seated changes which have taken place in the character of the Russian State and Government, the new confidence which has grown in our hearts towards Stalin – these have all had their effect. Most of all is the fact that the Russians may very soon be in physical possession of these territories, and it is absolutely certain that we should never attempt to turn them out. Moreover, at Teheran when Stalin talked about keeping East Prussia up to Königsberg we did not say anything about the Baltic States, which clearly would be comprised in the Russian Dominions in any such solution.

3. We are now about to attempt the settlement of the eastern frontiers of Poland, and we cannot be unconscious of the fact that the Baltic States, and the questions of Bukovina and Bessarabia, have very largely settled themselves through the victories of the Russian armies. At the same time any pronouncement on the topic might have disastrous effects in the United States in the election year, and there is no doubt that we should ourselves be subject to embarrassing attack in the House of Commons if we decided the fate of these countries.

4. In all these circumstances I should be very glad if you would let me have a note on the whole position of the Russian western frontier as you see it today. As far as I can make out the Russian claim in no way exceeds the former Tsarist boundaries, in fact in some parts it falls notably short of them ... It would be far better to shelve it all until we reach the discussions which we shall have to have after the defeat of Hitler ... ■

In February 1945 the 'Big Three' – Roosevelt, Stalin and Churchill – met at Yalta in the Crimea. Here, they discussed the postwar frontiers of Europe and the Far East, and confirmed their commitment to the enemy's unconditional surrender. Churchill accepted Stalin's right to safeguard Soviet security by creating a buffer zone in Poland and Eastern Europe, a pragmatic recognition of the fact that these areas were by now occupied by the Red Army. However, both Churchill and Roosevelt wanted to prevent the creation of a closed Soviet bloc, and insisted that 'free' elections should be held in Eastern Europe when possible.

The Yalta agreements eased Churchill's anxieties about Stalin. Although he subsequently had misgivings, he continued to hope that negotiation with the Soviet Union, rather than confrontation, would be feasible.

1.19   **'Report of the Crimea conference', 11 February 1945 (PRO PREM 3/51/10, ff. 44–52).**

■ POLAND

We came to the Crimea Conference resolved to settle our differences about Poland. We discussed fully all aspects of question [sic]. We re-affirmed our common desire to see established a strong free independent and democratic Poland. As a result of our discussion we have agreed on the conditions in which a new Polish Provisional Government of National Unity may be formed in such a manner as to command recognition by three major Powers. The agreement reached is as follows:–

A new situation has been created in Poland as a result of her complete liberation by the Red Army.

This calls for the establishment of a Polish Provisional Government which can be more broadly based than was possible before the recent liberation of Western Poland. The Provisional Government which is now functioning in Poland should, therefore, be reorganised on a broader democratic basis with the inclusion of democratic leaders from Poland itself and from Poles abroad. This new Government should then be called the Polish Provisional Government of National Unity ...

This Polish Provisional Government of National Unity shall be pledged to the holding of free and unfettered elections as soon as possible on basis of universal suffrage and secret ballot. In these elections all democratic and anti-Nazi parties shall have the right to take [part] and to put forward candidates.

When a Polish Provisional Government of National Unity has been properly formed in conformity with the above, the Government of the U.S.S.R. which now maintains diplomatic relations with the present Provisional Government of Poland, and the Government of the U.K. and the Government of the U.S. will establish diplomatic relations with the new Polish Provisional Government of National Unity, and will exchange Ambassadors by whose reports the respective Governments will be kept informed about the situation in Poland.

The three Heads of Government consider that the Eastern frontier of Poland should follow the Curzon line with digressions from it in some regions of five to eight kilometres in favour of Poland. They recognise that Poland must receive substantial accessions of territory in the North and West. They feel that the opinion of the new Polish Provisional Government of National Unity should be sought in due course on the extent of these accessions and that the final delimitations of the Western frontier of Poland should therefore await the peace Conference ... ■

Future international relations would be shaped to a great extent by the degree to which the Big Three kept to the agreement they had reached at Yalta. Doubts about Stalin's plans for Eastern Europe were already surfacing in March 1945, as the following extract from Sir John Colville's diary suggests.

1.20   **Sir John Colville, diary entry, 7 March 1945 (in Sir John Colville, *The Fringes of Power: Downing Street Diaries, Vol. Two: 1941–April 1955*, London, Sceptre, 1987, p. 211).**

■ During dinner I showed the P.M. a telegram from Roumania reporting that the new Russian-sponsored Roumanian Government may forcibly remove Radescu, the late Prime Minister, from the sanctuary which has been given him by the British Military mission. This inflamed the P.M. who saw that our honour was at stake. He subsequently spoke to Eden on the telephone. It seems that we may be heading for a show-down with the Russians who are showing every sign of going back on the Yalta agreement over Poland and of enforcing aggressive Communism on an unwilling Roumania. The P.M. and Eden both fear that our willingness to trust our Russian ally may have been vain and they look with despondency to the future. The P.M. is prepared to put the issue to the House and the Country with confidence in their support, but Eden, though nauseated, still hopes the Russians will not face an open breach with ourselves and the Americans. It looks as if Dr Goebbels' disciples may still be able to say "I told you so"; but, God knows, we have tried hard to march in step with Russia towards the broad and sun-lit uplands. If a cloud obscures the sun when we reach them, the responsibility is with Moscow and the bitter, though for the Germans empty, triumph is with Berlin. ■

The Allied onslaught on Germany continued throughout the early months of 1945. On 7 May Germany finally capitulated. Fighting in the Far East, however, dragged on until August 1945, ending only with Japan's unconditional surrender on 14 August, following the dropping of atomic bombs on Hiroshima and Nagasaki by the United States.

The seismic changes in Britain's world position which had occurred since 1939 were reviewed for the Foreign Office by one of its most senior figures, Sir Orme Sargent, in August 1945, shortly before the Japanese surrender. Sargent identified key themes which would preoccupy policy-makers in the postwar years. Most important was the problem of convincing the United States and the Soviet Union to accept Britain's continuing claims to Great Power status.

1.21   Sir Orme Sargent, memorandum, 'Stocktaking after VE-Day', August 1945 (PRO FO 371/50912, no. 5471).

■ The end of the war in Europe leaves us facing three main problems, none of which has any resemblance to the problems with which we were faced at the end of the last war. They are (a) the military occupation by Soviet troops of a large part of Eastern Europe, and the Soviet Government's future policy generally; (b) the economic rehabilitation of Europe so as to prevent a general economic collapse; and (c) the task of administering Germany and deciding on her future institutions in agreement with the Soviet, United States and French Governments.

2. Our own position, too, in dealing with these problems is very different from what it was at the end of the last war, when we and France shared and disputed, and eventually lost, control of Europe. This time the control is to

a large degree in the hands of the Soviet Union and the United States, and neither of them is likely to consider British interests overmuch if they interfere with their own and unless we assert ourselves.

3. Thus it suits us that the principle of co-operation between the three Great Powers should be specifically accepted as the basis on which problems arising out of the war should be handled and decided. Such a co-operative system will, it is hoped, give us a position in the world which we might otherwise find it increasingly difficult to assert and maintain were the other two Great Powers to act independently. It is not that either the United States or the Soviet Union do not wish to collaborate with Great Britain. The United States certainly find it very convenient to do so in order to fortify their own position in Europe and elsewhere; and the Soviet Union recognise in Great Britain a European Power with whom they will certainly have to reckon. But the fact remains that in the minds of our big partners, especially in that of the United States, there is a feeling that Great Britain is now a secondary Power and can be treated as such, and that in the long run all will be well if they – the United States and the Soviet Union – as the two supreme World Powers of the future, understand one another. It is this misconception which it must be our policy to combat.

4. We have many cards in our hands if we choose to use them – our political maturity; our diplomatic experience; the confidence which the solidarity of our democratic institutions inspires in Western Europe; and our incomparable war record. Unlike our two great partners we are not regarded in Western Europe either as gangsters or as go-getters. But we must do something about organising our side or we shall find our friends gradually drifting away from us. Time is not necessarily on our side. For this reason and because we are numerically the weakest and geographically the smallest of the three Great Powers, it is essential that we should increase our strength in not only the diplomatic but also the economic and military sphere. This clearly can best be done by enrolling France and the lesser Western European Powers, and, of course, also the Dominions, as collaborators with us in this tripartite system. Only so shall we be able, in the long run, to compel our two big partners to treat us as an equal. Even so, our collaboration with the Soviet Union, and even with the United States, is not going to be easy in view of the wide divergence between our respective outlooks, traditions and methods ... ■

CHAPTER TWO

Politics and Social Reform, 1940–5

THE domestic consequences of the Second World War were hardly less far-reaching than its impact on Britain's world position. The all-out military struggle required the maximum possible utilisation of the country's entire resources. To a much greater extent than during the First World War, the civilian population found themselves an integral part of total war, their homes and workplaces forming the 'Home Front'. Mobilisation of the economy and the population involved unprecedented government controls and growing state intervention in everyday life.

Politically, the war had major repercussions. Military reversals in 1940 and a loss of public confidence brought about the downfall of the National government, which had been in power since 1931, and demands for a new style of leadership and a true coalition. Winston Churchill, who had been isolated during the 1930s, returned to centre stage not only as the country's war leader but also as leader of the Conservative Party. The Labour Party, brought into Churchill's War Coalition, won the opportunity to shed the stigma of irresponsibility and incaution characteristic of the 1930s. Its leading figures became familiar and respected.

Superficially, at least, a new centre ground seemed to be developing in British politics, in which the two major parties discovered wide areas of policy on which they could agree. Whether this laid the foundations of a postwar political consensus is debatable. Although all parties were obliged to address the domestic economic and social issues which came to dominate politics, differences in their attitudes, for example on the role of the state in economic management and welfare provision, may have become muted but did not disappear.

This was revealed by contrasting party responses to the debates on reconstruction, given momentum by the landmark Beveridge Report of 1942 but already in progress before this. These tapped into and encouraged growing popular expectations of a better postwar social order and sweeping social reform, in part based on the success of wartime state intervention. Whether such hopes demonstrated a leftward shift in public opinion is also debatable; nevertheless, the Labour Party's general election victory in 1945 must in part be attributed to widened perceptions that Labour was more committed to domestic reform than were its rivals.

The Experience of Total War

Many lessons were learned by the government from the experience of the First World War. Comprehensive controls were soon introduced affecting the civilian population, for example in the spheres of food supply, transport and work. In order to avoid the tensions created by inequalities in food supplies during the First World War, rationing of many items was quickly begun.

In addition to the hardships of rationing, shortages, evacuation and dislocation, civilians faced the dangers of air raids by the Luftwaffe. One of the most devastating episodes was the attack on the Midlands industrial city of Coventry on 14 November 1940, in which 554 people died. Fireman George Kyrke later recalled his experiences that night when dealing with a blaze at one of the city's largest department stores.

2.1   **Auxiliary Fire Serviceman George Kyrke, memories of the bombing of Coventry, 14 November 1940 (in N. Longmate, *Air Raid: The Bombing of Coventry*, London, Hutchinson, 1976, p.114).**

■ When we arrived the building was well alight. All doors were locked. An iron grille delayed action by us. By the time we gained entry we realized that it was impossible to save the place from the inside so we played on the fire from a hydrant outside ... We had lost all sense of time [but] it must have been about midnight when we saw an object which appeared to be attached to a parachute falling in our direction. Four of my crew ran for shelter into Millets Stores' doorway, so Charles S., my deputy, and I took over the hose and continued to damp down the raging fires. A terrific explosion threw us to the ground and when we recovered ourselves, very dazed but not seriously hurt, we found the rest of the crew had disappeared. Charles and I tore away bricks, stone and rubble and after what seemed an interminable time we managed to free one of the buried crew. He was still alive and asked for a cigarette but before we could light it, he died. We struggled with our pump but could not get it going; it was badly damaged. Then, climbing over the piles of rubble, we found a pump at the bottom of Cross Cheaping unmanned. Using the murky water of the River Sherbourne we managed to get the pump working, only to be foiled by a leaking hose. There was nothing we could do so we decided to return to the Central Station – if it was still there. ■

As the chart shown as document 2.2 (overleaf) demonstrates, the worst years for air raid casualties were 1940 and 1941, 'the Blitz'. In 1944 casualties rose again as new German terror weapons, such as the V1 'doodlebug' and V2 rockets were brought into operation.

2.2   British civilian deaths resulting from the war, 1939–45 (chart derived from Central Statistical Office, *Statistical Digest of the War*, London, HMSO, 1951, pp. 37, 40).

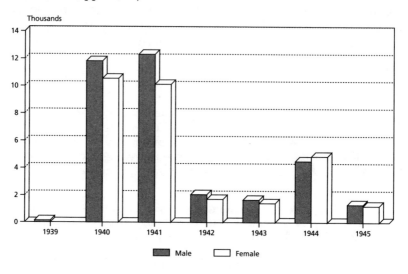

Male   Female

Maintaining civilian morale, to counter defeatism and rumour was considered vital to the war effort. The government, through the specially created Ministry of Information, devoted considerable energy to producing effective propaganda, using every available medium.

2.3   Government wartime propaganda, 'Careless talk costs lives: you never know who's listening!' and 'Dig for victory', undated posters (Imperial War Museum, London, PS252 and PS259).

Total war made labour a prime resource. In 1941 the government assumed the power to direct labour to essential war work. As in the First World War, the trade unions accepted the principle of 'diluting' labour, enabling skilled workers to be replaced by unskilled labour. Female workers increasingly became essential to the smooth running of the economy.

2.4 Philip Zec, 'Women of Britain come into the factories', undated poster (Imperial War Museum, London, PS263).

An important by-product of the full mobilisation of the country's economy for total war was the achievement of near-full employment, even in those industries which had been depressed in the inter-war years. Average wage rates rose also, although rationing and other constraints often meant there was little on which to spend this new disposable income.

2.5 **Average weekly earnings, 1938–45 (chart derived from W.K. Hancock and M.M. Gowing, *The British War Economy*, London, HMSO, 1949, p. 201).**

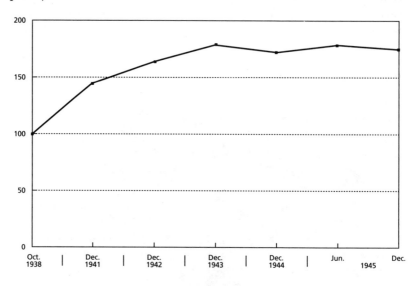

Many workers, especially those in the relatively well-paid munitions industries, were able to amass substantial savings for the first time in their lives. During 1940, in a series of articles in The Times, *the economist John Maynard Keynes advocated a system of compulsory saving, in which the higher incomes arising from the war would not be made available until afterwards, allowing the government to borrow during the war. When goods were more freely available after the war, workers would be able to draw on their savings, and their spending would help alleviate the expected postwar depression.*

2.6 **J.M. Keynes, 1940, *How to Pay for the War*, London, Macmillan, 1940, pp. 1, 10–12.**

■ It is not easy for a free community to organise for war. We are not accustomed to listen to experts or prophets. Our strength lies in an ability to improvise. Yet an open mind to untried ideas is also necessary ... Courage will be forthcoming if the leaders of opinion in all parties will summon out of the fatigue and confusion of war enough lucidity of mind to understand for themselves and to explain to the public what is required; and then propose a plan conceived in a spirit of social justice, a plan which uses a time of general sacrifice, not as an excuse for postponing desirable reforms, but as an opportunity for moving further than we have moved hitherto towards reducing inequalities ...

The first provision in our radical plan is ... to determine a proportion of each man's earnings which must be deferred; – withdrawn, that is to say, from immediate consumption and only made available as a right to consume after the war is over. If the proportion can be fixed fairly for each income group, this device will have a double advantage. It means that rights to immediate consumption during the war can be allotted with a closer regard to relative sacrifice than under any other plan. It also means that rights to deferred consumption after the war, which is another name for the National Debt, will be widely distributed amongst all those who are forgoing immediate consumption, instead of being mainly concentrated, as they were last time, in the hands of the capitalist class.

The second provision is to provide for this deferred consumption without increasing the National Debt by a general capital levy after the war.

The third provision is to protect from any reductions in current consumption those whose standard of life offers no sufficient margin. This is effected by an exempt minimum, a sharply progressive scale and a system of family allowances. The net result of these proposals is, to increase the consumption of young families with less than 75s. a week, to leave the aggregate consumption of the lower income group having £5 a week or less nearly as high as before the war (whilst at the same time giving them rights, in return for extra work, to deferred consumption after the war), and to reduce the aggregate consumption of the higher income group with more than £5 a week by about a third on the average.

The fourth provision, rendered possible by the previous provisions but not itself essential to them, is to link further changes in money-rates of wages, pensions and other allowances to changes in the cost of a limited range of rationed articles of consumption, an iron ration as it has been called, which the authorities will endeavour to prevent, one way or another, from rising in price.

A general plan like this, to which all are required to conform, is like a rule of the road – everyone gains and no one can lose. To regard such a rule as an infringement of liberty is somewhat silly. If the rule of the road is imposed, people will travel as much as before. Under this plan people will consume as much as before. The rule of the road allows people as much choice, as they would have without it, along which roads to travel. This plan would allow people as much choice as before what goods they consume. ■

An important consequence of near-full employment was an expansion of the tax base; since more people worked and paid taxes, government revenue rose accordingly. This, however, did not nearly meet the massive increase in government expenditure, most of which was war-related. While, in 1939–40, 45 per cent of public spending had been on defence, by 1944–5 the figure was 83 per cent. Early in the war it had been hoped that increased taxation and an export drive would pay for the war effort. The crisis of summer 1940 revealed the inadequacy of this approach. Henceforth, the government was forced to resort to heavy borrowing and the sale of overseas assets.

2.7   Central government expenditure and revenue, 1938–45 (chart derived from W.K. Hancock and M.M. Gowing, *The British War Economy*, London, HMSO, 1949, p. 200).

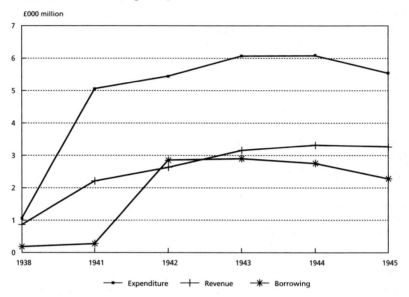

£000 million

—•— Expenditure   —+— Revenue   —✳— Borrowing

Wartime Politics

With the outbreak of the war, the three main political parties agreed on an electoral truce, which meant that they would not contest by-elections during the war. Prime Minister Neville Chamberlain attempted to broaden the composition of the Cabinet by including some of his former Conservative opponents, notably Winston Churchill and Anthony Eden. Nevertheless, the government was still heavily 'Chamberlainite' in character.

The Labour Party, still distrustful of Chamberlain, refused to join the government in 1939. Hugh Dalton, a senior Labour figure, recorded his colleagues' reasons in his diary.

2.8   Hugh Dalton on Chamberlain's War Cabinet, 6 September 1939 (in B. Pimlott (ed.), *The Political Diary of Hugh Dalton 1918–40, 1945–60*, London, Cape, 1986, p. 297).

■ I speak to Butler ...

He asks why we decline to join the Government. I tell him that I will answer this question quite frankly. Having regard to our frequently expressed views of the P.M. and Simon, we could not enter a Cabinet in which these two were Numbers 1 and 2. Moreover, we should require the influence of Sir

Horace Wilson to be eliminated. If we read that he had been appointed Governor of the Windward Islands and had already left England in order to take up this most respected position, we should be favourably impressed. (He asked whether we really attached as much importance to Wilson as this. I say, 'Yes, certainly, and I have so told a member of the War Cabinet, and one of my colleagues has so told another.') Continuing, I point out that if, for instance, members of the Labour Party were given, say, one seat in the Inner Cabinet, plus the Postmaster-General and the Secretaryship of State for Latrines, we should not only be uninfluential within, but we should lose most of our power to exercise influence from without, since we should be continually referred to as 'Your Mr So-and-So, who is now a Secretary of State'. Further, we should lose much of our own credit amongst our own people, who would be filled with suspicions at our official participation. He said that he agreed that these were weighty arguments. ■

During the so-called 'Phoney War', Chamberlain's government proved unable to offer inspiring leadership. Concern among the Labour Party, shared by some Conservatives, about Chamberlain's capacity crystallised in spring 1940, when British troops were obliged to withdraw from Norway, although the responsibility for this fiasco was Churchill's. In the resulting House of Commons debate, it became clear that Chamberlain had lost many Conservatives' confidence, and his government's majority fell from 200 to only 81. Leopold Amery, a veteran Conservative, later to be brought into the government as Secretary of State for India, delivered one of the most damning speeches.

2.9   Leopold Amery, speech in the House of Commons, 7 May 1940 (*Hansard*, 5th ser., 360: 1140–50).

■ We cannot go on as we are. There must be a change. First and foremost, it must be a change in the system and structure of our government machine. This is war, not peace. The essence of peace-time democratic government is discussion, conference and agreement; the Cabinet is in a sense a miniature Parliament. The main aim is agreement, the widest possible measure of agreement. To secure that it is necessary to compromise, to postpone, to rediscuss. Under those conditions there are no far-reaching plans for sudden action. It is a good thing to let policies develop as you go along and get people educated by circumstances. That may or may not be ideal in peace. It is impossible in war. In war the first essential is planning ahead. The next essential is swift, decisive action.

We can wage war only on military principles. One of the first of these principles is the clear definition of individual responsibilities – not party responsibilities or Cabinet responsibilities – and, with it, a proper delegation of authority ... What is our present Cabinet system? There are some 25 Ministers, heads of Departments, who have no direct chief above them except the Prime Minister. How often do they see him? How often can they get from him direct advice, direct impulse, direct drive? Who is to settle disputes between them? There should be someone, not chairmen of innumerable committees, but someone with authority over these Ministers and directly responsible for their efficiency ...

Believe me, as long as the present methods prevail, all our valour and all our resources are not going to see us through. Above all, so long as they prevail, time is not going to be on our side, because they are methods which, inevitably and inherently, waste time and weaken decisions. What we must have, and have soon, is a supreme war directorate of a handful of men free from administrative routine, free to frame policy among themselves, and with the task of supervising, inspiring, and impelling a group of departments clearly allocated to each one of them. That is the only way. We learned that in the last war ...

We must have, first of all, a right organisation of government. What is no less important to-day is that the Government shall be able to draw upon the whole abilities of the nation. It must represent all the elements of real political power in this country, whether in this House or not. The time has come when hon. and right hon. Members opposite must definitely take their share of the responsibility. The time has come when the organisation, the power and influence of the Trades Union Congress cannot be left outside. It must, through one of its recognised leaders, reinforce the strength of the national effort from inside. The time has come, in other words, for a real National Government ...

Just as our peace-time system is unsuitable for war conditions, so does it tend to breed peace-time statesmen who are not too well fitted for the conduct of war. Facility in debate, ability to state a case, caution in advancing an unpopular view, compromise and procrastination are the natural qualities – I might almost say, virtues – of a political leader in time of peace. They are fatal qualities in war. Vision, daring, swiftness and consistency of decision are the very essence of victory. In our normal politics, it is true, the conflict of party did encourage a certain combative spirit ... In recent years the normal weakness of our political life has been accentuated by a coalition based upon no clear political principles ... Surely, for the Government of the last 10 years to have bred a band of warrior statesmen would have been little short of a miracle. We have waited for eight months, and the miracle has not come to pass. Can we afford to wait any longer?

Somehow or other we must get into the Government men who can match our enemies in fighting spirit, in daring, in resolution and in thirst for victory ... It may not be easy to find these men. They can be found only by trial and by ruthlessly discarding all who fail and have their failings discovered. We are fighting to-day for our life, for our liberty, for our all; we cannot go on being led as we are. I have quoted certain words of Oliver Cromwell. I will quote certain other words. I do it with great reluctance, because I am speaking of those who are old friends and associates of mine, but they are words which, I think, are applicable to the present situation. This is what Cromwell said to the Long Parliament when he thought it was no longer fit to conduct the affairs of the nation:

'You have sat too long here for any good you have been doing. Depart, I say, and let us have done with you. In the name of God, go.' ■

By 9 May 1940 Chamberlain had concluded that he had to create a true coalition. Yet the Labour Party clearly would not serve under him as Prime Minister. Two possible successors emerged, Winston Churchill and Lord Halifax, the Foreign Secretary, either of whom Labour would accept. On 10 May, as Halifax later described in his memoirs, Churchill became Prime Minister.

2.10   The Earl of Halifax, *Fulness of Days*, London, Collins, 1957, pp. 219–20.

■ The Prime Minister recapitulated the position, saying he had made up his mind that he must go, and that either Churchill or I must take his place. He would serve under either. It would therefore be necessary to see the Labour people before they went to Bournemouth, where they were about to hold a party conference, and ask them whether they would, on principle, be prepared to join the Government (a) under the Present Prime Minister, or (b) under some other Prime Minister. David Margesson said that unity was essential and that he did not think this could be secured under Chamberlain. He did not at that moment pronounce definitely between Churchill and myself. I then said that I thought for the reasons given the Prime Minister must probably go, but that I had no doubt at all in my own mind that for me to succeed him would create a quite impossible situation. Apart altogether from Churchill's qualities as compared with my own at this particular juncture, what would in fact be my position? Churchill would be running Defence, and in this connection one could not but remember how rapidly the relationship between Asquith and Lloyd George had broken down in the first war, and I should have no access to the House of Commons. The inevitable result would be that, outside both these points of vital contact, I should speedily become a more or less honorary Prime Minister, living in a kind of twilight just outside the things that really mattered. I might if necessary have prayed in aid the experience of Lord Rosebery as Prime Minister with Sir William Harcourt leading the House of Commons, but Churchill, with suitable expressions of regard and humility, having said he could not but feel the force of my words, the Prime Minister reluctantly and Churchill evidently with much less reluctance finished by accepting my view.

So there we left it for the time being, Churchill and I having a cup of tea in the garden while the Prime Minister kept some other appointment, before we all saw Attlee and Greenwood together at 6.15 p.m. When we met, Chamberlain put the position to them, and it was finally agreed that they should consult their executive on the following day upon the two main points as to whether the Labour Party would join the Government either under Chamberlain or under somebody else. At six o'clock the following morning (10th May) the Belgian and Dutch Ambassadors presented themselves at my rooms at the Dorchester Hotel to report the invasion of their countries, and these new developments led Chamberlain for a short time to feel that reconstruction of the Government must stand over till the war situation was more stable. But this was plainly impossible, and the Labour Party having replied that they would not serve under him but would join in under somebody else, Chamberlain went to the King to resign his office and to advise sending for Churchill. ■

Churchill's appointment was popular. Some elements of the press had been calling for it since the outbreak of war. Now, it appeared, political differences could be set aside and a concerted war effort, based on national cohesion, could be forged. In a characteristically forceful piece of imagery, the cartoonist David Low sought to capture the new mood.

2.11   **David Low, 'All behind you, Winston',** *Evening Standard* **cartoon, 14 May 1940.**

The coalition under Churchill

Churchill initially formed a small War Cabinet of five members, although this was subsequently increased in size. Two senior Labour men, Clement Attlee and Arthur Greenwood, were included, along with two Conservatives, Chamberlain and Halifax. The government remained predominantly Conservative in membership, Labour having sixteen posts compared to the Conservatives' fifty-two.

Chamberlain was retained partly out of deference to his still substantial Tory following and because of Churchill's desire to minimise dissent. In October 1940 ill-health forced Chamberlain to resign. He died the following month. This strengthened the position of Churchill, who became leader of the Conservative Party.

As both Prime Minister and Minister of Defence, Churchill had overall responsibility for war strategy, and other Conservatives took key posts in the foreign, imperial and defence spheres. As a result, the Labour members of the Coalition, besides gaining valuable experience of office, also tended to become closely identified with the domestic issues so important to the electorate. The Coalition seemed to work well under Churchill, and the business of government acquired new drive and dynamism. Sir Edward Bridges, Cabinet Secretary between 1938 and 1947, later recalled Churchill's impact on government.

2.12   Sir Edward Bridges on Churchill as prime minister, 1968 (in Sir J. Wheeler-Bennet (ed.), *Action This Day: Working with Churchill,* **London, Macmillan, 1968, pp. 220–2, 228, 234–5).**

■ But, for all the calm and confidence which Churchill radiated, within a very few days of his becoming Prime Minister, the whole machinery of government was working at a pace, and with an intensity of purpose, quite unlike anything which had gone before. It was as though the machine had overnight acquired one or two new gears, capable of far higher speeds than had ever before been thought possible.

No doubt the acute crisis in the nation's affairs had something to do with this. But I believe that the main reason for the change lay in the vigorous sense of purpose which at once made itself felt, and in the methods which Churchill introduced. His experience of Government business enabled him to pick out the points on which prompt decisions were needed, and his authority to make sure that they were brought before him and that decisions were given without delay ...

Working for Churchill was unlike working for any other man. Perhaps the chief difference lay in the relationship which he established with those who worked for him.

It soon became clear that he liked to have about him a group of those whom he saw frequently. Chief of these, of course, were the senior Ministers, with some of whom he was in almost day-to-day consultation. On a different level were those who were called upon to provide him with help and services of various kinds ...

In these years there were no regular office hours. Nor indeed was there any frontier between the Prime Minister's office and the quarters in the New Public Offices overlooking Birdcage Walk in which he and Mrs Churchill lived for most of the war. We might find ourselves in his study or in his bedroom, or be called in to take some urgent orders while he was having a meal with his family. Before long he made us all feel that we had in some sense become honorary members of his domestic household ...

Throughout the war he sent a stream of Minutes to Ministers, and those in charge of particular branches of administration, putting questions – some of them on matters of great importance, others on minor issues. Many of these Minutes carried an 'ACTION THIS DAY' slip.

Churchill had several motives for these Minutes. The first – the more personal one – was his intense interest in and curiosity about everything which contributed to the nation's war effort. His vast energies found satisfaction in exploring each one of them, great and small.

The second and more important motive was his instinctive distrust of large organisations, whether civil or military. He was suspicious of what would happen to any question when it passed down the line into the depths of some great Department. How long might it not be before a decision was reached? And what processes of thought unknown to Ministers, or unacceptable to them, might not be brought into play in reaching a decision?

Moreover the Minister or official to whom the Minute was addressed had himself to look into the matter and produce almost immediately a short convincing answer, and this brought home his personal responsibility, in much the same way as Churchill established a special relationship with his own staff ...

The argument that politicians were not given sufficient scope cuts no ice. It is, however, true that during the Second World War Churchill inevitably occupied a far more dominating position than any other British Prime Minister for at least half a century. But this was due to the circumstances in which he became Prime Minister and to the fact that he alone had the qualities and authority needed to lead the country.

To anyone who still maintains that Churchill played an unduly dominating role in the war, I would reply: firstly, that relations between the politicians and the soldiers were infinitely better in the Second than in the First World War; and secondly, that I cannot recollect a single Minister, serving officer or civil servant who was removed from office because he stood up to Churchill and told Churchill that he thought his policy or proposals were wrong ... ■

While Churchill was preoccupied with strategy and diplomacy, and showed less interest in domestic issues, the Labour Party became identified with a growing awareness of the need for reform. Many contemporary commentators detected a swing to the political left among the British public during the war, an impatience with the traditional class structures, and a belief that the growth in state powers would make a transition to socialism virtually inevitable. The novelist George Orwell captured this mood in his essay The Lion and the Unicorn, *an early attempt to define the war's political goals. It was written in London at the height of the Blitz.*

2.13   **George Orwell on English socialism, 1941 (in George Orwell, *The Lion and the Unicorn*, London, Penguin, 1982, pp. 102–4, 112–13).**

■ The fact that we are at war has turned Socialism from a textbook word into a realizable policy.

The inefficiency of private capitalism has been proved all over Europe. Its injustice has been proved in the East End of London. Patriotism, against which the Socialists fought so long, has become a tremendous lever in their hands. People who at any other time would cling like glue to their miserable scraps of privilege, will surrender them fast enough when their country is in danger. War is the greatest of all agents of change. It speeds up all processes, wipes out minor distinctions, bring realities to the surface. Above all, war brings it home to the individual that he is not altogether an individual. It is only because they are aware of this that men will die on the field of battle. At this moment it is not so much a question of surrendering life as of surrendering leisure, comfort, economic liberty, social prestige. There are very few people in England who really want to see their country conquered by Germany. If it can be made clear that defeating Hitler means wiping out class privilege, the great mass of middling people, the £6 a week to £2,000 a year class, will probably be on our side. These people are quite indispensable, because they include most of the technical experts. Obviously the snobbishness and political ignorance of people like airmen and naval officers will be a very great difficulty. But without those airmen, destroyer commanders, etc. etc. we could not survive for a week. The only approach to them is through their patriotism. An intelligent Socialist movement will use their patriotism, instead of merely insulting it, as hitherto …

The swing of opinion is visibly happening, but it cannot be counted on to happen fast enough of its own accord. This war is a race between the consolidation of Hitler's empire and the growth of a democratic consciousness. Everywhere in England you can see a ding-dong battle raging to and fro – in Parliament and in the Government, in the factories and the armed forces, in the pubs and air-raid shelters, in the newspapers and on the radio. Every day there are tiny defeats, tiny victories. Morrison for Home Secretary – a few yards forward. Priestley shoved off the air – a few yards back. It is a struggle between the groping and the unteachable, between the young and the old, between the living and the dead. But it is very necessary that the discontent which undoubtedly exists should take a purposeful and not merely obstructive form. It is time for the people to define their war aims. What is wanted is a simple, concrete programme of action, which can be given all possible publicity, and round which public opinion can group itself …

Within a year, perhaps even within six months, if we are still unconquered, we shall see the rise of something that has never existed before, a specifically English Socialist movement. Hitherto there has been only the Labour Party, which was the creation of the working class but did not aim at any fundamental change, and Marxism, which was a German theory interpreted by Russians and unsuccessfully transplanted to England. There was nothing that really touched the heart of the English people ... Nations do not escape from their past merely by making a revolution. An English Socialist government will transform the nation from top to bottom, but it will still bear all over the unmistakable marks of our own civilization ...

It will not be doctrinaire, nor even logical. It will abolish the House of Lords, but quite probably will not abolish the Monarchy. It will leave anachronisms and loose-ends everywhere, the judge in his ridiculous horsehair wig and the lion and the unicorn on the soldier's cap-buttons. It will not set up any explicit class dictatorship. It will group itself round the old Labour Party and its mass following will be in the trade unions, but it will draw into it most of the middle class and many of the younger sons of the bourgeoisie. Most of its directing brains will come from the new indeterminate class of skilled workers, technical experts, airmen, scientists, architects and journalists, the people who feel at home in the radio and ferro-concrete age. But it will never lose touch with the tradition of compromise and the belief in a law that is above the State. ■

Reconstruction

The war gave rise to growing enthusiasm for a new social order after the war. This partly reflected the frustrated hopes of 1918 and of the wasted inter-war years. The sacrifices made by the civilian population, and shared equally by them, prompted calls for social inequalities to be reduced. Moreover, the growth of state intervention in everyday life fostered the belief that the same controls could be employed to address problems of social reform.

The writer J.B. Priestley, who broadcast a series of radio 'Postscripts' in 1940, was an early advocate of purposeful reconstruction, rejecting the negativism of the 1930s. The 'leftish' tone of his comments was not well received in Conservative circles.

2.14   **J.B. Priestley, 'Postscript', 28 July 1940 (in J.B. Priestley, *Postscripts*, London, Heinemann, 1940, p.38).**

■ I will tell you what we did for [servicemen] and their young wives at the end of the last war. We did nothing – except let them take their chance in a world where every gangster and trickster and stupid insensitive fool or rogue was let loose to do his damnedest. After the cheering and the flag-waving was over, and all the medals were given out, somehow the young heroes disappeared, but after a year or two there were a lot of shabby, young-oldish men about who didn't seem to have been lucky in the scramble for easy jobs and quick profits ...

No doubt, it's going to be all different this time, but... the same kind of minds are still about. Among bundles of very friendly letters just lately I've been getting some very fierce and angry ones telling me to get off the air before the Government 'puts you where you belong' – the real Fascist touch. Well, obviously, it wouldn't matter very much if I were taken off the air, but it would matter a great deal, even to these Blimps, if [the] young men of the R.A.F. were taken off the air; and so I repeat my question – in return for their skill, devotion, endurance and self-sacrifice, what are we civilians prepared to do? ... the least we can do is to give our minds honestly, sincerely and without immediate self-interest, to the task of preparing a world really fit for them and their kind – to arrange a final 'happy landing'. ■

The debates on postwar reconstruction gave a public platform to experts in many fields. In 1941 the popular magazine Picture Post *published a special edition devoted to the issue, for which it commissioned articles from leading figures in areas such as health, economic planning and education. Typical of these contributions was that by the rising architect and town planner Maxwell Fry, for whom reconstruction provided the opportunity to achieve improved living conditions for all through planned development.*

2.15 **Maxwell Fry, 'The new Britain must be planned',** *Picture Post,* **4 January 1941.**

■ The ordinary Englishman makes himself comfortable almost anywhere; and he doesn't bother much about the town he lives in, so long as his own kitchen and parlour are all right. That some of our bigger towns are inefficient and untidy to a degree which no woman would tolerate in her kitchen and no man in his workshop, may be news to many – and may not seem to matter much. But bad towns are an invisible burden on every citizen – damaging his health, his pocket, his enjoyment of life. And bad towns are unnecessary. It is a question of thought – of planning.

Given the will to plan, we could, in a quarter of a century or less, substantially transform our worst towns. Where they are black with soot, they could be at least partly green with trees and grass. We could bring the country into the town in great swathes of parkland never more than a step round the corner from the homes of the people. We could, by reorganisation, shorten the weary long journeys to work, and at the same time make the workplace itself more cheerful. We could replan and reconstruct many of our outworn public services, to stop the drain of money to no purpose.

A LAND PLEASANT TO LIVE IN

The main roads of the country can be tree-lined parkways, even into Wigan – yes, and right through it. The country can become real country, reserved for agriculture, instead of land not yet ripe for development. It can become a pleasure to leave a town and enter country where, to-day, it is a hope that at some point or other the mess of unplanned building and wretched advertisement will come to an end.

It can be a certainty that the heritage of beauty in downland, forest and

mountain will remain with us, and that we shall not through sheer care-
lessness lose the chief treasures of architecture and planning that have come
down to us from the past.

For industry, we can plan the pooled resources of power and transport, and
by combining the complementary interests of the community and industry,
bring more settled and happy conditions of labour and a richer life for all
concerned.

You may ask, knowing your England, how such transformations could be
brought about in a country already bunged up with building and overbur-
dened with debt. I ask you to remember how much we spent in the last
twenty-five years after an exhausting war. Was it all spent wisely? Economically? It was spent, and wherever housing was planned, it was well spent.
The planned town of Welwyn is nearly all sheer gain. But competitive development inside and out of towns will cost us millions to correct.

We Can Lead the Way

Another thing – England is a pioneer country. In the last century we produced one improvement after another in town building, and raised the possible level of living. Drainage, water supply, gas, electricity, railways, motor
transport, air transport. These things came in steady succession and many of
the first experiments are still working. Some of them are a hundred years
old; English antiques. Others, being below ground, are only assumed to be
working!

We practically invented the factory system, yet I have walked over an
important industrial plant, containing buildings of every period and decrepi-
tude, that could only be decribed as 'twenty acres of chaos'! And there are
plenty like it in the industrial centres, nearly always associated with housing conditions of equal squalor.

The nineteenth century, as you know, was an age of jungle-like competition, so that not only were these socially useful inventions frustrated by the
mass of unplanned buildings and streets growing everywhere into hopeless
congestion, but because congestion runs counter to healthy and economical
development, invention gradually dried up in England and the lead was
passed to other and better developed countries. To France, Germany and
Sweden, even to Finland, we are indebted for the latest developments of
drainage, sanitation and town-building machinery. We are in need of an
overhaul. The family car is choked up and wastes petrol and oil faster than
we can afford. Scrap it and buy the post-war model, in instalments, with
allowance for the old.

This, roughly, gives you the justification for replanning and rebuilding if
things were normal. They are not normal. As I write, bombs are dropping
on London and fire is raging. Some people imagine that what is destroyed is
a good riddance. This is mistaken, because bombing is haphazard, and the
bad street plan, which bombs never really destroy, is the root evil. But when
people say, as they do, that the East End of London is no loss to us, they

make a confession of real relief that they have no longer to answer their consciences for those slums and muddles. They hope to rebuild to better standards. They begin, in fact, to have a real 'will' to plan.

Town planning works from above and below – nationally and locally. It is for the Government to make up its mind what kind of a country we are, and to plan the larger issues accordingly. Thus it requires the national viewpoint to decide where industry should be induced to go in order that we should have a settled economy without areas of acute depression. Similarly, the lay-out of railway and trunk roads feeding industry and the ports are national in their scope although they affect localities incidentally.

Within a State policy of reconstruction lies the great work of rebuilding our towns and revitalising the country. For this we require the co-operation of industry and the State in a particular way. I have mentioned the inventive-ness of the nineteenth century and you will agree that, without it, we should not have been able to build our great cities. The problem is now more acute. After the war we must start rebuilding in a hurry, but to a long-term plan. ■

Social reform

The war has been seen by many commentators as advancing the cause of state responsibility for social reform. Certainly, the war appeared to raise popular expectations and enthusiasm for a more egalitarian future. The growth of state controls during the war seemed to indicate the possibilities for using govern-ment machinery to reduce social inequalities. During the war, the Coalition did introduce some measures of social reform, for example with the abolition of the despised Family Means Test in 1941, and the passage of the Butler Education Act of 1944. In the same year the government pledged its commitment to maintaining the highest possible level of employment.

Probably the most important episode in wartime discussions on social reform followed the publication in December 1942 of the report on social insurance by the distinguished academic Sir William Beveridge. The Beveridge Report, widely seen as the blueprint for the 'welfare state', quickly gained widespread popularity; unusually for an officially sponsored report, 100,000 copies were sold within a month of its publication.

·**2.16**   Sir William Beveridge, *Social Insurance and Allied Services: Report by Sir William Beveridge* (Beveridge Report), London, HMSO, November 1942 (Cmd 6404, PP VI, 1942–3, pp. 6–9, 11–12).

■ ...

7. The first principle is that any proposals for the future, while they should use to the full the experience gathered in the past, should not be restricted

by consideration of sectional interests established in the obtaining of that experience. Now, when the war is abolishing landmarks of every kind, is the opportunity for using experience in a clear field. A revolutionary moment in the world's history is a time for revolutions, not for patching.

8. The second principle is that organisation of social insurance should be treated as one part only of a comprehensive policy of social progress. Social insurance fully developed may provide income security; it is an attack upon Want. But Want is one only of five giants on the road of reconstruction and in some ways the easiest to attack. The others are Disease, Ignorance, Squalor and Idleness.

9. The third principle is that social security must be achieved by co-operation between the State and the individual. The State should offer security for service and contribution. The State in organising security should not stifle incentive, opportunity, responsibility; in establishing a national minimum, it should leave room and encouragement for voluntary action by each individual to provide more than that minimum for himself and his family.

10. The Plan for Social Security set out in this Report is built upon these principles. It uses experience but is not tied by experience. It is put forward as a limited contribution to a wider social policy, though as something that could be achieved now without waiting for the whole of that policy. It is, first and foremost, a plan of insurance – of giving in return for contributions benefits up to subsistence level, as of right and without means test, so that individuals may build freely upon it ...

12. Abolition of want requires, first, improvement of State insurance, that is to say provision against interruption and loss of earning power. All the principal causes of interruption or loss of earnings are now the subject of schemes of social insurance. If, in spite of these schemes, so many persons unemployed or sick or old or widowed are found to be without adequate income for subsistence according to the standards adopted in the social surveys, this means that the benefits amount to less than subsistence by those standards or do not last as long as the need, and that the assistance which supplements insurance is either insufficient in amount or available only on terms which make men unwilling to have recourse to it. None of the insurance benefits provided before the war were in fact designed with reference to the standards of the social surveys. Though unemployment benefit was not altogether out of relation to those standards, sickness and disablement benefit, old age pensions and widows' pensions were far below them, while workmen's compensation was below subsistence level for anyone who had family responsibilities or whose earnings in work were less than twice the amount needed for subsistence. To prevent interruption or destruction of earning power from leading to want, it is necessary to improve the present schemes of social insurance in three directions: by extension of scope to cover persons now excluded, by extension of purposes to cover risks now excluded, and by raising the rates of benefit.

13. Abolition of want requires, second, adjustment of incomes, in periods of earning as well as in interruption of earning, to family needs, that is to say, in one form or another it requires allowances for children. Without such allowances as part of benefit or added to it, to make provision for large families, no social insurance against interruption of earnings can be adequate. But, if children's allowances are given only when earnings are interrupted and not given during earning also, two evils are unavoidable. First, a substantial measure of acute want will remain among the lower paid workers as the accompaniment of large families. Second, in all such cases, income will be greater during unemployment or other interruptions of work than during work.

14. By a double re-distribution of income through social insurance and children's allowances, want, as defined in the social surveys, could have been abolished in Britain before the present war ...

17. The main feature of the Plan for Social Security is a scheme of social insurance against interruption and destruction of earning power and for special expenditure arising at birth, marriage or death. The scheme embodies six fundamental principles: flat rate of subsistence benefit; flat rate of contribution; unification of administrative responsibility; adequacy of benefit; comprehensiveness; and classification ... Based on them and in combination with national assistance and voluntary insurance as subsidiary methods, the aim of the Plan for Social Security is to make want under any circumstances unnecessary ...

20. Under the scheme of social insurance, which forms the main feature of this plan, every citizen of working age will contribute in his appropriate class according to the security that he needs, or as a married woman will have contributions made by the husband. Each will be covered for all his needs by a single weekly contribution on one insurance document. All the principal cash payments – for unemployment, disability and retirement – will continue so long as the need lasts, without means test, and will be paid from a Social Insurance Fund built up by contributions from the insured persons, from their employers, if any, and from the State. This is in accord with two views as to the lines on which the problem of income maintenance should be approached.

21. The first view is that benefit in return for contributions, rather than free allowances from the State, is what the people of Britain desire. This desire is shown both by the established popularity of compulsory insurance, and by the phenomenal growth of voluntary insurance against sickness, against death and for endowment, and most recently for hospital treatment. It is shown in another way by the strength of popular objection to any kind of means test. This objection springs not so much from a desire to get anything for nothing, as from resentment at a provision which appears to penalise what people have come to regard as the duty and pleasure of thrift, of putting pennies away for a rainy day. Management of one's income is an essential element of a citizen's freedom. Payment of a substantial part of the cost of benefit as a contribution irrespective of the means of the contributor is the firm basis of a claimant to benefit irrespective of means.

22. The second view is that whatever money is required for provision of insurance benefits, so long as they are needed, should come from a Fund to which the recipients have contributed and to which they may be required to make larger contributions if the Fund proves inadequate. The plan adopted since 1930 in regard to prolonged unemployment and sometimes suggested for prolonged disability, that the State should take this burden off insurance, in order to keep the contribution down, is wrong in principle. The insured persons should not feel that income for idleness, however caused, can come from a bottomless purse. The Government should not feel that by paying doles it can avoid the major responsibility of seeing that unemployment and disease are reduced to the minimum. The place for direct expenditure and organisation by the State is in maintaining employment of the labour and other productive resources of the country, and in preventing and combating disease, not in patching an incomplete scheme of insurance. ■

The financial implications of Beveridge's proposals alarmed sections of the Coalition, notably the (Conservative) Chancellor, Sir Kingsley Wood. Churchill, too, thought it dangerous to encourage expectations which might not be realisable, given the country's other likely expenditure commitments, and saw much of the reconstruction debate as a diversion of energy from the main task of winning the war. Such a lukewarm government response was politically dangerous. When the report was debated in the House of Commons, nearly every Labour MP voted against the government, the only occasion during the war when this happened.

In January 1943 a secret Conservative Party committee on Beveridge delivered its critical verdict on the report's proposals. The outcome was a severely pruned scale of provision, in which unemployment benefit would seldom be more attractive than the lowest-paid employment, and compulsory health insurance would not apply to the higher paid. Above all, the extent of reform would be dictated by postwar economic conditions.

2.17 **Conservative Party Beveridge Report Committee, report on the Beveridge proposals, 19 January 1943 (Conservative Party Archives).**

■ Sir William Beveridge's Report expresses the views of one man on a number of highly technical subjects, and although he had the advantage of the assistance of many eminent Civil Servants, the Report is his alone and does not contain, as is widely assumed, the recommendations of a well qualified expert Committee. There is no doubt, however, that the great publicity which the Report has received in the Press, on the platform and over the wireless has unfortunately led many people to assume that it represents Government policy and is likely to be carried into speedy effect as soon as the war is over. This does not make an approach to the problems any easier, since many hopes have been raised which it may not be possible to satisfy ...

There is much in the Report which is bound to commend itself to thought-ful people, and the country is under a great debt to the author for the way in which he has assembled in one document a great deal of material which is necessary for the study of the problem.

In spite, however, of the fact that he diagnoses various ills and attributes them to want, it must be realised at once that a great part of the money required for putting his scheme into effect is not devoted to curing want. Sir William is in search of a comprehensive and unified scheme of social secu-rity for the citizens of this country. Provision by the State of complete social security can only be achieved at the expense of personal freedom and by sacrificing the right of an individual to choose what life he wishes to lead and what occupation he should follow.

In so far however as it can be achieved, without loss of essential freedom, we agree with him in basing it on the fundamental conception of contribu-tion rather than State assistance, though in the working out of his scheme the contribution to be made by the taxpayer increases steadily as the years go by while the contributions to be paid by the insured persons or their employers do not rise. The scheme becomes more and more one for distrib-uting national income by means of taxation rather than a scheme based on the contributions of those who are to receive the benefits ... ∎

R.A. Butler, the Conservative education minister in the Coalition who successfully intro-duced educational reforms in 1944, later recalled some of the problems examined by the Cabinet Reconstruction Committee during the so-called 'white paper chase'.

2.18   **R.A. Butler on reconstruction, 1971 (in R.A. Butler, *The Art of the Possible: The Memoirs of Lord Butler*, London, Hamish Hamilton, 1971, pp. 124–5).**

∎ The crippling qualities of expense were much in the minds of my Coali-tion colleagues when they came to consider the further and wider problems of post-war reconstruction. 'We cannot initiate the legislation now or com-mit ourselves to the expenditure involved', was Churchill's initial reaction to the Beveridge Report. But, as with my plans for educational reform, a certain modification of view was produced by time and pressure. In November 1943 Lord Woolton, then still a non-party man who had won a large reputation as Minister of Food, became Minister of Reconstruction with a seat in the War Cabinet. A Reconstruction Committee was established under his chairmanship, with Sir John Anderson as its most influential member, Attlee, Bevin and Morrison as regular attenders from the Labour side, and 'Bobbety' Cranborne, Oliver Lyttelton, the Prof and I as the principal Conservatives. It framed a town and country planning measure and laid foundations of the post-war housing policy. It discussed and approved White Papers setting out the principles for a national health service and for post-war schemes of pensions, sickness and unemployment benefits, and workmen's compensation. It worked on the historic document which committed all parties to the 'maintenance of a high and stable level of employment after the war'. It was even tempted by Herbert Morrison to pledge itself to a public corporation structure for the electricity industry. The notes I made about these meetings at the time record that 'Morrison's cleverness increases every day', that 'electricity is the worst ground to fight upon' where nationalization was concerned, but that after a discussion between Conservative Ministers, enlivened rather than swayed by the vehemence of Max Beaverbrook, 'it was decided that we should attempt not to get involved in decisions about State ownership prior to the election'. My notes add: 'The fact is that the Committee has done a good deal of useful work in framing the future social and political structure of the country. The importance of its work can never be over-estimated. It will be seen that the work is of a type suitable to a National government.' Indeed, the Labour government which was swept to power in the summer of that year had, in the fields of social reform and reconstruction, only to complete the work which the Coalition had begun and in some cases to bring forward Bills already drafted. ■

One of the most popular topics in reconstruction discussions concerned future health care provision. Concern had been growing before the war about the inequalities obvious in this field. Successful wartime co-ordination of the health services, especially through the Emergency Medical Service, had encouraged debate on maintaining government intervention into peacetime. In 1944 the Coalition published its proposals for a national health service, in which the hospital sector would be co-ordinated with local medical care. The provisions for comprehensive medical care were hugely popular but met instant resistance from the British Medical Association, nervous about the future of private practice and the dangers of state control of the medical profession.

2.19 **Ministry of Health and Department of Health for Scotland,** *A National Health Service: The White Paper Proposals in Brief,* **London, HMSO, 1944.**

■ The Government have announced that they intend to establish a National Health Service, which will provide for everyone all the medical advice, treatment and care they require.

This new service represents the natural next development in the long and continuous growth of the health services of the country. Although it forms part of the wider theme of post-war reconstruction – and although it will form an essential part of any scheme of social insurance which may be adopted – it has to be seen in the light of the past as well as the future and to be judged on its own merits as part of a steady historical process of improving health and the opportunity for health among the people.

In considering the form which the new National Health Service should take, the Government have had the help of informal discussions ... with representatives of the major Local Authorities, the Medical Profession, the Voluntary Hospitals and others. They now put forward definite proposals for discussion in Parliament and in the country, but they do not at this stage put the proposals forward as fixed decisions. Indeed, they have promised that those concerned, professionally and otherwise, shall be fully consulted before final decisions are taken. The Government will welcome constructive criticism and they hope that the next stage – the stage of consultation and public discussion – will enable them to submit quickly to Parliament legislative proposals which will be largely agreed ...

The new service is designed to provide, for everyone who wishes to use it, a full range of health care. No one will be compelled to use it. Those who prefer to make their own arrangements for medical attention must be free to do so. But to all who use the service it must offer, as and when required, the care of a family doctor, the skill of a consultant, laboratory services, treatment in hospital, the advice and treatment available in specialised clinics (maternity and child welfare centres, tuberculosis dispensaries and the like), dental and ophthalmic treatment, drugs and surgical appliances, midwifery, home nursing and all other services essential to health. Moreover, all these branches of medical care must be so planned and related to one another that everyone who uses the new service is assured of ready access to whichever of its branches he or she needs.

The new health service in all its branches will be free to all, apart from possible charges where certain appliances are provided. Questions of the disability benefits payable during sickness at home or during periods of free maintenance in hospital are matters for the Government's later proposals on social insurance ...

A great deal of what is required is already provided in one or other of the existing health services. The problem of creating a National Health Service is not that of destroying services that are obsolete and bad and starting afresh, but of building on foundations laid by much hard work over many years and making better what is already good.

Yet there are many gaps in the existing services and much expansion and reorganisation are necessary to weld them into a comprehensive National Service. Despite the progress made it is far from true that everyone can get all the kinds of medical service which he requires. Nor is the care of health wholly divorced from ability to pay for it. To take one very important example, the first requirement is a personal or family doctor, available for consultation on all problems. The National Health Insurance scheme makes this provision for a large number of people, but not for wives or children or dependants – and it does not normally afford the consultant and specialist services which the general practitioner needs behind him. For extreme need, the Poor Law still exists. For particular groups, there are other facilities. But for something like half the population, the first-line service of a personal medical adviser depends on private arrangements.

So, too, in the hospital services, despite the well-known achievements of the voluntary hospital movement and more recently of the publicly provided hospitals of the local authorities, it is not yet true that everyone can be sure of the right hospital and specialist facilities which he needs, when he needs them.

Again, many existing services are provided – and excellently provided – by local authorities. But these services have grown up piecemeal to meet different needs at different times, and so they are usually conducted as separate and independent services. There is no sufficient link either between these services themselves or between them and general medical practice and the hospitals ...

Perhaps the most important point of all is the need for a new attitude towards health care. Personal health still tends to be regarded as something to be treated when at fault, but seldom as something to be positively improved and promoted and made full and robust. Much of present custom and habit still centres on the idea that the doctor and the hospital and the clinic are the means of mending ill-health rather than of increasing good health and the sense of well-being. While the health standards of the people have enormously improved, and while there are gratifying reductions in the ravages of preventable disease, the plain fact remains that there are many men and women and children who could be enjoying a sense of health and physical efficiency which they do not in fact enjoy; there is much sub-normal health still, which need not be, with a corresponding cost in efficiency and personal happiness ... ■

The 1945 General Election

By spring 1945, with the collapse of Nazi Germany drawing near, attention turned to the future of the Coalition government. In 1944 Churchill had suggested that, unless his partners were anxious to continue the Coalition, the defeat of Germany should determine the timing of the next general election. The Conservatives, banking on the electoral value of Churchill's wartime leadership, generally advocated an early poll, although Churchill himself would have preferred to maintain the Coalition until after the defeat of Japan. The Labour Party, suspicious of the Conservatives' attitudes towards social reform, had already decided late in 1944 not to prolong the Coalition, a view confirmed by the party's annual conference in 1945. Accordingly, soon after Germany's surrender on 7 May 1945, Churchill resigned (23 May) and formed a 'caretaker' government to preside until the election, set for July.

Tests of public opinion had shown a clear preference for the Labour Party from 1943 up until the demise of the Coalition in 1945. However, little attention had been paid to these indicators, which were widely thought to be unreliable.

2.20   **British Institute of Public Opinion (Gallup) general election forecasts, 1943–5 (chart derived from P. Addison, *The Road to 1945: British Politics and the Second World War*, London, Quartet Books, 1977, p. 248).**

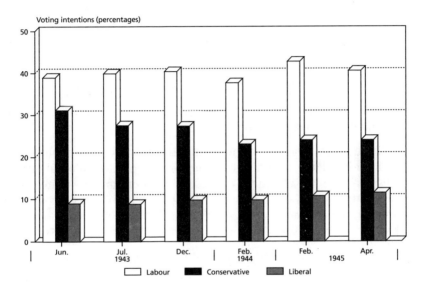

In its election campaign, the Labour Party sought to appear moderate. It was helped by the fact that the wartime state had extended considerable controls over the economy; Labour's nationalisation proposals therefore no longer seemed as radical as they had in the 1930s. The party's manifesto, Let Us Face the Future, *promised the nationalisation of the Bank of England, fuel and power, transport and iron and steel; it also promised economic planning, full employment and the creation of the National Health Service and a system of social security.*

2.21   **Labour Party, *Let Us Face the Future: A Declaration of Labour Policy for the Consideration of the Nation*, 1945 (in F.W.S. Craig (ed.), *British General Election Manifestos, 1900–1974*, London, Macmillan, 1975, pp. 123–9).**

■ VICTORY IN WAR MUST BE FOLLOWED BY A PROSPEROUS PEACE

Victory is assured for us and our allies in the European war. The war in the East goes the same way. The British Labour Party is firmly resolved that Japanese barbarism shall be defeated just as decisively as Nazi aggression and tyranny. The people will have won both struggles. The gallant men and women in the Fighting Services, in the Merchant Navy, Home Guard and

Civil Defence, in the factories and in the bombed areas – they deserve and must be assured a happier future than faced so many of them after the last war. Labour regards their welfare as a sacred trust.

So far as Britain's contribution is concerned, this war will have been won by its people, not by any one man or set of men, though strong and greatly valued leadership has been given to the high resolve of the people in the present struggle. And in this leadership the Labour Ministers have taken their full share of burdens and responsibilities. The record of the Labour Ministers has been one of hard tasks well done since that fateful day in May, 1940, when the initiative of Labour in Parliament brought about the fall of the Chamberlain Government and the formation of the new War Government which has led the country to victory ...

WHAT THE ELECTION WILL BE ABOUT

Britain's coming Election will be the greatest test in our history of the judgement and common sense of our people.

The nation wants food, work and homes. It wants more than that – it wants good food in plenty, useful work for all, and comfortable, labour-saving homes that take full advantage of the resources of modern science and productive industry. It wants a high and rising standard of living, security for all against a rainy day, an educational system that will give every boy and girl a chance to develop the best that is in them ...

The nation needs a tremendous overhaul, a great programme of modernisation and re-equipment of its homes, its factories and machinery, its schools, its social services.

All parties say so – the Labour Party means it. For the Labour Party is prepared to achieve it by drastic policies of replanning and by keeping a firm constructive hand on our whole productive machinery; the Labour Party will put the community first and the sectional interests of private business after. Labour will plan from the ground up – giving an appropriate place to constructive enterprise and private endeavour in the national plan, but dealing decisively with those interests which would use high-sounding talk about economic freedom to cloak their determination to put themselves and their wishes above those of the whole nation ...

INDUSTRY IN THE SERVICE OF THE NATION

By the test of war some industries have shown themselves capable of rising to new heights of efficiency and expansion. Others, including some of our older industries fundamental to our economic structure, have wholly or partly failed ...

Each industry must have applied to it the test of national service. If it serves the nation, well and good; if it is inefficient and falls down on its job, the nation must see that things are put right ...

There are basic industries ripe and over-ripe for public ownership and management in the direct service of the nation. There are many smaller businesses rendering good service which can be left to go on with their useful work ...

In the light of these considerations, the Labour Party submits to the nation the following industrial programme:–

1. Public ownership of the fuel and power industries. For a quarter of a century the coal industry, producing Britain's most precious national raw material, has been floundering chaotically under the ownership of many hundreds of independent companies. Amalgamation under public ownership will bring great economies in operation and make it possible to modernise production methods and to raise safety standards in every colliery in the country. Public ownership of gas and electricity undertakings will lower charges, prevent competitive waste, open the way for co-ordinated research and development, and lead to the reforming of uneconomic areas of distribution. Other industries will benefit.

2. Public ownership of inland transport. Co-ordination of transport services by rail, road, air and canal cannot be achieved without unification. And unification without public ownership means a steady struggle with sectional interests or the enthronement of a private monopoly, which would be a menace to the rest of industry.

3. Public ownership of iron and steel. Private monopoly has maintained high prices and kept inefficient high-cost plants in existence. Only if public ownership replaces private monopoly can the industry become efficient ...

HOUSES AND THE BUILDING PROGRAMME

... Housing will be one of the greatest and one of the earliest tests of a Government's real determination to put the nation first. Labour's pledge is firm and direct – it will proceed with a housing programme with the maximum practical speed until every family in this island has a good standard of accommodation. That may well mean centralised purchasing and pooling of building materials and components by the State, together with price control. If that is necessary to get the houses as it was necessary to get the guns and planes, Labour is ready ...

HEALTH OF THE NATION AND ITS CHILDREN

By good food and good homes, much avoidable ill-health can be prevented. In addition the best health services should be available for all. Money must no longer be the passport to the best treatment.

In the new National Health Service there should be health centres where the people may get the best that modern science can offer, more and better hospitals, and proper conditions for our doctors and nurses. More research is required into the causes of disease and the ways to prevent and cure it.

Labour will work specially for the care of Britain's nurses and their children – children's allowances and school medical and feeding services, better maternity and child welfare services. A healthy family life must be fully ensured and parenthood must not be penalised if the population of Britain is to be prevented from dwindling. ■

The Conservative Party's manifesto embodied the Coalition's apparently progressive consensus on key issues such as reconstruction priorities, the commitment to full employment and the National Health Service. Yet it was evasive on questions such as the postwar extent of government economic controls, perhaps betraying continuing internal party divisions on this point.

2.22   *Mr Churchill's Declaration of Policy to the Electors,* **1945 (in F.W.S. Craig (ed.),** *British General Election Manifestos, 1900–1974,* **London, Macmillan, 1975, pp. 113–23).**

■ I had hoped to preserve the Coalition Government, comprising all parties in the State, until the end of the Japanese war, but owing to the unwillingness of the Socialist and Sinclair Liberal Parties to agree to my proposal, a General Election became inevitable, and I have formed a new National Government, consisting of the best men in all Parties who were willing to serve and some who are members of no Party at all.

It is a strong Government, containing many of those who helped me to carry the burdens of State through the darkest days and on whose counsel and executive ability I have learned to rely.

We seek the good of the whole nation, not that of one section or one faction. We believe in the living unity of the British people, which transcends class or party differences. It was this living unity which enabled us to stand like a rock against Germany when she overran Europe. Upon our power to retain unity, the future of this country and of the whole world largely depends …

Having poured out all we could to beat the Germans, holding nothing back, we must now take stock of our resources and plan how the energies of the British people can best be freed for the work that lies ahead.

This is the time for freeing energies, not stifling them. Britain's greatness has been built on character and daring, not on docility to a State machine. At all costs we must preserve that spirit of independence and that 'Right to live by no man's leave underneath the law' …

FOUR YEARS' PLAN

More than two years ago, I made a broadcast to the nation in which I sketched a four years' plan which would cover five or six large measures of a practical character, which must all have been the subject of prolonged, careful and energetic preparation beforehand, and which fitted together into a general scheme.

This plan has now been shaped, and we present it to the country for their approval. Already a beginning has been made in carrying it out, and the Education Act for which our new Minister of Labour is greatly respected is already the law of the land ...

WORK

In the White Paper presented to Parliament by the late administration are sound plans for avoiding the disastrous slumps and booms from which we used to suffer, but which all are united in being determined to avoid in the future.

The Government accepts as one of its primary aims and responsibilities the maintenance of a high and stable level of employment. Unless there is steady and ample work, there will not be the happiness, the confidence, or the material resources in the country on which we can all build together the kind of Britain that we want to see.

To find plenty of work with individual liberty to choose one's job, free enterprise must be given the chance and the encouragement to plan ahead. Confidence in sound government – mutual co-operation between industry and the State, rather than control by the State - a lightening of the burdens of excessive taxation – these are the first essentials.

HOMES

In the first years of peace, the provision of homes will be the greatest domestic task.

An all-out housing policy will not only make a tremendous contribution to family life, but also to steady employment and to national health. All our energy must be thrown into it. Local authorities and private enterprise must both be given the fullest encouragement to get on with the job ...

NATIONAL INSURANCE

National wellbeing is founded on good employment, good housing and good health. But there always remain those personal hazards of fortune, such as illness, accident or loss of a job, or industrial injury, which may leave the individual and his family unexpectedly in distress. In addition, old age, death and child-birth throw heavy burdens upon the family income.

One of our most important tasks will be to pass into law and bring into action as soon as we can a nation-wide and compulsory scheme of National Insurance based on the plan announced by the Government of all Parties in 1944 ...

HEALTH

The health services of the country will be made available to all citizens. Everyone will contribute to the cost, and no one will be denied the attention, the treatment or the appliances he requires because he cannot afford them.

We propose to create a comprehensive health service covering the whole range of medical treatment from the general practitioner to the specialist, and from the hospital to convalescence and rehabilitation; and to introduce legislation for this purpose in the new Parliament ...

OUR PURPOSE

... We are dedicated to the purpose of helping to rebuild Britain on the sure foundations on which her greatness rests. In recent generations, enormous material progress has been made. This progress must be extended and accelerated not by subordinating the individual to the authority of the State, but by providing the conditions in which no one shall be precluded by poverty, ignorance, insecurity, or the selfishness of others from making the best of the gifts with which Providence has endowed him.

Our programme is not based upon unproved theories or fine phrases, but upon principles that have been tested anew in the fires of war and not found wanting. We commend it to the country not as offering an easy road to the nation's goal but because, while safeguarding our ancient liberties, it tackles practical problems in a practical way. ∎

If the Conservative manifesto was relatively uncontroversial, the party's campaign was more aggressive, warning of the dangers to liberty posed by a Labour government. Political capital was sought by Conservative supporters from the so-called 'Laski affair', sparked off by a statement by the Labour Party's chairman, Harold Laski, which seemed to imply that the Parliamentary Labour Party was subordinate to the party's more radical National Executive Committee. Most famously, in his election broadcast of 4 June 1945, Churchill, in what became known as his 'Gestapo speech', told the electors that the introduction of socialism in Britain would require government machinery similar to that employed in Nazi Germany. Attempts such as this to stigmatise Attlee and his colleagues as extremists were almost certainly counter-productive.

2.23   **Winston Churchill, election broadcast, 4 June 1945 (reported in** *The Times,* **5 June 1945).**

∎ My friends, I must tell you that a Socialist policy is abhorrent to the British ideas of freedom. Although it is now put forward in the main by people who have a good grounding in the Liberalism and Radicalism of the early part of this century, there can be no doubt that Socialism is inseparably interwoven with Totalitarianism and the abject worship of the State. It is not alone that property, in all its forms, is struck at, but that liberty, in all its forms, is challenged by the fundamental conceptions of Socialism.

Look how even today they hunger for controls of every kind, as if these were delectable foods instead of wartime inflictions and monstrosities. There is to be one State to which all are to be obedient in every act of their lives. This State is to be the arch-employer, the arch-planner, the arch-adminis-trator and ruler, and the arch-caucus-boss.

How is the ordinary citizen or subject of the King to stand up against this formidable machine, which, once it is in power, will prescribe for every one of them where they are to work; what they are to work at; where they may go and what they may say; what views they are to hold and within what limits they may express them; where their wives are to go to queue up for the State ration; and what education their children are to receive to mould their views of human liberty and conduct in the future?

A Socialist State once thoroughly completed in all its details and its aspects – and that is what I am speaking of – could not afford to suffer opposition ...

I declare to you, from the bottom of my heart, that no Socialist system can be established without a political police. Many of those who are advocating Socialism or voting Socialist today will be horrified at this idea. That is because they are short-sighted, that is because they do not see where their theories are leading them.

No Socialist Government conducting the entire life and industry of the country could afford to allow free, sharp, or violently worded expressions of public discontent. They would have to fall back on some form of Gestapo, no doubt very humanely directed in the first instance. And this would nip opinion in the bud; it would stop criticism as it reared its head, and it would gather all the power to the supreme party and the party leaders, rising like stately pinnacles above their vast bureaucracies of Civil servants, no longer servants and no longer civil. And where would the ordinary simple folk – the common people, as they like to call them in America – where would they be, once this mighty organism had got them in its grip? ■

From the Labour standpoint, Hugh Dalton some years later described in his memoirs the contrasting campaign styles of the two major parties. He also speculated on the signifi-cance of the servicemen's vote, which many contemporaries believed was crucial to the outcome of the election.

2.24 **Hugh Dalton, *The Fateful Years: Memoirs 1931–1945*, London, Muller, 1957, pp. 463–5.**

■ On the whole it was a quiet election. There was much evidence of a seri-ous mind among the electors and of a thoughtful interest in many questions, much more thoughtful and intelligent than before the war. I was very pleased with the form of many of our candidates. In a number of constituencies, where it would be close anyhow, I thought the personality of our candidate would just make the difference. On the other hand, but for the personality of the P.M., I thought we should trample the Tories under-foot and get a large majority. In fact, I much over-estimated the P.M.'s per-sonal influence on votes. The crowds which cheered him on his triumphal tours went into the polling booths and voted him down. And the soldiers, sailors and airmen voted overwhelmingly Labour.

As the war in Europe drew towards the end, the P.M., I heard, said to the Air Chief Marshal Harris: 'I suppose that, when the election comes, I can count on the votes of most of the men in the Air Force?' 'No, sir,' replied Harris, 'eighty per cent. of them will vote Labour.' 'Well at least that will give me 20 per cent.', said the P.M., sharply taken aback. 'No sir, the other 20 per cent. won't vote at all.'

'You can't trust the Tories' was a difficult slogan for Tories, at that time, to shout or argue down.

The Laski affair was most irritating, though I don't think it turned many votes against us, and it may have encouraged Churchill to launch his broad-cast attack on us as dangerous dictators, a new Gestapo, etc. This, followed by Attlee's quiet, reasonable and constructive reply, certainly turned many votes our way.

Laski, who had just become Chairman of the National Executive, had begun by declaring pontifically that Attlee should only go with Churchill to Potsdam 'as an observer', i.e. as a dumb figure at the Conference table. This would have been an impossible arrangement. Laski should not have inter-vened at all on Churchill's invitation to Attlee. He was not in touch with the Labour Parliamentary leaders, or he would have known that they had been consulted and agreed. Nor could we be 'bound' by decisions reached at Potsdam, now that we were no longer in the Government. Nor, on the other hand, was it very likely that we should wish to line up against anything agreed to, not only by Churchill, but by Stalin and Truman. It was a pity that his name was Laski and not Smith, and that he was a member of the National Executive but not a Member of Parliament. The question of the relationship of the National Executive to the Parliamentary Leaders is always potentially delicate. There was nothing new in this. But it was not a relationship, the public discussion of which usually helped us.

There was a further fuss, in the later stages of the campaign, as to whether Laski had said at a public meeting that we should, in certain circumstances, 'use violence' against our political opponents. Further discussion of this was, for the moment, stopped by the issue of writs, a very sensible move. But I had a strong suspicion that here, too, he had said something he should not. What was not sensible, was not to withdraw the writs after our great victo-ry. Withdrawal could have been presented either as a magnanimous or as a contemptuous gesture to those whose arguments, whether true or false, had been so overwhelmingly rejected by the electors. ∎

2.25   Conservative Party and Labour Party, 1945 general election posters (Conservative Party Archives).

The 1945 Results

The results of the 1945 election were a landslide victory for the Labour Party. A number of factors seem to have helped Labour. Around one-fifth of the electorate had never voted before, and many of these young voters probably chose Labour. Memories of the depressed 1930s and of appeasement hardly assisted the Conservatives, whereas Labour's recent record in government may have dispelled the party's reputation for irresponsibility, triggered by the collapse of the Labour government in 1931. Moreover, the electorate had had a long time to consider its choice; from 1942 onwards, ultimate victory seemed assured, and attention could focus on central issues such as housing, employment, health and social security. Ironically, Labour's victory was not entirely a rejection of Churchill. Many voters distinguished between Churchill and the Conservative Party. Some expected Churchill to remain in office even if a Labour government took power.

Whatever the 1945 election results may have indicated about popular views of Churchill, they were seen as providing the Labour government with an indisputable mandate to embark on its ambitious programme of reform.

2.26   General election results, 1945 (charts derived from D. Butler and
G. Butler (eds), *British Political Facts, 1900–1985*, London, Macmillan, 6th
edn, 1986, p. 226).

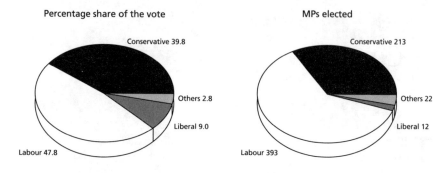

Percentage share of the vote

Conservative 39.8

Others 2.8

Liberal 9.0

Labour 47.8

MPs elected

Conservative 213

Others 22

Liberal 12

Labour 393

CHAPTER THREE

Labour in Power and Conservatism at Bay, 1945–51

THE outcome of the 1945 general election has traditionally been seen as a turning point in British history; for some observers, it marked a peaceful political revolution. For the first time, a Labour government enjoyed a parliamentary majority large enough to suggest a popular endorsement of its commitment to democratic socialism. The excitement generated by the victory meant inevitably that more would be expected of this government than of any predecessor in the twentieth century. Yet, as succeeding chapters suggest, the new Labour government faced enormous financial problems and constraints which, together with alarming developments overseas, greatly limited its freedom of manoeuvre.

Given the scale of the tasks ahead, and the personalities and differing political outlooks of leading ministers, it is perhaps not surprising that tensions developed not only within the government but also between the government and its supporters. Despite its problems, however, the government left office in 1951 apparently more popular than any other, before or since.

Electoral defeat had important consequences for the Conservative Party. Its prewar dominance of the political 'middle ground' had apparently crumbled in 1945, and the next six years would see a determined campaign to rebuild and modernise the party and its policies, and to convince electors of its commitment both to new styles of economic management and to the 'welfare state'.

Reactions to Labour's Victory

Many leading figures in the Labour Party appeared surprised by the result of the 1945 election. The poll gave Labour a parliamentary strength almost twice as large as it had enjoyed since 1935. Among the new intake of Labour MPs fewer were sponsored by trade unions, and more were from the professional middle classes. Twenty-one of the twenty-four women MPs in the new Parliament belonged to Labour. When Parliament assembled, the Labour ranks were understandably euphoric, shocking some of their Conservative colleagues by singing 'The Red Flag'.

One of the new Labour women MPs in 1945 was the outspoken young member for Blackburn, Barbara Castle. Regarded as being on the party's left, she later became a Cabinet minister under Harold Wilson and James Callaghan.

3.1 Barbara Castle, recollections of 1945 (in Barbara Castle, *Fighting All the Way*, London, Macmillan, 1993, pp. 125–7).

■ Despite the euphoria of the campaign, no one in the Labour Party, except Aneurin Bevan, believed that the party could snatch victory from the wartime Prime Minister. John [Edwards, fellow Labour candidate for Blackburn] and I were contending with Tory majorities of 3500 each and were not certain that we could win. Then on 26 July the news broke in an astonished press: Labour was in with an overall majority of 157 seats and nearly 3 million more votes than the Conservatives. John and I were both elected in Blackburn with majorities of over 8000 votes ...

Churchill never forgave the British people for what he considered their gross ingratitude. As leader of the Opposition, he concentrated his anger on the Labour government. For years to come the man who as wartime Prime Minister had declared that 'after the war this country will be bankrupt and the retiring soldier will have nothing to come back to' spent his time denouncing every piece of inevitable post-war austerity as due to the Labour government's mismanagement and every piece of our social legislation as 'socialist extravagance'. As I listened to him I became more and more in sympathy with Nye's [Bevan] attacks on Churchill, which had once seemed like treachery.

The Parliamentary Labour Party, which was summoned immediately to London to an excited meeting in the Beaver Hall, was unique in our history. The hall was spattered with young men in uniform, since sixty-eight Labour MPs, nearly a third of the new intake, had come straight from service in the forces, swamping the Tories' military claims. This, we pointed out, nailed Churchill's lie that Labour was less patriotic than the Conservatives ... Attlee was elected leader by acclamation and we all crowded outside for the press photographs. As the youngest woman Member I was pushed to the front between Herbert Morrison and Aneurin Bevan, where I stood shyly, looking as overwhelmed as I felt ...

With the Beaver Hall meeting over, I made my first contact with the Commons under Michael Foot's wing. Since Michael's father had been an MP many years earlier, Michael was less awed by the sacred precincts than I was and showed me round as though he had been an MP all his life. As he was proceeding to take me along the Members Only corridor we were stopped by a policeman who said to him, 'I am sorry, Mr Foot, you cannot take visitors there.' Michael replied haughtily, 'This isn't a visitor. She is Mrs Barbara Castle, MP.' The arrival of a record number of women MPs had obviously barely touched the consciousness of the guardians of this masculine institution.

I soon realized that this was not the only way in which the House of Commons was out of date. It was a relic of the days when government was run by wealthy amateurs. I had no desk, let alone an office, and had to stuff my working papers into one of the narrow lockers which lined the corridors and prepare my speeches in a corner of the overcrowded library. At £600 a year, the MP's salary was derisory. It was enough for me because I had a husband with whom to pool my finances, but it was penury for the married MPs from the provinces who had two abodes to keep – one in London and the other in the constituency – and had to cover their working expenses. One of the bravest things the new Labour government did was to increase the MP's salary immediately to £1000 a year, a modest enough sum in any case ... ■

Reginald Maudling joined Conservative Central Office in 1945, working closely with R.A. Butler on remodelling the party's policies and image. He entered Parliament in 1950 and held numerous ministerial posts before resigning in 1972.

3.2   Reginald Maudling, recollections of 1945 (in Reginald Maudling, *Memoirs*, London, Sidgwick & Jackson, 1978, p.38).

■ In the result we were heavily defeated. I suppose we should have expected this. Certainly when the Forces' vote, which on that occasion was counted early, came through, we could see the way things were going. There was a desire for change, a determination not to go back to the pre-war days. The Conservative Party had not much to offer at that time to those who wished to see change, and we relied heavily on the personality of Winston Churchill. There was no doubt about his popularity, or, indeed, the reverence in which people held him, but as it turned out we overestimated the effect this would have on their voting. People distinguished between Churchill the War Leader, and the Conservative Party as a peacetime Government. It may well be that the strange political instinct of the British people proved right again on that occasion. When I was working for Winston in the late 1940s, he told me that after his defeat in the 1945 election, Lady Churchill had said to him, 'Well, Winston, it may be a blessing in disguise', and how he had replied, 'If it is, it is a pretty effective disguise.' But, he added, 'On looking back on it, I think she was probably right.' There had not been an overthrow of individual liberty, which many, including Winston, had feared, and while he fought tooth and nail against the Socialists, I think he realized, as other lesser minds do not, that this country cannot permanently be governed by one Party, that we must operate within a framework where change is possible, and that what is essential is to ensure that change takes place within an agreed acceptance of basic political liberty, thereby leaving the opportunity always for further change when the electorate so desire. ■

The Attlee Governments

Tensions within the Labour leadership surfaced early. Clement Attlee's long-standing rival, Herbert Morrison, felt that he ought to have become Prime Minister, and advised Attlee to seek the Parliamentary Labour Party's approval before attempting to form a government. Comfortable in the support of his loyal ally Ernest Bevin, Attlee did not waver. In composing his Cabinet, Attlee could draw from an unusually able and experienced team, in marked contrast to Ramsay MacDonald's position in 1924 and 1929. Attlee himself had been Deputy Prime Minister between 1942 and 1945. Bevin, Arthur Greenwood and Morrison had been members of the War Cabinet, and Stafford Cripps and Hugh Dalton had also held important posts during the war. While familiar with the workings of government, these men had already endured several years of heavy responsibility; perhaps partly as a result, fatigue and illness dogged Attlee's government in its later years.

In shaping his team, Attlee needed to keep a balance between left and right, and between trade union and middle-class figures. He also needed to include politicians who might be more troublesome if outside the government. Bevin became Foreign Secretary; Dalton, who had coveted that post, went instead to the Exchequer; and Morrison was made Deputy Prime Minister and Lord President of the Council, kept busy timetabling the government's legislative programme. The former renegade Stafford Cripps, expelled from the Labour Party in 1939 for advocating a popular front with the Communists, became President of the Board of Trade, later Minister of Economic Affairs and, after Dalton's resignation in 1947, Chancellor of the Exchequer. The government's most charismatic personality, the leftish Welsh ex-miner Aneurin Bevan, became Minister of Health. Morrison later reflected on Attlee's political style.

3.3   **Herbert Morrison, autobiography, 1960 (Lord Morrison, *Herbert Morrison: An Autobiography*, London, Odhams Press, 1960, pp. 248–9).**

■ Forming a government involves considerations beyond those of a simple choice of specialized experts, self-appointed or otherwise. It should be balanced and be broadly representative of the Party. It should also be able to work as a team, even though personalities and ideas may be varied.

This, I think, Attlee admirably achieved. The Trade Unions, the Co-operative movement, and the 'left-wing' had their share of ministerial influence, but always with regard to their ability and experience. Considering the years since the Party had had to take governmental responsibility, the talent at our disposal was considerable.

Attlee showed himself at home as prime minister. His experience as deputy prime minister during the war, when at all times he handled for the prime minister a range of matters not directly concerned with military operations, and his duties as acting prime minister during the considerable periods when Churchill was out of the country or ill, had, of course, been invaluable training for him. He delegated much to me.

At meetings of ministers it was Attlee's usual custom to wait till the general discussion was over, the principal minister concerned opening the discussion. The Prime Minister's practice enabled him to gauge what would be the most generally acceptable decision for the meeting to take. The general opinion that Attlee was quite oblivious to the regard of his ministers and of the rank and file was not really correct. A more legitimate criticism would be that he tended to follow rather than lead.

In relationship with his colleagues of cabinet ministerial rank the Prime Minister was courteous and considerate, despite his staccato and monosyllabic comments which gave the impression of brusqueness to others. But with ministers whose position did not justify cabinet rank and with parliamentary secretaries he could be, often without justifiable cause, schoolmasterly and rather contemptuous. Those who merited it (even at times when they did not) might find themselves rolling in the dust, having completely misjudged the capabilities of withering comment by this ostensibly mild man. ■

Attlee had an unusually clear grasp of the complexities of Cabinet government and was reputedly an effective chairman in Cabinet. He reformed the structure of Cabinet, introducing a system of complementary and interconnected Cabinet committees, which formed a pyramid at the top of which were Attlee himself and the most senior Cabinet ministers. The following extract from Attlee's memoirs illustrates his characteristically reticent, undramatic style.

3.4   Clement Attlee, autobiography, 1954 (*As It Happened*, London, Heinemann, 1954, pp. 151–2).

■ For many years I had given a good deal of thought to the problem of the machinery of government, having realised that the old pattern needed reforming in the light of the wide extensions of Government activity and the inevitable increase in the number of departmental Ministers. In 1940 it had been thought right, for war purposes, to have a small Cabinet. This was in accordance with the precedent set in 1916 after experience had shown the need for it. The question I had to answer was, 'What should be the size and composition of the Cabinet in peace-time?' After the First World War there had been a return to pre-war practice for a Cabinet composed of twenty or even more Ministers. Its composition was largely on traditional lines. Certain offices were held to carry Cabinet rank, and therefore the holders must be included. Sometimes holders of the offices were included because of their personal standing, but there was no definite theoretical basis.

I was aware that there was a view held in some quarters that a Cabinet should be composed of only a few members without departmental responsibilities – a Cabinet of 'overlords' – its function being essentially that of dealing with large matters of policy. It was to be an instrument of decision. I had myself been attracted by this idea though I was well aware that considerations – both political and personal – would make it difficult to adopt it in its entirety. Having had experience of the working of a system in which senior Ministers were given a general oversight over a range of functions, and being aware of the crucial problem of securing supervision without blurring the responsibility of departmental Ministers, I approached my task of forming a Government with all these considerations in mind. ■

Attlee had been elected leader of the Labour Party in 1935, defeating Greenwood and Morrison, largely because he was not seen as a strong personality who might lead the party towards the same fate bequeathed by MacDonald. A reserved, taciturn man, he struck some as being cold and remote. Not all the government's sympathisers found Attlee sufficiently dynamic as a leader. In the cartoon below, David Low modified his famous 'flying wedge' formation to reflect these misgivings (cf. doc. 2.11).

3.5   David Low, 'Giving a lead', *Evening Standard* cartoon, 12 August 1947.

Of great symbolic importance for the entire labour movement was the repeal, in 1946, of the Trades Disputes Act. This had been passed in 1927 in the wake of the General Strike, and had been regarded as vindictive. As a result of the repeal, trade unionists who did not want to pay a political levy to the Labour Party had henceforth to 'contract out' (hitherto, the situation had been the reverse). During the debate on repealing the Act, the Attorney-General, Sir Hartley Shawcross, provided the government's rationale.

3.6   Sir Hartley Shawcross, speech to the House of Commons, 12 February 1946 (*Hansard* 5th ser., 419: 192 ff).

■ **The Attorney-General:** In so far as this Bill improves, as it undoubtedly will improve, the atmosphere in industry – [Interruption]. Hon. Members should try to view this matter with detachment, and free from political prejudice, and they would do well to remember that for 20 years the Act of 1927 has been a sore, a small sore, it may be, but a running sore, which has debilitated our industrial body politic, and, to the extent that we remove it and improve the atmosphere in industry, this Bill will make strikes even less likely than they are at the present time. If this country should ever be faced – and I hope it will not – with the misfortune of a recurrence of a general strike, then at least this Bill will avoid a conflict with the law which, in existing circumstances, the law would inevitably lose with grave constitutional results.

Those who say, as Conservative propagandists outside this House have from time to time been saying, that this Bill is an attack upon the freedom and liberty of the individual, are saying something which they must know to be completely untrue. This Bill, in fact, restores certain hard-won and important individual freedoms, and it does so without threatening the liberty of any one in the slightest degree. Those who pretend, as Conservative propagandists outside this House have pretended, that this Bill is designed to compel people to contribute to political funds when they do not desire so to do, are saying that which is a grotesque travesty of the facts as established by previous experience ... This Bill plays only an indirect, and, in some senses, a psychological part in the Government's programme, but what it will do – and at least it will do this – will be to remove from the Statute Book an Act of Parliament, the perpetuation of which, in existing circumstances, is an undoubted and historical injustice.

Quite frankly, looking back at the 1927 legislation now, one can see that it very largely failed the purposes for which its supporters hoped and which many of its opponents feared. It had no practical effects whatever on the exercise of the right to strike – not a scrap. It imposed some inconvenience on the organisation of the trade unions. Also, although it resulted in what I suggest to the House was a wholly unjustifiable but not really significant diminution in the political funds of the trade unions, it did nothing to prevent the trade unions and the Labour Party going on from strength to strength. What it did do – and this is its importance, because we must get rid of this, if we are to maintain and strengthen the better feeling between both sides of industry which manifested itself during the war – was to create among the great mass of working people of this country a bitter sense of injustice, a feeling that the courts of this country had been turned against them, a belief that the law had been vindictively manipulated to their disadvantage, and a feeling that their hard-won right to withhold their labour if they chose, which, after all, is the inalienable right of every free man, had been whittled away. It is to remove that sense of injustice, to do away with these unwarranted restrictions upon the rights of individuals as individuals, or in association together, that this Bill is presented to the House. ■

In 1948 the government passed the Representation of the People Act, which finally reformed the electoral system, by abolishing the business premises qualification to vote and the anachronism of university seats. At last, each adult had one vote. Continuing the trend begun by Asquith's government in 1911, Labour further trimmed the powers of the House of Lords in 1949, reducing their ability to delay bills from two years to one. This was done partly in anticipation of opposition to the government's nationalisation programme, particularly the nationalisation of the steel industry.

3.7   Cabinet discussion on amending the Parliament Act, 14 October 1947 (PRO CAB 128/10 CM 80(47)1).

■ The Cabinet first discussed whether it was expedient that such legislation should be introduced at the present time. In the Declaration of Labour Policy issued before the last General Election the statement of the Party's domestic policy had been prefaced by the declaration: 'We give clear notice that we will not tolerate obstruction of the people's will by the House of Lords.' Having been returned to power on the basis of that declaration, the Government had a clear right to limit the powers of the House of Lords if those powers were used to prevent the passage of Government legislation. Hitherto, however, the House of Lords had not rejected any Government Bill and had in fact passed a number of important socialisation measures. It would, therefore, be argued that, as the House of Lords had not obstructed the passage of Government legislation, the situation envisaged in the Party's Declaration of Policy had not in fact arisen and the Government had no mandate from the electorate to introduce legislation amending the Parliament Act. There might be a demand that this issue should be specifically referred to the electorate, and moderate opinion throughout the country might be alienated. Moreover, it should not be assumed that the House of Lords would necessarily become more inclined to obstruct Government legislation in the remaining Session of this Parliament than they had been in the first two Sessions. There were some grounds for believing that the House of Lords were apprehensive of the political consequences of exercising their powers under the Parliament Act; and it was arguable that on this account they would refrain from rejecting even a Bill for the socialisation of the iron and steel industry, especially if the Bill reached them towards the end of the life of the present Parliament. A few ministers felt that in these circumstances it might be bad political tactics for the Government to introduce at this stage, without any provocation from the House of Lords to delay the passage of Government legislation.

On the other side it was argued that because the House of Lords had refrained from obstructing Government legislation in the first two Sessions of this Parliament it could not be assumed that they would be equally reasonable throughout the remaining Sessions. Hitherto, they had acted in the knowledge that the Government had power to enforce the passage of legislation amending the Parliament Act. If such legislation were not introduced in the coming Session, the House of Lords could prevent its becoming law before the next General Election; and, once the threat of such legislation had been removed, there might be a change in the attitude of the House of Lords towards Government legislation. Account must also be taken of the strength of the political feeling which would be aroused by the Iron and Steel Bill. This would cause far more controversy than the earlier socialisation measures which had been accepted by the House of Lords; and a number of Peers who did not normally attend the sittings of the House of Lords might be provoked to attend and vote for the rejection of the Bill. If that situation arose it was unlikely that the more moderate counsels of the Leaders of the Opposition Parties in the House of Lords would prevail ... ■

Public Ownership

At the heart of the government's legislative programme was the promise to bring substantial sectors of the economy into public ownership. For many Labour supporters this, and the tool for economic management which it would give governments, was the acid test of the party's commitment to socialism. The party's constitution, after all, spoke of 'common ownership' as a fundamental goal. Attlee's government began with the energy and transport industries, pride of place being reserved for coal mining, nationalised in 1946. Partly on the basis of successful wartime state intervention, nationalisation was justified as a way of preventing unemployment, rationalising production and fostering improved industrial relations.

Although the Conservatives attacked all measures of nationalisation on principle, their opposition was half-hearted in relation to industries such as coal mining, where the need for reorganisation was accepted across the party divide. It was when proposals emerged to nationalise industries which were competitive and profitable that resistance was strongest. During a debate on the government's economic policies in December 1945, Attlee responded to an attack by Churchill on the nationalisation programme.

3.8   **Clement Attlee, speech to the House of Commons, 6 December 1945**
(*Hansard*, 5th ser., 416: 2562–3).

■ I must turn now to the right hon. Gentleman's main indictment:

'these gloomy vultures of nationalisation hovering over our basic industries.'

I have no doubt that the right hon. Gentleman knows all about vultures. The vultures never fed on him because he kept alive, fortunately for us all; vultures feed on rotten carrion. Is it his view that our basic industries are so rotten that they attract the vultures? Is that his view of private enterprise? He talks about growing uncertainty. There is no growing uncertainty whatever. [HON. MEMBERS: 'Oh.'] Well, really, if hon. Members are uncertain, they have been asleep for a long time. Our party has stood for nationalisation programmes for 40 years or more, and even an hon. Member opposite might have realised that when we got a majority we should naturally go in for nationalisation. At the same time, we put it quite clearly in the King's Speech that we intended to nationalise certain industries. Reassurances were given to others by Ministers, and particularly by my right hon. Friend the Lord President of the Council [Morrison], and really there is no growing uncertainty. [An HON. MEMBER: 'No, no.'] If the hon. Member instead of shouting 'No, no,' would read the speeches of intelligent industrialists like the president of the F[ederation of]. B[ritish]. I[ndustries]., and many others, they [sic] would find that they know a great deal more about their business than he does. I noticed with interest the difference between the wild and whirling words of the right hon. Gentleman opposite … Characteristically, he continues to tread the middle way, while the right hon. Gentleman right back in the Conservative Party goes down the primrose path, which everybody remembers, leads to the eternal bonfire.

The right hon. Gentleman says that our proposals on nationalisation divert the Government from the immediate task. That is an example of a static mind. The idea is that private enterprise is the only way in which our economic affairs can be managed. The right hon. Gentleman has grown up with that idea and he cannot get it out of his head. I am quite sure, had he been born in one of those countries where the railways had, from the start, belonged to the State, he would have thought it a perfectly natural thing … The right hon. Gentleman's general position seems to be that things should be left as they are. Is he satisfied with the coal industry? Has he been satisfied at any time in the last 25 years with the organisation of the coal industry? Whatever happens, something has to be done with the coal industry, on the admission of the people who run it. It is a question as to which is the best way to deal with that particular piece of economic machinery, our way or their way. We have had 20 years and more of fiddling about with their way, and in consonance with the view of every authoritative commission, we now intend to take our way. ■

Iron and steel nationalisation

During 1948 and 1949 divisions grew between government ministers, and among Labour Party members, over the issue of extending the public sector. For some, like Aneurin Bevan, the early programme of nationalisation was only the first step towards a more far-reaching penetration of manufacturing industry. On the party's right, however, others, like Morrison, felt that the party should consolidate the position it had achieved. Increasingly, nationalisation was justified on pragmatic grounds, rather than as an article of socialist faith.

The real test case for the government's belief in nationalisation arose over the iron and steel industry. Here was an industry, vital to other sectors in manufacturing, which had already been rationalised in the 1930s. The government, unable on political grounds to retreat from the question, pressed ahead with plans for nationalisation. There followed a prolonged and bitter parliamentary struggle, lasting some two years, in which the government had to defend every section of the Bill.

The extent to which ministers were already having misgivings about the nationalisation of iron and steel is demonstrated by the following extract from a Cabinet discussion on the problem in August 1947. Morrison and the Minister of Supply, John Wilmot, had produced compromise proposals (referred to in the extract as CP(47)212), which stopped short of outright nationalisation of the industry. While Attlee and Bevin advocated caution, some ministers, notably Bevan and Dalton, urged that nationalisation should go ahead, not least as a signal to Labour's supporters that the government was committed to socialist policies.

3.9 Cabinet discussion on nationalising the steel industry, 7 August 1947 (PRO CAB 128/10 CM 70(47)6).

■ *The Chancellor of the Exchequer* said that he remained in favour of the policy of full nationalisation. He felt, however, that it would be most unwise for the Cabinet to attempt to decide at the present time what, if any, legislation on the subject of the iron and steel industry should be included in the 1947–48 Legislative Programme. The Government should, therefore, inform their supporters that it was very doubtful whether it would be possible to legislate on the subject in the 1947–48 Session. At the same time, it should be made clear that a measure to nationalise the iron and steel industry would remain part of the Government's programme of legislation for the present Parliament; and he believed there was a good chance of the Government's being able to deal with the matter in the 1947–48 Session …

The Minister of Fuel and Power said that in principle he favoured the complete nationalisation of the iron and steel industry. He recognised, however, that nationalisation would not produce any beneficial result in increased steel output for some considerable time and that the introduction of legislation to carry out the scheme … would have a disturbing effect …

The Foreign Secretary said that, after further consideration, he remained opposed to the scheme of control outlined in C.P.(47)212. On the other hand, he did not think that the Government should commit themselves to legislation to nationalise the industry in the 1947–48 Session. He did not see why the Government should be forced to state their intentions at this stage, and he would prefer to leave the position open for at least a few weeks. The Cabinet might then consider the matter afresh, possibly after taking further soundings among their supporters …

The Prime Minister said that the Cabinet were bound to take account of the administrative tasks which they had undertaken in order to deal with the present economic situation. To proceed with the original scheme might lead to considerable disturbance in the industry and would add substantially to the heavy burdens already imposed by the Ministry of Supply. For these reasons he would favour an announcement that the Government did not intend to proceed with the scheme in the 1947–48 Session. He realised, however, that any such announcement would cause disappointment among Government supporters, and he felt that the predominant view in the

Cabinet was in favour of stating that, while the scheme still remained in the programme for the present Parliament, it was doubtful whether it would be possible to introduce the necessary legislation in the 1947–48 Session. ■

Although the Act to nationalise steel was finally passed in 1949, the political problems involved in securing its passage through Parliament strengthened the position of Labour's 'consolidationists' against the left wing. While the party's election manifestos in 1950 and 1951 both promised further nationalisation, privately the leadership doubted how practicable this would be. The iron and steel industry, under threat of nationalisation, mounted a vigorous opposition campaign, backed by the Conservatives. This led industrialists to engage in fund-raising for political purposes on a scale not seen before.

3.10   **British Iron and Steel Federation, anti-nationalisation advertisement,** *Daily Express,* **26 November 1949.**

WHY

is the steel industry delivering the goods?

The question is answered by the facts.

The British steel industry is composed of five hundred independent firms, working under Government supervision and in competition with each other. To-day the efficiency of the industry is such that:

1 Output has achieved an all-time record.

2 Exports of goods made from steel are now double pre-war.

3 Steel prices are among the lowest in the world.

What produced these results?

The team spirit in the industry, the stimulus of competitive enterprise, and the sense of public responsibility on the part of both workers and management.

STEEL is serving you well

BRITISH IRON AND STEEL FEDERATION ⸺⸺⸺⸺

Critics on the Left

The steel nationalisation episode was one example of growing tensions between the left and right wings of the Labour Party. In 1947 fifteen MPs had formed the 'Keep Left' group, criticising the government's economic and foreign policies. Those impatient with the government's progress towards socialism became increasingly vocal, a foretaste of the bitter divisions the party would face in the 1950s. For many on the left, Aneurin Bevan appeared to be a natural leader, in contrast to Attlee, who seemed to personify middle-class values.

George Brown entered the Commons in 1945, having served as a trade union official. A colourful character on the right wing of the Labour Party, he held minor office in the Attlee government and was a Cabinet minister under Harold Wilson. The characteristically unrestrained language of the following extract indicates the passionate divisions within the Labour Party.

3.11 **George Brown, recollections of the Labour left (in** *The Political Memoirs of Lord George-Brown*, **London, Gollancz, 1971, p. 53).**

■ Those years of Labour Government were bedevilled by rows with a group of 'left-wingers' in the Parliamentary Party, already beginning to be called 'Bevanites'. They were always an odd mixture, and although they took their name from Aneurin Bevan and it flattered him to be regarded as their leader, he didn't really share the views of most of his followers: indeed Aneurin would probably have been about the first man sent to Siberia if the rest of them had ever had their way.

The Bevanite row in the Labour Party was partly endemic in the philosophical differences between theoretical Socialism and the approach of those of us who were in the Labour movement to secure practical reforms; and partly it was concerned with personalities. Aneurin Bevan was no Marxist, though he tended to be surrounded by theorists and the natural descendants of the I.W.W. – the International Workers of the World, or the 'wobblies', as they were called in America. Despite all the evidence to the contrary, and even if they themselves were not Communists, they still believed that pretty well everything that came out of the Russian Revolution was somehow good. Even when millions of people, including their own friends, suffered from Russian actions, they still believed that the Russians were 'goodies' standing up to the 'baddies' of all the rest of the world. This was not logical reasoning, it was sheer illogical belief … ■

Labour and Communism

In addition to criticism within its own ranks, the Labour government became increasingly concerned about the activities of the Communist Party. Although unsuccessful electorally, the Communists had come to occupy important positions within the trade union movement, for example in the National Union of Mineworkers and the Amalgamated Engineering Union, and among the London dockworkers. As the cold war developed, the Communist Party's initially favourable stance towards the Labour government became hostile. Britain's clear orientation towards the emerging Western Alliance was taken as proof that Attlee and his colleagues sought partnership with the 'imperialist' bloc. Domestic policies, such as the attempt to introduce an incomes policy in 1948, and continued rationing were attacked as penalising the working class. Such criticism produced a strong government response and attempts to limit the Communist Party's influence. Labour Party members were forbidden to co-operate with Communists, and some Labour MPs were expelled for advocating the Communist Party line. In 1948, shortly after the Prague coup and the deterioration of the cold war, the government purged the civil service of Communists. With the outbreak of the Korean War in 1950, there was much alarmist talk about the danger of Communist sabotage at home.

Tensions within the labour movement led the veteran Communist and MP William Gallacher to write a clear statement of Communist principles and policies, in which the Labour government was inevitably singled out for attack.

3.12   **William Gallacher, views on the Labour Party, 1949 (in William Gallacher, *The Case for Communism*, Harmondsworth, Penguin, 1949, pp. 163–4).**

■ The idea is quite clear. The Labour leaders simply want to fill the gap left by the Liberals. Politics, for them, is not a question of leading the working class to power against the capitalist class, for the ending of capitalism and the establishment of Socialism. To them, politics is simply the struggle for positions in the existing capitalist State between two political groups. They and the Tories will argue and throw mud at each other. That is all part of the political game. But at bottom, they are united in purpose, determined to preserve capitalism, to prevent further inroads into the power of the capitalist class, and to get the workers to accept heavy sacrifices.

This is the outcome of the famous 'middle-road' – neither Communism nor Toryism – ending up on the side of the Tories. With this effort of theirs the F[ederation of] B[ritish] I[ndustries] and the Tory Party are in most complete sympathy. It is even possible to get the General Council of the T.U.C. to fall into line. But the Communists, and what they call 'subversive' elements in the working class, keep on making demands of one kind and another, which, if persisted in, would completely upset the balance and possibly create a situation leading to a revolutionary struggle for power. At all costs, that must be avoided, so these alleged Socialists find themselves more and more drawn into the camp of the enemies of the working class, holding back any advance towards Socialism, and directing all their venomous hatred at the Communists and those who associate with them. Having been accepted into, and become part of, the social life of the capitalist system, they have reached the ultimate. Only those who are mad or bad, the 'subversive' few, could desire to change the happy social relations that obtain in this country.

At all costs, these social relations must be preserved from attack. They are the ideal and couldn't possibly be bettered. Mr Morrison has publicly declared the preservation of the Tory Party is essential to 'our' democratic system. On the other hand, the Communist Party is a menace to 'our' democratic system and must be purged, banned and spat upon as an enemy of all that is good and desirable ...

Thus the right-wing Labour leadership seeks to build up barricades to stop the onward march of the movement. Pitiful little creatures, puffed up with their own make-believe importance. In a few years they're gone, and immediately forgotten, but the cause they tried to halt will go forward with ever-increasing rapidity till final victory crowns the efforts of those who kept the faith and held the banner high ... ■

The Conservatives in Opposition

The election defeat in 1945 came as an undoubted shock to many Conservatives, whose morale plummeted. Churchill's disappointment was intense, and he turned to writing for consolation. In these circumstances, the party could initially offer only half-hearted opposition in Parliament. Some Conservatives blamed their party's campaign in 1945 for the setback, believing that too little stress had been placed on policies and the popularity of reform, and perhaps too much on Churchill's leadership and attacks on Labour. Moreover, the party was still bedevilled by the image of having been responsible for Britain's inter-war problems and the now vilified policy of 'appeasement'.

A widely held view was that Labour had won the 1945 election because it was the better organised party. In order to modernise the Conservative Party, Churchill made the popular wartime Minister of Food, Lord Woolton, party chairman in 1946. Woolton succeeded in developing a much more professional constituency party organisation, partly by strengthening the position of local party agents. He worked hard to revive party workers' morale, set them high membership and fund-raising targets, and gave them once more a sense of purpose. More generally, the party tried to democratise itself. Following recommendations by David Maxwell-Fyfe, whose committee on party organisation reported in 1949, finance became a less important consideration in the selection of candidates.

3.13   **Earl of Woolton, on Conservative retrenchment (in** *Memoirs of the Rt Hon. The Earl of Woolton,* **London, Cassell, 1959, p. 334).**

■ I soon found that the primary need of the whole of the Conservative Party, but in particular of the Central Office, was that it should believe in itself, and in its capacity to convert the electorate to Conservatism. We had our backs to the wall: we had been heavily defeated: we had very little money: the Party was depressed. The political Press of the country was largely staffed, on its reporting sides, by members of the Labour Party, and everywhere there was a slant towards Socialism and a disbelief that in the new post-war world this old Conservative Party could ever govern the country again. Large numbers of Conservatives were trying to find a new name for the party because 'conserving' seemed to be out of joint with this new world that was demanding adventure and expansion and a rejection of the economic restraints of the pre-war life of this country under a Conservative administration, though it was a mystery to me to see why they thought they could get freedom under a Socialist Government.

The word 'Conservative' was certainly not a political asset when compared with the Socialist word 'Labour'. The man who first called the Socialist Party the 'Labour Party' was a political genius, for indeed the word 'labour' implied the party that would look after the best interests of 'labour'; this word 'labour' had nothing to do with the Socialist conception that all labour should be employed by the State – a bureaucratic conception lacking in all the warmth that comes from human relationship – whether it be the warmth that comes from affection or the heat that comes from conflict.

I made up my mind that we should call the Government the 'Socialist Party'. This was their true description; it was on the Socialist dogma of the nationalization of the means of production, distribution, and exchange that they had based the programme on which the Party had been elected to Parliament. I would have liked to call the Conservative Party the 'Union Party'. That, indeed, is its proper title, representing the unity of the Empire, the essential unity between the Crown, the Government, and the people, and embracing the idea that is certainly true of this country, that we dislike class conflict almost as much as we dislike either the vague internationalism of the political sentimentalist or the foreign creeds of Marxian Socialism or Russian Communism. We are very like a family – indulging in times of security in much diversity of opinion; in times of pressure, or emergency, or of danger, quickly and strongly united. That is what the people of this country want. ■

Tory policy revision

The shock of 1945 forced the Conservatives to reconsider their policies. Historians have questioned how thoroughgoing this policy revision was, and some have concluded that the process was more cosmetic than real. Under R.A. Butler, the wartime Minister of Education, the Conservative Research Department, which had been largely dormant during the war, became a major influence on policy-making.

One of the most important policy documents produced by the Conservatives was the Industrial Charter, *unveiled by Butler in May 1947. This was soon followed by statements on agriculture, Scotland, Wales, the empire and women. Butler later conceded that the* Industrial Charter *was broad in scope and vague in character. This reflected Churchill's reluctance to be bound by detailed policy commitments. The charter sought to demonstrate the Conservatives' commitment to a mixed economy and improved welfare provision. However, while accepting the case for state intervention, it also called for a regenerated private sector. As such, the charter went little further than the Conservatives' 1945 election manifesto.*

3.14   **R.A. Butler on the** *Industrial Charter,* **1947 (in R.A. Butler** *The Art of the Possible: The Memoirs of Lord Butler,* **London, Hamish Hamilton, 1971, pp. 145–7).**

■ Rarely in the field of political pamphleteering can a document so radical in effect have been written with such flatness of language or blandness of tone. This was not wholly unintentional. We were out-Peeling Peel in giving the Party a painless but permanent face-lift: the more unflamboyant the changes, the less likely were the features to sag again. Our first purpose was to counter the charge and the fear that we were the party of industrial go-as-you-please and devil-take-the-hindmost, that full employment and the Welfare State were not safe in our hands. We therefore took our cue less from our historic philosophy, though that would indeed have been relevant, than from the existing complexity of modern industry and Britain's position as a debtor country which made reversion to *laissez-faire* impossible. 'In economic matters the government has very important functions', we insisted in the accents of Keynesianism. 'Foremost among these are its general powers to collect and distribute information to an extent beyond that of any private undertaking, its duties to take decisions on the scale of national expenditure and taxation, its power to control monetary policy and to guide overseas trade. It has responsibilities for stimulating industrial efficiency, in particular by assisting research and making the results more readily available to small firms. But perhaps its greatest duty is to ensure that such main priorities as the maintenance of employment and our well-developed social services are fulfilled before subsidiary objectives are sought and that the tasks set are not beyond the capacity of the resources available.' The Charter was, therefore, first and foremost an assurance that, in the interests of efficiency, full employment and social security, modern Conservatism would maintain strong central guidance over the operation of the economy.

Our second purpose was to present a recognizable alternative to the reigning orthodoxies of Socialism – not to put the clock back, but to reclaim a prominent role for individual initiative and private enterprise in the mixed and managed economy. It has been argued that the Charter was largely concerned with economic problems that were to be irrelevant in the 'fifties and that we did not therefore act upon it at all obviously when we got back into power. In so far as it was dealing with the current crisis and stress through which the country was passing there is, of course, some truth in the criticism that the emphases of the Charter were quickly dated. Yet, if it is read with this qualification in mind, what stands out very plainly is the extent to which we foresaw and foreshadowed the characteristically Conservative measures of the post-1951 period, with many of which I was myself to be associated as Chancellor – the improvement of incentives through reduced taxation, the encouragement of a high level of personal savings, the steady and orderly reduction of physical controls, the overhauling of the top-heavy administrative machine and the shrinking of the Civil Service, the reopening of the commodity markets, the sharpening of competition by bringing what we called 'the floodlight of publicity' to bear upon restrictive practices, and the empirical approach to denationalization. All these are to be found in the Charter; and, if they were not the ingredients which gave it its most distinctive flavour, this was because an assertion of freedom may be taken for granted in the Conservative faith, whereas our imperative need was to establish what was then very far from being taken for granted: the Conservative intention to reconcile individual effort with a proper measure of central planning and direction and, no less important, to 'point to a way of life designed to free private endeavour from the taint of selfishness or self-interest' ... ■

Harold Macmillan, the Conservative MP for Stockton, lost his seat in 1945 but was returned later in the year as MP for Bromley. In the 1930s he had been identified with the progressive wing of the Conservative Party as an advocate of the political 'middle way'. He was a member of the committee which produced the Industrial Charter. *Many Conservative colleagues felt uneasy about Macmillan's ideas, and he did not re-establish himself securely in their ranks until 1951 and the return of Churchill to office.*

3.15   Harold Macmillan on the Conservatives in opposition (in H. Macmillan, *Tides of Fortune 1945–55*, London, Macmillan, 1969, pp. 43–5).

■ The House of Commons before and immediately after the Second World War was less highly organised or regimented than it is today. Nowhere was this more marked than in the conduct of the Opposition. There were a number of advisers to the leader (often a former Prime Minister), which the Press had christened after 1929 by the name of 'Shadow Cabinet'. But its members were not – as in a real Cabinet – allocated to particular posts. In selecting this body Churchill followed the traditional system, for he was a great believer in precedent. It consisted of Privy Councillors who sat by right on the Opposition front bench. Others, not Privy Councillors, he gradually promoted; or, since our numbers were so thin at the beginning of the Parliament before such defeated ex-Ministers as Bracken, Richard Law and I began to get back, one or two were asked to help from the very start. All these met each Wednesday in the Leader of the Opposition's room to discuss the immediate business and to allocate the different tasks accordingly ... But none of us were designated by the title of 'Shadow' Minister of this or that. In the work of dealing with the main Bills, both on Second Readings and in Committee as well as in more general debates, some of us concentrated on particular issues … The incongruity of calling someone 'Shadow' Minister of Transport or 'Shadow' Postmaster-General was avoided. The new fashion, which has sometimes included appointing even 'Shadow' Under-Secretaries, was adopted by the Labour Party in their long years of Opposition from 1951 to 1964, and was later followed by the Conservatives. There are grave disadvantages in this formality. Only from the Opposition benches is it possible for Members, including ex-Ministers, to speak on a whole variety of subjects. The chief compensation for a party being in Opposition is that it can train individuals in a wide range of subjects, so that they obtain practice and experience over a broad field. In office men have to be, to some extent, circumscribed within the walls of their own Ministry. Out of office let them wander free and unencumbered. This at least was Churchill's plan. Once a fortnight he entertained us – about fourteen in all – at an imposing luncheon at the Savoy Hotel. This sometimes took the place of and was sometimes followed by the more formal Wednesday meeting. Naturally conversation was sometimes more about the immediate past than about the immediate future; but these were occasions not to be forgotten, forever cherished by those few who can remember them, where we could enjoy the genius as well the hospitality of our beloved leader.

Nevertheless, there were, as was no doubt to be expected in view of the magnitude of our defeat, some grumbles. Some complained of the laxity of Churchill's attendance at the House. He certainly did not think it necessary to intervene every day at Questions or to make a statement in the country every weekend. These were, of course, the days before television and the fashion for 'instant' politics. Others thought that he had lost touch with the House and that his speeches no longer struck a modern note. Yet as he gradually attuned himself to the spirit of the new House and when he spoke in the country, more especially at the great party conferences, his power and authority were easily re-established … Whether he was successful, or – as often happened – worsted in these engagements, the boyish enthusiasm with which he plunged into these affrays disarmed criticism. He loved a good Parliamentary row. Nor was there any occasion, whether in public speech or private conferences, which was not illumined by some pregnant phrase which showed how carefully he was studying the present and the future in the light of the past. In many ways this old man was the youngest and the most up-to-date of us all. ■

The following cartoons address a key problem in assessments of the postwar Conservative Party: how far did the party really change its ideas after 1945? Was it, at heart, essentially the traditional party of the inter-war years, or had it really absorbed the new thinking on managing the economy and welfare provision? The cartoonist 'Vicky' implies that little has changed, while David Low takes the analysis further, asking how the Conservatives can reconcile continued levels of public spending with promises of tax cuts.

3.16 'Vicky', 'Love me – love my horse', *News Chronicle* cartoon, 3 October 1949.

3.17 David Low, 'This is the road', *Evening Standard* cartoon, 27 January 1950.

The 1950 General Election

The Labour government had good reason to be confident as it faced the people in 1950. It had a solid record of achievements, and had not lost a single by-election contest since 1945. Opinion polls gave no indication of large-scale disenchantment among the electorate. Nevertheless, public attitudes were shifting perceptibly by 1950 in favour of greater consumer freedom, exemplified by the 'housewives' campaigns' against rationing, which had received Conservative support. Both Labour and the Conservatives saw the election as an important test; for Labour, success would indicate that the 1945 result was no freak, and that a new political age had dawned.

Labour's 1950 election manifesto was based squarely on the Attlee government's record, and on the need to defend its achievements. There was little new in the document, which emphasised welfare, full employment and 'fair shares'.

3.18   **Labour Party general election manifesto,** *Let Us Win Through Together,* **1950 (in F.W.S. Craig,** *British General Election Manifestos 1900–1974,* **London, Macmillan, 1975, pp. 152–61).**

■ When the Labour Party published Let Us Face the Future in 1945 those five words were more than the title of the Election Manifesto; they were five words which crystallised the minds of the people at that time. By hard work, good sense and self-discipline the people have laid the foundations of a future based on free social democracy. They have helped Parliament and Government to carry into effect all the main proposals in that Manifesto.

Now in 1950 the country is facing another General Election. We ask our fellow citizens to assert in their free exercise of the franchise that by and large the first majority Labour Government has served the country well. The task now is to carry the nation through to complete recovery. And that will mean continued, mighty efforts from us all. The choice for the electors is between the Labour Party – the party of positive action, of constructive progress, the true party of the nation – and the Conservative Party – the party of outdated ideas, of unemployment, of privilege.

THE NEW MORAL ORDER

Socialism is not bread alone. Economic security and freedom from the enslaving bonds of capitalism are not the final goals. They are means to the greater end – the evolution of a people more kindly, intelligent, free, co-operative, enterprising and rich in culture. They are means to the greater end of the full and free development of every individual person. We in the Labour Party – men and women from all occupations and from every sphere of life – have set out to create a community that relies for its driving power on the release of all the finer constructive impulses of man. We believe that all citizens have obligations to fulfil as well as rights to enjoy.

In contrast, the fainthearted feel that only fear of poverty will drive men to work for the nation. 'Empty bellies', one Tory has said, 'are the one thing that will make Britons work.' Labour for its part declares that full employment is the corner-stone of the new society.

The Labour Government has ensured full employment and fair shares of the necessities of life. What a contrast with pre-war days! In those days millions of unwanted men eked out their lives in need of the very things they themselves could have made in the factories that were standing idle.

Even when at work each man often feared that the next pay-day would be the last. The wife feared that the housekeeping money would suddenly vanish. Often it did. Her husband was handed his cards, he drew the dole, then she had to make do with a fraction of her previous money – and despite all her sacrifices the children suffered. The queue at the Labour Exchange was repeated in the queue of small traders at the bankruptcy court. Clerks and professional people saw their hopes destroyed and their savings swept away by the slump.

Big Business did not believe in Britain – it believed only in profit. So money went into cinemas, not coal; into luxury flats, not looms for Lancashire; into land speculation, not into agriculture.

Whatever our Party, all of us old enough to remember are in our hearts ashamed of those years. They were unhappy years for our country and our people. They must never come again … ■

For the Conservatives, the 1950 campaign was an opportunity to convince voters that the party was committed both to full employment and to welfare. At the same time, much emphasis was placed on the need to liberalise the economy and respond to consumers' wishes. The party's election manifesto was based on the Conservative Research Department's policy document, The Right Road for Britain, *published in 1949.*

3.19   **Conservative Party general election manifesto, 'This Is the Road: The Conservative and Unionist Party's Policy, 1950' (in F.W.S. Craig, *British General Election Manifestos 1900–1974*, London, Macmillan, 1975, pp. 139–52).**

■ The policy of the Conservative Party, expressed in 'The Right Road for Britain' is to restore to our country her economic independence and to our citizens their full personal freedom and power of initiative. Unless Britain can hold her place in the world, she cannot make her full contribution to the preservation of peace, and peace is our supreme purpose. Britain, wisely led, can bring together the Commonwealth and Empire, Western Europe and the Atlantic Powers into a partnership dedicated to the cause of saving world peace and of preserving democratic freedom and the rule of law.

PRESENT DANGERS

We can only import the food and raw materials on which we depend by paying for them in goods, services or cash. For the first few years after the war every country wanted all that Britain could make, almost regardless of price. That time is passing. Now Britain can sell abroad only if her goods are high in quality and competitive in price.

Since 1945, Britain has received in gifts and loans from the United States and the nations of the Commonwealth the vast sum of nearly £2,000 millions. But Marshall aid will end by 1952. From that time forth we must pay for all we buy from overseas or suffer the consequences in low standards of living and high unemployment.

The duty of the Government from their first day in office was to husband the national resources, to evoke the greatest efforts from all, to give every chance to enterprise and inventiveness and above all, not needlessly to divide the nation.

THE SOCIALIST FUTURE

But the Socialists have failed in their duty. National resources have been squandered. Individual effort has been discouraged or suppressed. National unity has been deeply injured. The Government have shrunk from the realities of the situation and have not told the people the truth.

THE SOCIALIST DECEPTION

From the time they acquired power they pretended that their policy was bringing the prosperity they had promised. They tried to make out that before they got a majority the whole history of Great Britain, so long admired and envied throughout the world, was dark and dismal. They spread the tale that social welfare is something to be had from the State free, gratis and for nothing. They have put more money into circulation, but it has bought less and less. The value of every pound earned or saved or paid in pensions or social services has been cut by 3s. 8d. since they took office. It is not a £ but 16/4.

There is no foundation for the Socialist claim to have brought us prosperity and security. Ministers themselves have declared that but for American Aid there would have been two million people unemployed.

During these bleak years Britain has lurched from crisis to crisis and from makeshift to makeshift. Whatever temporary expedients have been used to create a false sense of well-being, none has effected a permanent cure. Devaluation is not the last crisis nor have we seen the worst of it yet.

SOCIALIST MISMANAGEMENT

In 1945, the Socialists promised that their methods of planning and nationalisation would make the people of Britain masters of their economic destiny. Nothing could be more untrue. Every forecast has proved grossly over-optimistic. Every crisis has caught them unawares. The Fuel Crisis cost the country £200 millions and the Convertibility Crisis as much. Ambitious plans have gone awry. Nearly thirty million pounds have already been muddled away on the Groundnuts Scheme. Railway engines were converted to burn oil because coal was scarce and then converted back again because oil was even scarcer. With the same labour force as before the war little more than half as many houses are being built. Despite the promise of the Minister of Health that 'when the next Election occurs there will be no housing problem in Great Britain for the working class', waiting lists for council houses in many districts are longer now than they were five years ago.

Socialism has imposed a crushing burden of taxation amounting to eight shillings of every pound earned in this country. Enterprise and extra effort have been stifled. Success has been penalised. Thrift and savings have been discouraged. A vote for Socialism is a vote to continue the policy which has endangered our economic and present independence both as a nation and as men and women ... ■

3.20   **Labour Party and Conservative Party posters, 1950 general election (Conservative Party Archives).**

More people voted in 1950 than in the 1945 election. Labour retained, and even increased, its following, but its majority was reduced to only six. The Conservatives had apparently benefited from a toughening of middle-class opposition. Inevitably, the result posed serious problems for Labour. The reinforced Conservative opposition was now filled with young, energetic backbenchers anxious to attack the government, whose members were ageing and ailing, in some cases after ten continuous years in office. It was widely expected that the government's small majority could not endure for long, and that a fresh contest would soon follow.

3.21   General election results, 1950 (charts derived from D. Butler and G. Butler (eds), *British Political Facts, 1900–1985*, London, Macmillan, 6th edn, 1986, p. 226).

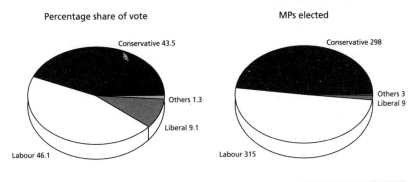

Percentage share of vote

Conservative 43.5
Others 1.3
Liberal 9.1
Labour 46.1

MPs elected

Conservative 298
Others 3
Liberal 9
Labour 315

Labour divided

By 1950 Attlee's government appeared to be losing momentum in its domestic programme. One of Labour's successes, the National Health Service, ironically precipitated a crisis within the government. As Chapter 4 will describe, the scale of the demand for free treatment far exceeded both expectations and the finances originally provided, and ministers became increasingly concerned that the health budget was jeopardising spending in other areas.

Divisions in the government crystallised when the Chancellor, Hugh Gaitskell, urged in his 1951 Budget the introduction of charges for dentures and spectacles; these charges were intended to generate some revenue, but more importantly to discourage abuse of the system. This seemed to be an attack on the NHS's fundamental principle of free provision, creating a precedent which Bevan, the minister responsible for the NHS, could not countenance. Attlee and the rest of the Cabinet supported Gaitskell, the young, rising star of the party's consolidationist wing. Bevan, increasingly disenchanted with his colleagues over a range of issues, therefore resigned, followed by the President of the Board of Trade, Harold Wilson, in April 1951. Bevan explained his position following the Budget speech.

3.22   **Aneurin Bevan, speech to the House of Commons, 25 April 1951 (*Hansard* 5th ser., 487, 34–43).**

■ I listened to the Chancellor of the Exchequer with very great admiration. It was one of the cleverest Budget speeches I had ever heard in my life. There was a passage towards the end in which he said that he was now coming to a complicated and technical matter and that if Members wished to they could go to sleep. They did. Whilst they were sleeping he stole £100 million a year from the National Insurance Fund. Of course I know that in the same Budget speech the Chancellor of the Exchequer said that he had already taken account of it as savings. Of course he had, so that the re-armament of Great Britain is financed out of the contributions that the workers have paid into the Fund in order to protect themselves. [HON. MEMBERS: 'Oh!'] Certainly, that is the meaning of it. It is no good my hon. Friends refusing to face these matters. If we look at the Chancellor's speech we see that the Chancellor himself said that he had already taken account of the contributions into the Insurance Fund as savings. He said so, and he is right. [Interruption]. Do not deny that he is right. I am saying he is right. Do not quarrel with me when I agree with him.

The conclusion is as follows. At a time when there are still large untapped sources of wealth in Great Britain, a Socialist Chancellor of the Exchequer uses the Insurance Fund, contributed for the purpose of maintaining the social services, as his source of revenue, and I say that is not Socialist finance. Go to that source for revenue when no other source remains, but no one can say that there are no other sources of revenue in Great Britain except the Insurance Fund.

I come now to the National Health Service side of the matter. Let me say to my hon. Friends on these benches: you have been saying in the last fortnight or three weeks that I have been quarrelling about a triviality – spectacles and dentures. You may call it a triviality. I remember the triviality that started an avalanche in 1931 ...

The Chancellor of the Exchequer in this year's Budget proposes to reduce the Health expenditure by £13 million – only £13 million out of £4,000 million ... If he finds it necessary to mutilate, or begin to mutilate, the Health Services for £13 million out of £4,000 million, what will he do next year? Or are you next year going to take your stand on the upper denture? The lower half apparently does not matter, but the top half is sacrosanct. Is that right? If my hon. Friends are asked questions at meetings about what they will do next year, what will they say?

The Chancellor of the Exchequer is putting a financial ceiling on the Health Service. With rising prices the Health Service is squeezed between that artificial figure and rising prices. What is to be squeezed out next year? Is it the upper half? When that has been squeezed out and the same principle holds good, what do you squeeze out the year after? Prescriptions? Hospital charges? Where do you stop? ...

After all, the National Health Service was something of which we were all very proud, and even the Opposition were beginning to be proud of it. It only had to last a few more years to become a part of our traditions, and then the traditionalists would have claimed the credit for all of it. Why should we throw it away? ...

I say this, in conclusion. There is only one hope for mankind – and that is democratic Socialism. There is only one party in Great Britain which can do it – and that is the Labour Party. But I ask them carefully to consider how far they are polluting the stream. We have gone a long way – a very long way – against great difficulties. Do not let us change direction now. Let us make it clear, quite clear, to the rest of the world that we stand where we stood, that we are not going to allow ourselves to be diverted from our path by the exigencies of the immediate situation. We shall do what is necessary to defend ourselves – defend ourselves by arms, and not only with arms but with the spiritual resources of our people. ■

The 1951 General Election

Attlee was reluctant to continue in office without a clear mandate, especially once Britain had become involved in the Korean War. For some observers, this was a typical example of his placing national before party interests. Although the signs were not very favourable, given the still fresh wounds caused by Bevan's departure, Attlee opted for an election in October 1951. The campaign was a tough one, in which both parties vied for the all-important former Liberal vote. Whereas in 1950 there had been 475 Liberal candidates, who between them attracted 2.6 million votes, in 1951, because of a shortage of funds, only 100 Liberals stood. The Labour Party defended its record but perhaps failed to offer the electors anything new. As it had done in 1945, Labour called into question whether the Conservatives really meant what they said. By 1951 it seemed to many that the Conservatives were committed to the new political 'consensus'.

Although in 1951 neither party could challenge the goal of full employment, especially since Labour had achieved it since 1945, there were nevertheless significant differences in the two parties' election manifestos. For Labour, it was essential to protect the economic and social policies introduced since the early 1940s. For the Conservatives, the emphasis was on stemming the tide of socialist advance. Yet the Conservatives made few promises to undo what Labour had achieved, save for commitments to denationalise the iron and steel and road haulage industries. It was after 1951 that commentators began to talk of a blurring of party differences and the birth of 'Butskellism'. But Labour was arguably mistaken in stressing the risks attached to a Conservative government, implying that Churchill could not be trusted to maintain peace, given the troubled international background.

3.23   **Labour Party general election manifesto, 1951 (in F.W.S. Craig, *British General Election Manifestos 1900–1974*, London, Macmillan, 1975, pp. 173–6).**

■ Labour – proud of its record, sure in its policies – confidently asks the electors to renew its mandate.

Four major tasks face our nation: to secure peace; to maintain full employment and increase production; to bring down the cost of living; to build a just society. Only with a Labour Government can the British people achieve these aims ...

FULL EMPLOYMENT AND PRODUCTION

Full employment through six years of peace is the greatest of all Labour's achievements. It has never happened before. It has meant a revolution in the lives of our people. To-day, there are half a million unfilled vacancies at the employment exchanges. Under Labour – more jobs than workers. Under the Tories – more workers than jobs ...

We shall do everything possible to stimulate at home and to expand our exports. We shall press on with the development of new sources of raw materials, particularly within the Commonwealth.

We shall attack monopolies and combines which restrict production and keep prices and profits too high. We shall prohibit by law the withholding of supplies to traders who bring prices down.

We shall take over concerns which fail the nation and start new public enterprises wherever this will serve the national interest. We shall help industry with scientific and technical aid.

We shall establish Development Councils, by compulsion if necessary, wherever this will help industrial efficiency.

We shall associate the workers more closely with the administration of public industries and services ...

SOCIAL JUSTICE

Contrast Britain in the inter-war years with Britain to-day. Then we had mass unemployment; mass fear; mass misery. Now we have full employment.

Then millions suffered from insecurity and want. Now we have social security for every man, woman and child.

The dread of doctors' bills was a nightmare in countless homes so that good health cost more than most people could afford to pay. Now we have a national health scheme which is the admiration of the post-war world.

Then we had the workhouse and the Poor Law for the old people. Now we have a national insurance system covering the whole population with greatly improved pensions and a humane National Assistance scheme ...

There has, indeed, been progress, but much more remains to be done in the redistribution of income and of property to ensure that those who create the nation's wealth receive their just reward. Half of Britain's wealth is still owned by 1 per cent of the population ...

FORWARD WITH LABOUR OR BACKWARD WITH THE TORIES

We ask the electors to renew their vote of confidence in the Labour Party. It is a simple choice – Labour or Tory.

Look first at the past records, for we have both made history. But what kind of history? To-day, after six years of Labour rule and in spite of post-war difficulties, the standard of living of the vast majority of our people is higher than ever it was in the days of Tory rule. Never have the old folk been better cared for. Never had we so happy and healthy a young generation as we see in Britain to-day ...

Welfare at home, peace abroad, with a constant striving for international co-operation – this is Labour's aim. The Tories with their dark past, full of bitter memories for so many of our people, promise no light for the future. They would take us backward into poverty and insecurity at home and grave perils abroad. ■

The Conservatives' campaign in 1951, like that in 1950, showed that the party was drift-ing away from its earlier, apparently interventionist position. Their slogan in 1951, 'Set the people free', was an attempt to capitalise on a public mood tiring of austerity and rationing. As the Labour government itself set the tone in the later 1940s by dismantling some economic controls, so Conservatives could feel more comfortable with the lan-guage of politics. Although they did not jettison the Industrial Charter, *the Conservatives emphasised a very different style of economic management in 1951.*

3.24 *Manifesto of the Conservative and Unionist Party,* **1951 (in F.W.S. Craig,** *British General Election Manifestos 1900–1974,* **London, Macmillan, 1975, pp. 169–73).**

■ We are confronted with a critical Election which may well be the turn-ing point in the fortunes and even the life of Britain. We cannot go on with this evenly balanced Party strife and hold our own in the world, or even earn our living. The prime need is for a stable government with sev-eral years before it, during which time national interests must be faithful-ly held far above party feuds or tactics. We need a new Government not biased by privilege or interest or cramped by doctrinal prejudices or inflamed by the passions of class warfare. Such a Government only the Conservative and Unionist Party can to-day provide.

There must be no illusions about our difficulties and dangers. It is better to face them squarely as we did in 1940. The Conservative Party, who since victory have had no responsibility for the events which have led us to where we are now, offers no bribes to the electors. We will do our best to serve them and to make things better all round, but we do not blind ourselves to the difficulties that have to be overcome, or the time that will be required to bring us back to our rightful position in the world, and to revive the vigour of our national life and impulse ...

Contrast our position to-day with what it was six years ago. Then all our foes had yielded. We all had a right to believe and hope that the fear of war would not afflict our generation nor our children. We were respected, honoured and admired throughout the world. We were a united people at home, and it was only by being united that we had survived the deadly perils through which we had come and had kept the flag of freedom flying through the fateful year when we were alone. There, at any rate, is a great foundation and inspiration. Everyone knows how the aftermath of war brings extraordinary difficulties. With national unity we could have overcome them. But what has happened since those days?

The attempt to impose a doctrinaire Socialism upon an Island which has grown great and famous by free enterprise has inflicted serious injury upon our strength and prosperity. Nationalisation has proved itself a failure which has resulted in heavy losses to the taxpayer or the consumer, or both. It has not given general satisfaction to the wage-earners in the nationalised industries. It has impaired the relations of the Trade Unions with their members. In more than one nationalised industry the wage-earners are ill-content with the change from the private employers, with whom they could negotiate on equal terms through the Trade Unions, to the all-powerful and remote officials in Whitehall.

Our finances have been brought into grave disorder. No British Government in peacetime has ever had the power or spent the money in the vast extent and reckless manner of our present rulers. Apart from the two thousand millions they have borrowed or obtained from the United States and the Dominions, they have spent more than 10 million pounds a day, or 22 thousand millions in their six years. No community living in a world of competing nations can possibly afford such frantic extravagances. Devaluation was the offspring of wild, profuse expenditure, and the evils which we suffer to-day are the inevitable progeny of that wanton way of living.

A Conservative Government will cut out all unnecessary Government expenditure, simplify the administrative machine, and prune waste and extravagance in every department …

The Nation now has a chance of rebuilding its life at home and of strengthening its position abroad. We must free ourselves from our impediments. Of all impediments the class war is the worst. At the time when a growing measure of national unity is more than ever necessary, the Socialist Party hope to gain another lease of power by fomenting class hatred and appealing to moods of greed and envy … ■

3.25 Labour Party and Conservative Party posters, 1951 general election (Conservative Party Archives).

Although the Conservatives won the 1951 election, they did not do as well as some had hoped, securing a majority over Labour of twenty-six seats. The bulk of Conservative gains probably reflected the rightwards shift of the old Liberal vote and the fact that only 100 Liberal candidates stood throughout the country. By 1951 the Liberal Party appeared to be almost a spent force, having only six seats in Parliament, though it resisted attempts to be brought into an anti-socialist alliance with the Conservatives. This decision partly guaranteed the Liberals' survival into the next decade. The Conservatives were also helped by the organisational reforms they had made since 1945. Yet the Labour Party achieved more votes than the Conservatives, and only the vagaries of the 'first past the post' electoral system allowed Churchill to claim victory. Crucially, the Conservatives had succeeded in tapping into disgruntled middle opinion, the basis of their success in the 1930s.

3.26 **General election results, 1951 (derived from D. Butler and G. Butler (eds), *British Political Facts, 1900–1985*, London, Macmillan, 6th edn, 1986, p. 226).**

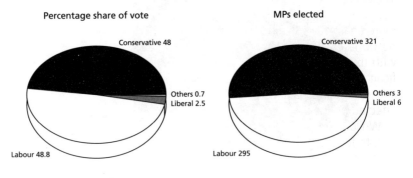

Percentage share of vote

Conservative 48
Others 0.7
Liberal 2.5
Labour 48.8

MPs elected

Conservative 321
Others 3
Liberal 6
Labour 295

CHAPTER FOUR

Towards the 'New Jerusalem'? The Economy and the Welfare State, 1945–51

THE TASK of returning the British economy to a peacetime footing would have been a formidable one for any government. But the newly elected Labour government had set itself ambitious additional goals including the elimination of unemployment through economic 'planning', public ownership of key sectors of the economy, an attack on poverty and the construction of a more egalitarian, healthier society. Throughout its life, the government was to be buffeted by external developments and constraints, and these, together with the still imprecise tools of economic management, made it extremely difficult to maintain consistent economic policies. Above all, there was the problem of Britain's balance of payments, especially its dollar deficit, disastrously affected by the war.

While helped by a loan from the United States, and later by US 'Marshall aid', to feed itself, Britain had to restore its exporting capacity as quickly as possible, to earn precious dollars from whatever means available; and this was achieved with remarkable success, even if in the process the British public was obliged to endure continuing austerity and scarcity. Nevertheless, full employment, the touchstone of wartime thinking on reconstruction for a better world, was secured. In the social sphere, too, much of the fear endemic in the decades between the wars was eliminated by the introduction of a comprehensive social insurance system; while by no means flawless, this represented, in combination with the provision of free health care, a revolution in the lives of the majority of the population.

Britain's Postwar Economic Outlook

When Japan was defeated in August 1945, the United States government unexpectedly terminated 'Lend-Lease', which had been a vital prop to Britain's wartime economy. Britain had accumulated wartime debts of £4.7 billion, and had been obliged to sell £1.1 billion worth of overseas assets. This would restrict Britain's future 'invisible earnings' capacity, just as the wartime emphasis on military production at the expense of exports would impair the country's balance of payments position. Fresh US financial aid seemed to be essential if Britain was to deal with the transitional problems of adjusting to peace.

In August 1945 John Maynard Keynes, economic adviser to the Treasury, provided a bleak summary of the country's financial circumstances.

4.1   Lord Keynes, memorandum, 'Our overseas financial prospects', 13 August 1945 (PRO CAB 129/1, CP(45)112, Annex).

■ **27.** It seems, then, that there are three essential conditions without which we have not a hope of escaping what might be described, without exaggeration and without implying that we should not eventually recover from it, a financial Dunkirk. These conditions are (a) an intense concentration on the expansion of exports, (b) drastic and immediate economies in our overseas expenditure, and (c) substantial aid from the United States on terms which we can accept. They can only be fulfilled by a combination of the greatest enterprise, ruthlessness and tact.

28. What does one mean in this context by 'a financial Dunkirk'? What would happen in the event of insufficient success? That is not easily foreseen. Abroad it would require a sudden and humiliating withdrawal from our onerous responsibilities with great loss of prestige and an acceptance for the time being of the position of a second-class Power, rather like the present position of France. From the Dominions and elsewhere we should seek what charity we could obtain. At home a greater degree of austerity would be necessary than we have experienced at any time during the war. And there would have to be an indefinite postponement of the realisation of the best hopes of the new Government. It is probable that after five years the difficulties would have been largely overcome.

29. But in practice one will be surprised if it ever comes to this. In practice, of course, we shall in the end accept the best terms we can get. And that may be the beginning of later troubles and bitter feelings. That is why it is so important to grasp the reality of our position and to mitigate its potentialities by energy, ingenuity and foresight.

30. Shortage of material goods is not going to be the real problem of the post-war world for more than a brief period. Beyond question we are entering into the age of abundance. All the more reason not to mess things up and endanger the prizes of victory and the fruits of peace whilst crossing the threshold. The time may well come – sooner than we may yet have any right to assume – when the sums which now overwhelm us may seem chicken-feed, and an opportunity to get rid of stuff without payment a positive convenience. ■

US aid

After tough negotiations, in which Britain's case was forcefully argued by Keynes, Washington agreed to write off Britain's Lend-Lease debts in return for $650 million, and to make available a loan of $3.75 billion. For its part, Britain had to agree to co-operate in implementing the 1944 Bretton Woods agreements on creating a system of stable currency exchange rates, and to make sterling freely convertible on the world's foreign exchanges. Behind the second condition lay Washington's accurate belief that, at a time when only the US economy could supply goods in short supply, most of the world's holders of sterling would be anxious to convert their pounds into dollars. The loan was eventually agreed; and throughout the life of the Attlee government, Britain was to remain dependent on US aid in various forms.

The postwar loan conditions angered many commentators in Britain, where it was felt the Sterling Area was to be dismantled in the interests of American exporters. When the loan was debated in Parliament, the government faced bitter attacks. The Conservative MP Robert Boothby was a particularly fierce critic of the terms imposed by the United States.

4.2　Robert Boothby, speech on the US loan conditions, 12 December 1945 (*Hansard*, 5th ser., 417: 457–66).

■ I submit that the conditions put forward for our approval are far too onerous. It is not untrue to say that comparable terms have never hitherto been imposed on a nation that has not been defeated in war. To get through, and pay our debt, on the admission of the Government, we shall have to increase our exports by 75 per cent.; not 50 per cent. any more, but 75 per cent., over prewar. If ever there was any chance of our achieving this aim, it has been removed by the conditions attached to the Loan which is now being given us … Look at the inevitable effect of our convertibility undertaking – to convert dollars freely, sterling into dollars – on our trade. No doubt hon. Members on both sides of the House have read the extremely able letter of Sir Hubert Henderson in 'The Times' this morning. He wrote:

'… all incentive to other countries to buy from us because we buy from them will be removed in about a year from now. Moreover, any part of the huge accumulated sterling balances which countries in the sterling area are allowed to spend at all must be made equally available for dollar as for sterling purchases.'

I was told only yesterday that some of our engineering firms have orders from countries in the sterling area up to 1950 and 1951 for capital goods and machinery, for delivery two, three, four, even five years hence. As soon as this process begins, a very considerable number of these contracts will be transferred immediately to the United States. Can you imagine, for example, that India, or Egypt, as soon as they get convertible currency in exchange for their sterling balances, will not go straight to the United States of America; not because they dislike this country particularly, but because they can get the goods more quickly delivered. For the United States are well on the way to complete reconversion; in fact, they have already practically converted their industries to a peace basis, and we have a long way still to go in this direction.

As I have already said, in order to obtain the necessary imports to pay our debts, we shall have to increase our exports by 75 per cent. a year ... Our trade, imports and exports, must be on an incomparably higher scale in the future than they were prior to 1938; and it is axiomatic, if we are to increase the export trade to the extent envisaged, that we must also greatly increase imports over the prewar figure. To say we cannot do this is tantamount to saying that our export target is unattainable ...

I want now to put two propositions to the Chancellor of the Exchequer. The first is that multilateral trade and free convertibility, to which this Agreement admittedly commits us, are impractical in the modern world ... The philosophy underlying the old Liberal doctrine of enlightened self-interest and the free-market economy depended for its success on the existence of empty spaces and continually expanding markets. The spaces are filling up. The era of uncontrolled capitalist expansion is drawing to a close ...

My second proposition is that we cannot have a planned national economy with international economic anarchy ... Is everybody so absolutely confident in the economic stability of the United States of America and of their system? Do hon. Members opposite feel such faith and reliance in the steady development of free, knock-about Capitalism that they think there can never be another depression in the United States? ... I think there may possibly be a slump there. And if there is, His Majesty's Government are, by these measures, depriving us of every weapon by which we might protect ourselves from its most dire consequences ... ■

Exports and austerity

The balance of payments difficulties which dogged the country after 1945 resulted in a special emphasis being placed on rebuilding British exports in order to pay for vital imports. This led the government to launch an export drive. It was especially important to increase exports which would earn dollars, as these could then be used to buy imports not available from non-dollar sources. Inevitably, the needs of consumers had to take second place. At the end of the war, it was assumed that food supplies would return to normal and that rationing could be terminated. In the event, rationing was to become more severe than in wartime, and some items not rationed during the war, such as bread and potatoes, were rationed. This unexpected austerity gave rise to criticism of government policy.

In 1947 the government published its economic forecast for the year ahead. This analysed economic trends and set a series of targets, in which the need to maximise exports featured prominently.

4.3 *Economic Survey for 1947*, **February 1947 (London, HMSO, Cmd 7046, PP XIX, 1946-7, pp. 16–17, 20).**

■ **61.** The central fact of 1947 is that we have not enough resources to do all that we want to do. We have barely enough to do all that we *must* do. Whether we reckon in man-power, coal, electricity, steel, or national production as a whole, the conclusion is unavoidable. To get all we want, production would have to be increased by at least 25 per cent. This is clearly impossible in 1947.

62. There is no reason for surprise about this. We have come through six years of all-out effort. We lost less than some of our Allies; we were saved from enemy occupation. But our losses, though less obvious, are very real, and are now making themselves felt – first, in our import–export problem and, second, in the need for rebuilding our basic industries. We must find means to pay for imports which we formerly got in return for our overseas investments, and we must make up six years' arrears of industrial equipment. These are basic things, and to put them right is a huge job of work – especially as we must at the same time rebuild our battered housing, restore our depleted flocks and herds and produce more clothing and household goods.

63. We could live without new radio sets and furniture, but we cannot live without imported food. We could indeed at a pinch live without new houses and holidays, but our national existence becomes quite impossible if we cannot produce enough coal and electric power.

64. Those things which are fundamental to our national life must come first. The danger in our present situation is that there is so much that we want to do, and so much that seems important that too little effort will be concentrated on the things that are really vital.

65. The Government has examined the national needs for 1947, and has decided that first importance must be attached to payment for imports and to basic industries and services, particularly coal and power ...

66. Imports and exports are of fundamental importance, now and for some years to come. Failure to build up our export trade in the next two or three years so that we can afford to buy enough imports would mean continued food rationing, much less smoking and private motoring, widespread unemployment for lack of raw materials and inability to re-equip industry with the most modern machinery.

67. We need more imports in 1947. In the last year we have been getting 70 per cent. of the 1938 quantities, and have had to draw on stocks. The 1947 import programme provides an expansion to 80–85 per cent. of 1938 volume. But much more than that would be needed to increase rations considerably.

68. Our imports are limited both by what is available and by what we can afford in foreign exchange. At present, our imports of food (up to the requirements for a certain basic consumption level), feeding-stuffs and essential raw materials are limited by world shortages. Our imports of additional food beyond the basic level, tobacco, petrol and consumers goods are determined by what we can afford. Both considerations affect our imports of machinery and equipment for industry, agriculture, mining, shipping, &c., but normally import is permitted if the machine is of essential importance and cannot be supplied in comparable conditions from United Kingdom production. As world supplies improve, our imports will be fixed entirely by what we can afford. We must continue to control their total volume tightly ...

81. The basic fact of our position over the next few years, and indeed in the longer-term future, is that we must devote at least 25 per cent. of our manufacturing capacity to the production of exports. This means a smaller supply for the home market, unless production is increased. We shall indeed require to export more than this if we are to get the imports which we need for improving our standards of living. But 25 per cent. of our production of manufactured goods must be a first charge. A large part of our production is exclusively for the home market; this means that the industries which can export will have to plan for a much larger long-term export proportion than 25 per cent. and a far larger proportion than they devoted to exports before the war. There is nothing temporary about our need for exports; concentration upon exports must become a permanent part of our normal industrial life. Without exports, we cannot get food and we cannot get raw materials, and without these, we cannot hope to increase our standard of living – or even maintain it ... ■

The year 1947 was to be one of crisis for Britain. It began with an extremely harsh winter, the worst for over sixty years, which disrupted transport, aggravated the shortage of coal and other fuels and resulted in closures of factories and a temporary surge in unemployment. It was against this background that major decisions about Britain's overseas commitments were taken, as will be discussed in Chapter 5. In his memoirs, the Chancellor of the Exchequer, Hugh Dalton, quoting his own diaries, recalled the fuel crisis and its effects. Like numerous commentators, he blamed the unanticipated shortage of coal, and the failure to build up adequate stockpiles, on the Minister of Fuel and Power, Emanuel Shinwell.

4.4   Hugh Dalton on the fuel crisis, 1947 (in Hugh Dalton, *High Tide and After: Memoirs 1945–1960*, **London, Muller, 1962, pp. 203–5).**

■ *February 6th*

'We are having an exceptionally bad run of weather and our coal and electricity supplies are in a pretty poor way. It will be a great relief to get through March, and into the period when more coal is being produced, and then we shall have to make firm plans for stocking up well in advance of next winter.

'Shinwell is the most mercurial of Ministers, and, according to all accounts, a very bad administrator. He seems incapable of settling down to a close and objective study of the facts, or of following a steady line in regard to the many very tricky issues in his department.'

Friday, February 7th

'Today, at this morning's Cabinet, Shinwell suddenly asks permission to tell the House of Commons this afternoon that all electricity must be cut off from industry in London, South-East England, the Midlands and the North-West, and from all domestic consumers all over the country between nine and twelve, and between two and four each day. This is a complete thunder-clap, following the usual rather hopeful tales we have had from him during the past week. Only two days ago he was saying that he supposed we ought to give a priority to keeping all the generating stations well supplied, even if this meant cutting off some other people. The weather has been very bad, but the root cause of all this trouble is the insufficient stocks with which we started the winter' ...

Monday, February 10th

... 'The next few days, and weeks, were plagued by fuel shortage and con-tinuing bad weather. Shinwell does not excel in the team spirit. Most people blame *him* primarily for the crisis, since he didn't clearly foresee it or make any plans to meet it in advance and lessen its impact. But he had to face, from the start, some almost insoluble departmental problems. For all the efforts to solve these, he and all his Cabinet colleagues must share responsibility. But he won't face facts squarely. I hear that in the late summer of last year the P.M. sent for him and showed him some very dis-quieting figures about coal stocks, actual and prospective. But Shinwell replied, "You mustn't let yourself be led up the garden by all these statist-ics. You must consider the imponderables."' ...

The crisis lasted three weeks. Unemployment, which, just before the crisis, had been 397,000 or $2\frac{1}{2}$ per cent of insured workers, quickly rose to a peak of 2,300,000 or $15\frac{1}{2}$ per cent on February 22nd, then gradually declined to 785,000 or 5 per cent on March 12th, when all the restrictions imposed when the crisis began had been removed. This had not been the end of the world, as some panic-mongers had expected. But it was certainly the first really heavy blow to confidence in the Government and in our post-war plans. This soon began to show itself in many different and unwelcome ways. Never glad, confident morning again! ∎

Convertibility and Marshall Aid

As part of the US loan agreement, Britain had agreed to make sterling con-vertible by July 1947. The Treasury and the Bank of England hoped that convertibility would demonstrate the strength of the pound, and so encourage greater confidence in sterling overseas. This optimism overlooked the fact that Britain did not possess sufficient financial reserves to back convertibility, and the fact that Britain still depended on the US loan. Two-thirds of that loan had been exhausted within a year, partly because of the convertibility commitment, and partly because of Britain's own heavy overseas defence spending. In the summer of 1947 the drain on London's dollar reserves reached crisis levels, such that if convertibility had been allowed to continue, the original loan would have evaporated by late September. On 20 August 1947 the government announced the suspension of convertibility.

The convertibility crisis forced the government to reduce imports, especially those bought with dollars, and to renew its calls for an expansion of exports. In September 1947 the President of the Board of Trade, Stafford Cripps, explained to his Cabinet colleagues that the country would have to expand its exports to 140 per cent of their 1938 volume by mid-1948, and to 160 per cent by the end of 1948. Inevitably, this would place severe constraints on the domestic economy.

4.5   Stafford Cripps, memorandum on the export programme, 5 September 1947 (PRO CAB 129/20 CP(47)250).

■ **2.** The most important prerequisite of success in our export drive is that individual requirements of fuel and power should be met in full. This means that over the winter months it will be necessary for the Government and the National Coal Board to take steps to ensure that industry receives at least $24\frac{1}{4}$ million tons of coal even if other consumers go short ... If the requirements of industry are not met in full we shall require to discriminate in favour of industries and firms of special importance to the export trade ...

4. I am particularly concerned that the export programme should not be wrecked by lack of steel. In terms of employment, 60 per cent. of those who are at work on export orders are in the metal and engineering industries; and the shortage of steel is seriously reducing the productivity of those workers by interrupting the flow of materials and components. An increase in the supply of steel to the engineering industries would provide us with additional exports of the most acceptable type without any increased call on man-power and without detraction from the re-equipment of British industry. But if the steel requirements of those industries cannot be met, even the most drastic curtailment in the domestic supply of machinery and plant might fail to bring exports to the level which we hope to achieve ...

13. It has not been possible to draw up the export programme without making provision for a substantial reduction in civilian consumption in many directions, until such time as overall production can be materially increased. The largest and most important reduction will be in textiles. Although the issue of clothing coupons has been successively reduced to a level which is about 50 per cent. of pre-war, it will be necessary, if we are to take full advantage of our export opportunities and to ensure that exports reach the target of 160 per cent. of 1938, that even this low rate of issue should be cut still further ...

18. The export programme will call for an increased consumption of imported raw materials, some of them from hard currency areas ... I have assumed that the foreign exchange necessary for the supply of these raw materials will be forthcoming even if this deprives us of other imports ... ■

Britain's need for dollars with which to buy vital imports was extreme. This is why the government was so relieved when Washington announced, in June 1947, its massive European Recovery Programme of 'Marshall aid', effective from April 1948. In order to safeguard political stability in economically stricken Western Europe, the United States was prepared to supply some $12 billion in aid between 1948 and 1950, Britain receiving the largest single share, $2.7 billion. Marshall aid enabled Britain to continue importing raw materials, which kept industry working, and so helped to maintain full employment.

As the officials of the 'London Committee', created in London to orchestrate Britain's response to Marshall aid, concluded, the need for British participation in the scheme was unarguable.

4.6   London Committee on European Economic Co-operation, notes on the need for Marshall Aid, 4 October 1947 (PRO CAB 129/21 CP(47)279).

■ *Do we need American assistance?*

The position of the United Kingdom is a very difficult one. The policies upon which we are now entering are designed to enable us to balance our payments with the outside world. We calculate that if we can sell sufficient of the goods we are making available for export at the cost very largely of our own home consuming public – we shall be able very nearly to bring about an overall balance in our trade by the middle of next year. But owing to the inconvertibility of other currencies this will still leave us with a very serious dollar shortage.

This arises from the fact that a large proportion of the foodstuffs and raw materials that we require must come from the Western Hemisphere, while we cannot sell a sufficient proportion of our goods in dollar markets to bring about a dollar balance. This situation has always existed, but before the war we earned dollars by our surpluses with other countries. To-day the world shortage of dollars is such that these surpluses are not convertible into dollars. It is this that makes it impossible for us to balance our dollar payments even though we obtain an overall balance of payments.

This means that some time – probably early – next year we shall in the absence of aid have still further to cut off the purchase of foodstuffs, tobacco, films and raw materials from the Western Hemisphere. Alternative supplies will probably not be obtainable elsewhere, and substitute foods will not be available. We shall therefore have to go without and our already low standards will perforce be further reduced, and this not because we cannot produce enough in the United Kingdom to pay for the supplies we need but because we cannot sell our goods in the market from which our supplies alone can come ...

Such a situation may well lead to a progressive frustration of our efforts to get ourselves back on to our feet. Our productive power will be reduced, first by lack of foodstuffs to nourish our people, second by non-availability of raw materials.

This is the situation which Mr. Marshall foresaw, and to meet which the Marshall Plan was designed. We are now beginning a series of bilateral negotiations designed to secure our supplies at the minimum cost to our reserves. As the situation becomes more acute, further cuts are made in our imports, and our gold and dollar reserves dwindle, these efforts to secure our supplies are certain to lead to a further distortion of the world economic structure and a breakdown of even that part of multilateral trading which still survives. The sort of multilateral world which we and the Americans have been seeking to achieve since the end of the war would be postponed for an indefinite period.

We are setting out to develop our colonial and Commonwealth resources but this must be a long term matter. In time we can expect to develop sources of supply within the Empire of goods we must now buy for dollars, so that some relief from the problem of the dollar deficit in the future can be expected. Equally our own agricultural programme will in time save us dollars. But none of these will relieve the immediate dollar problem ...

The answer then must clearly be that we need assistance from the United States, and we need that assistance in 1948 if not sooner. ■

The Sterling Area

One of the most clearly sustained policies in the government's postwar economic strategy was to rebuild Britain's position in international finance, shattered by the war, and to use the Sterling Area as one of the main vehicles towards this goal. In 1945 Britain owed the members of the Sterling Area a total of around £3.5 billion. Yet, because these debts were in sterling, and so could only be used to buy sterling goods, and because they enabled Britain to buy goods from the Sterling Area on credit, officials in London regarded them as assets to the British economy, which should be encouraged to accumulate, not diminish.

In view of Britain's continuing dollar shortage, even after the introduction of Marshall aid, government ministers became increasingly interested in the production of vital commodities within the British empire and the Sterling Area, which Britain could either sell to earn dollars or import in place of goods bought with dollars. When the governors of

Britain's African colonies gathered in London in November 1947, Cripps took the oppor-
tunity to explain the important contribution the colonies could make to Britain's finan-
cial recovery.

4.7   **Sir Stafford Cripps, speech to African governors' conference,**
       12 November 1947 (PRO CO 852/989/3).

■ You will, I have no doubt, have read and studied the recent statements
made in the House of Commons and elsewhere which have given the details
of our present situation; I need therefore only recapitulate them very
shortly.

The sterling area – and indeed the rest of the non-dollar world – has got
itself completely out of balance with the Dollar countries, and with the
United States of America in particular.

This is partly due to an acceleration of the tendency towards unbalance
which was in evidence even before the first world war, and which was much
more obvious between the two wars. The rapid rise in productive capacity
of the American Continent was already in those days making it difficult to
balance its contribution to the rest of the world against what it took from the
rest of the world.

Partly too, of course, it is due to the very great upset caused by the two
world wars and the consequent setback to European productive capacity.

This lessened European productive capacity meant in effect a slower
development of all those areas in Africa that are primarily dependent upon
European capital goods manufactured for their capital development.

To some extent all the European countries were obliged to neglect capital
development both at home and in their Colonies in their attempt to balance
their overseas payments. That tendency is unfortunately accentuated by the
present much higher degree of unbalance.

This unbalance is not merely or primarily in the manufactured products of
the U.S.A. but also, more importantly, in the foodstuffs and raw materials
that members of the sterling group are compelled to obtain from the U.S.A.,
Canada or S. America (all of which must be considered as dollar countries)
simply because they are not obtainable anywhere else. The degree of unbalance has risen to extraordinary levels …

The direct trade of Great Britain with the U.S.A. has always shown a great
excess of exports from over imports to the U.S.A., but before the war this
was precariously balanced by the dollars we received from third parties, particularly members of the Commonwealth and Empire.

This enabled the sterling area as a whole to maintain a balance and so preserve the convertibility of sterling, thus permitting a very wide area of multilateral trade throughout the world.

Our own set-back in production consequent upon war devastation and our inability to buy foodstuffs and raw materials from the sterling area or non-dollar countries, coupled to the need of other sterling countries to buy manufactured goods from the U.S.A., has resulted in the very heavy adverse balance of dollars running at the rate of between £600 and £700 millions a year for the sterling area.

It is the problem of righting this tremendous unbalance which now confronts us ... I know you will all want to help in this matter but it is still vitally important that the great gravity of the common danger should be realised and the need for every unit in the sterling area to make the greatest possible contribution to overcoming it. In facing that problem we must have it quite clearly in our minds that this is not merely a short-term difficulty; it is one that, unless tackled fundamentally and on a long-term basis, will never be solved at all. We believe that provided we can sell our goods abroad there is no insuperable difficulty in our manufacturing in this country enough goods for export to enable us to pay for all the imports that we need by the end of next year. That is within our capacity. But there remains the proviso that we can sell our goods abroad and sell them – if we want to balance our overseas payments – in the right markets.

The right markets must obviously be those from which we can get an immediate return in the form of essential foodstuffs and raw materials. This same principle of course applies to all the countries in the sterling area since we desire to make the sterling area as little dependent as possible upon supplies from the dollar area.

We must therefore not only expand our exports but at the same time we must cut down our dollar imports. This means a reduction in our total volume of imports for the simple reason that we cannot at present buy elsewhere the goods we must stop purchasing for dollars. It is only however because they come from a dollar source that we must do without them; if we could get them for sterling we could still afford to have them, because as I have said we can make enough goods to export to balance our total imports.

Our trouble is that the U.S.A. cannot take enough either raw materials or manufactured goods from the Sterling Area to anything like balance her capacity to export to that area. We must, therefore, while doing all we can to increase imports into the U.S.A. from the sterling area, at the same time reduce our imports from the U.S.A. If we are to maintain even the present standard of living for our people in Great Britain, we must be able to find other sources of those kinds of foodstuffs and raw materials or their equivalents, the importation of which from the Western Hemisphere we want to cut off.

We have for a long time talked about the development of Africa but I do not believe that we have realised how from the point of view of world economy that development is absolutely vital.

The economies of Western Europe and Tropical Africa are so closely interlocked in mutual trade, in the supply of capital and in currency systems that their problems of overseas balance are essentially one. Tropical Africa is already contributing much, both in physical supplies of food and raw materials and in quite substantial net earnings of dollars for the sterling area pool. The further development of African resources is of the same crucial importance to the rehabilitation and strengthening of Western Europe as the restoration of European productive power is to the future progress and prosperity of Africa. Each needs and is needed by the other. In Africa indeed is to be found a great potential for new strength and vigour in the Western European economy and the stronger that economy becomes the better of course Africa itself will fare.

It is the urgency of the present situation and the need for the Sterling Group and Western Europe both of them to maintain their economic independence that makes it so essential that we should increase out of all recognition the tempo of African economic development. We must be prepared to change our outlook and our habits of Colonial development and force the pace so that within the next 2–5 years we can get a really marked increase of production in coal, minerals, timber, raw materials of all kinds and foodstuffs and anything else that will save dollars or will sell in a dollar market ...

We are interested in every method and device that will yield a few thousand tons more of any valuable crop or material. We want the small things followed up as well as the big prospects and we want the spirit of improvisation, invention and adventure to permeate the whole of our colonial economic policy. In the course of this work if it is carried through energetically we shall expect failures as well as successes. An occasional failure is the necessary price of adventurous development and we must not allow safety first to be the keynote of our work.

The situation is far too urgent for that, for the whole future of the sterling group and its ability to survive depends in my view upon a quick and extensive development of our African resources ... ■

Devaluation

As the convertibility crisis of 1947 had shown, Britain overestimated the strength of the pound in the postwar period. At the same time, the country's dollar shortage remained a major preoccupation. By 1949 Britain's sterling debts, continuing overseas speculation against the pound and the uncompetitive position of British exports suggested the need to devalue the pound, that is, to lower its value compared to the dollar. Delays during 1949 only served to aggravate the situation, and a looming recession in the United States eroded the dollar value of British exports. Eventually, in September 1949, the decisive step was taken, and the value of the pound was reduced from $4.03 to $2.80. Although devaluation made British exports more competitive, it also meant that more goods had to be exported in order to pay for the same volume of imports.

Indications of an impending financial crisis arose throughout the summer of 1949. In June, Cripps was already warning his colleagues of the seriousness of the situation.

4.8   Stafford Cripps, memorandum on the dollar situation, 22 June 1949 (PRO PREM 8/1412 Pt 2).

■ 1. I gave, last week, some figures to show how serious the dollar drain had become for reasons largely outside our control and I undertook to bring forward measures for dealing with the situation.

2. Meanwhile we have stopped or postponed all possible dollar expenditure as from the beginning of this week, as a temporary measure, and have communicated with the Prime Ministers of the Commonwealth countries informing them of the seriousness of the situation and suggesting a meeting of Finance Ministers in London for July 11th.

The Dollar Drain

3. The drain continues at about the same rate. The figures for the last two weeks are $48.2 millions and $53.2 millions; this week's figure is likely to be about $85 millions … The reserves at June 30th are still estimated at £400 millions on which basis we shall have lost over £70 millions in three months …

5. To meet this situation we must take measures at once which will

   (a) restore confidence in sterling throughout the world.
   (b) reduce the dollar drain both by the U.K. and the rest of the sterling area to manageable proportions.
   (c) enable us to reverse the trend despite the continued recession in U.S.A. and its likely repercussions in other countries.

6. In order to restore confidence in the £ sterling we must be able to show that we are masters of the situation and that we can avert the drain before any further damage is done. It is for that reason that we took immediate steps to reduce all dollar expenditure. It would be desirable by the end of the next quarter (September 30th) to show a very marked improvement by a lessening of the drain and maintenance of our reserves, but I must emphasise that it will take time for results to show.

7. This entails first of all a maximum effort in every direction to earn dollars or gold, but this is not likely to yield very much very quickly especially in view of the worsening world conditions resulting from U.S.A. recession.

8. We must therefore get the immediate effect by the cutting out and postponement of dollar expenditure to an amount capable of achieving our objective. There is no doubt that a part of the extra drain of the last few weeks has been due to the devaluation talk and the consequent loss of confidence in sterling. It is not possible to calculate how much this has been but it has no doubt been appreciable in amount. Once confidence can be

restored this quasi-capital (loss of floating capital) should cease and there should gradually be some return of it. I have taken measures to tighten up exchange control, and to prevent any avoidable loss on this score ... ■

Britain's balance of payments position fluctuated violently after 1945, as document 4.9 illustrates. Ignoring 1945, distorted by the last phase of the war, the crisis year of 1947 stands out clearly in the chart, but, the position was much improved by 1948. This was partly because costly overseas commitments in India and the Middle East had been shed, partly because of the impact of Marshall aid and partly, too, thanks to an impressive increase in British exports. The successful consequences of devaluation in 1949 can be seen in the very healthy position attained in 1950. However, rearmament triggered by the Korean War, and the resulting need to import more raw materials, at artificially high prices, plunged the trade balance back towards crisis in 1951.

4.9   **Britain's balance of payments, 1945–51 (chart derived from D. Butler and G. Butler (eds),** *British Political Facts, 1900–1985,* **London, Macmillan, 6th edn 1986, p. 386).**

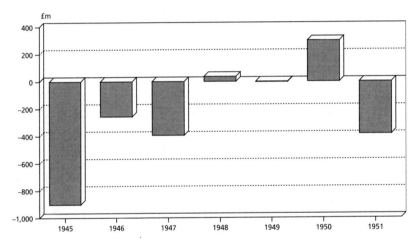

Economic Management

One of the major legacies of the war was a conviction, widely found among economists, civil servants and many politicians, that the country's economy could be 'managed' so as to prevent the seeming anarchy of the inter-war years, when millions of people had been victims of the Depression. The war seemed to many to have proved what the state could achieve in controlling production and distribution. Initially in the postwar years there was much talk of 'planning' the economy, although precisely what this meant was not always clear. Many wartime economic controls were allowed to continue, and it was only gradually that more sophisticated, and less direct, forms of economic management, influenced by Keynesian ideas, found favour within the government.

Labour's commitment to extending public ownership through the nationalisation of key sectors of the economy was given a variety of justifications. It was expected to help prevent unemployment, to achieve some redistribution of wealth, to assist in the rationalisation of production and to promote easier industrial relations. Soon after it came to office, the Labour government embarked on its ambitious nationalisation programme. How far nationalisation represented a real shift in the distribution of economic power in Britain is debatable. Most of the sectors taken into public ownership were service industries, such as energy and transport. Since nationalisation involved the underwriting of their losses by the state, it was a form of subsidy to the remainder of the private economy. Strikingly, the government's plans made no provision for greater worker participation in the management of these industries. Frequently, those running the industries after nationalisation were the same managers who had done the job before nationalisation, since no one else appeared competent for the role.

In November 1945 Herbert Morrison, the minister responsible for organising the government's legislative programme, outlined his colleagues' plans for future nationalisation.

4.10   Herbert Morrison, speech to the House of Commons, 19 November 1945 (*Hansard*, 5th ser., 416: 34–6).

■ His Majesty's Government believe that it is in the public interest that they should give a general indication of the further Measures they propose to introduce during the life of the present Parliament to bring certain essential services under public ownership. This statement, which follows the clear indication of Government policy contained in the King's Speech at the beginning of the Session, will enable the Ministers concerned to enter into consultation with the industries affected.

As stated in the Gracious Speech, the Government will introduce a Bill during the present Session to nationalise the coal-mining industry. At a later stage in the lifetime of this Parliament the Government intend to introduce Measures to bring under national ownership the electricity supply industry and the gas industry. This will implement the concerted plan for the co-ordination of the fuel and power industries which were foreshadowed in the King's Speech.

It is in the intention of the Government to introduce, during the life of the present Parliament, measures designed to bring transport services, essential to the economic well-being of the nation, under public ownership and control. Government policy in regard to civil aviation and telecommunications services has already been announced. In regard to inland transport, powers will be taken to bring under national ownership the railways, canals and long distance road haulage services ...

Dock and harbour undertakings will be brought within the scope of the national scheme. The most suitable form of public ownership is under examination, as is also the question of including certain appropriate ancillary activities.

It is not the intention of the Government to propose the nationalisation of the shipping industry, and we shall rely on the industry to have full regard to the public interest ...

The Coalition Government invited the iron and steel industry to submit a report on the improvements required to put the industry on an efficient basis. The Government propose to await this report, which is expected shortly, before taking final decisions on the future organisation of the iron and steel industry ...

The compensation payable will have regard to any extent to which an undertaking has not been maintained up to the time of transfer, and the Government will naturally take precautions in its legislation to protect the acquiring authority against any transactions entered into in the interim period, whether by way of contract or otherwise, which may prejudice that authority.

The proposals outlined in this statement involve important changes in the ownership and organisation of a series of industries vital to the national wellbeing – changes which were approved by the people at the General Election. The policy issues involved must be taken as having been decided and approved by the nation, and it will be for Parliament, Government and the active leaders and workers of the industries concerned to pull together in a high public spirit so that these great changes may be carried through smoothly and successfully, thereby promoting the wellbeing [of] the nation, including efficient service for the wide range of privately owned industries to which the successful operation of those industries coming under public ownership is vital ... ■

Public corporations

The mechanism chosen to implement state control of the nationalised industries was the public corporation, already familiar before the Second World War when it was introduced to administer the BBC, the London Passenger Transport Board, the Central Electricity Board and other public bodies. Public corporations were intended to be semi-independent, responsible to Parliament for major policy issues through the appropriate government minister, and to the Treasury for their capital investment plans, but otherwise enjoying, theoretically, the freedom of action of a commercial organisation.

Walter Citrine, general secretary of the Trades Union Congress from 1926 until 1946, was appointed chairman of the newly nationalised Electricity Board. As he explained in the following extract from his autobiography, there had been little detailed preparation for nationalisation.

4.11   Walter Citrine on public ownership (in Lord Citrine, *Two Careers*, London, Hutchinson, 1967, pp. 263–4).

■ Nationalisation had long figured in the programme of the labour movement, both political and industrial. But the methods by which the industries would be acquired had not been thought out with any real precision. Originally, it had been assumed that when an industry was transferred to the State, it would be operated by a Government department, something like the Post Office. But as the years passed, it became evident that a greater measure of freedom from party political control was desirable. So arose the public corporation as we know it today. It was intended that these corporations should operate on broad commercial principles and not be sacrificed to political expediency. The members of its governing body, appointed by a Minister responsible to Parliament, would be chosen because of their competence and ability to run the industry efficiently in the public interest. Provision was made for the representation of the interests of the workers in the composition of the governing Boards. Ultimate responsibility for the nationalised industries would be vested in a Minister, who would be responsible for the proper co-ordination of their policies.

I have said that this form of structure was designed to give the nationalised industries a measure of independence of the Government. I had been warned that there would probably be a tendency for the Government departments to encroach on the functions of the nationalised Boards and I resolved to keep alert to maintain their freedom as far as possible. I knew that complete independence was an impossibility, and that the electricity supply industry, like the other public corporations, must to some extent become an instrument of Government policy. But I wanted to keep Party politics out of it, while being amenable to the national requirements as interpreted by the Government of the day, whether Labour, Conservative, or (with a lofty flight of imagination) Liberal. ■

Control and decontrol

The wartime growth of state intervention in the economy had involved the physical control of industrial production, through the allocation of manpower and materials. Because of recollections of the experience of a brief inflationary boom after 1918, it was widely agreed that there should be no precipitous dismantling of economic controls after 1945. In any case, the Labour government initially saw these controls as useful in the longer term, in order to prevent unemployment and to ensure an equitable distribution of goods and services. This reflected the government's faith in economic planning over the unpredictability of a market economy, a faith strengthened by wartime experience of apparently successful government intervention. A wide range of economic controls persisted after 1945, including controls over investment and the allocation of raw materials, over imports and foreign exchange transactions, and over prices and consumer rationing. However, with the gradual easing of the conditions of scarcity which had required controls, there was growing pressure on the government to lift them as quickly as possible.

Partly influenced by electoral considerations, and by the belief that greater freedom within the economy would be popular, the government embarked on a campaign to reduce the number of controls. On 5 November 1948, appropriately, the President of the Board of Trade, Harold Wilson, announced a 'bonfire of controls'. This was followed by further measures of liberalisation in the spring of 1949. Left-wing critics tended to see this as a mistake, a sacrifice of one of the most useful tools in constructing a fairer economic system.

4.12   Harold Wilson, speech to the House of Commons, 5 November 1948 (*Hansard*, 5th ser., 457: 1223–5).

■ It has been suggested that some of the work placed upon the higher officials arose because of Ministers' doctrinaire preoccupation with certain economic theories, but I want to make it clear that every one of those Measures was important and essential for the economic recovery of this country in the particular industry with which it was concerned. Not one of them could be described as in any way a doctrinaire Measure …

It is common ground, I think, that under any Government under present, post-war conditions, we must have a much closer preoccupation with economic policy, a much closer control of industry than we had before the war …

Some say that we ought to remove controls … As the hon. Member knows, yesterday we removed a considerable number of controls. Here again we have had to do it entirely on our own, without any help from those who for the last three years have been demanding the removal of controls. While I am still awaiting, and most anxiously awaiting, a report of the committee which was appointed by the Conservative Central Office in 1946, which was to publish a list of controls which we ought to remove and has so far not published anything, we have been getting on with the job and yesterday we removed a very large number of controls …

De-control takes even more time and even more attention on the part of higher officials than the maintenance of controls. That is not an argument for keeping controls on unnecessarily. As a matter of fact I am only too anxious to remove them, but when we are concerned with the removal of a control, often against the advice and wishes of the trade association concerned, and often involving the removal of protection and safeguards from certain parts of an industry, it frequently takes more of the time of officials than does the continuation of the control from day to day.

The hon. Member asked a question which I think he was absolutely right to ask and which I will try to answer. He asked if these higher officials had time to think and to get down to the job of clearing up what he described as 'the growing jungle of control.' It is not growing, but is in fact being cleared away as fast as we can clear it ... ■

Planning, industrial relations and inflation

Although the government and its advisers were committed to a 'planned' economy, they were not always clear about what this entailed, or about how much could practicably be achieved. As Chancellor, Stafford Cripps understood the importance of clear priorities in the allocation of manpower, materials and money. As already seen, the government initially preferred physical controls and was suspicious of 'market forces', giving rise to its austere regime of price-fixing and rationing and to a huge volume of administrative work, referred to by Wilson in his 'bonfire' speech. It was only after Cripps's appointment as Chancellor in 1947 that the Treasury regained overall control over economic policy. Even then, it took time for Keynesian ideas of demand-management to be absorbed. By 1950–1 concepts of planning the economy on the basis of relatively crude physical controls were in retreat.

In 1947 the government appointed a chief planning officer, Sir Edwin Plowden, who became head of a new planning 'think-tank', the Central Economic Planning Staff, inside the Cabinet Office. In his autobiography, Plowden described the shift in official thinking on planning.

4.13   **Sir Edwin Plowden on economic planning (in Sir Edwin Plowden,** *An Industrialist in the Treasury: The Postwar Years*, **London, Deutsch, 1989, pp. 166–8).**

■ Various factors underpinned this success in economic policy-making. First, was the fact that for much of the time the government had the co-operation and support not only of management, but also of the trade unions and the general public ...

Second, there was the fact that from November 1947, economic policy was run from a single department ... A division of responsibility for macroeconomic policy between two departments, as existed in the first two post-war years, causes many problems ...

Third, ministers were soon convinced that to try to plan the economy in minute and elaborate detail over the long term and outside a war situation was an error. In a free democratic society, when supplies are sufficient, the price mechanism must eventually be allowed to allocate the lion's share of resources. Efforts to circumvent this process, and to retain controls for their own sake, result only in frustration on the part of the consumer and failure on the part of the government.

At the same time, however, it was important to recognise that in the situation of recovery from a war, attempts to move too soon towards the free play of market forces could, in themselves, throw up problems and were to be avoided ...

With this in mind, after 1947 planning came increasingly to be expressed in terms of the management of demand in a Keynesian macroeconomic manner in order to counterbalance the natural cyclical behaviour of the economy. This, in turn, further secured the position of the Treasury as the epicentre of economic policy-making. Direct controls were dropped as supplies became sufficient to render them unnecessary ... The unthought-out and nebulous concept of 'democratic planning', with its implication of detailed intervention which Labour had propounded in 1945, fell by the wayside, not just when the Tories came to power in late 1951, but gradually from late 1947 ... ∎

The issue of industrial relations was particularly sensitive for a Labour government. A number of wartime controls over labour were retained after 1945, such as the ban on strikes, in place until 1951 but impossible to apply. In 1947 the trade unions agreed to the resurrection of state powers to direct labour to particular kinds of work, but only in exceptional circumstances. Afraid of inflation, the government called for voluntary restraint in pay claims. In January 1947 the Minister of Labour and National Service, George Isaacs, related the country's economic position to the need for co-operation between the two sides of industry, and stressed the importance both of increasing the country's productivity and of making Britain's exports competitive.

4.14 George Isaacs, *Statement on Economic Considerations Affecting Relations between Employers and Workers*, **January 1947 (Cmd 7018, PP XIX, 1946–7, p. 3).**

∎ 2. The position of Great Britain is extremely serious. We have in the course of the last seven years deliberately distorted and unbalanced our economic system, suffered the loss and permitted the depreciation of our capital resources, sold at least half our external capital assets and gone into debt abroad – all for the purpose of enabling the country to concentrate its fullest efforts upon the war and in an endeavour to maintain reasonable standards of living ...

3. It is clear that we must – and, indeed, very quickly – begin to maintain and seek to improve our standards of living entirely by our own efforts. We cannot continue indefinitely to meet our deficits by external credits. We must soon begin to repay some of the external borrowings by means of which we are at present able to maintain existing standards. It is therefore highly imperative that we secure a speedy and substantial increase in the output of the products of British industry whilst maintaining their quality. That is the kernel of the economic and industrial policy of the British Government.

4 The fulfilment of this policy requires improvements in the efficiency and the productivity of British industry, and these are not the responsibility of

the Government alone but of industrial management and workers alike. It is for all concerned with industrial production to apply themselves to this task of improved efficiency and output in the realisation that the common good of the country as a whole depends very considerably upon their efforts.

5. During the war in a number of industries machinery was developed for joint consultation between management and workpeople on production problems. The extension and further development of this practice would be of advantage.

6. Until the output of British industry is considerably increased there is bound to be some fear of our ability to maintain the stability of prices and the orderliness within our industrial system which have characterised Great Britain throughout all the difficulties of the war and the transition from war to peace. The nature of our industrial relations system entails responsibilities on both sides to work together not only for the common good of the industry on which both depend, but also for the common good of the country as a whole. The responsibilities are greater to-day than they have ever been ... ■

For all its problems, the postwar Labour government managed to maintain full employment, thereby setting the political agenda for the next thirty years. Its control of inflation was also impressive. There was no repetition of the disastrous inflationary boom which had followed the First World War. Food prices, for example, were deliberately held down by the use of government subsidies. To a great extent, controlling inflation required the consent of the trade unions to wage restraint. Although average wages did rise by some 46 per cent between 1945 and 1951, this figure was perhaps not unduly high, given the strong position of the trade unions, whose membership continued to grow in this period. Generally speaking, the Trades Union Congress loyally backed the government's calls for wage restraint, but by 1950, with the cost of living rising due to devaluation and the effects of the Korean War, this position could no longer be adhered to.

4.15 **Living standards and industrial relations, 1939–51 (charts derived from D. Butler and G. Butler (eds), *British Political Facts 1900–1985*, London, Macmillan, 6th edn 1986, pp. 357, 381; H. Pelling, *A History of British Trade Unionism*, Harmondsworth, Penguin, 1976, p. 295).**

Average weekly earnings

Men aged 21+   Women aged 21+

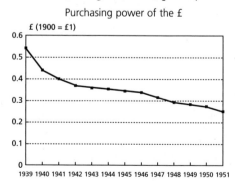

Purchasing power of the £

Trade Union membership

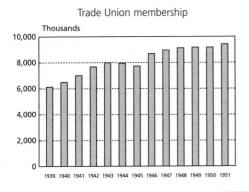

Strikes

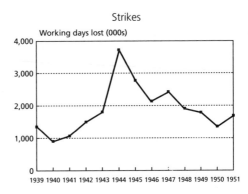

The Festival of Britain

Against a background of continuing domestic austerity and drabness, the government attempted to raise morale by organising the Festival of Britain in 1951, 100 years after the Great Exhibition at the Crystal Palace. Like its predecessor, the festival was intended to be a showpiece of the best of British science, technology and culture. The main focus of the festival was London's South Bank, where various buildings, such as the *Dome of Discovery*, were erected.

One of the most popular festival installations was the Skylon, a graceful aluminium structure which seemed to defy gravity. Reputedly loathed by Churchill, it was summarily bulldozed on the Conservatives' return to office. Meanwhile, it provided a metaphor for the ailing Labour government (see Chapter 3) which the cartoonist Illingworth could not resist. He depicts Attlee and Morrison admiring the festival site from the north bank of the Thames.

4.16   L.G. Illingworth, 'No visible means of support', *Punch* cartoon, 14 March 1951.

Building the Welfare State

The Second World War had encouraged great hopes about future welfare provision. In some respects, the omens for the fulfilment of these hopes were good in 1945. A Labour government had been elected, committed to implementing much of the comprehensive Beveridge programme. Moreover, there was no economic depression in the postwar period, as there had been after the First World War. For most people, the welfare reforms of the Labour government far outweighed in significance its economic experiments

The Labour Party had endorsed the Beveridge Plan enthusiastically, and the welfare legislation of the Attlee government drew heavily on Beveridge's proposals. The centrepiece of the reforms was the 1946 National Insurance Act; this brought the entire population into a comprehensive and unified system which provided insurance covering unemployment, sickness, old age and death. The state provided the initial capital of £100 million for the National Insurance Fund, and this was to be supplemented by contributions from employers and workers. For many newly insured people, the effects were dramatic. Before the war, old age and unemployment insurance had been patchy; the unemployed faced the hated 'means test'; and the poor might still be consigned to the workhouse.

Michael Stewart became a Labour MP in 1945 and was appointed Secretary of State for War in 1947. He held various ministerial appointments in Harold Wilson's government from 1964 to 1970. In his autobiography, he reflected on the impact of the National Insurance Act, and of James Griffiths, the Minister for National Insurance. As Stewart commented, Labour's reforms, while impressive, were only a partial remedy, and in the 1950s and early 1960s commentators were to 'rediscover' poverty in a series of disturbing reports.

4.17 **Michael Stewart, recollections of the National Insurance Act (in Michael Stewart, *Life and Labour: An Autobiography*, London, Sidgwick & Jackson, 1980, pp. 68–70).**

■ The aim of the Labour Party is to create a Socialist community by the method of parliamentary democracy, and it was the Government's task to take the first steps along this road. By Socialism I understand first, a state of society in which differences of wealth are limited in scope and strictly related to function – if A is richer than B, it should be because either his contribution to society is more valuable, or (by virtue, say, of disablement or a large family) he needs more. The two principles 'to each according to what he produces' and 'to each according to his needs' have to be blended. This result cannot be achieved if most of the sources of wealth are privately, and unequally, owned: a community which relies mainly on private investment to produce wealth must always defer to the wishes of the wealthy about the sharing of wealth and the level of taxation. My second proposition about a Socialist community, then, is that there should be enough public ownership of land and industry to ensure the just distribution of income. This does not mean 100 per cent public ownership, or anything like it, but it does mean more than today and certainly more than in 1945. Third, I believe that differences in the provision of health and education should be minimal, since it is in these fields that wide differences do most injury to the welfare and personality of the least fortunate …

In the light of these goals, what did Clem Attlee's government achieve? Jim Griffiths took the pre-war piecemeal social legislation and fashioned it into the comprehensive National Insurance system which still exists, with many improvements, today. The Tories had prepared a less generous plan, but at the second reading of Jim Griffiths' Bill only one voice, that of the indomitable right-winger, Sir Waldron Smithers, was raised against it. The Speaker asked those opposing the Bill to rise in their places. Sir Waldron stood alone, to an accompaniment of ironic cheers from the Labour side and vexed silence from his own. But the rules require at least two objectors if a vote is to be taken. 'The Ayes have it' said Mr Speaker, adding, with a stony stare at Smithers, 'nemine contradicente.'

Jim Griffiths not only brought this great scheme into existence, but infused a new spirit into the administration of benefits. Before the 1939–45 War, civil servants who dealt with the claims to benefits by disabled ex-servicemen were instructed not to inform their clients of any extra or special benefits to which they might, by law, be entitled, but which, being unaware of their rights, they had not claimed. Many such officials dealt with this problem by dropping anonymous letters through their clients' letter-boxes. Jim Griffiths established the principle, now generally accepted, that rights to benefit should be publicized: his determined humanity permeated right through to the local offices of his Ministry with very favourable effects on the treatment of claimants …

Much, however, remained to be done. The removal of mass poverty by the 1946 Act highlighted the unhappy position of certain groups: single-parent families; those whose disabilities made them immobile; those in need of constant attendance at home. Over the years, through constituency work, I have come to realize a special significance in the saying, 'The poor (or at any rate, the needy) ye have always with you'. Every general improvement raises the standard of compassion in society and makes us aware of needs previously unnoticed. Welfare legislation is a continuous process and it is right, at every stage, to point out deficiencies: but it would be wrong to belittle the basic achievement of the Griffiths Act … ∎

The National Health Service

Perhaps Labour's proudest achievement after 1945 was the creation of the National Health Service. As in the case of unemployment insurance, prewar health provision had been uneven, with a complex mixture of local authority hospitals and 'voluntary' hospitals funded on a charitable and fee-paying basis. The war had resulted in a radical streamlining of medical care which many believed should be continued after the war.

The National Health Service Act of 1946 effectively nationalised most of the country's hospitals, placing them under the administration of regional hospital boards, though teaching hospitals were to enjoy considerable autonomy. This created a unified hospital system aiming to provide adequate care throughout the country. Aneurin Bevan, the Minister of Health, envisaged a health service available to all citizens, providing comprehensive care free of charge. In most respects, he succeeded, though not before confronting opposition from the doctors' professional body, the British Medical Association.

In the months before the National Health Service came into operation in July 1948, relations between the government and the British Medical Association, backed in Parliament by the Conservatives, deteriorated. A BMA survey, conducted as late as February 1948, revealed that doctors still opposed the NHS scheme by a majority of eight to one. The BMA eventually extracted concessions from Bevan, ensuring that doctors did not become salaried state employees and permitting consultants to continue treating private patients. Bevan refused, however, to give way over the sale of doctors' practices, which was believed to have given rise to wide geographical discrepancies in general practitioner provision.

4.18   **Aneurin Bevan, speech to the House of Commons, 9 February 1948**
(*Hansard*, 5th ser., 447: 35–41).

■ During the last six months to a year there has been a sustained propaganda in the newspapers supporting the party opposite, which has resulted in grave misrepresentation of the nature of the Health Service and of the conditions under which the medical profession are asked to enter the Health Service. There has been even worse misrepresentation, sustained by a campaign of personal abuse, from a small body of spokesmen who have consistently misled the great profession to which they are supposed to belong. I make a distinction ... between the hard-working doctors who have little or no time to give to these matters, and the small body of raucous voiced people who are alleged to represent the profession as a whole.

So much misrepresentation has been engaged in by the B.M.A. that the doctors who have voted or are voting in the plebiscite are doing so under a complete misapprehension of what the Health Service is. It has been frightening to speak to some doctors and to learn the extent to which their representatives have failed to inform them about the facts of the case ...

From the very beginning, this small body of politically poisoned people have decided to fight the Health Act itself and to stir up as much emotion as they can in the profession ...

It has been suggested by the spokesmen of the B.M.A. that we have not negotiated with them sufficiently, that if we had only been more approachable things would have been different. But there were long negotiations with Mr. Brown and long negotiations with Mr. Willink, and on every occasion the B.M.A. rejected the advances made ...

There are four main issues on which the B.M.A. say they join issue. They say, in the first place, that they cannot accept the abolition of the sale and purchase of practices. The abolition of the sale and purchase of practices was recommended by the profession's own health commission. They voted for the abolition in their own plebiscite and all I have done, and all the Government and the House have done, is to put in the Act recommendations about this step based on the best medical information. We regard it as being inconsistent with a civilised community and with a reasonable health service for patients to be bought and sold over their heads. When I am told that all they desire is that patients should have the best medical treatment, how can that be argued when a doctor succeeds to another doctor's panel not on account of personal qualifications but on the size of his purse? How can it be reasonably be argued that there is any effective free choice of doctor when the doctors negotiate the terms between themselves and the patient knows nothing at all about it? This system exists in no other country in the world. It is a blot upon our medical system ...

The doctors have said that their second objection – indeed, many of them said that this is the one thing that is offending them – is that they will not accept a basic salary as part of their remuneration. The first time that a full-time salaried practitioner service was put before the medical profession was in 1943, in the days of the Coalition Government. It came from Mr. Ernest Brown. I hope the Opposition will note that ...

We not only desire in this scheme to relieve patients of financial anxiety; we desire to relieve the doctor of financial anxiety when he approaches his patients. It is one of the most deplorable features of the existing system that young doctors, when they go into practice ... they have financial burdens put upon them. We consider, therefore, that a salary, only of £300 – but, nevertheless, a salary of £6 a week – plus what he can get from capitation fees, would be a financial support for the young doctor whilst he is building up his practice ... ∎

The National Health Service was hugely popular, but few had anticipated how great the demand for its facilities would be, and there was considerable concern within the government at the unexpectedly large cost of the service. It was doubly unfortunate that these revelations came at a time when the government was already under financial pressure, committed to rearmament and to participation in the Korean War.

4.19   **Gross expenditure on the National Health Service, 1948–51 (chart derived from C. Webster, *The Health Services since the War, Vol. I*, London, HMSO, 1988, p. 135).**

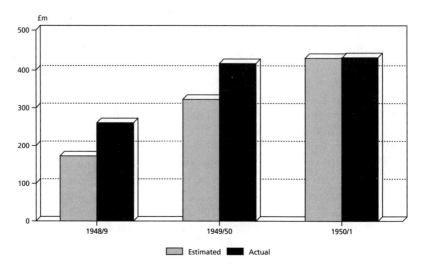

Resisting his colleagues' wish to limit health expenditure, Bevan commissioned Sir Cyril Jones, an independent expert, to investigate the finances of the NHS. His report, produced in July 1950, emphasised the rocketing cost of the hospital sector, the largest single area of spending. Jones recommended greater centralised control of the hospitals, which, ironically, had been Bevan's position in 1945. Bevan continued to resist growing calls within the government for prescription and other charges to be imposed. When he was overruled, in April 1951, he resigned from the government.

4.20   **Sir Cyril Jones, report on the finances of the National Health Service, 15 July 1950 (PRO PREM 8/1486 Pt 1 NH(50)17).**

■ **7.** Much of the rapid growth of expenditure is readily explainable. On the General Practitioner Services' side, by the back-log of demand and the unexpectedly great amount of work which can be done under the unceasing pressure of long waiting lists, especially with personal remuneration calculated over most of the field on an items-of-service basis applicable to more normal conditions. On the hospital side, by the urge to overtake arrears of maintenance of buildings and equipment hanging over from the war and early post-war years, and to carry out overdue expansions and developments; expansion of medical, nursing, domestic and administrative staffs; the introduction with retrospective effect of improved salary scales and conditions of service; and a continuous rise in prices. It is quite certain, however, that legitimate grounds have been accentuated by the new mentality created by a new free Health Service paid for out of the general revenues of the State. This applies to the hospital administering authorities no less than to the general public and has led, at the best, to subordination of financial considerations and an impatience at financial control, and at the worst to positive but definite abuse. An incidental effect is an almost total disregard of relative priorities at all levels which can hardly be allowed to continue when the financial burden of the Service has about reached the limit of what the country's economy can bear. To those who have at heart the welfare and success of the new Service the tragedy is that that stage should have been reached while so much yet remains to be done on the Hospital side. It is thus of the first importance, in the public interest, that a system of control be devised, or modifications made in the administrative set-up, which will ensure that practicable economies be achieved and realised, that extravagance and waste be uncovered and eliminated, and, above all, that available funds be directed into those channels where they can best serve the most urgent health needs of the community. ■

CHAPTER FIVE

Compromise and Co-operation: Maintaining Britain's World Role, 1945–51

DURING the six years following the end of the Second World War, The increasingly embattled British government took major decisions affecting British foreign policy. It is striking that, at a time of considerable financial difficulty, during which domestic public spending commitments were enlarged, not least in constructing the 'welfare state', the government chose not to reduce Britain's world role considerably. Thus, defence spending remained steady, before being massively increased at the end of this period with a new programme of rearmament. Typical of the government's outlook was the secret decision to develop nuclear weapons, as proof of Britain's continuing status as a great power. The cold war did much to reinforce Britain's pretensions to a world role; above all, it ensured that the United States would not again retreat into diplomatic isolationism, but rather would become the major element in the emerging Western Alliance. United States defence commitments to Western Europe enabled Britain to concentrate on maintaining its wider, global role. In turn, Britain set great store by its 'special relationship' with the United States, and sought to maintain it, making concessions to Washington wherever these were considered prudent.

Although this period saw challenges to Britain's imperial authority and witnessed Britain's retreat from India and Palestine, the imperial system remained intact; most notably, those colonies occupied during the war had all been regained. It was a priority for the British government to consolidate the ties of empire, by devising a new framework for the Commonwealth, and by promoting faster economic, social and ultimately political development in the colonies.

Cold War Strategy

Between 16 July and 2 August 1945 the leaders of the Grand Alliance, meeting at Potsdam in Germany, held the last of their wartime summit conferences. The chief topics of discussion were future Allied control of Germany, the question of German reparations, Soviet entry into the war against Japan and the settlement of the postwar Polish–German border. As at Yalta, the Soviets made promises about holding free elections in Poland, and, temporarily at least, the differences between the Soviet Union and its Western allies were concealed.

During the conference, Clement Attlee became Prime Minister of Britain, replacing Winston Churchill, who had originally headed the British delegation. At the end of the conference, Attlee wrote privately to Churchill, summarising its outcome.

5.1 Clement Attlee, letter to Winston Churchill, 1 August 1945 (PRO PREM 8/109).

■   MOST SECRET

The Conference is ending to-night in a good atmosphere. I would like to let you know the broad results before the communiqué is issued.

We have, of course, been building on the foundation laid by you, and there has been no change of policy.

It was clear, when the Conference was suspended that the vital points were Reparations and the Polish Western Frontier. On the former the Russians were very insistent on their pound of flesh. We were firm on the need for supplies of food etc. from the Eastern zone for the rest of Germany and on not allowing reparations to have precedence of maintaining a reasonable economy in Germany. On Poland the Russians insisted on the Western Neisse and eventually the Americans accepted this. We were, of course, powerless to prevent the course of events in the Russian zone. We have tied the Poles down as closely as we can with specific pledges on elections, press facilities and repatriation of fighting Poles. We therefore agreed on the Western Neisse as the western boundary of Polish administration pending the Peace Conference decisions. Other questions proved soluble when these major matters were disposed of.

Uncle Joe [Stalin] was not in a good mood at the start caused I think by an indisposition which kept him in bed for two days. Thereafter he was in good form. The President [Truman] was very co-operative. My having been present from the start was a great advantage, but Bevin picked up all the points extremely quickly and showed his quality as an experienced negotiator in playing his hand. I think that the results achieved are not unsatisfactory having regard to the way the course of the war had dealt the cards. I hope you have been able to get some rest. If you would care to come and see me to hear more details I should be delighted … ■

Immediately after the war, the Foreign Office hoped that co-operation between the 'Big Three' wartime allies would continue. Officials tended to assume that the Soviet Union was preoccupied with its own security rather than with ideas of expansion. British military planners, however, were more pessimistic and had been warning since the later stages of the war that the Soviet Union was becoming a threat to Britain. During 1945 and 1946 relations with the Soviet Union became increasingly strained. The view gained ground in London that

Moscow was failing to honour the Yalta agreements, which had provided for free elections in Eastern Europe. Communist control of Poland, Bulgaria and Romania alarmed the British government, while the Soviet insistence on large-scale reparations from Germany delayed a peace settlement. Moreover, there was growing fear of Communist influence in West European countries such as France and Italy, which both had large Communist parties.

By 1946 the Foreign Office's attitude towards the Soviet Union had become suspicious. Particularly worrying was the strong Soviet military position in Europe. Parallels were drawn between Josef Stalin and Adolf Hitler, reinforcing arguments against appeasing Moscow. Ironically, Stalin had respected his wartime undertakings, had not intervened in the bitter civil war in Greece and generally did not take advantage of the Communist parties' strength in Western Europe. An important role in shaping London's view of the Soviet Union was played by Sir Frank Roberts, Britain's Minister in Moscow. In March 1946 he gave London an alarming summary of the situation as he saw it.

5.2   Sir Frank Roberts, dispatch to the Foreign Office, 14 March 1946 (PRO FO 371/56763, N4065/97/38).

■ ... The present state of Soviet relations with the outside world, and more particularly with Britain, is very different from what we had hoped for on the morrow of our joint victory, and after we have made so many concessions to meet Soviet security requirements. Instead of the Soviet Union gradually settling down to a more normal and friendly relationship with its allies, we are faced with a Soviet policy designed to advance Soviet interests at every possible opportunity, regardless even of treaty obligations. Instead of telling a weary and sorely tried population that, the Fascist menace having now been removed, the peoples of the Soviet Union can settle down in peace to work for the improvement of their standards of living, Soviet propaganda is actively instilling suspicions and distrust of the outside world, of which the Soviet public is being kept in complete ignorance. In recent telegrams I have endeavoured to explain the ever-increasing emphasis laid here upon Marxist-Leninist ideology as the basis for Soviet internal and for-eign policy and to show the abnormality of the Soviet Government in its dealings with other governments. The bonds forged by common interests in the war against Germany and Japan are now so visibly parting that the question must be asked whether the Soviet Government still attribute importance to continued cooperation among the Big Three, to the Anglo-Soviet Alliance, and even to the U.N.O. except in so far as this provides a convenient machinery for advancing Soviet interests. In view of the con-tents of the election speeches by the Soviet leaders which laid down policy in the months ahead, it may even be asked whether the world is not now faced with the danger of a modern equivalent of the religious wars of the 16th century, in which Soviet communism will struggle with Western social democracy and the American version of capitalism for domination of the world. Turning to more immediate and concrete issues, and having regard to the latest developments in Persia, we may even ask ourselves whether the Soviet rulers are not preparing some military adventure in the Spring – for example, against Turkey. At times it might seem that Soviet successes have gone to the heads of the Politburo, that they feel that everything is possible and that they can advance their designs throughout the world without fear of serious opposition; or there may simply be a great sense of urgency to achieve as much as possible before resistance becomes too strong. In other words it is not yet clear how far present Soviet actions and statements are purely tactical and how far they represent the first steps in a carefully considered long-term offensive strategy. When such questions are asked, there is clearly a danger that we may swing from the extreme of optimism about the future of Anglo-Soviet relations, cherished during the war, to the opposite extreme of pessimism in which the Anglo-Soviet Treaty would appear a mere dead-letter … ∎

One of the turning points in the public acknowledgement of the growing East–West divide was Churchill's famous 'Iron Curtain' speech, delivered in March 1946. Churchill, now Leader of the Opposition, had been invited to visit Westminster College in Fulton, Missouri, and took the opportunity to describe the European situation as he saw it. When delivered, the speech caused an outcry in the United States, where opinion was not yet convinced that relations with the Soviet Union could not be salvaged. President Harry Truman subsequently distanced himself from Churchill's views, although he had read the speech in advance.

5.3   **Winston Churchill, 'Iron Curtain' speech, 5 March 1946 (in D. Cannadine (ed.),** *The Speeches of Winston Churchill,* **London, Penguin, 1990, pp. 303–4).**

∎ A shadow has fallen over the scenes so lately lighted by the Allied victory. Nobody knows what Soviet Russia and its Communist international organization intends to do in the immediate future, or what are the limits, if any, to their expansive and proselytizing tendencies. I have a strong admiration and regard for the valiant Russian people and for my wartime comrade, Marshal Stalin. There is a deep sympathy and goodwill in Britain – and I doubt not here also – towards the peoples of all the Russias and a resolve to persevere through many differences and rebuffs in establishing lasting friendships. We understand the Russian need to be secure on her western frontiers by the removal of all possibility of German aggression. We welcome Russia to her rightful place among the leading nations of the world. We welcome her flag upon the seas. Above all, we welcome constant, frequent and growing contacts between the Russian people and our own people on both sides of the Atlantic. It is my duty, however, for I am sure you would wish me to state the facts as I see them to you, to place before you certain facts about the present position in Europe.

From Stettin in the Baltic to Trieste in the Adriatic, an iron curtain has descended across the Continent. Behind that line lie all the capitals of the ancient states of Central and Eastern Europe. Warsaw, Berlin, Prague, Vienna, Budapest, Belgrade, Bucharest and Sofia, all these famous cities and the populations around them lie in what I must call the Soviet sphere, and all are subject in one form or another, not only to Soviet influence but to a very high and, in many cases, increasing measure of control from Moscow. Athens alone – Greece with its immortal glories – is free to decide its future at an election under British, American and French observation. The Russian-dominated Polish Government has been encouraged to make enormous and wrongful inroads upon Germany, and mass expulsions of millions of Germans on a scale grievous and undreamed-of are now taking place. The Communist parties, which were very small in all these Eastern States of Europe, have been raised to pre-eminence and power far beyond their numbers and are seeking everywhere to obtain totalitarian control. Police governments are prevailing in nearly every case, and so far, except in Czechoslovakia, there is no true democracy ... ■

During 1946 there was growing concern in Britain about Soviet aims in the Mediterranean and the Middle East, regions seen as vital to British imperial interests. Moscow had sought an agreement on control over the Dardanelles, which would have given the Soviet navy access to the Mediterranean; it staked a claim to Italian colonial territory in North Africa; and, contrary to an earlier agreement, it did not remove the troops which it had stationed in Iran in 1941. Also in 1946 a major disagreement over British strategy developed between Attlee and the Chiefs of Staff. Attlee had hoped that a *modus vivendi* could be reached with the Soviet Union, reducing tension and enabling Britain to spend less on defence. Whereas the conventional view, reinforced by wartime experience, was that the Middle East and the Near East were areas vital to British strategic interests, Attlee had become sceptical, particularly about the significance of the Eastern Mediterranean, including Greece and Palestine. He feared that, by strengthening its presence in the Eastern Mediterranean, Britain might provoke the Soviet Union. Moreover, he believed that the traditional preoccupation with this region was outdated, given the imminence of Indian independence and the advent of air power. The Chiefs of Staff disagreed entirely; for them, changes in military technology made the Middle East even more important than in the past, because from here Britain could, in a war, mount air attacks on the southern Soviet Union.

In January 1947 Attlee renewed his criticism of existing military strategy, calling for a thorough reappraisal of British policy. He backed down only when the Chiefs of Staff, led by Field Marshal Montgomery, threatened to resign. As the cold war deepened during 1948, Attlee's views were modified further. Although Britain was forced, for financial reasons, to vacate Palestine and to cease aid to Greece and Turkey, the Middle East remained a region of key significance to British policy-makers, as their concern to maintain a foothold in Egypt in the early 1950s was later to demonstrate.

5.4   **Clement Attlee, minute to Ernest Bevin, 5 January 1947, 'Near Eastern policy' (PRO FO 800/476, ff. 2–9).**

■ 1. The broad conclusions of the Chiefs of Staff and of the Imperial Defence College are:–

(a) That the U.K. which is the heart of the Commonwealth is extremely vulnerable to modern attack by long range weapons and that our present knowledge does not provide any effective method of passive defence.

(b) Therefore the only way to prevent such an attack is by a threat of counter attack so formidable that a potential enemy will be deterred through fear of his own losses.

(c) The only possible enemy is Russia.

(d) The only bases from which Russia could be attacked are situated in the Near East.

(e) Therefore the maintenance of British influence and consequently British forces in the Near East are essential to our safety.

(f) As a corollary we must secure our oil supplies in the Middle East and endeavour to secure our communications through the Mediterranean, if at all possible.

2. The consequence of this appreciation means heavy military commitments which must be considered in relation to our man power and our economic resources.

It also means that we have to support a number of states in the Near East. Turkey, Greece, Iraq, Persia, Lebanon, Syria, Egypt and Transjordan and also to maintain our position in Palestine.

This brings us into a sphere of competition for political and economic influence with the U.S.S.R.

This needs very careful consideration.

3. What is in our view a necessary measure of defence will inevitably seem to the U.S.S.R. the preparation for an offensive which according to their ideology is a natural course to be adopted by any State which does not accept the communist philosophy.

They may react by:–

(a) Pressing forward with a westward penetration in order that they may be in a position to strike more effectively at the U.K. than we can at them.

(b) Pressing forward their penetration in the Near East in order to deny us possible bases for an attack against their vulnerable points. This would be in consonance with their general policy of seeking to construct a glacis round their homeland.

(c) They may do both.

4. I understand that it is not considered now possible for us to put sufficient forces on the Continent in order to give support to a Western block of Powers. Therefore the prevention of a rapid penetration to the Atlantic Coast by the U.S.S.R. must depend on the extent of the resistance likely to be offered by the countries of Western Europe.

In my view such resistance will only be possible after a period of some years in which the economic revival of Europe has made good progress and has been accompanied by a falling off in the attraction which Communism offers to countries in a state of economic depression. I mean in effect that a period of peace will permit the strengthening of western conceptions of democracy to gain strength. I should expect that the more international tension relaxes the less possible will it be to maintain in the U.S.S.R. the war mentality and war economy that has persisted since the revolution. The best hope of enduring peace lies in a change in the character of the regime in the U.S.S.R.

5. The countries which we have to support in the Middle East if we are to use that area as a potential base against the U.S.S.R. are weak …

6. Our position is, therefore, made very difficult before the world and our own people. We shall constantly appear to be supporting vested interests and reaction against reform and revolution in the interests of the poor. We have already that difficulty in Greece. The same position is likely to arise in all these other countries.

We can only gain the position we require by military agreements as in Egypt and Iraq. We have no base of our own except in Cyprus.

We have the difficult position in Palestine where we have either to offend the Arab States and probably Turkey and Persia as well or offend world Jewry with its powerful influence in the U.S.A.

7. We, therefore, endeavouring to keep our influence over this congeries of weak, backward and reactionary States have to face the U.S.S.R. organised under an iron discipline, equipped with the weapon of a revolutionary doctrine liable to attract the masses, strategically well placed for penetration or attack and with only a limited number of its key points open to our attack.

8. In order to gain this advantage we shall be committed –

(*a*) To the maintenance of considerable forces overseas. Two divisions in Palestine. Powerful Air Forces somewhere in the area for a striking force.

(*b*) The control of the Mediterranean with naval forces and with air forces sufficient to keep the route open. We should have to try to keep the Dardanelles closed. We should have to watch for the development of naval forces in Jugo-Slavia and Albania. We should have only Malta and Cyprus of our own to depend on. We should have to be on good terms with Spain.

(*c*) In the event of failure which I consider possible if not indeed probable we should have to supply these forces from around the Cape. It is unlikely that we shall be able to use India as a base.

(*d*) We shall have to spend large sums of money in bolstering up these weak States. Even if we can provide the resources it will take a long time for them to fructify. Meanwhile the U.S.S.R. will not be idle.

9. For the reasons set out above I regard the strategy outlined above as a strategy of despair. I have the gravest doubts as to its efficacy. The deterrent does not seem to me to be sufficiently strong. I apprehend that the pursuit of this policy so far from preventing may precipitate hostilities ... ■

One of the most far-reaching decisions of the early postwar years was the government's secret decision in 1947 to develop a British atomic bomb programme. Britain had worked closely with the United States and Canada during the war to produce the first atomic bombs, and in November 1945 President Truman promised continued co-operation. However, the McMahon Act, passed by Congress in 1946, effectively blocked atomic collaboration, angering the British government. At a time when the country's financial position was rapidly deteriorating, it was nevertheless judged essential to Britain's claims to be a great power that it should possess this new form of weaponry. Neither Attlee nor the Foreign Secretary, Ernest Bevin, doubted that a British bomb programme should proceed; and their view, grounded in status considerations, was supported by the conclusion of the Chiefs of Staff that, since Britain was now so vulnerable to attack, the best form of defence was nuclear deterrence.

5.5 Meeting of ministers to decide on construction of a British atom bomb, 8 January 1947 (PRO CAB 130/16).

■   TOP SECRET

GEN.163/1st Meeting

MEETING OF MINISTERS

CONFIDENTIAL ANNEX, MINUTE 1

(8th January, 1947 – 3.0 p.m.)

RESEARCH IN ATOMIC WEAPONS

The meeting had before them a Memorandum by the Minister of Supply covering a Note by the Controller of Production (Atomic Energy), (GEN.163/1) asking for directions on two points:–

(*a*) Whether research and development work on atomic weapons was to be undertaken;

(*b*) If so, whether special arrangements conducive to secrecy (outlined in paragraph 6 of the Memorandum) should be adopted.

LORD PORTAL said that so far as he was aware, no decision had yet been taken to proceed with the development of atomic weapons. He had discussed the matter with the Chiefs of Staff who were naturally anxious that we should not be without this weapon if others possessed it. About three years' work would be needed to solve the problems of nuclear physics and engineering involved in developing the bomb mechanism. If this matter were handled through the ordinary agencies responsible for weapon development, the result would inevitably be that a large number of persons in the Service Departments and in the Ministry of Supply would be made aware of what was being done. The alternative would be to make special arrangements whereby research could be carried on by the Chief Superintendent of Armament Research (Dr. Penney). He would set up a special section at Woolwich, the work of which would be described as 'basic high explosive research'. He would be responsible for this work to Lord Portal, who would arrange for the necessary contacts with the Atomic Energy Department and with the Chiefs of Staff in such a way as to ensure the maximum secrecy.

THE FOREIGN SECRETARY said that in his view it was important that we should press on with the study of all aspects of atomic energy. We could not afford to acquiesce in an American monopoly of this new development. Other countries also might develop atomic weapons. Unless therefore an effective international system could be developed under which the production and use of the weapon would be prohibited, we must develop it ourselves.

THE MINISTER OF DEFENCE agreed and said that in his view the arrangements suggested by Lord Portal should be effective in securing the greatest possible secrecy.

THE MINISTER OF SUPPLY said that a considerable amount of work would have to be done, particularly on the engineering side. In two years' time, the staff of all grades which would be employed would amount to about 180 people.

THE MEETING:–

(1) Agreed that research and development work on atomic weapons should be undertaken;

(2) Approved the special arrangements for this purpose, outlined in paragraph 6 of the Memorandum circulated by the Minister of Supply (GEN.163/1). ■

Partly through fear of political and social instability arising from Europe's economic problems in 1947, the United States unveiled the Marshall Plan in June 1947, a massive programme of aid. Theoretically, this aid was available to the Soviet Union and Eastern Europe, but Moscow's refusal to participate in the scheme accelerated the deepening division of Europe into opposing camps. Relations deteriorated further in December 1947, when negotiations over the future of Germany broke down. Then, in February

1948, Communists took power in Czechoslovakia. For a lifelong opponent of Communism like Bevin, this was the last straw; in March he warned his Cabinet colleagues of the threat to the West from Soviet expansionism. As the cold war deepened throughout 1948, Bevin's attitude hardened.

5.6 Ernest Bevin, memorandum, 'The threat to Western civilisation', 3 March 1948 (PRO CAB 129/25, CP(48)72).

■ The fast increasing threat to western civilisation which Soviet expansion represents impels me once again to examine the extent to which the Soviet Government appear to be achieving their aims, together with the steps we should now take in order to frustrate them …

3. It will be remembered … that ever since the European Recovery Programme was devised, the Soviet Government have been carrying on a war of nerves and behind it resolutely using the Communist Party to achieve dictatorship. It is their intention to endeavour to expand their activities to cover the whole of Europe at the earliest possible date. So far as we are concerned, we have been proceeding on the basis, which we made quite clear to Stalin, that just as the Russians had built up in the east what they called security, we intended to develop a good-neighbourly policy in the west, not aimed against Russia but inspired by the sheer necessity of economic revival and development and of security … It has really become a matter of the defence of western civilisation, or everyone will be swamped by this Soviet method of infiltration. I ask my colleagues, therefore, to give further consideration to the whole situation and decide whether our policy should not now be broadened so that we can proceed urgently with the active organisation of all those countries who believe in parliamentary government and free institutions, and devise methods which will cope with this quickly moving stream of events …

There is only one conclusion to draw. After all the efforts that have been made and the appeasement that we have followed to try and get a real friendly settlement on a four-Power basis, not only is the Soviet Government not prepared at the present stage to co-operate in any real sense with any non-Communist or non-Communist controlled government, but it is actively preparing to extend its hold over the remaining part of continental Europe and, subsequently, over the Middle East and no doubt the bulk of the Far East as well. In other words, physical control of the Eurasian land mass and eventual control of the whole World Island is what the Politburo is aiming at – no less a thing than that. The immensity of the aim should not betray us into believing in its impracticability. Indeed, unless positive and vigorous steps are shortly taken by those other states who are in a position to take them, it may well be that within the next few months or even weeks the Soviet Union will gain political and strategical advantages which will set the great Communist machine in action, leading either to the establishment of a World Dictatorship or (more probably) to the collapse of organised society over great stretches of the globe …

Recommendations

(1) We should pursue on as broad a basis as possible in co-operation with our French allies, the conclusions of a treaty or treaties with the Benelux countries. We should aim as a matter of great urgency at negotiating multi-lateral economic, cultural and defensive pacts between the United Kingdom, France and the Benelux countries, which would be left open for accession by other European democracies ...

(2) Simultaneously with this, the whole problem of the co-ordination of efforts for the cultural, social, economic and financial revival and develop-ment of the West and for the defence of western civilisation with the sup-port of all friendly western Powers and of course of the Commonwealth should be proceeded with at once. Having in mind Soviet tactics from Yalta onwards, we should decide what common arrangements can be made and what consultations should be entered into to prevent Soviet tactics succeed-ing on an even wider basis than hitherto and to halt any further expansion of Soviet dictatorship. The issue upon which we should consult with like-minded countries is not so much that of Communism as of the establish-ment of dictatorship as against parliamentary government and liberty. In this connection we cannot limit ourselves to Europe. We must bring in the Commonwealth and the Americas, and eventually every country outside the Soviet group ... ∎

The British Empire–Commonwealth

By 1945 the fortunes of the British empire had improved astonishingly since the nadir of 1942. At the end of the war, all the colonies occupied by Japan had been retrieved and the wartime spectre of international trusteeship over colonies had largely receded. Although the empire was to face problems after 1945, there was no question, in the minds of Attlee and Bevin, of Britain aban-doning this foundation of its world influence. If anything, the empire's resources were valued even more highly after 1945. Furthermore, the empire was gradually evolving; not only did Attlee's government give India indepen-dence in 1947 and begin to consider preparing other colonies for self-govern-ment, but the Commonwealth, formerly restricted to the 'white' Dominions, was enlarged to include countries like India and Pakistan. The Commonwealth came to be seen as a flexible, multiracial community and as a vital means through which Britain could maintain its influence in the world.

India

India had traditionally been regarded as the most valuable component of the British empire, and its possession as proof of British world power. Yet the war had strained Britain's capacity to govern the country, leading to a British com-mitment to discuss Indian self-government after the war. Given Britain's problems of postwar readjustment, the cost of remaining in India became unacceptably high. However, the transition to independence was not smooth. Britain failed to achieve a constitutional settlement which both the Indian National Congress and the Muslim League could accept, and communal tensions between Hindus and Muslims erupted into violence which the British could not quell, and in which many thousands of Indians died.

By late 1946 the British authorities in India had effectively lost control, and the Viceroy, Lord Wavell, advocated withdrawal. In February 1947 Attlee announced that Britain would leave India no later than June 1948. The new Viceroy, Lord Mountbatten, dispatched from London to supervise the transfer of power, quickly concluded that there was no alternative to partition, arrangements for which were made hastily in preparation for India's independence in August 1947. Although delighted that both India and Pakistan chose to remain within the Commonwealth, the British government failed to conclude a defence treaty with India, which had been one of its prime objectives.

5.7 Cabinet discussion on India, 10 December 1946 (PRO CAB 128/8, CM 104(46)3).

■ In the course of the Cabinet's discussions on the results of the recent visit of Indian leaders to this country, *The Prime Minister* said that it was impossible to be confident that the main political parties in India had any real will to reach agreement between themselves. Pandit Nehru's present policy seemed to be to secure complete domination by Congress throughout the government of India. If a constitution was framed which had this effect, there would certainly be strong reactions from the Muslims. Provinces with a Muslim majority might refuse to join a central Government on such terms at all; and the ultimate result of Congress policy might be the establishment of that Pakistan which they so much disliked. The Prime Minister warned the Cabinet that the situation might so develop as to result in civil war in India, with all the bloodshed which that would entail. There seemed to be little realisation among Indian leaders of the risk that ordered government might collapse.

The Cabinet felt that, however much the Indian politicians might abuse the British Raj, there was always at the back of their minds the sense that the Army was there and would be able to deal with civil disorder. This dulled their sense of responsibility for the consequences of their political policies. Apart from this, however, such confidence in the authority of the Army was no longer fully justified. The strength of the British Forces in India was not great. And the Indian Army, though the Commander-in-Chief had great personal influence with it, could not fairly be expected to prove a reliable instrument for maintaining public order in conditions tantamount to civil war. One thing was quite certain viz., that we could not put back the clock and introduce a period of firm British rule. Neither the military nor administrative machine in India was any longer capable of this.

Some Ministers felt that in the event our only course might prove to be to evacuate India and to leave the Indians to find, after a period no doubt of chaos, their own solution to their own problems. The Cabinet were assured that plans were being made for evacuating, in an extreme emergency, both British troops and civilians from India. Other Ministers felt, however, that even if such evacuation were practicable as a military operation – and it would not be an easy operation to carry out – it was not, politically, realistic to suppose that we should be able to adopt that course. Would it be acceptable to Parliament and to public opinion that we should leave India in chaos, having obtained no guarantee of fair treatment for the Muslims or for the other minorities? That would indeed be an inglorious end to our long association with India. World opinion would regard it as a policy of scuttle unworthy of a great Power.

There was general agreement that so grave a decision could not be taken without the most anxious thought. The decision need not be prejudged at this stage. Matters might not reach so serious a pass. It was certainly the wish of the great masses of the Indian people that there should continue to be ordered government throughout India and the leaders of the political Parties in India might well be forced to take account of this.

For the moment, the important thing was to secure that these leaders faced the difficulties which inevitably accompanied major constitutional changes in India. We should do anything that we could to bring home to them the heavy weight of responsibility which rested on them. ■

Palestine

One of the most serious problems within the prewar empire was the Palestine question. During the First World War, Britain had made promises about a National Homeland for the Jews in Palestine which were incompatible with the commitments it had made to the region's Arab populations. Jewish immigration into Palestine in the 1920s and 1930s triggered Arab–Jewish violence which the British authorities, responsible for the Palestine mandate, found difficult to control. To win Arab favour, Britain declared in 1939 that future Jewish immigration would be restricted, but after the Second World War, especially because of the Holocaust, Jewish pressure for a National Homeland increased and was difficult to resist.

After 1945 Arab–Jewish tensions worsened. While British military planners argued that Palestine was strategically vital to Britain, the problem increasingly became an international one, given the United Nations' ultimate responsibility for the territory. President Truman, under pressure at home, demanded continued Jewish immigration and an independent Jewish state. Unable to secure United States co-operation, and facing growing Jewish violence against its forces in Palestine, the British government decided in February 1947 to refer the entire question to the United Nations, hoping that the pro-Arab majority there might produce a solution which would safeguard British interests.

In September 1947 the United Nations proposed the partition of Palestine. Britain responded by declaring that it could not be responsible for implementing the plan, and instead prepared to withdraw.

5.8   Ernest Bevin, memorandum on withdrawal from Palestine, 18 September 1947 (PRO CAB 129/21, CP(47)259).

■ ...

18. The present situation in Palestine is intolerable and cannot be allowed to continue. His Majesty's Government have themselves failed to devise any settlement which would enable them to transfer their authority to a Government representing the inhabitants of the country. If the Assembly should fail, or if it were to propose a settlement for which His Majesty's Government could not accept responsibility, the only remaining course would be to withdraw from Palestine, in the last resort unconditionally.

19. The threat of British withdrawal within a specified time, coupled with an offer to assist in giving effect to any agreement reached between the Arabs and the Jews before our departure, might conceivably have the result of inducing them to co-operate in order to avoid the otherwise inevitable civil war. But a withdrawal, if decided upon, should not be made conditional on such an agreement.

20. Withdrawal in the absence of Arab–Jewish agreement has disadvantages which should not be underestimated. There would be an interval between the announcement of our intention to withdraw and the actual withdrawal, an interval in which the task of the Administration might be more difficult than in any previous period. In the absence of a Government to which power could be transferred, the consequences of our evacuation would be unpredictable. Some or all of the Arab States would probably become involved in the resulting disorders; they might even quarrel among themselves over the country's future. In any event it is likely that the situation would before long be brought to the attention of the Security Council.

21. On the other hand our withdrawal from Palestine, even if it had to be effected at the cost of a period of bloodshed and chaos in the country, would have two major advantages. British lives would not be lost, nor British resources expended, in suppressing one Palestinian community for the advantage of the other. And (at least as compared with enforcing the majority plan or a variant of it) we should not be pursuing a policy destructive of our own interests in the Middle East ... ■

The colonial empire

The need to improve colonial living standards had been recognised before the Second World War. The British government passed Colonial Development and Welfare Acts, intended to help pay for this development, during the war and amended them thereafter. There was a continuing, and growing, need to improve the international image of British colonial rule, which after 1945 became a target for Soviet criticism. Above all, the government sought to develop the colonial economies in order to assist Britain's economic recovery. Colonial development was seen by the British government as a lengthy process of preparing the colonies for eventual self-government, and it remained confident that it could control this evolution.

In 1947 the government unveiled a new colonial policy, bringing forward the goal of self-government, and emphasising the need to prepare the ground politically, by identifying Westernised groups in the colonies to whom power could be transferred. In 1951, by then no longer in office, Arthur Creech Jones, Labour's reforming Colonial Secretary between 1946 and 1950, reflected on the broad purposes of the policy he had helped to introduce.

5.9 Arthur Creech Jones, 'British colonial policy with particular reference to Africa' (in *International Affairs*, XXVII, 2, April 1951, pp. 176–83).

■ In the last five years many colonial constitutions have been overhauled. Some had become ill-fitted to prevailing conditions and their amendment was long overdue. It was inevitable that, as a result of the great acceleration of change and development in our territories during and since the last war, constitutions should be made more liberal and better adapted to political requirements. The experiences which came to tens of thousands of colonial soldiers in the war years released influences and stimulated ideas which were incalculable. They became more racially aware of themselves; new political notions dawned and spread among people who had previously been conscious only of kinship and tribal association. The effects of the war must also be coupled with the thoughts and hopes of men who had, through education, shared in a wider experience than that offered by the customary life to which they belonged ...

The agitation for advance in self-government is often described as nationalism or self-determination. Nationalism, as we understand it in Europe, however, has little relevance in African tribal society, among people who have as yet hardly realized their common interest and community. The boundaries of most of our African territories are artificial; little regard was shown to ethnic requirements when they were divided up. These territories have often had to be manoeuvred into some semblance of administrative unity, with little or no community of race, culture, and language. Nevertheless, it would be folly to discount the fact that a political ferment is at work. The desire for participation and responsibility in government has found expression among an increasing and influential minority. The natural resentment against the alien will ferment unless the thought and energies of the minority can be turned to better account.

It is no virtue for an administration to refuse obvious political adjustment when a deep and widely felt uneasiness about the need for change exists and when people begin to feel that only the use of force will serve to bring it about. This is not to say that we should yield to premature demands of noisy political groups. But as I see it, constitutions should reflect the developing life of the people and be subject to amendment to fit changing conditions. We do not ask people to distort themselves to fit into a constitution, and only seldom do we apply time schedules to constitutional changes; we are instructed by experience, and believe in orderly and progressive adaptation ...

Constitutional changes should, however, be seen in a right perspective. In recent years in Africa there have been marked changes. Formerly, Colonial Governments were content to interfere as little as possible with indigenous institutions and customs, and to let traditional structures and practices adjust themselves to altering needs. The economic and political forces in the modern world, however, could not fail to influence and change much of the life of the old societies. Not only did educational development result in the emergence of Africans without tribal privilege and status, but the traditional forms were shown to be insufficiently adaptable for modern needs – indeed some have disintegrated under the pressure of the new influences. Colonial Governments began to see themselves, therefore, not as mere administrations based on traditional structures, but as instruments of social and economic progress and as organs of political expression. Today the Colonial Government must accept active responsibility for promoting and controlling changes in order that tribal societies may develop into modern forms ...

Critics may assert that means of gaining experience in government have not been adequately formulated, that responsibility is being devolved on an African minority, that local government fails to receive the consideration its importance merits, that the composition of the local authorities is not being liberalized sufficiently by the admission of popularly selected representatives; the truth is that the counterpart of central government in the colonies is being evolved and that formerly backward tribal people are being led some way towards a working knowledge of the forms and processes of democratic government on both a local and national scale.

It is this more comprehensive picture of political advance which should be kept in mind, particularly when it is alleged that these developments are outstripping economic and social progress in our African territories, and responsible ministers and officials, instead of yielding to clamour, should concentrate on economic development and attempt to integrate economic and social advance with the political changes already conceded. In recent years there has been the maximum of effort to strengthen the economies of the territories. Colonial Governments have been trying with all possible expedition to fulfil the programmes made possible by the Colonial Development and Welfare Acts. No previous period in our history has witnessed a similar concentration of energy and resources in building up social standards, improving agriculture and public works, establishing new utilities and enterprises, and attending to such matters as irrigation, soil conservation, water supply, afforestation, research, surveys, and higher education. The record is more than impressive. Indeed it became necessary that political adjustment should not lag behind it. These developments are only possible if the people's representatives are associated with them and cooperate in their achievement ... ∎

Western Europe

After 1945 there was evidence of a new attitude towards Western Europe in British official circles. Co-operation with European governments, possibly assuming the leadership of Western Europe, seemed to offer a means by which Britain could strengthen its position in relation to the 'superpowers'. In 1947 Britain concluded a military alliance, the Treaty of Dunkirk, with France. Prior to this, Bevin and his Foreign Office advisers had been enthusiastic about proposing a Western European customs union. When the United States announced its programme of Marshall Aid to promote European economic recovery in June 1947, Britain provided the co-ordination in Europe demanded by Washington as a condition of the programme. As the cold war deepened early in 1948, Bevin concluded that Western Europe had to be protected from Soviet expansionism, and in June he advised Washington that some form of Western union was needed, with both United States and British backing. To convince Washington, Bevin had already concluded the Brussels Pact with France, Belgium, the Netherlands and Luxembourg, and given a commitment to maintain British troops in Europe.

Cold war tensions were accentuated when, in June 1948, the Soviet authorities, apparently aiming to prevent the creation of a West German state, blockaded all traffic between Berlin and the west. For almost a year the British co-operated with the Americans in mounting a huge airlift of supplies to Berlin. The Berlin Crisis precipitated the transformation of the Brussels Pact into the more comprehensive Atlantic Treaty (April 1949), which created the North Atlantic Treaty Organisation. Crucially important was the fact that the formation of NATO finally secured the involvement of the United States in European affairs. Meanwhile, Washington sought to encourage Western European economic integration, seeing Britain as the region's potential leader. Britain, however, was still more interested in developing ties with the Sterling Area than in becoming part of a European tariff-free zone. Anglo-American differences were encapsulated in the two countries' attitudes to the Organisation for European Economic Co-operation (OEEC), set up to administer Marshall Aid. Whereas Washington sought integration through 'supranational' structures, Britain proposed much looser intergovernmental arrangements.

Britain's attitudes towards Western European integration in the late 1940s were shaped by wider, global considerations. Although interested in integration, especially if this would draw France and West Germany closer together, Britain's own priorities lay with the Commonwealth and the Sterling Area, the latter importing twice as much British produce as did Western Europe. Thus, when the French economist and government adviser Jean Monnet visited London early in 1949 and raised the possibility of an Anglo-French economic union, the British response was cool. ■

In October 1949 Bevin reviewed policy towards Europe over the previous two years. In the past, he had talked in terms of Britain, its empire and Western Europe together constituting a 'third force' in the world, capable of matching the strength and influence of the two 'superpowers', and of maintaining an independent course in world affairs. However, the cold war had drawn Bevin increasingly to the conclusion that this was an unrealistic goal, and that the security of Britain and Western Europe required a clear orientation towards Washington, hence his relief when NATO was formed.

5.10   Ernest Bevin, memorandum on European policy, 18 October 1949 (PRO CAB 129/37/1, CP(49)208).

■ This paper, which is circulated for the information of my colleagues, discusses the question whether the aim of European policy should be the creation of a third world power or the consolidation of the Western World.

I. INTRODUCTION

Until about the end of 1947, when the Great Power system known as the Council of Foreign Ministers broke down, it was assumed, with decreasing confidence, that the general structure of peace would be based essentially on co-operation between the United States, the Soviet Union and the United Kingdom, which to some extent might be taken as representing the British Commonwealth and Empire. The breakdown on the question of Germany, however, destroyed this conception, perhaps temporarily, perhaps for ever. Although the United Nations was maintained as a kind of symbol of a real world system, and no doubt in the expectation that it would ultimately prove possible to revert to it, it was then clearly necessary to cast around for some alternative system of security which would be capable of maintaining peace for a long time to come.

2. This process of consolidating the non-Communist world really began in June 1947 with the announcement of the Marshall Plan and my acceptance of it. It passed from the economic to the political and military sphere early in 1948. At that time I envisaged action in three stages. The first stage was the conclusion of the Brussels Treaty, described as the hard core of the European system. The second stage was its reinforcement by the power and wealth of North America. The third stage was the extension of the European system. The first stage was completed by the signature of the Brussels Treaty on 17th March, 1948. The second stage was completed by the signature of the Atlantic Pact, which, for the first time, committed the United States and

Canada to the defence of Western Europe. The third stage has now been initiated with the signature of the Statute of the Council of Europe. It therefore seems desirable to consider carefully what is to be the ultimate aim of this policy...

4. This concept of a Third World Power has had many advocates. In this country it has appealed particularly to those who find American capitalism little more attractive than Soviet Communism, and to those who feel a natural dislike of seeing this country in a dependent position. But the policy is not without its advocates in the United States itself. These have included, at one time at any rate, the Planning Section of the State Department, who thought that the best way to consolidate the Western world was to build up another power-unit with a strength equivalent to that of America and Russia. It has also found favour among the isolationists, who feel that if this unit came into existence it would provide America with an excuse for retiring into her shell and leaving the task of containing Russia to the Third World Power.

5. Another school of thought, more common perhaps on the Continent of Europe than in the United States or the United Kingdom, has suggested that a Third World Power of this kind, even if its physical power were less than that of either of the other two great Powers, would by remaining neutral develop an influence out of proportion to its strength, since it could hope to be courted by both sides. The ability of a weak State to exploit its neutrality in this manner is illustrated by the conduct of Bulgaria in 1914–15 and Italy in 1939–40, though the subsequent experiences of these two countries are not encouraging ...

II. POSSIBLE COMPOSITION OF A THIRD WORLD POWER

7. The first question that requires consideration is what the composition of a Third World Power might be. The only serious suggestions that have been made are that it should consist of the Commonwealth, or of Western Europe (including the United Kingdom) with its overseas territories, or of these groups combined ...

Commonwealth

(a) Political

8. There are no political tendencies in the Commonwealth to-day which suggest that it could successfully be consolidated as a single unit. The Commonwealth is not a unit in the same sense as the United States or the Soviet Union. It has no central authority and is unlikely to create one, and its members are increasingly framing their policies on grounds of regional or local interests. The only member of the Commonwealth which might assume a position of leadership within it is the United Kingdom, and it seems unlikely that any proposals originating in London for a closer co-ordination of Commonwealth policy would be welcomed at present ...

(*b*) Economic

9. Since the creation of the O.E.E.C. machinery, the economic planning of the United Kingdom is tending to become more closely tied in with Western Europe than with the Commonwealth. The general trend of O.E.E.C. planning has so far been satisfactory to the sterling members of the Commonwealth ... There is little sign that the other members of the Commonwealth would accept collective planning arrangements for the Commonwealth similar to O.E.E.C., but we may well hope to persuade them increasingly to discuss their long-term problems individually with the United Kingdom. Even so, Commonwealth countries are likely to take the view that their needs for investment capital for industrial development cannot be met by co-operation with the United Kingdom and Western Europe alone but that dollar assistance will be needed. The Americans have shown reluctance in the past to use the United Kingdom as a channel for extending dollar aid to the rest of the Commonwealth.

(*c*) Military

10. The military picture is similar. As a result of the Brussels Treaty the United Kingdom has gone much further in military planning with Western Europe than it has with the Commonwealth. Moreover, the Commonwealth is not a strategic unit, and here again it must be clear to other Commonwealth members that their defence cannot be assured without United States support. For example, the Commonwealth, even with the help of Western Europe, will not in the foreseeable future be strong enough to hold the Middle East, which is vital to its security.

(*d*) Conclusion

11. Despite the possibility of improved economic consultation, there seems little prospect of the United Kingdom being able to unite the Commonwealth as a single world power. The attraction exerted by the pound sterling and the Royal Navy is now less strong than that of the dollar and the atom bomb. An attempt to turn the Commonwealth into a Third World Power would only confront its members with a direct choice between London and Washington, and though sentiment might point one way interest would certainly lead the other ... ■

After Britain's rejection of Monnet's proposal, the French Foreign Minister, Robert Schuman, unveiled the plan for a European Coal and Steel Community, embracing France and West Germany. In addition to stimulating economic recovery, it was hoped that the ECSC would strengthen French security, since this supranational body would effectively control German heavy industry. Anticipating British resistance, France had given London no prior warning of its plans, insisting that interested parties should accept in advance the principle of a supranational authority before negotiations began. In Britain, opposition to the plan came from the recently nationalised coal industry and from steel producers keen to develop worldwide, not merely European, markets. Above all, the British government disliked the idea of surrendering national sovereignty to a supranational authority.

On 2 June 1950 the Cabinet met to decide its response to the Schuman Plan. Ministers assumed that negotiations would in fact break down, but the ECSC talks forged ahead, and the Community was formed in April 1952. The government took a similar line in response to the Pleven Plan of October 1950, a proposal to create a Western European army. Both Attlee and Bevin rejected British participation in the plan, which subsequently collapsed due to French opposition.

5.11 Cabinet discussion on the Schuman Plan, 2 June 1950 (PRO CAB 128/17, CM 34(50)).

■ *The Minister of State* said that, in spite of the numerous diplomatic exchanges which had taken place during the past few days, it had proved impossible to reach agreement with the French Government about the terms on which the United Kingdom could join in the examination of the French proposal for the integration of the coal and steel industries of Western Europe. The French Government were insisting that all Governments participating in the proposed examination of the proposal should commit themselves in advance to accepting the principle of the scheme before it was discussed in detail ...

In discussion there was general agreement that the United Kingdom could not participate in the proposed discussion of the French proposal on the basis of the communiqué suggested by the French Government ... This would commit us to accepting the principle of the French proposal before any of its details had been made known to us. No British Government could be expected to accept such a commitment without having had any opportunity to assess the consequences which it might involve for our key industries, our export trade and our level of employment ...

Other points made in the discussion were:–

(*a*) The bulk of public opinion in this country, as reflected in Parliament and in the Press, was likely to support the view that the Government could not be expected to commit themselves in advance to accepting the principle of this proposal before they knew what practical shape it would take and what it was likely to involve. There would doubtless be some criticism from groups which were disposed to favour almost any scheme for European integration; but most people would think that the course now proposed was not unduly cautious.

(*b*) There was some risk that our attitude might be regarded by public opinion in the United States as a further sign of our reluctance to promote European union; and it was especially important from this point of view that, if the French decided to hold their conversations without our participation, the reasons for their attitude should be made clear without delay.

(c) It was important that, as proposed by the Foreign Secretary, a further attempt should be made to dissuade the French from going forward on the basis proposed without our participation. It was unreasonable that we should have been presented with an ultimatum that, if we did not concur in their proposal within 24 hours, the French would proceed without us; and it should be made clear to the French Government that we were surprised to receive such summary treatment in a matter of this importance ...

(d) Some Ministers thought that the French Government must have some underlying political motive for urging this precipitate acceptance of integrating the coal and steel industries of Western Europe. They might perhaps envisage this plan as a means of avoiding the additional commitments for the defence of Western Europe which had been foreshadowed in the recent meeting of the North Atlantic Council. Alternatively, they might be strengthened by knowledge that the United States Government would support their efforts to secure agreement on the principle of their plan.

(e) Although the other European Governments invited to participate in the discussions had accepted the latest French formula, some of them had done so with reservations. It would, however, be undesirable for the United Kingdom Government to take this course: for nothing would be more likely to exacerbate Anglo-French relations than for us to join in the discussions with mental reservations and withdraw from participation at a later stage.

(f) Our position was different from that of the other European countries by reason of our Commonwealth connections; and we should be slow to accept the principle of the French proposal without consultation with other members of the Commonwealth, especially as it appeared to involve some surrender of sovereignty ... ■

The Korean War and Rearmament

British defence policy after 1945 contrasted strongly with the position Britain had adopted after 1918. Whereas after the First World War there soon followed drastic cuts in public spending, notably in the defence sphere, the post-1945 years saw sustained, and even enlarged, expenditure on defence. For example, in 1947 Parliament approved the continuation of conscription, unusual in peacetime, which was subsequently extended to eighteen months in 1948, and to two years in 1950.

In June 1950 the Chiefs of Staff produced their report on Britain's defences and strategic priorities. Fundamental changes had taken place since their last review in 1947. The cold war was now indisputably the dominant theme in world affairs; NATO had been formed, giving the promise of United States military assistance; and, alarmingly, the Soviet Union had exploded its first atomic bomb in 1949, several years earlier than had been expected in the West.

5.12 Chiefs of Staff report, 'Defence policy and global strategy', 7 June 1950 (PRO CAB 131/9, DO(50)45).

■ 1. Since our last review in 1947 of the strategic situation many changes have taken place, notably the formation of Western alliances under the Brussels and North Atlantic treaties and the discovery by Russia of the atomic bomb. We now submit for the consideration of the Defence Committee a fresh review of Defence Policy and Global Strategy written in the light of these changes and from the joint point of view of a partner in a Western Alliance and a member of the British Commonwealth.

2. The British Commonwealth and the Continental Powers, whether individually or collectively, cannot fight Russia except in alliance with the United States; nor could the United States fight Russia without the help of the British Commonwealth. To-day it makes no sense to think in terms of British strategy or Western European strategy as something individual and independent. Full collaboration with the United States in policy and method is vital. This truth is recognised in the most important area of conflict by the North Atlantic Treaty. But the Cold War against Russian Communism is a global war as a hot war would inevitably be. After stabilisation of the European front the next most important object should be to secure an agreed Allied military strategy in the Middle East and East Asia theatres – and the machinery to implement it. It is also clearly necessary to obtain the fullest possible political, economic and military collaboration in the British Commonwealth as a whole – if possible including the countries of the Indian sub-continent, but if necessary without them ...

4. The first essential is to define clearly the political and military aim in the struggle against Russian communism. The enemy's aim is quite clear – it is a communist world dominated by Moscow. Allied defence policy has been confused by a lack of clear definition of what we are fighting for and by a failure to recognise that our aim in this struggle, in its present 'cold' phase as well as in a possible 'hot' phase, must be consistent.

5. Allied defence policy cannot be divided into water-tight compartments of 'cold' and 'hot' strategy. The former is largely conditioned by our ability in the last resort to defend our interests against armed aggression; while our readiness to fight defensively is inevitably affected by the demands of the cold war. Our aim must be to reduce to the minimum the extent to which it is so affected, but not to the fatal compromise of our ability to win the cold war which is rightly our first defence priority.

6. It is essential to our ability to win the cold war, which we cannot do without an increasing assumption of the offensive in the political and economic fields, that Allied foreign policy should not be cramped by the fear that if we

go too far we could not defend ourselves against armed attack. In this respect Western superiority in atomic air power and the security of the United Kingdom against air attack are vital factors. Cold War policy must therefore be related to military strength. The war of nerves by Hitler from 1933 to 1939 was in many ways similar to the present cold war, and the history of that period is eloquent proof of what happens if foreign policy and military preparedness do not march closely in step.

7. The overall policy must be defined by the Governments of the Allied nations. We submit that this should be as follows:

> 'To ensure the abandonment by Russia and her satellites of further military and ideological aggression, and at the same time to create conditions in which nations with different methods of government can live together peacefully.'

It is necessary to translate this policy into practical aims both for the cold war and for open hostilities.

The Aim in the Cold War

8. This aim, which must be achieved if possible without real hostilities, involves first a stabilisation of the anti-communist front in the present free world and then, as the Western Powers become militarily less weak, the intensification of 'cold' offensive measures aimed at weakening the Russian grip on the satellite states and ultimately achieving their complete independence of Russian control.

The Aim in the Hot War

9. If real hostilities are forced upon the Western Allies the aim will remain broadly the same. Our first preoccupation must be to ensure survival in the face of the initial onslaught. Our ultimate military aim must be to bring the war to the speediest possible conclusion, without Western Europe being overrun, by bringing about the destruction of Russian military power and the collapse of the present régime ... ∎

The attitudes expressed by the Chiefs of Staff above account for Britain's reactions to the outbreak of the Korean War. In June 1950 forces from Communist North Korea invaded South Korea, with the approval, the Foreign Office assumed, of Moscow. This caused a dramatic heightening of cold war tensions, to which both the United States and British governments agreed there had to be a firm response. Washington secured United Nations approval for intervention on South Korea's behalf, and Britain agreed to contribute troops.

The Korean War entered a new, more dangerous phase when Communist Chinese forces intervened on North Korea's behalf in November 1950. They quickly pushed back the United Nations forces under General Douglas MacArthur, who in turn seemed to favour action against China itself. This created fears of an escalation of the war into a direct East–West conflict. In particular, the British government was alarmed by casual remarks by Truman about the possible use of atomic weapons in Korea. Attlee rushed to Washington for consultations and extracted reassurances from Truman. London's continuing anxiety about MacArthur's strategy was summarised by the Foreign Office official, Sir Pierson Dixon, in April 1951.

5.13 Sir Pierson Dixon, memorandum, 9 April 1951 (in *British Documents on Policy Overseas*, series II, vol. 4, no. 142, London, HMSO, 1991).

■ Much as we may criticise General MacArthur, it must be admitted that there is an underlying ambiguity as to the political objectives governing the military conduct of the campaign in Korea and this ambiguity, I think, partly justifies the Supreme Commander's attitude though not his indiscretions.

The truth is we are in a jam in Korea, and perhaps inevitably, cover this up by not openly facing the ambiguity.

The fact is that we can neither get out nor get on. We can only get out, that is liquidate the Korean affair honourably and without further fighting, if China negotiates. We can only get on, that is conquer and hold the whole of Korea up to the Yalu, if we attack Chinese bases, supply centres and communications in China. That at any rate seems to be General MacArthur's thesis based no doubt on the experience of his last disastrous general offensive. We do not want to do this because war with China might bring in the Russians and develop into a general war.

We are thus on the horns of a dilemma, which H.M.G. try to solve by harping on the possibility of negotiations (as a means of getting out), and MacArthur, with some support now from the administration, by harping on the need to attack China proper (as a means of getting on).

While insisting that the war must not be extended to China, we continue to insist that our objective is a free and independent Korea. If the Chinese would negotiate with the same objective in view, well and good. But it seems highly unlikely that the Chinese will agree to negotiate so long as we maintain that objective, because they know that we are stuck and on the horns of a dilemma.

If then the Chinese continue to refuse to negotiate, and we maintain our objective of a free and independent Korea, are we to go on and try to conquer and hold all Korea by force as the sole means of attaining our political objective? If it is decided to do so, General MacArthur will have some justification in saying that in order to attain the political objective he must attack China.

The real solution of the dilemma, it seems to me, is to modify our political objective. This would mean abandoning the concept of a free and independent Korea and accepting the concept of a divided Korea. This objective could be translated into action in two ways: first, by accepting a military stalemate along the general line of the 38th Parallel and, secondly, by publicly stating this change of objective as a means of inducing a more reasonable frame of mind on the part of the Chinese towards a negotiated settlement. ■

One important consequence of the Korean War was pressure on Britain from the United States for an increase in defence expenditure. Following Attlee's visit to Washington in December 1950, the Cabinet discussed this question and agreed to comply with American wishes. The defence budget for 1951–3 rose from £2.3 billion to £3.6 billion, and again in January 1951 was further increased to £4.7 billion. This represented an increase in defence spending from 8 per cent of Britain's gross national product to 14 per cent.

5.14 Cabinet discussion on defence spending, 18 December 1950 (PRO CAB 128/18 CM(50)87th conclusions).

■ 1. *The Prime Minister* recalled that when, on 12th December, he had made his report to the Cabinet on his talks with President Truman he had said that he had undertaken to consider the President's request that this country should increase its defence effort. Since his return from Washington he had been considering this matter in the light of the continuing gravity of the international situation and, after discussions with the Foreign Secretary and the Minister of Defence, he had come to the conclusion that some acceleration in the pace of defence preparations was now unavoidable. The war planning of Departments generally was still based on the assumption that there would be no major war before 1957, though some of the Departments had adjusted some of their preparations to take account of the earlier date of 1954 to which the Medium Term Defence Plan of the North Atlantic Treaty Organisation was related. The United States were now accelerating their own preparations on the basis that major war might occur in 1952 or even 1951 … If Departments were told to plan on the basis that a major war was inevitable within the next two or three years very large expenditure would be involved (e.g. on civil defence), and he believed that a satisfactory hypothesis could be framed on the basis that the aim was to strengthen the active defences of this country for the purpose of preventing a major war. Some increase in defence expenditure over the next two years appeared, however, to be unavoidable. The existing programme would have to be accelerated in some respects, and there would be need for quicker progress with the completion of paper plans. The Chiefs of Staff were examining as a matter of urgency the measures which would be required: they were likely to recommend the calling up of reserves in batches for special training, increased production of weapons and equipment, and the completion of plans for the expansion of war production in the early stages of a war …

Meanwhile, it had been learned that, at the meeting of the North Atlantic Council on 19th December, the United States Secretary of State intended to make a statement calling on European Governments to increase their defence effort. He would announce that the United States Government aimed to complete their share of the Medium Term Defence Plan in two years instead of three, and that the United States aid towards European military effort would be continued in 1952 at the same rate as in 1951 ($5,000 million). He would estimate that Europe's contribution to the accelerated Medium Term Defence Plan should be between $15,000 and $18,000 million in the period to 30th June, 1953, and on this basis he would ask European countries to double their pre-Korean rate of defence expenditure. In his talks in Washington, the Prime Minister had persuaded the Americans to accept Anglo-American partnership as the mainspring of Atlantic defence. Much of the advantage we had gained would be lost if we were now to be treated as merely one of the European countries which were being urged by America to make a larger contribution to the common defence effort. We should align ourselves with the Americans in urging the others to do more. One could not ignore the risk, however remote it might seem, that the United States might lose interest in the defence of Europe, if her allies in the North Atlantic Treaty Organisation failed to play their proper part.

The Prime Minister accordingly proposed that the Foreign Secretary should express general agreement with all that the United States Secretary of State was to say about the urgency of building up the military strength of the West: that he should also emphasise the substantial contributions which the United Kingdom Government had already made: but that he should be authorised to go on to say that the United Kingdom Government, in view of the disturbed and dangerous international situation, had decided to increase and accelerate their defence preparations still further, with the sole object of assisting the Atlantic community and the other nations of the free world to resist aggression and to secure their own safety and freedom, and were now considering the form and direction which this additional effort should take … ∎

5.15 **Defence spending, 1945–51 (chart derived from D. Butler and G. Butler (eds), *British Political Facts, 1900–1985*, London, Macmillan, 1986, 6th edn, pp. 390–1).**

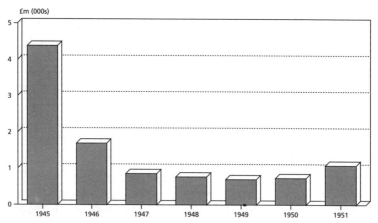

A Great Power Still?

As Attlee's government entered its final months, there were grounds for satisfaction with Britain's relationship with the wider world. Having survived the Second World War, Britain now appeared to be secure under the mantle of United States defence; it was on the road to becoming one of the elite band of nuclear powers; it had embarked on a course of decolonisation; and it still had high hopes for the developing Commonwealth.

In 1951 the senior diplomat Sir Roger Makins, who would later become Britain's Ambassador in Washington, attempted to take stock of Britain's world position. While candidly accepting Britain's dependence on the United States, Makins betrayed assumptions about the continuing scope for British influence in the world which would increasingly be tested as the 1950s progressed.

5.16 Sir Roger Makins, memorandum, 'Some notes on British foreign policy', 11 August 1951 (PRO FO 371/124968 no. 24/2).

■ Periodically, we all have qualms about the soundness of our foreign policy and need to be reassured. Since some of these qualms have been expressed recently, it may be useful to examine the grounds for reassurance.

2. It is a truism to say that the object of British policy is to secure peace, because it is the case that a peaceful world is a major British interest. All our actions should be subject to this major purpose.

3. Foreign policy is based on national strength, and cannot safely get too much out of line with the resources, moral and material, which a country can control. British foreign policy in recent years has sought to recognise this fact, and has rested on the basic assumption that neither the United Kingdom and Commonwealth alone, nor the United Kingdom and Western Europe alone, nor even the United Kingdom, Western Europe and the Commonwealth alone, possess sufficient resources to resist the forces arrayed against them. The second basic assumption is that these forces are those controlled by the Soviet Union and are being used to weaken, undermine and ultimately to dominate the democracies of Western Europe, by all means short of war, and, in certain circumstances possibly even by war itself. The resources and support of the United States of America are therefore essential to the security of the United Kingdom and indeed to the free world.

4. We believe that the British 'way of life', which is a convenient expression to use for our political and social system, is more enlightened than that of other countries; we believe also that British influence is on the whole moderately and wisely exercised in the world, and consistently used to promote the peaceful development and economic welfare of our own and other peoples. So long as we believe this (and if we cease to believe in our mission we

shall soon go down) it must be our objective to maintain our position as a great Power, and this has, indeed, been our main purpose since 1900, when British power was at its zenith. It can be argued, and it was so argued before the last war, that our resources are no longer equal to this task, and that we ought to content ourselves with a more modest role; and if we survey the resources which we physically own, there is something to be said for this view. But our resources are not only physical; they are in large measure intangible and imponderable: our prestige, our technical and political skill, our reputation for fair dealing and wise counsel, our national will, and consequently the support which we obtain not only from the Commonwealth and Empire but also from foreign countries. Secondly, if we accepted a lesser role, it would be so modest as to be intolerable. We have plenty of enemies and if we relaxed our grip scarcely a British interest outside the United Kingdom would survive.

5. It follows that we must continue to aim at the maintenance of our power and influence in the world at the highest possible level.

6. The strategy we are following in the pursuit of these objectives is four-fold –

(*a*) to maintain the maximum cohesion in the Commonwealth and Empire, and to hold the sterling area together;

(*b*) to maintain a partner relationship with the United States;

(*c*) to promote the cohesion of Western Europe;

(*d*) to strive for the fullest measure of economic independence and strength for the United Kingdom ...

Conclusion

18. The policy we are following is, in its broad lines, the only feasible one for the United Kingdom if we are to avoid sinking to the level of a second or third class Power. But there should, of course, be appropriate changes of emphasis and modification of tactics (such as we are now making in regard to federal trends in Europe).

19. This policy is a bold one. It strains our resources, both material and moral, to the full, and needs firm resolve, strong nerves, the highest degree of political and diplomatic skill and the support of public opinion. United Kingdom policy needs to be lively, adaptable, and imaginative, and we should take the lead where we can. And we cannot afford to make mistakes.

20. In particular the policy involves –

(*a*) a substantial effort from the British people on the basis of 'Peace before Plenty';

(*b*) the avoidance of an economic crisis in the United Kingdom leading to failure in production and exports or to a balance of payments situation in which the United Kingdom will need general economic aid. ■

CHAPTER SIX

Economic and Social Policy, 1951–64

THE economic outlook at the beginning of the 1950s was grim. The enormous scale of the rearmament programme adopted under Labour had contributed to a balance of payments crisis which seemed serious indeed when the Conservatives took power at the end of October 1951. But conditions steadily improved over the following two years, and the rest of the decade has been remembered as an age of affluence and prosperity. There remained, however, troubling problems in economic policy. Already by the middle of the decade, Britain's economic policy-makers were steering a jerky 'stop–go' course between overheating and recession. The continued official determination to maintain a fixed exchange rate for sterling was another source of strain and controversy in these years. Full employment, economic growth and rising standards of living were encouraging; but Britain's performance compared to other Western economies was not. By the early 1960s a mood of pessimism had begun to replace the optimism of the previous decade.

Prosperity itself raised several important areas of public debate. On the left, the Labour Party was divided increasingly from the mid-1950s over the extent to which further nationalisation and planning were either necessary or desirable. On the right, there were many voices advocating a more radical challenge to the mixed economy and the welfare state. While industrial harmony was prioritised in the 1951–5 government, strained relations with the trade unions were increasingly apparent by 1956, as the government became increasingly determined to control rising wages and public spending.

But prosperity in the 1950s also allowed successive Chancellors to phase out rationing and other economic controls left over from the war, to cut taxation and to maintain comparatively high levels of public expenditure at the same time. While some long-term planning was apparent, for example over the expansion of the higher education sector, critics of Conservative economic policy charged with increasing frequency that important opportunities to invest in the modernisation and development of the manufacturing sector had been forsaken in order to appease the voting consumer.

Crisis and Controversy

The scale of the balance of payments crisis came as a shock to Winston Churchill's Cabinet. The new Chancellor of the Exchequer, R.A. ('Rab') Butler, was forced to take a series of economising measures upon coming into office, and over the following weeks even more extreme measures were contemplated. It was a depressing start for a government with a small majority.

The first memorandum considered by the Churchill Cabinet after the 1951 election stressed the ominous economic situation.

6.1   **R.A. Butler, Cabinet memorandum on the economic position, 31 October 1951 (PRO CAB129/48, C(51)1, pp. 1–8).**

■   THE ECONOMIC POSITION: ANALYSIS AND REMEDIES

Memorandum by the Chancellor of the Exchequer

I wish to put before my colleagues an analysis of the present economic position of the United Kingdom, as evidenced in our Balance of Payments with the dollar area and the rest of the world. I also suggest in this memorandum certain measures for their consideration: I believe that we should take these measures in order to remedy the situation.

I. THE DETERIORATING POSITION AND OUTLOOK

2. We are in a balance of payments crisis, worse than 1949, and in many ways worse even than 1947. Confidence in sterling is impaired, as witness the large discounts on forward sterling in New York, and speculation against it is considerable, increasing the deficits and the drain on our gold and dollar reserves ...

II. THE NEED TO RESTORE CONFIDENCE

6. This very serious deterioration in our position, coming as it does at the inception and not during the full impact of the rearmament programme, threatens the whole position of sterling and of the United Kingdom and sterling area. It is a clear indication not only that there are serious underlying weaknesses in our position, but also that foreign confidence in our ability to deal with these weaknesses is greatly impaired ...

III. THE URGENT NEED FOR A COMPREHENSIVE STATEMENT OF GOVERNMENT POLICY

7. The restoration of confidence requires, in my view, an early and comprehensive statement by the Government which shows that it is both ready and able to grip the situation ...

V. THE CONTENT OF THE STATEMENT ...

11. The following are the broad headings of the measures which I ask my colleagues to consider ...

A. IMPORT CUTS. I recommend that immediate action be taken, and announced, to reduce external expenditure by £350 million a year ... The following are my detailed proposals to achieve this:–

(*a*) Savings of £150 million by direct cuts on a selected list of imports from European and other non-sterling sources ... This list should include:–

  (i)   Private imports of unrationed food ...

  (ii) Government imports of unrationed food ...

  (iii) Private imports of manufactures ...

  (iv) Private imports of raw materials ...

(*b*) Savings of £50 million by cutting the 1952 import programme of rationed foods ...

(*c*) Limiting imports of timber to maintain present consumption only ...

(*d*) Saving of £100 million by suspension of strategic stockpiling programme....

(*e*) Saving of £15 million by reducing tourist ration from £100 to £50 ...

(*f*)   General tightening up of external expenditure ...

B. MONETARY MEASURES. I am satisfied that it has now become necessary to remove the rigidity in short term interest rates of the last few years, which has limited the power of the authorities to exercise sufficient pressure upon credit policy.

C. REDUCTIONS IN GOVERNMENT EXPENDITURE. We need an urgent review of all Government expenditure so as to cut out waste, and – far more important – to cut out and slow down expenditure on work which is valuable but not essential in times of crisis. We may have to go further and take some big steps of a kind which no one can welcome ...

D. INVESTMENT. The present building programe authorised for 1952 is ten per cent higher than the work actually carried out in 1950. But in the first half of 1951 the building industry achieved about 4 per cent less than in 1950. This was due to bad weather, shortage of steel, and an attempt to achieve too much with limited labour and materials ... The industry is already overloaded and the first essential is to limit severely any more work being started under the present programme until the overload has been worked off ... ■

The speculation which preceded Butler's first Budget was intense; it was thought that the Chancellor would be forced to take a series of unpopular measures which could fatally undermine confidence in Conservative promises to 'set the people free'. In fact, the Cabinet considered but ultimately rejected a highly controversial scheme, dubbed 'ROBOT' after the initial letters of the names of the three civil servants with whom it was most closely associated, which was designed to ease the pressure on sterling by allowing it to float in the international money market.

6.2   R.A. Butler, draft memorandum on the 'ROBOT' scheme, 26 February 1952 (PRO PREM 11/140).

■ 1. The drain on the gold reserves continues unchecked. In January, the loss was $297 million; in the first three weeks of February, a further loss of $224 million – a loss of $521 million in eight weeks, bringing the reserves to $1,800 million (£650 million) – equivalent to $3\frac{1}{2}$ weeks' turnover of the sterling area's transactions with the rest of the world ...

4. I feel I should disclose the January and February losses in my Budget speech; even if I did not do so, I should have to announce the first quarter's loss early in April. These are bound to deal a heavy blow at confidence in sterling. I intend to introduce a Budget which will show that we are dealing vigorously with our internal problems, but I do not believe that this alone could arrest the loss of confidence ...

6. The decision which we have to take is this. Should we wait until our gold reserves are in effect exhausted and until we are forced to take the action in circumstances in which we should no longer have the power to influence the situation? ...

7. My own view is that we should act now, in the most effective and drastic way which is open to us. I am supported in this view by the Governor of the Bank of England and by my official advisers ...

15. The proposal is in five parts:–

(i) *Exchange Rate.* The official parity of $2.80 remains but we abandon the existing margin ($2.78–$2.82) and the Exchange Equalisation Account will be used to intervene constructively so as to secure the maximum stability of the international value of sterling. The above would be announced publicly.

But for our own purposes we should decide that we shall initially seek, so long as this does not dangerously weaken the reserves, to keep the rate within the limits of, say, 15 per cent either side of the official parity, i.e. about $2.40–$3.20 ...

(ii) All foreigners' sterling balances would be blocked (except for American and Canadian Accounts, which are already convertible into dollars). Ten per cent of Central Bank balances would be reclassified as 'external sterling';

this, and any sterling which they acquired subsequently, would be convertible into gold or dollars, or any other currency in the market, at the ruling rate.

(iii) The present structure of the sterling area would be maintained ...

(iv) Arrangements would be made to ensure that not less than 80% of sterling balances held by independent sterling area countries' Central Banks are, in effect, held in funded form and therefore could not be immediately used.

(v) The London Gold Market will be re-opened so as to provide a single market at the highest possible price for sterling area newly-mined gold. The price will not be related to the official dollar price of gold, but will fluctuate freely ...

19. The effect is that the gold reserves cease to take the full strain of the balance of payments deficit of the sterling area. The strain would then be taken by the exchange rate unless the reserves are used ...

20. Depreciation of the exchange rate would, of course, fall immediately and directly on the internal economy, in rising prices of food and raw materials ... The more effective our own action to deal with our balance of payments deficit, the higher will be the rate, and the lower the cost of living ...

22. It is true to say, on the other hand, that this process itself sets up forces which, in the long run, will tend to bring the economy into balance. The rise in the price of imports would reduce the consumption of imports, and a fall in the exchange rate would increase the competitive power of our exports, and would encourage the concentration of industry on exports. But of course the balance would be at worse terms of trade – we should have to export more goods in order to get fewer imports. If we continue to use industrial resources for other purposes – defence, housing, etc. – thus preventing the diversion of resources to export work, the rate would continue to fall ...

46. It will be seen that this new course in our external economic policy requires a complete re-thinking of the whole of the economic policies which have been in operation, fundamentally with the support of all parties, during the last few years. We cannot pretend to predict just what its consequences will be. ▪

Butler's first Budget was masterful, avoiding unpopular cuts in the social services by slashing food subsidies. The senior backbench Conservative MP Henry Channon recalled the Chancellor's reception in his diary.

6.3 Henry Channon, diary, March 1952 (in R.R. James (ed.), *Chips: The Diaries of Sir Henry Channon*, London, Weidenfeld & Nicolson, 1967, pp. 466–7).

■ *11 March [1952]*

To the House for the Budget; crowded and excited. Rab looking sleek, calm and well ... spoke for nearly two hours, and he was clear, concise, calm, good-tempered. His performance was magnificent. He played politely with the Opposition, who revealed themselves in a really despicable light. They only cheered bad news, as when Rab announced cuts in food subsidies. When tax cuts were revealed they were glum and grim. His is a brilliant bourgeois budget; instead of being stern there is something in it for everybody – even the rich. He was cool, calculating and clever. He is like a Howitzer and mows down the Opposition, in their awkward embarrassed attempts to make 'phoney' attacks ... Dalton was disgusting; he is the most — biped, all in all, that I have ever met. Rab had a great triumph, and afterwards smiled broadly, blandly. It was a bold bid for the floating middle-class vote and possibly for the Premiership. A wave of enthusiastic relief has surged over the House and later over the City. There is a new festival spirit about. A young Queen; an old Prime Minister and a brave buoyant Butler budget. Has he put us in for a generation? ■

Return to the Free Market?

The Conservatives were elected in 1951 on a manifesto which promised to remove restrictions and controls from the economy and to place more emphasis on the free market. Although many controls remained in place longer than the party had envisaged, a shift in style and emphasis of social and economic policy did occur.

Easing economic conditions permitted food rationing to end in the summer of 1954. Housing policy was another example; as the chart shown as document 6.5 indicates, housing provision under the Conservatives shifted steadily back towards the private sector between 1951 and 1964.

6.4 Giles, 'I suppose you realise that now they can get steaks like foreigners, British sportsmen have no excuse for not winning everything', *Daily Express* cartoon, 6 July 1954.

6.5 Housing provision, 1951–64 (chart derived from D. Butler and G. Butler (eds) , *British Political Facts, 1900–1985*, London, Macmillan, 6th edn, 1986, p. 332).

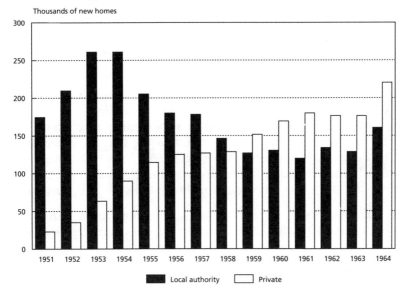

Thousands of new homes

Local authority   Private

While the Conservatives did succeed in their desire to return some elements of economic and social activity to the private sector, broadly speaking the postwar emphasis on the state provision of social services remained unchanged in the 1950s. The government consistently attempted to find ways to cut the cost of the welfare state, but in practice there was little scope for reduction without taking drastic and unpopular policy de-

cisions. The Royal Commission of Enquiry into the cost of the National Health Service, chaired by Claude Guillebaud, for example, concluded in 1956 that state provision of health care was cost-efficient and recommended further capital investment in the service. Similarly, the rising proportion of elderly people in the population dictated that expenditure on pensions and National Assistance must rise.

6.6   *Report of the Committee of Enquiry into the Cost of the National Health Service* (Guillebaud Report), January 1956 (London, HMSO, Cmd 9663, PP XX, 1955–6, pp. 46, 249, 268–9).

■   ## THE CURRENT COST OF THE NATIONAL HEALTH SERVICE IN ENGLAND AND WALES DURING THE PERIOD 1948 TO 1954

General

[92] (1) In England and Wales, the current net cost of the National Health Service in productive resources was £$371\frac{1}{2}$ million in 1949–50. In subsequent years it rose by roughly £15 million each year, reaching £$430\frac{1}{2}$ million in 1953–54 ...

(2) The rise of £59 million in the current net cost of the Service over the four years was the combined result of a larger rise (£77 milion) in gross costs, offset by a saving of £18 million arising from new or increased charges to beneficiaries ...

(3) Expressed as a proportion of total national resources (the 'gross national product') the current net cost of the Service fell from $3\frac{3}{4}$ per cent in 1949–50 to $3\frac{1}{4}$ per cent in 1953–54 ...

(4) During the period under review there was a considerable general rise in prices. An attempt has been made to estimate the effect of price increases on the cost of the Service, recalculating expenditures at constant (1948–49) prices and wages. The current net cost of the Service, expressed in 'real' terms in this way, was only £11 million greater in 1953–54 than in 1949–50. Thus, the net diversion of resources to the National Health Service as a whole since 1949–50 has been of relatively insignificant proportions ...

(5) There was a rise of nearly 2 per cent in population during the period under review. Allowing for this and for changes in the age structure of the population, the cost *per head* at constant prices was almost exactly the same in 1953–54 as in 1949–50 ...

[735] (4) *Our Final Comment*

Having concluded that in practice there is no objective and attainable standard of 'adequacy' in the health field, and that no major change is needed in the general administrative structure of the National Health Service, we have sought to ascertain where, if anywhere, there is opportunity for effecting substantial savings in expenditure, or for attracting new sources of income, within the existing structure of the Service; but we have found no opportunity for making recommendations which would either produce new sources of income or reduce in a substantial degree the annual cost of the Service. In some instances – and particularly with regard to the level of hospital capital expenditure – we have found it necessary, in the interests of the future efficiency of the Service, to make recommendations which will tend to increase the future cost.

In considering the more distant future there are a large number of factors at work, some of which will lead to an increase in the cost of the Service, while others will operate in the opposite direction. It is quite impossible at the present time to forecast which of these tendencies will ultimately prevail; though it is obvious that, so far as financial cost is concerned, in the sense of the amount of money spent on the Service, a great deal will depend upon what happens to the value of money and therefore upon the future trend of prices and wages.

There are defects in the present organisation and administration of the National Health Service to which we have drawn attention throughout our Report; but these weaknesses apart, we have reached the conclusion that the Service's record of performance since the Appointed Day has been one of real achievement. The rising cost of the Service in real terms during the years 1948–54 was kept within narrow bounds; while many of the services provided were substantially expanded and improved during the period. Any charge that there has been widespread extravagance in the National Health Service, whether in respect of the spending of money or the use of manpower, is not borne out by our evidence. ▪

Affluence and Consumerism

By 1953 economic conditions in Britain had eased considerably. The drop in world commodity prices from 1952 which followed the end of the war in Korea, combined with the delayed effects of the 1949 devaluation, which made exports more competitive, improved the terms of British trade with the outside world. This allowed for the generally expansionist tone of economic policy for the rest of the decade.

The increased spending power of the consumer in the mid-1950s was brought about through rising wages and tax cuts. In his address to the Conservative Party Conference in 1954, Butler held out the promise of a doubled standard of living in twenty-five years. But he warned of the conflict between the government's objective of reduced taxation and continued high levels of public spending.

6.7   R.A. Butler, speech to the party conference, Blackpool, 7 October 1954 (National Union of Conservative and Unionist Associations, *Seventy-Fourth Annual Conference Official Report*, London, Conservative Party, 1954, pp. 64–6).

■ … The way to deal with the cost of living is really to go on increasing production and bringing about greater plenty. If we have greater plenty we shall have cheaper prices. I am glad to tell you that production now stands, both in industry and agriculture, under our Government at the highest level ever recorded in the history of our country.

By expanding and developing production we can best help those in need. They are the people, the pensioners, and others, on fixed incomes, the retired people, and those who have had legacies left to them of a very small amount; those are the people on fixed incomes whom we must try to help, and especially the old-age pensioners and the ex-servicemen and their wives. This then is the attitude we should adopt towards the cost of living.

This question of doing something for somebody leads me to the problem of expenditure … We shall make further economies … with a view to reducing taxation. But there are limits to what I can achieve, if we are at the same time to have the booms of full employment and social welfare. In fact, the public cannot have it all round.

If we are to have the social welfare benefits, and to maintain full employment without inflation, which has been done by this country in the last two years, and has hardly ever been achieved before by any economy in the world, if we are to have those benefits which you ought to push on every platform, we cannot have massive reduction of taxation as well …

When I approach this problem of expenditure, I reflect with some whimsicality that our financial policy must have a heart as well as a head, and as long as I am responsible for our financial policy it is going to have both those vital organs, a heart and a head. The difficulty is to find the exact relationship between the two …

… we are consuming in this quarter, compared with the same quarter last year, 4 per cent more household goods, 6 per cent more food, and 7 per cent more clothing. I see no reason why, in the next quarter of a century, if we run our policy properly and soundly, we should not double our standard of living in this country … ■

As the chart shown as document 6.8 indicates, the growth of consumerism in the 1950s was indeed dramatic. The best-known phrase associated with the affluence of the period, 'You've never had it so good', was paraphrased from Harold Macmillan's speech at Bedford in the summer of 1957. Less well remembered are his accompanying warnings against the continued growth of public expenditure and wage rates.

6.8   The growth of consumerism, 1952–63 (Chart derived from D.E. Butler and A. King (eds), *The British General Election of 1964*, London, Macmillan, 1965).

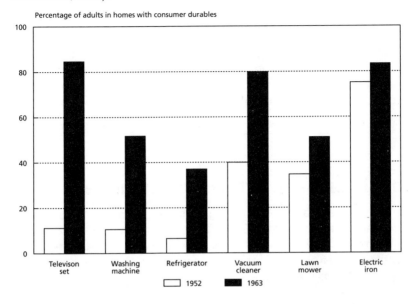

Percentage of adults in homes with consumer durables

1952 · 1963

Televison set · Washing machine · Refrigerator · Vacuum cleaner · Lawn mower · Electric iron

6.9   **Harold Macmillan, speech at Bedford, 20 July 1957 (reported in *The Times*, 22 July 1957).**

■ … These increased earnings come from the increasing production of most of our main industries – steel, coal, motor cars; a large part of the increase in output is going to exports or to investment. That is all to the good. Indeed, let us be frank about it: most of our people have never had it so good. Go around the country, go to the industrial towns, go to the farms, and you will see a state of prosperity such as we have never had in my lifetime – nor indeed ever in the history of this country.

What is beginning to worry some of us is, is it too good to be true? – or perhaps I should say, is it too good to last? … Our constant concern to-day is, can prices be steadied while at the same time we maintain full employment in an expanding economy? Can we control inflation? This is the problem of our time. Our first duty at a time when there is more money about than goods to spend it on is to keep down Government expenditure. We have already done a lot. In terms of 1951 prices this year's Budget is nearly £400m down and we have achieved this in spite of increases in education, pensions and health. We have reduced the Civil Service by over 50,000 and we have now embarked upon a new plan to secure greater efficiency and economy in local government expenditure …

Monetary policy, restriction of credit, acceleration or retardation in the investment programmes over which the Government has control – these are the measures which we have to intensify or relax according to the state of the economic barometer. All these steps are good and all of them are necessary, but in the long run there is only one answer to the 64,000 dollar question – to increase production. That is the answer, that is where the real hope lies ...

Government action is needed and is being taken, but by itself it cannot solve the problem. This is a combined operation; we are all in it – Government, industry, the general public. What we need is restraint and common sense – restraint in the demands we make and common sense on how we spend our income. But the only form of restraint which can work in a free society is self-restraint ... ■

Revisionism and Orthodoxy on the Left

The emergence of a period of strong economic performance posed a dilemma for socialist theorists in the 1950s. If capitalism under the Conservative Party could provide full employment, a welfare state and rising incomes, then what was the point of orthodox Labour economic policy? The Labour Party was bitterly divided over these issues.

The most significant intellectual critique of orthodox Labour policy in the 1950s was Labour economist Anthony Crosland's The Future of Socialism. *Crosland accepted that the economic crises which had characterised the interwar years were a thing of the past; in postwar Britain, he argued, socialism should focus on increasing equality and social justice in society through vigorous policies on taxation, education, social security and industrial democracy.*

6.10   **C.A.R. Crosland,** *The Future of Socialism,* **London, Cape, 1956, pp. 515–29.**

■ We stand, in Britain, on the threshold of mass abundance; and within a decade the average family will enjoy a standard of living which, whether or not it fully satisfies their aspirations, will certainly convince the reformer that he should turn his main attention elsewhere ...

Traditionally, or at least since Marx, socialist thought has been dominated by the economic problems posed by capitalism: poverty, mass unemployment, squalor, instability, and even the possibility of the imminent collapse of the whole system. These were problems of the most severe and urgent character; and it was correct to argue that major economic changes must precede the execution of socialist policy in other fields.

But it is gradually ceasing to be correct to-day. Capitalism has been reformed almost out of recognition. Despite occasional minor recessions and balance of payments crises, full employment and at least a tolerable degree of stability are likely to be maintained. Automation can be expected steadily to solve any remaining problems of under-production. Looking ahead, our present rate of growth will give us a national output three times as high as now in 50 years – an increase capable of sustaining not only a generous rise in home living standards, but also a level of investment in the under-developed areas fully as high as they can physically accommodate. The pre-war reasons for a largely economic orientation are therefore steadily losing their relevance; and we can increasingly divert our energies into more fruitful and idealistic channels, and to fulfilling earlier and more fundamental socialist aspirations ...

These have been defined in this book primarily in terms of social welfare and social equality ...

As these objectives also are gradually fulfilled, and society becomes more social-democratic with the passing of the old collective grievances and injustices (and perhaps as automation carries us towards the 30- or even 20-hour week), we shall turn our attention increasingly to other, and in the long run more important, spheres – of personal freedom, happiness, and cultural endeavour: the cultivation of leisure, beauty, grace, gaiety, excitement, and of all the proper pursuits, whether elevated, vulgar, or eccentric, which contribute to the varied fabric of a full private and family life ...

We need to make Britain a more colourful and civilised country to live in. We need not only higher exports and old-age pensions, but more open-air cafes ...

This becomes manifest when we turn to the more serious question of socially-imposed restrictions on the individual's private life and liberty. There come to mind at once the divorce laws, licensing laws, prehistoric (and flagrantly unfair) abortion laws, obsolete penalties for sexual abnormality, the illiterate censorship of books and plays, and remaining restrictions on the equal rights of women. Most of these are intolerable, and should be highly offensive to socialists, in whose blood there should always run a trace of the anarchist and the libertarian, and not too much of the prig and the prude ... We do not want to enter the age of abundance, only to find that we have lost the values which might teach us how to enjoy it. ■

Within a Labour Party led by the right-winger Hugh Gaitskell, Croslandism was an important influence on the formulation of new policies. In policy statements such as Industry and Society, *Labour demonstrated a newly flexible approach to issues like public ownership. Capitalism, it seemed to be saying, if managed well, could be used to the benefit of all the people.*

6.11 **Labour Party,** *Industry and Society,* **London, Labour Party, 1957, pp. 55–8.**

■ ... there has emerged, as the dominant institution, a distinctive form of business organisation – the large firm. It is the dominant institution because, measured by any yardstick, large firms already control the greater part of economic resources in the private sector. It is distinctive on several counts: size is the first; stability – one could say permanence – is the second; professional, managerial control is the third; the capacity to accumulate capital and finance its own development is the fourth ...

In these large firms the functions of private ownership have declined – or are declining – to the point where it has no further part to play ... No one can convincingly argue that ... if private shareholders ceased to exist, the companies would to the smallest extent be harmed ...

Nevertheless, the shareholders still retain the legal rights of ownership and the financial rewards that accompany them ... What is more, these gains accrue for the most part to a very small section of the population.

Thus we have – from the socialist viewpoint – the paradox of a substantial sector of industry in which private ownership has ceased to be necessary and yet is still a major bulwark of inequality of wealth in our society.

Public ownership as a means of achieving greater equality of wealth is a recognised part of Party policy.

... in the case of the larger firms, no difficulties of finance, incentive or management stand in the way of a transfer from private to public ownership. At the same time, such a transfer would contribute powerfully towards a better distribution of wealth.

There are several ways of giving effect to this conclusion. First ... death duties can be paid in shares and land as well as in cash. Further, as we have already described, the National Superannuation Fund will be able to invest its growing surplus ...

The need for State planning and control to maintain full employment is no longer seriously disputed. But there are other objectives relating to the balance of payments, the level of investment and the expansion of output which industry must also be made to serve.

... we reserve the right to extend public ownership in any industry or part of industry which, after thorough enquiry, is found to be seriously failing the nation ...

We also propose that the State should participate in expansion and development which is desirable from the national viewpoint by the provision of capital. In the past this has been done on a small scale, and generally in the form of loans. In future we believe that the State should also participate through the provision of equity capital. In this way the fruits of any enterprise would be shared by the community through an extension of public ownership.

The problem of control is given new emphasis by the emergence of large firms as the dominant institution in the private sector. Their special significance and greater public obligations are already recognised by the State in various ways. We do not wish to subject these firms to detailed supervision:

the great majority, indeed, are serving the nation well. But in view of their immense economic power, the community is entitled to satisfy itself that these independent boards act in conformity with the needs and interests of the nation. We propose to review the Companies' Acts with this end in view.

Finally there is the problem of what has been called 'social power'.

... As vast disparities in individual wealth begin to disappear, we do not wish to see a new order of privilege, based upon the control as distinct from the ownership of corporate wealth, taking its place. Nor do we wish to see the sharp distinctions of opportunity and status which in the past have been largely based on personal wealth, replaced by new and equally sharp distinctions determined by the social policies of corporate managers. ■

Crosland's economic and political analysis, however, was not universally accepted on the left. From the late 1950s a school of New Left thought began to emerge. Scathingly critical of the underlying inequality and continued dominance of a traditional class system in modern Britain, voices on the far left became increasingly influential as the optimism of the mid- to late 1950s gave way to the introspection and cynicism of the early 1960s.

6.12   Stuart Hall, 'Crosland territory', *New Left Review*, 1, 1, January and February 1960, pp. 2–3.

■ ... The errors in the argument fall into two categories. In the first place, the analysis of capitalism and its trends appears to us wrong: wrongly conceived, and not borne out by the facts. In the second place, the picture of prosperity is false, couched in individualist and Tory terms, and accepted on their face value, without a rigorous examination from socialist assumptions.

We have passed through a period of post-war prosperity. We have also passed through a period of post-war inflation, never dipping into the deep troughs of a major slumps, but oscillating, with alarming regularity, between jumping prices and industrial recession. The inflation question is still on the agenda – unresolved.

What is more, the managerial revolution is not what it seems ... the circle of the system remains the accumulation and investment of private wealth, and the making of profits ...

Can we really accept, at this stage in history, the definition of 'prosperity', of 'the Good Life', which is now the most popular Tory 'image'? If it is true, as we argue, that the system has not [provided] and cannot provide for what we may generally call the public, social, and community needs of the society ... how is it that we have been driven into the position of basing a socialist case on a capitalist view of life, a propertied interpretation of human 'needs'? If socialism has roots anywhere, it is in the concept of a community of equals, in the moral principle of sharing and co-operation, in the planned command of skills and resources so that they can be made to serve the full needs of the community. If we abandon this we have abandoned everything for which socialism stands ...

The 'ends' are contained by the 'means', then. If it is really a classless society we want, we must face up to the fact that the system which we are trying to tame, which provides Mr Macmillan's kind of 'prosperity' on the one hand, is what generates class power on the other. Behind the back of the Welfare Revolution, a revival of the class system has silently taken place: and the more profitable it is to supply the consumer needs of the community, the more robust the owners, controllers and managers of the system will become, the sounder their social position, the more stable their personal prospects, the greater the gaps in income and privilege, the more divided the society ... ■

6.13   Philip Zec cartoon, *Daily Herald*, 8 April 1959.

Trouble on the Horizon

Conservative policy objectives after 1951 remained fairly consistent: to reduce taxation and public expenditure, to raise productivity and exports, and to control inflation. Politically, it was essential to maintain a high level of employment and to maintain the social services which had proved so popular with the middle as well as the working classes. All of these aims were possible in the short term, given the unique set of circumstances in the international economy from 1952. But voices within the government and the Treasury warned consistently that reduced taxation, rising wages, high public expenditure and low inflation were simply unsustainable. These problems were addressed with increasing urgency in the 1951–64 period, but with limited success.

While Churchill was Prime Minister, 'appeasement' of the trade unions was prioritised by the government, in spite of Treasury fears over the pace of wage rises. In document 6.14 Butler recalls how Churchill and his Minister of Labour, Walter Monckton, settled a threatened rail strike in 1953.

6.14   **R.A. Butler,** *The Art of Memory,* **London, Hodder & Stoughton, 1982, p. 137.**

■ The railway crisis of 1953 was one of the most important problems with which Walter had to deal. I had several talks with Winston about this and he said to me, 'We cannot have a railway strike, it would be so disturbing to all of us. You will never get home, nobody will be able to see their wives.' I said at the time that it was rather important from the point of view of the economy that we should not have wage increases which we could not afford. Winston, typical of his more human side, firmly backed Walter in his efforts to avoid a railway strike which would have paralysed the country over Christmas. He averted the crisis in masterly fashion and was much praised. Many considered it the greatest triumph of Monckton's political life, although the *Economist* struck a sombre note with its suggestion that 'the railway rumpus' had been handled with 'sympathy, patience and funk'.

In the case of myself, I had an interesting experience. I was rung up about midnight by Winston Churchill who said, 'Walter and I settled the railway strike so you won't be troubled any more.' I said, 'On what terms have you settled it?' and Winston answered me, 'Theirs, old cock! We did not like to keep you up.' I was up nearly every night until one o'clock doing my boxes. Of course I could have been present. ■

After the 1955 general election, which increased the government's majority, Conservative fears for the economy were more openly addressed. In 1956 the decision was taken to publish a white paper on full employment, which warned bluntly of the dangers of inflation and called for wage restraint.

6.15   *The Economic Implications of Full Employment,* **March 1956 (London, HMSO, Cmd 9725, PP XXXVI, 1956, pp. 2–11).**

■ 1. The White Paper on Employment Policy (Cmd. 6527), issued by the Coalition Government in May 1944, set out the policies to be pursued after the war to maintain a high and stable level of employment and to combine this with a rising standard of living. These policies have been applied with considerable success. Full employment has, in fact, been maintained in most parts of the country over practically the whole of the past ten years, and we are to-day consuming more as a nation than we have ever done before. But full employment has brought with it one problem to which we have not yet found a satisfactory solution: yet, unless we do find the solution, it will be more difficult to achieve a further advance in living standards, and full employment itself may be threatened. The problem is that of continually rising prices. It affects everyone, and everyone must contribute if it is to be solved ...

19. Our overseas earnings must be increased if we are to pay for the imports needed to sustain an expanding economy, to provide for overseas investment, and to build up our reserves. The necessary expansion of exports will depend for its realisation on two factors – first, a continuing growth of production and trade throughout the world; second, our own ability to secure a sufficient share of this growing trade ...

20. An adequate volume of exports will depend above all upon the competitive strength of our goods in overseas markets. That strength is itself the outcome of many factors – the quality of the product, promptness of delivery, effective salesmanship, good after-sales service, and so forth. But the basic factor is price. Unless our prices are fully competitive, our exports will be inadequate for our vital national needs, our currency will not retain its value in world markets, and unemployment will result from shortage of imported raw materials ...

23. A weakening of the balance of payments is the most obvious and immediate consequence of a disproportionate rise in costs and prices. But such a rise, if it persists, has other, and no less serious, effects at home. The future growth of the economy will depend upon a sustained expansion of investment; and the rate of investment which we can afford will depend on our willingness to save ... This willingness itself derives from a basic confidence that money will broadly retain its value ...

24. But the effects of a rising price level have a much more direct and more immediately personal impact. Continually rising prices are an obvious social evil. For many people this evil is obscured by the fact that they either are, or believe themselves to be, able to secure increases in their incomes to offset the rise in prices; and although their pressure for higher incomes itself adds to the pressure on prices and they do not in fact gain very much from the rise in incomes, at least they do not lose very much from the rise in prices ...

26. In order to maintain full employment the Government must ensure that the level of demand for goods and services is high and rises steadily as productive capacity grows. This means a strong demand for labour, and good opportunities to sell goods and services profitably. In these conditions it is open to employees to insist on large wage increases, and it is often possible for employers to grant them and pass on the cost to the consumer, so maintaining their profit margins. This is the dilemma which confronts the country. If the prosperous economic conditions necessary to maintain full

employment are exploited by trade unions and business men, price stability and full employment become incompatible. The solution lies in self-restraint in making wage claims and fixing profit margins and prices, so that total money income rises no faster than total output …

27. How fast output rises depends on our success in raising productivity. The achievement of a sustained increase in productivity calls for contributions from both management and labour. Management must strive to ensure the maximum expansion of output by progressive investment in the most efficient capital assets, by the introduction of the most modern industrial techniques and by the elimination of all restrictive practices which inhibit the economic growth of production. The contribution of labour lies in cooperating to the full in the adoption of new methods of working and in setting aside all practices which, however much they may have been justified in the past as means of safeguarding status, conditions of work, or the security of employment itself, are not appropriate in conditions of full employment. ■

Frank Cousins, leader of the Transport and General Workers' Union, expressed the growing anger of many trade unionists in 1956, when he moved a motion at the Trades Union Congress which lashed out at government calls for wage restraint to control inflation. Inflation, he argued, must not be brought under control at the expense of the working-class standard of living, which was easily eroded as the retail price index rose.

6.16   **Frank Cousins, speech to the Trades Union Congress, 1956** (*Report of the Proceedings of the Eighty-Eighth Annual Trades Union Congress, London, TUC, 1956, pp. 399–400*).

■ … I would suggest that a motion of the character that we put forward, endorsed and adopted with some additions by some of the most responsible unions in this country, demonstrates what they collectively feel about this economic problem. Secondly, the motion does not portray a sudden upheaval of thought within the Trade Union Movement. It is a cumulative development. It is a recognition of a situation which has been created by this Government …

We do not share the view that it is not of any great consequence which political party is in power when you are facing an economic problem. We think it matters very much. We think that a Government which, by its very nature, represents labouring groups and is pledged by its election policies to look after the interests of the working class, and in making those policies, intends to carry them out, is more ready to discuss and examine properly with us the effects of those policies. You will know, of course, that Mr Macmillan has said several times recently that there is a medium by which the trade unions can talk with the Government: through the TUC and the Joint Advisory Council such representations as they may wish to make can be made at any time. Of course they can. Of course they have been made; and of course no notice has been taken of them ...

Now if you turn to the second paragraph of the motion you will see that we ask Congress to assert 'the right of Labour to bargain on equal terms with Capital and to use its bargaining strength to protect the workers from the dislocations of an unplanned economy'. We mean that. We assert that right. We say that we want to preserve that right. We accept that in a period of 'freedom for all' we are part of the 'all'. When listening to Government pronouncements which talk of sharing sacrifices among us all, we sometimes wonder whether the word has a double meaning. The plurality of 'all' will be accepted by us as grammatically correct. Let them go ahead with their 'freedom'. We have told them where it will take them: it will take them straight into the arms of the next Labour Government. But in the intervening period we are not prepared to sit down and see our members' conditions worsened.

... In the period while high profits are being taken and prices are being raised without any regard to the overall economic problem of the country – the export markets – we shall do all we can to protect the rights of the people we represent ...

We are not being asked by the Chancellor of the Exchequer to agree that the standard of living of the people we represent should remain as it is; we are asked to agree that it should be worse. There is no purpose in their policy if that is not so. They have told us that if they could save £750,000,000 on the Defence Bill they would be economically sound. Then let them save it there, not on wages.

Finally, let us say to them, not only by our words to-day but by our actions in the future, that we are not impressed by a Chancellor of the Exchequer who says he would like to come here and address the TUC. What does he think it is – a film festival? We will welcome a Chancellor of the Exchequer but we will wait for one – we will wait for a Labour Chancellor of the Exchequer. ■

A sudden and severe speculative run on Britain's gold reserves in the late summer of 1957 led to a new determination to maintain the value of sterling at home and abroad, by confronting what some saw as the underlying problems of wage-push inflation and high public spending. In a sudden change of policy the Chancellor, Peter Thorneycroft, introduced a series of deflationary measures in September. Moreover, he determined to halt – and even reverse in real terms – the rise in public expenditure and fought within the Cabinet over the following months to reduce the budget estimates. Frustration over Macmillan's failure to support this policy ultimately led to the resignation of Thorneycroft and two of his junior ministers at the Treasury, Enoch Powell and Nigel Birch, in January 1958. The minutes of the Cabinet meeting which preceded the resignations give some indication of the battle raging inside the government at this time.

6.17　**The wage–price 'spiral', 1951–64 (chart derived from R. Taylor, *The Trade Union Question in British Politics*, Oxford, Blackwell, 1993, p. 385).**

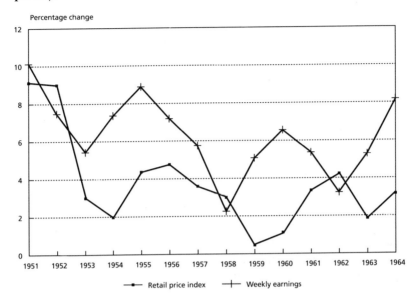

6.18　**Cabinet minutes, 5 January 1958 (PRO CAB 128/32 I, CC(58)3rd, pp. 5–7).**

■ *The Chancellor of the Exchequer* said that he conceived it to be his duty not to accept Departmental Estimates foreshadowing an increase of Government expenditure in 1958–59 over the level of 1957–58. The course of the discussion had shown that the Cabinet were not agreed, as he had hoped, on the importance of eliminating this increase … if the Government were wholly determined to press through their disinflationary policy … the cut of £76 millions which had already been secured would be increased by savings of £30 millions on the welfare services and a further reduction of some £22 millions on Service Votes. The total of nearly £130 millions would represent an approximation to his purpose of eliminating the whole of the £153 millions increase in expenditure; but he would still require the support of the Cabinet in searching, over the whole range of the remaining civil Estimates, for further economies in an effort to approach still more closely to this objective.

At this point *The Prime Minister* adjourned the meeting in order to enable Ministers to give further consideration to the issues involved.

When the discussion was resumed, *The Prime Minister* said that the Cabinet must seek to share with the Chancellor of the Exchequer the heavy burden of managing an economy which, though potentially prosperous, was precariously balanced ... But disinflation, if enforced to the point at which it created a stagnant economy or provoked a new outbreak of industrial unrest, would defeat its own ends; and, if the individual measures proposed by the Chancellor had been criticised, this criticism was evidence of the concern of other members of the Cabinet that a gain in respect of one aspect of the Government's policies should not be offset by a loss in respect of others.

... it was unreasonable that Ministers should be expected, at very short notice, to give a firm undertaking to enforce economies of £30 millions in the welfare services together with further unspecified economies on the other civil Votes ...

The defence Estimates had already been severely cut, and it was doubtful whether they could properly and safely be expected to suffer any further reductions ...

The Chancellor of the Exchequer said that he had never wavered in his view that Government expenditure in 1958–59 should not substantially exceed the level in 1957–58 and that, although he was well aware of the difficulties entailed by some of the measures to this end which he had proposed, he must now consider his own position in light of the Prime Minister's summary of the issues at stake. ■

The continued difficulties of fighting such Cabinet battles on an annual basis, and growing dissatisfaction with the 'stop–go' style of economic management, led to consideration of alternative methods of economic control. In 1959, for example, the Radcliffe Report on the workings of the monetary system considered the value of controlling the money supply, that is, the amount of money in circulation, in stabilising the economy. The report played down the use of such instruments as a magic cure for economic ills; this conclusion would prove increasingly controversial over the following years, as monetarist economics began to be taken more seriously.

6.19 *Committee on the Working of the Monetary System: Report* (Radcliffe Report), August 1959 (London, HMSO, Cmnd 827, PP XVII, 1958–9, p. 183).

■ 514. It will be seen that our review of monetary measures has not led us to any positive and simple recommendations. No method, new or old, provides the remedy for all our troubles. We do not find any solution of the problem of influencing total demand in more violent manipulation of interest rates; we find control of the supply of money to be no more than an important facet of debt management; we cannot recommend any substantial change in the rules under which the banks operate; we do not regard the capital issues control as useful in ordinary times; and we believe that there are narrow limits to the usefulness of hire purchase controls. On the other hand, we believe that the authorities could make more deliberate use of interest rates. The level of these is relevant to the working of the economic system and, although many effects of changes in them are slow to work, some effect comes fairly rapidly through liquidity disturbances created by these changes … But, when all has been said on the possibility of monetary action and of its likely efficacy, our conclusion is that monetary measures cannot alone be relied upon to keep in nice balance an economy subject to major strains from both without and within. Monetary measures can help, but that is all. ■

Stagnation and the New Vogue for Planning

In the years following the 1959 election, concern over Britain's poor economic performance continued to grow. Already by 1961 the complacency of the affluent society had been replaced by deep-seated concern over Britain's sluggish growth rate.

The publication of the economic journalist Michael Shanks's critique, The Stagnant Society *in 1961 was one example of the new mood of self-examination.*

6.20 **Michael Shanks, *The Stagnant Society,* Harmondsworth, Penguin, 1961, pp. 232–3.**

■ What sort of an island do we want to be? This is the question to which we come back in the end. A lotus island of easy, tolerant ways, bathed in the golden glow of an imperial sunset, shielded from discontent by a threadbare welfare state and an acceptance of genteel poverty? Or the tough dynamic race we have been in the past, striving always to better ourselves, seeking new worlds to conquer in place of those we have lost, ready to accept growing pains as the price of growth?

It is easy to pose this challenge rhetorically. It is less easy to bring ourselves to acccpt all the implications that a decision to opt for growth would entail. One does not achieve expansion simply by deciding that it would be a good thing to have …

If we are to succeed, it will be because we are determined as a nation to succeed, and because we are prepared to subordinate all other considerations – personal or sectional – to this national aim …

This does not mean that we must embrace a thoroughgoing materialist philosophy, accepting much wider differences in wealth as the rewards of a more competitive society. On the contrary, expansion demands as we have seen a greater social discipline, a greater willingness to sacrifice personal gain in the common interest. Nothing about this will be easy, nothing immediately congenial. At every stage of the journey there will be the temptation to refuse the hurdle, to take the easy way out, to go back to the lotus land and impoverishing gentility, to turn in on ourselves and try to forget the bustling, menacing, ungrateful world outside.

For let us be clear about the alternative. The choice between growth and stagnation, though it will underlie every one of the agonizing decisions which will face the British people over the next few years, will seldom if ever be posed directly in black and white. There will always be extraneous issues intruding, special complications or mitigating factors. And if we refuse the hurdle – if the unions or the Labour Party or the British people as a whole duck the challenges before them – the consequences will not be immediately catastrophic. The trumpet of doom will not sound at once. It may be some time before the consequences become noticeable at all. All that will happen is that the slow slide towards impotence and failure will be accelerated – slowly at first, then faster and faster – until we see the blue waters below us, and it is too late to do anything about it. ■

In 1960 and 1961, under the Chancellorship of Selwyn Lloyd, new machinery for nation-al planning was introduced in an attempt to address the problem of economic 'decline'. It was clear by then that short-term measures of economic management, such as hire-purchase restrictions, unacceptably undermined business confidence and were clumsy in application. There was an increasing belief both inside and outside the government that steady and even growth could be achieved only by forecasting economic performance and expenditure over a period of several years. In particular, Lloyd proposed the estab-lishment of an independent forum, the National Economic Development Council (NEDC, or 'Neddy'), in which ministers, business and trade union leaders could consult each other regularly on important issues. Many ministers and officials hoped that the NEDC would make an incomes policy a political feasibility. The need for tripartite discussion on the pace of wage rises had become clearer with the controversy and unpopularity which had surrounded Lloyd's introduction of a public sector 'pay pause' between July 1961 and April 1962.

6.21 Selwyn Lloyd, letter proposing the establishment of the NEDC, 16 September 1961 (PRO CAB 129/106, C(61)136, pp. 1–2).

■ Following upon my meetings with both sides of industry about a new approach to economic planning on a national scale, I have given careful thought to the various suggestions which have been made. In order to for-ward our joint consideration of these matters I set out in this letter, as promised, some specific proposals.

I believe that the time has come to establish new and more effective machinery for the co-ordination of plans and forecasts for the main sectors of our economy. There is a need to study centrally the plans and prospects of our main industries, to correlate them with each other and with the Government's plans for the public sector, and to see how in aggregate they contribute to, and fit in with, the prospects for the economy as a whole, including the vital external balance of payments. This should be of assis-tance in the promotion of more rapid and sustained economic growth, both by the creation of a climate favourable to expansion and by directing atten-tion to the correction of weaknesses in our economic structure.

I am anxious to secure that both sides of industry, on whose co-operation the fulfilment of our objectives must significantly depend, should participate fully with the Government in all stages of the process. I hope they would, under the arrangements proposed below, obtain a picture, more continuous and comprehensive than has hitherto been available, of the long-term problems in the development of our economy: and this should enhance the value of their advice on, and efforts in, the search for solutions. They would also have better opportunities to help in the moulding of the economic policies of the Government at the formative stage.

Clearly, we shall need some new machinery for this work. I envisage that this might take the following form. First, I propose the creation of a National Economic Development Council. The Chancellor of the Exchequer would be the Chairman and one or two other Ministers, such as the President of the Board of Trade and the Minister of Labour, would be members. The other members of the Council, who would be appointed by the Chancellor after appropriate consultations, would be drawn from the trade unions and from the management side of private and nationalised industry, with perhaps some independent members. I would aim at a total membership of, say, about twenty.

The functions of the Council would be to consider, and if necessary commission, studies relevant to the economic objectives which I have indicated earlier in this letter and to give advice to the Government and to industry on the policies to secure these objectives. The Council would be free and indeed would be expected to comment on the conditions necessary for faster economic growth and on measures whereby such conditions might be created. Responsibility for final decisions on matters of Government policy must of course remain with the Government, but I have no doubt that the Council's recommendations would carry great weight, not only with the Government, but with all others concerned. I would expect that the recommendations and advice of the council would normally be made public: how this could best be done will need further discussion … ■

The need to overcome structural weakness in the British economy had a knock-on effect on social as well as economic policy. For example, in 1963 the Robbins Report on higher education recommended a rapid increase in the number of student places, paving the way for the expansion of the university sector. By 1966 seven new universities had been established.

6.22   Committee on Higher Education, *Higher Education: Report of the Committee Appointed by the Prime Minister under the Chairmanship of Lord Robbins,* **September 1963 (London, HMSO, Cmd 2154, PP XI, 1963, pp. 268, 276).**

■ 1. Our terms of reference instructed us to review the present pattern of higher education and to make suggestions for improving it. Our first task, therefore, after some preliminary discussion of principles, was to make a thorough survey of the existing situation in higher education in Great Britain and the historical trends of which it is the outcome ...

2. Comparisons with conditions abroad reveal a situation of some complexity. In the United States of America, the Soviet Union and certain Commonwealth countries the provision of higher education greatly exceeds our own ... when we compare published plans for future development many other countries are far ahead of us. If, as we believe, a highly educated population is essential to meet competitive pressures in the modern world, a much greater effort is necessary if we are to hold our own.

3. Our calculation of the future requirement for places in this country is based on an estimate of the numbers of young people who, on the present basis of student grants, will both be able to satisfy suitable entrance requirements for higher education and will wish to be admitted. Our investigations have suggested the existence of large reservoirs of untapped ability in the population, especially among girls ... we have arrived at a requirement of about 560,000 places for full-time students in all higher education in 1980/1, and of about 390,000 places in 1973/4, compared with 216,000 in 1962/3 ...

38. The Report concludes by drawing attention to an educational emergency now confronting higher education because of the arrival at the ages of seventeen and eighteen of the very large numbers of children born immediately after the second world war. In our judgment, this is an emergency of the same importance as the emergency produced by demobilisation after the last war and demanding the same type of extraordinary measures to meet it. If the needs of this situation are not adequately met by immediate government action, many of our plans for long-term expansion will be seriously endangered. ■

CHAPTER SEVEN

Conservative Hegemony: Politics, 1951–64

WHEN the Conservative Party entered office in October 1951, there were no widespread expectations that the victory would last. But the Conservatives, aided in particular by the favourable turn of economic events discussed in Chapter 6, went on to increase their majority in the general election of 1955, and they won again in 1959. The final years of this period of Conservative administration saw the rapid erosion of public support for a government which seemed increasingly out of touch with the aspirations of white-collar workers, and this accounted for a brief revival of Liberal Party fortunes in the early 1960s.

Nevertheless, between 1951 and 1964 Britain experienced thirteen years of uninterrupted Conservative political hegemony. Part of the explanation for this lies in the failure of the Labour Party to present a united platform to the electorate. Indeed, the divisions which had erupted over the cost of rearmament in 1950 continued to characterise Labour's internal politics in these years. The third election loss in a row, in 1959, was the catalyst for renewed debate over the first principles of Labour's brand of democratic socialism. After Hugh Gaitskell's untimely death in January 1963, the party settled uneasily under the leadership of the centre-left leader Harold Wilson.

In the mid-1950s new issues on the political agenda began to take over from those inherited from the wartime Coalition government. The unanticipated public controversy which surrounded the arrival of New Commonwealth immigrants in Britain from the late 1940s was debated with urgency from the late summer of 1958, following a series of attacks on West Indian communities in London and Nottingham. The advent of the hydrogen bomb led to the formation of the Campaign for Nuclear Disarmament earlier the same year, as discussed in Chapter 11. The success of CND as a mass movement of protest led to a wave of New Left criticism of British society which prepared the ground for the protest movements of the following decade.

Historians continue to argue over the extent of 'consensus' between the Conservative and Labour parties in the 1951–64 period. The ease of the transition to Conservative government in 1951, and the superficial absence of radical policy departures from Labour's agenda, led to the invention of 'Mr Butskell' in 1954 (see below). Increasingly, explanations for this policy convergence has come to focus on the structural features of the British political system in this period, as opposed to any unusual degree of agreement between the parties over the aims and objectives of policy.

The Conservatives in Power

When Winston Churchill was returned to No. 10 Downing Street in October 1951 he was determined to prevent domestic conflict at a time of increasing international tension. The electoral defeats of 1945 and 1950 and the clear popularity of many of the postwar reforms introduced by Clement Attlee's Labour government meant that the new administration took care to stick to a popular domestic agenda. Churchill was determined to create a broad mandate for his new administration. The government was careful to introduce potentially controversial policies gradually and with minimal disruption.

The diaries of Churchill's Joint Private Secretary, Sir John Colville, give some indication of the Prime Minister's domestic policy considerations.

7.1   **John Colville, diary, 1952 (in John Colville, *The Fringes of Power: Downing Street Diaries, 1939–1955*, London, Hodder & Stoughton, 1985, pp. 643–4).**

■ *Saturday, March 22nd–Sunday, March 23rd*

Drove to Chequers with the PM … In the long gallery on Sunday night, after the rest had gone to bed, he told Christopher [Soames] and me that the programme of the Tory Party must be: 'Houses and meat and not being scuppered'. He didn't feel quite happy about the latter though he does not himself think war probable unless the Americans lose patience. As he subsequently added, perhaps 'not being broke' is going to be our major difficulty and preoccupation …

Friday, April 4th

… This morning the results of the LCC elections, which went strongly for the socialists, were published. The PM took them well though he found them a shock. The reason, I have no doubt, is that the country hoped a Tory Government would mean relaxations and more food: in fact it has meant controls as stringent as ever and severer rationing. ■

The government's position was precarious. As the chart shown as document 7.2 illustrates, the Conservatives ran consistently behind Labour in the opinion polls until the spring of 1953; and indeed, throughout the 1951–5 period the government proved unable to make a popular breakthrough. Unfavourable local and by-election results led to considerable restlessness within the Conservative Party. Churchill was criticised for failing to take a dynamic policy lead, relying instead upon mostly ageing wartime colleagues whom he appointed as peacetime 'overlords' to oversee major areas of policy.

7.2   **Public opinion polls on voting preferences, 1952–5 (chart derived from D. Butler and G. Butler (eds), *British Political Facts, 1900–1985*, London, Macmillan, 6th edn, 1986, pp. 254–5).**

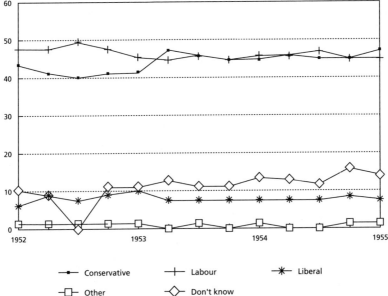

Voting intentions (percentage)

7.3   **'Political diary', (Hugh Massingham), *Observer*, 22 June 1952.**

■ A pamphlet recently issued by the Conservative Central Office tersely puts in its headlines the dilemma which faces the Government. At the top, on the front page, are the warning words, THE CRISIS. And below comes the more hopeful reflection, AND MR BUTLER'S BENEFITS.

The document then goes on to make an able synthesis of what many people feel, perhaps wrongly, are two irreconcilable conceptions. Nor is it only the ignorant public that is confused.

The real reason why the Conservative back-benchers are so touchy and rebellious is that the Government seems to them to be offering an unbalanced diet of gruel and caviar.

The point was admirably put yesterday by Mr Aubrey Jones, who sits for one of the Birmingham constituencies. 'For the time being,' he said, 'but for the time being only, the Government has restored confidence. Now it has to do more: it has to prove that the confidence is justified.

'How can it best be done? Certainly not by tacking from severity to softness and back again. Either the Government can do what it thinks right in the country's interest or it can do what it is told the country likes. If it just does the second, not only Britain will go down: the Conservative Party will go down too, for Labour will outbid it every time. The alternative is that the Government must steer a straight, even, at times, a severe, course, and the party in the country must see that it does not waver.'

These words faithfully express the attitude of many moderate Conservatives in the House, and some of them have reacted as one might have expected – they are saying that Mr Churchill is the real cause of all the indecision. Certainly Mr Churchill must take part of the blame if the Government has been weak and vacillating – there has never been a Premier who has dominated his colleagues as he has done ...

Up to now Ministers cannot be said to have handled their rank and file very cleverly. No real attempt has been made to explain policy. Whenever the snarling off-stage has penetrated to the Cabinet, the usual decision seems to have been to feed the back-benchers with an overlord. The genial and gracious Lord Leathers will probably never be the same since he went through this hair-raising experience ...It is reported that since he met the 1922 committee he has become hopelessly gun-shy ...

Mr Churchill no doubt has his faults, but he is still a giant and makes many of his colleagues look like pygmies. There are, too, some MPs who are by no means certain that Mr Eden would be an improvement, even though supported by Mr Butler and Mr Macmillan. For the crisis in the Conservative Party is not only over policy, but also over men, and Mr Eden's personal entourage hardly encourages the belief that he is a good judge of character ...

But although it is impossible to believe in any organised rebellion – at least, at the moment – it does not follow that Mr Churchill can entirely ignore the genuine disquiet among his rank and file. There is always the chance of an accidental explosion if the Prime Minister allows things to drift too far. ∎

Although the profile of the Cabinet grew younger as the government continued, Churchill's physical frailty became increasingly obvious after he suffered a major stroke in June 1953. Speculation over his retirement and the appointment of a successor further weakened his authority. Churchill was finally prevailed upon to retire in April 1955, but resisted standing down until the last moment. His successor, Anthony Eden, gives in his diary a flavour of the backstage machinations which proved necessary to unseat the great man.

7.4   Anthony Eden, diary, 1952 (quoted in R.R. James, *Anthony Eden,* London, Weidenfeld & Nicolson, 1986, pp. 392–3).

■ *21 December*

… Set out for No. 10 at 9.30. Found Clemmie there with W. She was charming & worried at my colour. W. said he supposed I had been living too well in Paris. Then when Clemmie had gone after a long pause he said 'What do you want to see me about?' in his most aggressive tone.

I said that he had had my letter and said he would be ready to discuss it. And slowly the argument began. At first he would have nothing. All was as well as possible. There was no hurry for an election or for him to hand over, the end of June or July would do very well. Laboriously I explained first that the new administration should have a chance to establish itself with the public. This gave us none. Second that it would place me in a much stronger position if I could take over in a month when an election was possible. Then, if my authority or mandate was challenged I would have the option either to fight it out in Parliament or to say very well let the country judge, & go to the country. This I could not do in July.

He wasn't much interested in this but when I had made it quite clear that I was not interested either in taking over at the end of June he eventually agreed to meeting at 3 pm with the people I chose. But it was all most grudging. There was much rather cruel 'divide et impera'. For instance, he asked me how I got on with Harold [Macmillan]. I said 'very well, why?'. He replied 'Oh, he is very ambitious'. I laughed.

22 December

Meeting of Ministers at 3 pm on lines I had asked for last night. Not a pleasant business … After a certain amount of further desultory conversation & explanation of value of an option to a new Govt, W. rounded on me and said it was clear we wanted him out. Nobody contradicted him …

At the end W. said menacingly that he would think over what his colleagues had said & let them know his decision. Whatever it was he hoped it would not affect their present relationship with him. Nobody quailed. James [Stuart] said afterwards to me that it had been painful but absolutely necessary. He had to be told he could not pursue a course of 'such utter selfishness'.

… What the result of all this may be I cannot tell except that the old man feels bitterly towards me, but this I cannot help. The colleagues are unanimous about drawling Cabinets, the failure to take decisions, the general atmosphere of 'après moi le déluge' & someone had to give a heave. ■

7.5 **L.G. Illingworth, 'On the Premier's probable retirement',**
Punch **cartoon, 3 February 1954.**

In the course of preparing for the general election of May 1955, the Conservatives targeted the undecided middle-class voter. Both Conservative and Labour maintained a solid base of support; the vote of the 10 to 15 per cent of the electorate which was undecided determined the outcome of an election. The Research Study Group set up by the Conservative leadership to prepare a manifesto considered how to capture this middle ground. The paradox was in trying to deliver more spending on health and education while at the same time reducing taxation.

7.6 **Conservative Party Research Study Group minutes, 13 October 1954 (CPA CRD2/49/30).**

■ *Note of the 26th Meeting of Research Study Group*

13 October 1954

Present: Mr Brooke, Mr Macleod, Mr Fraser, Mr Dear, Mr Goldman, Mr Graham, Miss Naismith.

....

The Middle Classes

A discussion on the Middle Classes arose from RSG/61. Mr Macleod thought it was essential that we should become increasingly selective in our policy and do more to help the middle classes. Mr Goldman drew attention to Ivor Jennings's 'Middle Slice' of the nation, to whom we should make our appeal. Mr Fraser suggested the £500 to £1000 income group. Mr Brooke agreed with Mr Macleod; there were other deserving people besides the Old Age Pensioners who have already been promised help.

Various suggestions were made. Mr Macleod thought it logical to go ahead with his scheme for concessions to private patients and felt strongly that certain proposals of the kind should go into the manifesto. Mr Fraser suggested income tax relief for those who wished to educate their children privately. (Mr Macleod said that he had been 'converted' on this point.) Mr Dear suggested greater ability to opt out of the Health Service and implementation of some of the small tax concessions ... Mr Goldman wanted more spent on health and education – in his view the middle classes had benefited more from the Health Service than from any other single piece of social legislation, but the service had been starved of money.

Mr Macleod felt that useful points that could not be covered by immediate legislation should be put in the manifesto and suggested that the Department should prepare notes on the specific questions of help to the middle classes. Mr Fraser undertook to have these produced for the next meeting. ■

7.7 **Conservative Party general election poster, 1955 (Conservative Party Archives).**

Eden's victory in the May 1955 election increased the Government's majority to fifty-eight. The victory was partly due to the popularity of R.A. Butler's April 1955 Budget, which by cutting income taxes did nothing to check an economy that was showing clear signs of overheating. When Butler had to introduce an emergency Budget in the autumn to rectify matters, the opposition scornfully charged that the government had put electoral considerations before the health of the economy.

7.8   Hugh Gaitskell, speech on the Budget proposals, 27 October 1955 (*Hansard*, 5th ser., 545: 390, 399–400, 405–6).

■ The people of this country were generally surprised when they heard the announcement of an autumn Budget. Today, having heard its contents, they are even more surprised. An autumn Budget is, of course, a most unusual event and admittedly, in most cases, an unpleasant event. It signifies the need for emergency action, because in this country chancellors of the Exchequer are normally expected to budget for a year ahead and not to chop and change in the middle. If they do chop and change there must be good reason for it …

The evidence is complete and convincing. The Chancellor has made a number of grave errors of policy. He has persistently and wilfully misled the public about the economic situation and he has done it for electoral reasons. This Budget which we are considering is necessary because the April Budget – a masterpiece of deception – actively encouraged instead of damping down additional spending. Now, having bought his votes with a bribe, the Chancellor is forced – as he knew he would be – to dishonour the cheque. Last night, on television, he said he did not believe in making promises. He is much cleverer than that. He simply gives the money away at the time of the Election and then takes it back afterwards …

This Budget would not have been necessary if the April Budget had been an honest Budget. It is no answer to say that it is investment that has increased more than consumption, because that would and could have been taken into account in an honest Budget in April. Who was it, however, who gained in April from the tax concessions? …

… This was a Budget, the April Budget, which was overwhelmingly in favour of the better-off half of the community. [*Interruption.*] Yes, the better-off half of the community …

… It gave the general impression of great prosperity and it benefited a very large number of people. I would even concede this, that it is quite likely that not 50 per cent. but 52 per cent. of the population were better off as a result of it. It was very neatly devised – just enough to give the government the majority they wanted … ■

The Suez Crisis of 1956 destroyed Eden's health and his career. Before he resigned, however, he circulated a short memorandum on the general position of the country in the wake of the crisis. This 'last will and testament' from a man whose intimate involvement with British politics and foreign policy had begun well before the Second World War is a sobering indication of the pressures on British policy-makers in this period.

7.9   Anthony Eden, memorandum, 28 December 1956 (PRO PREM 11/1138).

▨ We have to try to assess the lessons of Suez. the first is that if we are to play an independent part in the world, even on a more modest scale than we have done heretofore, we must ensure our financial and economic independence. Since we have no raw materials but coal, this means that we must excel in technical knowledge. This in its turn affects our military plans.

Too many of our scientists are working for the fighting Services. I think that I have seen a figure of two-thirds. Anything of this order must be unacceptable at the present time. On the other hand, some progress with the military aspects of the development of the hydrogen bomb can no doubt be useful for civil purposes also. It seems therefore that we have need to keep the balance between civil and military development, leaning rather more towards the former in our nuclear programme.

In the strategic sphere we have to do some rethinking about our areas of influence and the military bases on which they must rest. Some of the latter seem of doubtful value in the light of our Suez experience ...

... one of the lessons of Suez is surely that we need a smaller force that is more mobile and more moderate in its equipment. This probably means that we have in proportion to our total army too much armour and too much infantry and too small a paratroop force. We cannot contemplate keeping an army in Germany which is numerically much more that half its present numbers and the cost will have to come down proportionately ...

The most anxious fact on the home front is I think the alarming increase in the cost of the welfare state. Some of this, e.g. education, is a necessary part of our effort to maintain a leading position in new industrial developments. Other aspects of this spending are less directly related to our struggle for existence. I have long been anxious, as I know have the Lord Privy Seal and the Chancellor, to do something to encourage our younger and gifted leaders in science and industry to stay with us. The present burden of taxation leaves them with little incentive except patriotism. We shall not have adjusted our problems until the younger generation here can feel that they live in a community which is leading in industrial development and can reasonably expect a fair reward for their brains and application.

The conclusion of all this is surely that we must review our world position and our domestic capacity more searchingly in the light of the Suez experience, which has not so much changed our fortunes as revealed realities.

While the consequences of this examination may be to determine us to work more closely with Europe, carrying with us, we hope, our closest friends in the Commonwealth in such development, here too we must be under no illusion. Europe will not welcome us simply because at the moment it may appear to suit us to look to them. The timing and the conviction of our approach may be decisive in their influence on those with whom we plan to work. ■

After Eden's resignation in January 1957, Harold Macmillan became Prime Minister. Macmillan's style of premiership was far more successful than Eden's had been. Within months of the Suez Crisis, he had successfully asserted a more purposeful and well-managed sense of direction within the Cabinet.

7.10   David Maxwell Fyfe, *Political Adventure: The Memoirs of the Earl of Kilmuir*, London, Weidenfeld & Nicolson, 1962, p. 308.

■ On the home political front, it was clear by the end of 1957 that the Government had turned the corner. It is impossible to over-emphasize the personal. contribution of the Prime Minister to this renaissance. From the very beginning of his Premiership there had been a new 'feel' about the Government. Eden's chronic restlessness, which had sensibly affected all his colleagues, was replaced by a central calmness which provided a wonderful contrast with 1955–56. Macmillan's approach to Cabinet business was businesslike and firm; all important issues would be dealt with by the Cabinet, to remove the very real possibility that some unconsidered independent action by a junior Minister might damage the Government as a whole. He was always accessible to his colleagues, and sedulously nursed the Party in the House of Commons. On the whole, he interfered less in Departmental matters than Eden, unless he judged that they merited Cabinet consideration. He always gave the impression, even in the darkest hours, that everything was going according to plan. He refused to be shaken by unexpected and unfortunate reverses, of which the Devlin Report and the deaths at Hola Camp were two examples. He imparted confidence to his colleagues and the Party in Parliament, and their confidence spread to the constituencies. It was a remarkable example of how a political revival must start from the top. ■

Macmillan's success was derived from a mood of affluence and optimism which characterised the last years of the decade. Although meant initially as a political criticism, the cartoonist Vicky's invention of the character 'Supermac' soon became a positive factor in his public image. In spite of the recent pain of Suez, the Conservative Party entered the general election campaign of 1959 in a good position. Labour ran a strong campaign under the leadership of Hugh Gaitskell, but the Conservatives nevertheless managed to increase their majority.

7.11 'Vicky', 'Supermac', *Evening Standard* **cartoon, 6 November 1958.**

7.12 *The Next Five Years,* **Conservative Party election manifesto, 1959 (Conservative Party Archives).**

■ THE CONSERVATIVE RECORD

Eight years ago was a turning point in British history. The Labour Government had failed in grappling with the problems of the post-war world. Under Conservative leadership this country set out upon a new path. It is leading to prosperity and opportunity for all.

The British economy is sounder today than at any time since the first world war. Sterling has been re-established as a strong and respected currency. Under Conservative government we have earned abroad £1,600 million more than we have spent. Our exports have reached the highest peak ever. Overseas, mostly in the Commonwealth, we are investing nearly double what we could manage eight years ago. Capital investment at home, to build for the future, is over half as large again. To match this, and make it possible, people are saving more than ever before.

The paraphernalia of controls have been swept away. The call-up is being abolished. We have cut taxes in seven Budgets, whilst continuing to develop the social services. We have provided over two million new homes and almost two million new school places, a better health service and a modern pensions plan. We have now stabilised the cost of living while maintaining full employment. We have shown that Conservative freedom works. Life is better with the Conservatives.

In the international field, thanks to the initiative of the Conservative Government, the diplomatic deadlock between East and West has now been broken. The Prime Minister's visit to Russia in February began a sequence of events which has led to the present easing of tension. The proposed exchange of visits between President Eisenhower and Mr Khrushchev is the most recent proof of this. It is our determination to see that this process continues and to make a success of the important negotiations which we trust will follow.

The main issues at this election are therefore simple: (1) Do you want to go ahead on the lines which have brought prosperity at home? (2) Do you want your present leaders to represent you abroad? ■

7.13   **Trog (Wally Fawkes), 'Well, gentlemen, I think we all fought a good fight ...',** *Spectator* **cartoon, 16 October 1959.**

Labour in Opposition

After being returned to opposition at the end of 1951, the Labour Party continued to be beset by the divisions between its left and right wings, led respectively by the former Cabinet ministers Aneurin Bevan and Hugh Gaitskell. Debate within the party centred at first on the causes of defeat and future electoral strategy.

Doctrinal tension within the Labour Party was fuelled by the organisation of Bevanite MPs on a more formal basis in 1952. The Bevanite left argued that the party should stick to its traditional policy objectives of public ownership and planning, as well as develop a distinctly 'socialist' foreign policy. At the Labour Party Conference of 1952, held in Morecambe, the left captured all of the constituency section of the National Executive Committee. Hugh Dalton and Herbert Morrison both lost their seats on the NEC as a result. In document 7.14 the journalist and Bevanite MP Michael Foot describes the group sympathetically, in a passage from his biography of Bevan.

7.14   Michael Foot, *Aneurin Bevan: A Biography, Vol. II: 1945–1960*, London, Davis-Poynter, 1973, pp. 358–9, 373.

■ Since the opening of the new session [in January 1952] the Bevanites had sought to organize themselves into a more effective parliamentary group. On the suggestion of Ian Mikardo and on the precedent of the Keep Left group, it was agreed to elect a regular chairman – Harold Wilson was the first – and to meet at a regular time in the parliamentary week: 1.30 on Mondays. None of those participating in these secret rites thought at the outset that they might be indulging in some scandalous Mau Mau activity ... Unofficial groups had existed in Parliament ever since the first Witenagemot, and the Bevanites of the early 1950s imagined they were following a more recent precedent set by others, notably the XYZ Club, which had been talking politics over exclusive dinner tables since its foundation by Douglas Jay and a few others in the early 1940s. No one, after all, had ever suggested that the Keep Left group should be outlawed.

... In fact the group was considerably less organized than outsiders imagined and several insiders desired. What exact role the group should perform and what relationship it should seek with the rest of the Party was a perpetual subject of discussion within its own ranks. In the main, Ian Mikardo and Dick Crossman were the protagonists favouring a stronger, more tightly-knit group, while Bevan himself was more sensitively aware of the soreness this might provoke within the rest of the Party, and this disagreement impinged on another, the perpetual complaint that the group in general and Bevan in particular was much too slow in embarking on the thorough task of devising a complete new policy for the left. These discussions continued all through that year while a few of the newspapers gave the impression that Bevan, a mixture, say, of Cassius and Joseph Chamberlain, was engaged with his fellow conspirators in a relentless plot against the leaders. ■

The backbench pressures on the front-bench leaders of both main parties to adopt a more radical course in economic policy led to the invention of the character of 'Mr Butskell' in an article in the Economist *in 1954. The name was a humorous combination of 'Butler' and 'Gaitskell' – the latter being the last Labour Chancellor, under Attlee. The Chancellor of the Exchequer in modern Britain, it was argued, had two roles. First he was a policy moderator, admonishing extreme opinion within his party. Secondly, he had a duty as the chief economic policy-maker not to give in to political pressures, but to be brave enough to take the steps necessary to keep the economy on course. 'Mr Butskell's dilemma' was that he rarely showed the courage to do the right thing.*

7.15 'Mr Butskell's dilemma', *Economist*, 13 February 1954, p. 440.

■ Mr Butskell is already a well-known figure in dinner table conversations in both Westminster and Whitehall, and the time has come to introduce him to a wider audience. He is a composite of the present chancellor and the previous one ... Whenever there is a tendency to excess Conservatism within the Conservative party – such as a clamour for too much imperial preference, for a wild dash to convertibility, or even for a little more unemployment to teach the workers a lesson – Mr Butskell speaks up for the cause of moderation from the Government side of the House; when there is a clamour for even graver irresponsibilities from the Labour benches, Mr Butskell has hitherto spoken up from the other.

This admonitory role in Parliament is only one facet of his composite personality. It is in his policy-making – as distinct from policy-moderating – role that he runs into his perennial dilemma. He is willing to bolster up demand when there is slack in the economy, or to trim down demand a little (a very little) when there is a danger of inflation. But – and this is the secret – he has not yet shown himself to be a really strong character in the face of adversity; political pressures stand in his way. If ever external economic events make it necessary to cut down demand very ruthlessly, he is quite likely to run away; and the result is apt to be an economic crisis, which redounds to the disadvantage of the half of him that is in office and to the advantage of the half that is not. ■

By 1955 Bevan's disruptive behaviour culminated in an attempt, led by the Gaitskellites, to have him expelled from the Labour Party. This move was not supported by Attlee and failed narrowly. The episode contributed temporarily to a more harmonious climate within the party, and increasing speculation over the likely date of Attlee's retirement concentrated minds on the leadership elections to come. Even a chastened Bevan proved more willing to accept party discipline. In document 7.16 Gaitskell gives an account of the NEC meeting at which the expulsion was discussed.

7.16 Hugh Gaitskell, diary, 25 March 1955 (in P.M. Williams (ed), *The Diary of Hugh Gaitskell*, London, Cape, 1983, p. 389–91).

■ It became known in the course of the evening that Attlee had seen Bevan. I was afraid that this meant some new development, that Clem [Attlee] would spring a surprise. But it was not so. After Knight had moved the expulsion without making a speech, Clem at once intervened to say that Bevan had come to see him, but only for four minutes, to say that if he were expelled he would raise the question of Privilege ... There was a brief discussion after Clem had explained the situation ... But there was a strong reaction from all the non-Bevanites, who were justly indignant with Bevan for trying this bit of blackmail at the last minute. The discussion then proceeded. Jack Cooper made a strong and impressive speech, going to some extent into Bevan's past. Haworth then produced his amendment, which was a fantastic affair, more or less preventing Bevan from ever saying anything at all anywhere. It went in fact much too far, and nobody could have seriously expected him to sign it. He was supported by Gooch. It was, I think, at this point that Attlee intervened, as I had expected he would, saying that we ought to see him, and proposing that we should do so. He did not speak for long, and left it to Jim Griffiths, who followed him, to make the usual rather passionate and alarmist speech about the consequences in the country if we expelled him with an election coming up, etc., etc. I think Herbert [Morrison] came next, putting the case for expulsion quite reasonably, though not perhaps replying adequately to Attlee's amendment. He was followed by Sam Watson, who was excellent as usual, forthright and absolutely firm. There were then a series of Bevanite speeches ... There was little discussion of Bevan's behaviour. It was all mostly talk about what the consequences would be. There was a good deal of talk as well about the attitude of the Parliamentary Party, and claims were made that they were really not in favour of expulsion. I then spoke more or less winding up for our side ... I ... opposed the Attlee motion on the grounds that delay would be fatal, and that we must face it that if we accepted it, it was almost certain that we would not expel him ... I thought that if we did not expel him the Tories would certainly claim that he was indispensable, and indeed the future leader of the Party & that they would use this against us in the Election. I admitted that we should lose some support in the constituency party membership, but I thought this would be balanced by the gain from the marginal voters. Percy Knight then spoke very briefly, and the vote was taken. Fourteen for Attlee's amendment and thirteen against. ■

The results of the 1955 election, which increased the Conservative majority in the House of Commons, were not unexpected within the Labour Party. At this time, nine members of the party's shadow Cabinet were over the age of sixty-five. With Attlee nearing retirement, the feeling grew that a younger generation of activists was needed to carry Labour back into power. But it was not simply a matter of cultivating a youthful image. By the mid-1950s Labour Party politics was confronting a situation in which economic prosperity was being delivered by the Conservatives under a capitalist economic system. In such circumstances, it was unclear how to proceed; as discussed in Chapter 6, a new approach to economic policy issues was signalled with the publication of Anthony Crosland's The Future of Socialism *in 1956. In document 7.17 the Bevanite backbencher Richard Crossman describes the despondency within the party in the months following the 1955 election.*

7.17   Richard Crossman, diary, 15 July 1955 (in Janet Morgan (ed.), *The Backbench Diaries of Richard Crossman*, London, Hamish Hamilton and Cape, 1981 p. 437).

■ The fact is that the results of the Election are already proving far more profound and pervasive than anybody expected. Not only is the Labour

Party ideologically disintegrated by the fact that Keynesian welfare capitalism is proving, for the time being, quite an adequate substitute for Socialism. Each of us, individually, is being changed. During the last three weeks, when I have come home to dinner and then just dropped into the House to vote, I have begun to realize how ordinary politicians, for generations, have regarded politics – not as a mission or vocation, but as a rather pleasant public service, which one takes on in addition to one's main interests and one's private life but without permitting it to tyrannize over the others ...

Others are behaving in the same way but in different environments. Ian is now immersing himself in his business, Nye is out on his farm or drinking and merely playing his part as a politician in the shadow Cabinet. 'Things fall apart, the centre cannot hold.' And, ironically enough, all this happens to the Labour Party because people in Britain are more prosperous and more contented and because peace is breaking out all over the world. We suddenly feel that our mission to save people from cataclysm and disaster has come unstuck. We are missionaries without a mission, or missionaries more and more dubious about the mission. ■

Under the leadership of Gaitskell, who replaced Attlee in 1955, Labour made a concerted attempt to limit the damage which its public infighting had inflicted. Party propaganda was careful to stress the unity of the Labour leadership.

7.18   Labour Party general election poster, 1959 (Conservative Party Archives).

Labour's failure in the 1959 general election resulted in a period of crisis and division over strategy and policy. A public opinion survey commissioned in the wake of the defeat suggested several reasons for the party's failure. In the published version, Rita Hinden, editor of the party journal Socialist Commentary, *summarised its findings.*

7.19   Rita Hinden, 'Commentary' on the defeat of the Labour Party, 1960 (in M. Abrams and R. Rose, *Must Labour Lose?*, Harmondsworth, Penguin, 1960, pp. 100–1).

■ Why is the tide of opinion set against Labour at the present time? The survey suggests three main reasons. The first is that Labour is thought of predominantly as a class party, and that the class which it represents is – objectively and subjectively – on the wane. This stamps it with an aura of sectionalism and narrowness, at a time when people see opportunities for advancement opening before them as never before. It is the Conservatives who have the wider appeal. They are regarded by the majority as the champions of material prosperity, the natural home for the young, the ambitious, the successful. And, foremost – apart from working for world peace – among the qualities which the majority look for in a political party, is that it should ensure prosperity ...

The second reason for Labour's unpopularity is its identification with nationalization. It is not that public ownership is condemned outright: people are discriminating and are quite prepared to say that certain publicly-owned industries have been a success. Nor, as the survey reveals, do people want to retreat to the times of *laissez-faire*: they understand that a considerable measure of government control is necessary. But their attitude reveals the empiricism for which British people are renowned. They will judge each case on its merits, and, in so far as Labour appears to be doctrinaire on this subject of ownership, it saddles itself with a liability.

The third factor telling against Labour is the impression of weak, divided leadership. Hugh Gaitskell is admired as a decent kindly man – there is nothing against him as a person; but Harold Macmillan is thought to be stronger˙ and more capable of taking unpleasant decisions. Labour is seen as lacking a united team of leaders; the Conservatives have it. And it is this strength and unity that is valued. Apparently, British people are not afraid of unpleasant decisions; the capacity to take them is wanted in a political leader. ■

Nationalisation, which had already been debated within the Labour Party, as discussed in Chapter 6, became the focus of an impassioned debate at the 1959 special party conference in Blackpool. At issue was Clause IV of the party constitution, which lists among the objects of the party the securing of 'the common ownership of the means of production, distribution and exchange'. In the face of widespread trade union opposition to any change, the National Executive Committee quietly rejected the abandonment of Clause IV. At the conference, Barbara Castle presented the political case for the retention of a policy of nationalisation, while Gaitskell spoke against.

7.20　Barbara Castle, speech to the party conference, Blackpool, 1959
(*Report of the Fifty-Eighth Annual Conference of the Labour Party*, London, Labour Party, 1959, pp. 84–5).

■ ... We are told that we have succeeded so well in reforming capitalism that we have made it, not only civilised, but indestructible. Our best bet, therefore, we are told, is to accept it almost completely in its present modified form, to abandon the attempt to take over any more industries and to use public ownership merely to ensure that the community gets a cut at the capitalist cake. Such a policy, it is urged, would enable us to concentrate on social reforms and the sort of moral issues which will rally the radicals. Thus by uniting all progressive forces we should sweep back into power.

Let us by all means examine this argument carefully, for only in that way shall we find where it would lead. And in my view it would lead us slap-bang into a fallacy. That fallacy is the belief that you can separate moral issues from economic ones. We are not prigs in the Labour Party; of course we believe that people should have a good time, but we also believe deeply and enduringly in the good life. And we have spent 50 years of political life proving to the people of this country that economic and social morality go hand in hand. That was the force that gave us our dynamic and has enabled us to set an indelible impress on the course of history. The lesson of the 1930's that it took us so long to teach, was that social crimes are also economic ones: poverty, for example, and unemployment ...

We don't want to take over industries merely in order to make them more efficient, but to make them responsible to us all. And I believe that one of the reasons why the idea of public ownership alienated people in the last election is that we have not yet presented the real case for it. To say, for instance, that the State should acquire shares in private industry on the strict understanding that it exercises no control over it is like legalising the Burglars Union on condition that we share the swag. Nor are the existing nationalised industries exactly a model of public accountability. They are not really accountable to their workers, to the consumers, or even to Parliament. And until they are, they are not Socialist ... ■

7.21　Hugh Gaitskell, speech to the party conference, Blackpool, 1959
(*Report of the Fifty-Eighth Annual Conference of the Labour Party*, London, Labour Party, 1959, pp. 110–13).

■ ... we must face the fact that nationalisation as such will not be positively popular until all these industries are clearly seen to be performing at least as well as the best firms in the private sector. When this goal has been achieved, then we can face the country with complete confidence on this issue. Our fellow-citizens are more likely to judge the value of the public sector by their experience of it than from theoretical arguments in speeches or Labour Party pamphlets.

Some suggest that we should accept for all time the present frontiers between the public and private sectors. We cannot do that. It would imply that everything works so perfectly in the private sector that we shall never want to intervene ... At the same time I disagree equally with the other extreme view that nationalisation or even public ownership is the be all and end all, the ultimate first principle and aim of socialism. I believe that this view arises from a complete confusion about the fundamental meaning of socialism and, in particular, a misunderstanding about ends and means ...

As I have already said, I am against starting on a new election programme now. But I do think that we should clear our minds on these fundamental issues and then try to express in the most simple and comprehensive fashion what we stand for in the world today.

The only official document which embodies such an attempt is the Party Constitution, written over 40 years ago. It seems to me that this needs to be brought up to date. For instance, can we really be satisfied today with a statement of fundamentals which makes no mention at all of colonial freedom, race relations, disarmament, full employment or planning? The only specific reference to our objectives at home is the well-known phrase:

> To secure for the workers by hand or by brain the full fruits of their industry and the most equitable distribution thereof that may be possible, upon the basis of the common ownership of the means of production, distribution, and exchange ...

Standing as it does on its own, this cannot possibly be regarded as adequate. It lays us open to continual misrepresentation. It implies that common ownership is an end, whereas in fact it is a means. It implies that the only precise object we have is nationalisaton, whereas in fact we have many other Socialist objectives. It implies that we propose to nationalise everything, but do we? Everything? – the whole of light industry, the whole of agriculture, all the shops – every little pub and garage? Of course not. We have long ago come to accept, we know very well, for the foreseeable future, at least in some form, a mixed economy; in which case, if this is our view – as I believe it to be of 90 per cent of the Labour Party – had we better not say so instead of going out of our way to court misrepresentation?

I knew I should say some things that would not be palatable to everybody this afternoon. It would have been very nice in some ways to have made a speech which contained so many bromides and so little controversial matter that it was certain of a very large number of cheers. But I do not conceive that to be my duty today. I would rather forgo the cheers now in the hope that we shall get more votes later on. I do not want deliberately to advise a course of action which could only involve me in leading this Party to another electoral defeat, and I will not do so. ■

Immigration Becomes a Political Issue

While legislative instruments for the restriction of foreign immigration into Britain dated from the Edwardian period, until the end of the 1950s there was no legal bar to the entry of citizens from Commonwealth countries. This policy was considered by many to be essential for good relations within the Commonwealth. From the late 1940s, however, full employment and growing prosperity in Britain resulted in the arrival of growing numbers of people from the colonies and Commonwealth countries. In particular, Afro-Caribbean immigrants from the 'New Commonwealth' countries began to come in significant numbers for the first time, often recruited for low-paid unskilled work, as in the health service. By the late 1950s this phenomenon had become a major political issue, raising the subject of race relations and the possibility of restricting immigration from within the Commonwealth for the first time.

The first wave of new immigrants came primarily from the West Indies. Economic conditions there were deteriorating, and the wartime experiences of many ex-servicemen encouraged them to seek work abroad. Nevertheless, emigration out of Britain continued to match or exceed overall immigration levels; and immigration from Ireland and the Old (predominantly white) Commonwealth countries still outweighed colonial and Commonwealth immigration.

7.22   Claude Ramsey, oral testimony concerning arrival in Britain from Barbados, 1988 (in *Forty Winters On: Memories of Britain's Postwar Caribbean Immigrants*, London, Lambeth Council, *The Voice* and *South London Press*, 1988, pp. 37–8).

■ As War ended I found myself back in Barbados with its poverty and lack of opportunities. I was married in 1950 and worked as a civil servant in the Department of Agriculture until 1956 when I moved to Britain. My reasons for leaving were simple – the Barbadian economic depression, and the greater employment prospects in Britain. I arrived in Britain … aboard the SS *Antilles*, and although expecting arrangements to have been made by the Salvation Army to accommodate me, I discovered that no booking had been made. And so I was left alone to fend for myself, at a very late hour, on my first night in England. Although a bit apprehensive, I could not help noticing what a well lit place England was, that was the first thing that struck me.

But there was also a dullness about Britain, and the people were much more remote than I was used to in the West Indies. As the 'Mother country' I expected to find the people more open and welcoming. It took me about a year to get used to the climate – I remember, during that winter, being surprised at actually seeing my own breath coming out of my mouth.

My first home in England was a house in Notting Hill Gate shared with about 30 other people, with only one bath and toilet between us. The conditions were appalling, and it cost me £3 a week in rent …

The racist exploitation of West Indians was to be seen everywhere. There were signs saying 'no coloureds please' on various advertisements for flats. As a result, our choice of where to live was extremely limited. The employment situation was equally restrictive and most of us were only allowed to do portering or cleaning jobs in stores or hospitals … ■

7.23 **Migration into Britain, 1953–68 (charts derived from House of Commons Library Research Division, Background Paper No. 56, *Commonwealth Immigration into the United Kingdom from the 1950s to 1975 – A Survey of Statistical Sources*, unpublished, 1976, pp. 11, 17).**

The balance of migration

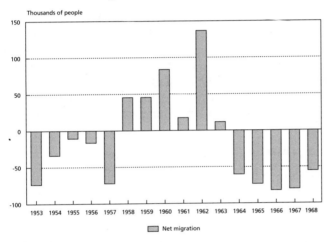

Net immigration from the Colonies and Commonwealth

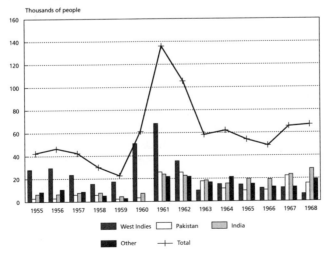

The official response to rising levels of black immigrants was mixed. In Cabinet, while there was concern over the long-term implications of multiracial immigration, the balance of ministerial opinion before 1958 was still in favour of maintaining an open-door policy.

7.24 **Cabinet Committee, 'Colonial immigrants', 22 June 1956 (PRO CAB 129/81, CP(56)145, pp. 6–7).**

■ ...

The Case for Early Legislation

21. The principle that the United Kingdom should maintain an open door for British subjects grew up tacitly at a time when the coloured races of the Commonwealth were at a more primitive stage of development than now. There was no danger then of a coloured invasion of this country. In the meantime circumstances have changed. Coloured people are better educated, they can find the passage money, and transport facilities are better developed ... We clearly cannot undertake to absorb in such a densely-populated island inhabited by a different racial strain all the coloured immigrants who may wish to come here. It therefore seems inevitable that a time will come when this immigration will give rise to problems which outweigh the difficulties of, and objections to, enacting legislation to control it. There is a danger that we may be faced with the need for urgent action when it has already become too late ... the prudent course would therefore be to legislate without delay ...

The Case Against Early Legislation

23. From the economic point of view the nation has benefited up to the present from the arrival of coloured workers. Moreover, the problem is to some extent self-regulating: the immigrants will not come here if there is no work. Control which might amount to virtual prohibition of immigration might impose severe difficulties on the authorities in the West Indies at a time when the Caribbean Federation would be struggling to get on its feet. In the field of thought, a decision to impose control would come as a shock to liberal opinion. However disguised, it would be represented as discrimination on grounds of race and colour ...

Recommendations

We all agree that coloured immigration has become an ominous problem which cannot now be ignored. The majority of the Committee, while taking the view that some form of control over coloured immigration will eventually be inescapable, consider that the balance of advantage lies against taking steps to impose that control at the present time. They think that the situation should be kept under regular review and should be remitted for further examination in perhaps a year's time. Indeed, in view of current trends in the employment situation it may well prove necessary to review the possibility of controlling coloured immigration at an earlier date than a year from now.

The Lord President dissents from the view that the balance of advantage is against taking action now. He considers that, as the arguments advanced in the Report itself seem conclusive in favour of action at some point, the longer we delay the worse the position is bound to become. Nor does he accept the assumption (in paragraph 23) that the Government would not have a strong body of public opinion behind them if they acted now. He would therefore favour action being put in hand forthwith. ■

The balance of opinion on black immigration began to shift in the autumn of 1958. A series of highly publicised attacks on the Afro-Caribbean communities in London and Nottingham in the late summer of that year propelled the issue into the national press. There was widespread condemnation of the attacks; the Labour Party, for example, quickly issued a policy statement on racial discrimination in time for the party conference of that year, and firmly opposed the introduction of immigration controls. Within the Conservative Cabinet, however, the 'disturbances' appear to have marked a shift of opinion in favour of legislation.

Concern that affluence and full employment would lead to a dramatic rise in black immigration; the government's subsequent failure to persuade Commonwealth governments voluntarily to restrict the number of passports issued; and increasing pressure from the constituency level: all led to the passage of the Commonwealth Immigrants Act in 1962. The legislation meant that citizens of the Commonwealth who did not hold a United Kingdom passport, or who were not born in the UK, had to apply for a limited number of vouchers before gaining permission to enter the country.

7.25 Labour Party, *Racial Discrimination*, London, Labour Party, 1958, pp. 2–4.

■ The Labour Party utterly abhors every manifestation of racial prejudice, and particularly condemns those instances which have recently occurred in this country ...

The new Commonwealth, which has grown up since 1945, represents the greatest multi-racial association the world has ever known. Yet the Commonwealth is continually sensitive about race relations. Failure in these relations can destroy all hopes of peace and international friendship. Unless peoples of different races and colours can learn to live together in harmony, the future for our children in this rapidly shrinking world will be one of extreme danger ...

Britain has become symbolically and practically the heart of the Commonwealth. To an important extent this is due to the fact that all Commonwealth citizens are welcomed to our midst. If our position is to continue, the welcome must be whole-hearted and unreserved ...

However, difficulties inevitably arise when a large number of immigrants settle in one place. Housing shortage, periodic unemployment, and differing social customs may combine with natural strangeness to exaggerate community tensions ...

It should be realised that the immigrants also have their difficulties. They often come from countries which have been ruled by Britain for centuries, frequently to the benefit of the British people. Poor housing, unemployment, low standards of living, are common to many of these countries, and are at least partially the responsibility of the British people ...

Although we believe that the fundamental and long term solution of this problem is educational, nonetheless there are public manifestations of racial prejudice so serious that they must be dealt with by legislation. The Labour Party therefore urges Her Majesty's Government now to introduce legislation, making illegal the public practice of discrimination ...

We are firmly convinced that any form of British legislation limiting Commonwealth immigration to this country would be disastrous to our status in the Commonwealth and to the confidence of the Commonwealth peoples. ■

7.26   **Cabinet discussion on the Nottingham and London riots, 8 September 1958 (PRO CAB 128, CC 69(58)3, pp. 1–2).**

■ 3. *The Home Secretary* said that the police were confident that they could control the racial disturbances which had recently occurred in Nottingham and in the Notting Hill area of London. It would be necessary, however, to give further consideration to the circumstances which provoked these outbreaks of violence between white and coloured people. They appeared to originate largely in competition for housing and casual employment, and they were aggravated in some cases by disputes about women. It would be desirable to seek to establish some form of control over the emigration of coloured people from their countries of origin, similar to the measures which we had recently persuaded the Governments of India and Pakistan to introduce; and it might be appropriate, as an initial step, to discuss this possibility with the Federal Government of the West Indies. In addition it would be desirable to reconsider the possibility of taking statutory powers to deport undesirable immigrants from other countries of the Commonwealth and of implementing certain of the recommendations of the committee on Homosexual Offences and Prostitution. ■

The general election of 1964 confirmed that immigration from the New Commonwealth, increasingly now from India and Pakistan, had become a hot political issue in Britain. Most infamously, the Labour MP for the Smethwick division of Birmingham, Patrick Gordon Walker, who had been closely involved with opposition to the introduction of immigration controls, was unseated by an overtly racist Conservative candidate.

7.27   **A.W. Singham, 'Immigration and the election', 1965 (in D.E. Butler and A. King (eds), *The British General Election of 1964*, London, Macmillan, 1965, p. 364).**

■ Smethwick itself belongs to the bleak industrial complex stretching beyond Birmingham. No one knows exactly how many immigrants live there. Estimates vary between 4,000 and 7,000. The overwhelming majority are Indians – mostly Sikhs – and most of the rest West Indians. Long before the town became the focus of national attention its inhabitants had been made acutely aware of the immigration issue by the local weekly newspaper, the *Smethwick Telephone*. In 1963 the *Telephone* devoted approximatey 1,650 column inches of space to immigrants – mostly of an extremely unfavourable nature. The paper's activities helped substantially to create a highly-charged political atmosphere.

The Smethwick campaign was not a short three-week affair, but started in earnest as early as 1961. Mr Peter Griffiths, who had fought the seat in 1959, was also active in local government and spearheaded the drive which resulted in the spectacular overthrow of the formerly Labour-dominated council … He used essentially the same techniques and organisation in fighting Mr Gordon Walker … He proposed a ban on all immigration for at least five years and the summary deportation of any immigrant who had a criminal record or remained unemployed for more than a certain period. He also sponsored a plan for separate school classes for immigrant children who had difficulty in speaking English, and opposed the rehousing by the local authority of anyone who had lived in Smethwick for less than ten years. He almost invariably linked immigration with violence, crime and disease. At his adoption meeting he asserted that Smethwick must not become 'a dumping ground for criminals, the chronic sick and those who have no intention of working'. His attitude towards the integration of the immigrants was equivocal. He said that he himself preferred to use the term 'peaceful co-existence' … ■

The Decline of the Conservative Government

By 1962 Macmillan's premiership seemed to have lost much of its lustre. Popular approval of the affluence of the late 1950s was increasingly giving way to national self-doubt over relatively poor economic performance and cynicism towards institutions which were loosely described as the 'establishment'.

Liberal revival

Until the Labour Party began to make genuine headway in the opinion polls from 1962, it seemed that the Liberal Party might be poised to become a serious political alternative for the first time since the early 1920s.

In March 1962 the Liberal by-election victory in the suburban seat of Orpington in Kent fuelled speculation that a revived Liberalism could find a substantial constituency in the white-collar workers of the lower middle class. As document 7.28 from the satirical magazine Private Eye *illustrates, the Conservatives were widely perceived to have become increasingly out of touch with this section of the electorate. The Liberal surge proved to be a temporary phenomenon, however, as illustrated by contemporary opinion poll findings.*

7.28 'Conservative Central Office market research report on white-collar voters', satire in *Private Eye*, 6 April 1962.

■ After the Orpington incident last March, it was brought to our notice that the unfortunate number of Conservative abstentions could be attributed to a certain discontent among the large quantity of so-called 'White Collar Workers' living in the area.

We received a memorandum from the Cabinet enquiring as to who these people were. But no one at Central Office, with the exception of our Mr Goldman, could ever remember having met one.

It was obviously vital that, before preparing our advertising campaign for the next General Election, we should conduct a thorough investigation. We therefore called in Probes Ltd, the well-known market research consultancy which recently conducted the enquiry into 'Why the Working Classes don't use Harrods', to go down to Orpington and give us a full report. To talk to these 'White Collar Workers' in their own homes, even to live with them for a few days, and to find out exactly what was on their minds. ■

7.29 Voting intentions, 1960–4 (chart derived from D. Butler and G. Butler (eds), *British Political Facts, 1900–1985*, London, Macmillan, 6th edn, 1986, pp. 258–9).

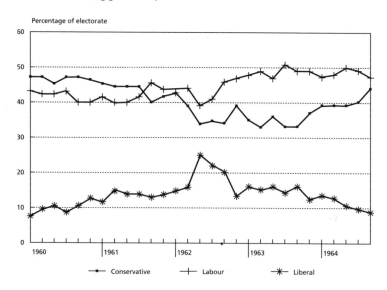

Macmillan's faltering premiership

Macmillan attempted throughout 1962 to rejuvenate his government's flagging image. But in spite of his efforts to seize the political initiative, support for the Conservatives continued to decline.

The official record of Macmillan's preliminary remarks to the Cabinet in May 1962 is one of the rare documents in existence which record the verbatim text of a Cabinet address. In particular, he addressed the problem of appealing to the 'Orpingtonians' and the strains of attempting to maintain simultaneously full employment, high public spending, low inflation and economic growth.

7.30 **Harold Macmillan, remarks to the Cabinet, 28 May 1962 (PRO PREM 11/3930).**

■ We have four objectives – to retain full employment; to secure if we can stable prices; to have a strong pound which means a favourable balance of payments both on current and on capital accounts; and to gain growth and expansion in the economy. So far as I know these four objectives have never been sustained for any length of time by any nation. Nor have they been so clearly the purpose of political economic policy at any period in the history of nations …

… They are like four balls in one of those puzzles we had as children – you can get three into the holes and when you get the fourth in, out pops one of the others. If you get the balance of payments right, then you don't get growth; if you get full employment, then the prices begin to go up. How can you get them all in? …

… In a modern society with all its pressures and in our island in particular with all its economic hazards, if all four objectives are to be satisfactorily maintained, full employment, the stable prices, the balance of payment and the strong pound and above all growth, we must have a permanent incomes policy …

… it must be part of a package, which I call the new approach.

First the working classes as we are apt in this room to call them, but I suppose there's some new name for them now. If they are to accept an incomes policy however promulgated by whatever Government or by a wider body, in my view the time has come now to state definitely we can no longer accept the difference of status between the wage earner and the salary earner … That involves the abolition of the day contract or even in some cases the hour contract … I think we have also got to make better arrangements for redundancy, partly because it is fair and partly because it helps movement and mobility which is what we want. And we have got to get better methods for retraining. We must examine health and welfare arrangements and see in what degree there are still two nations – those of the manual day-to-day workers and those of the staffs … If the working classes are to play in this hand they must feel that they play as full members of the team and not fighting for their strength and therefore tending to abuse their strength. Secondly the middle classes – the Orpingtonians. At present they feel the victims of both sides, pushed about between large industry and the Trade Unions to whom they see us what they call surren‑ der. They have immensely to gain from an incomes policy and it shouldn't be difficult to persuade them. Stability which is the biggest thing they can have and a sense of order and decency in the kind of world they want to have. They suffer in a free for all unless of course we were to throw the full employment ball away and go for a violently deflationary policy somewhat like that between the wars, when undoubtedly the standard of living of the middle classes was high. However I don't think anybody seriously suggests the conscious creation of unemployment ... nor do I think any Government is likely to survive it, so that really cannot be a hope for the middle classes. They want stability, they want steady prices and if we can get the expansion and the other benefits that would follow the acceptance of some kind of the new incomes policy in its larger field, they would get the biggest boon they can get, which is a reduction in the long term interest rate. This should be pushed on as soon as we feel it is sound to do so. It is the heavy cost of bor- rowing – which they all do, especially the young people – to which they are very susceptible.

... Therefore we must widen the appeal, add to it a new attitude towards the unity of the nation as a whole and their different claim upon each other, to try to create a kind of moral position on which it is almost anarchical and indecent to oppose this line of thought ... ■

Macmillan attempted to bolster the strength of his government on 13 July 1962 by reshuffling the Cabinet in an extreme move which was irreverently dubbed 'the night of the long knives'. Seven ministers, one-third of the Cabinet, were removed from office, and nine others were to follow in the coming days. It seemed a gesture of panic and it undermined much of the Prime Minister's support within his own Party. The Conservative press reacted critically.

7.31 Peregrine Worsthorne, 'His own executioner?', *Sunday Telegraph*, 22 July 1962.

■ By far the most striking result of the Cabinet reshuffle so far has been the drastic decline of the one man who really matters in a Government – the Prime Minister himself. Most of the other high offices of state have been substantially strengthened by the changes. But the top office of all has been severely weakened.

This strikes me as the fatal flaw in the whole operation. The limbs of gov- ernment have been fortified at the expense of the head. Mr Macmillan has brightened the face of the administration, but only by blackening his own name. No man could more truly say of himself, 'Mine Own Executioner' ...

This is not a question primarily of age, although it is perhaps worth noting that Mr Macmillan is now the only member of the Government who fought in the First World War. Much more is it a question of the Prime Minister having destroyed the trust and respect which his followers previously held him in. Not a single Tory member I talked to last week had a kind word to spare, and even the promoted Ministers seemed to find it difficult to show any gratitude ...

But more damaging to the Prime Minister than the disgruntling of the back benchers is the growing disquiet among officials in the Central Office as they read one by-election post-mortem after another, all emphasising the extent of Mr Macmillan's personal unpopularity among the electorate as a whole ... leaving little room to doubt that 'Supermac' is today the weakest link in the Tory chain. And what is more, all the indications available to the Central Office suggest that this trend has been spectacularly augmented by the indecorous and flappable way in which the reshuffle was conducted ...

A bee stings its victim and then dies. It is not impossible that Mr Macmillan may politically suffer the same harsh fate. ■

The government was weakened further by a series of sex and espionage scandals in 1962 and 1963. Of these the most notorious was the Profumo Affair. The Secretary of State for War, John Profumo, was forced to resign after admitting an affair with the call-girl Christine Keeler, whose other lovers included a Russian diplomat. The details of the case, which proved wonderfully rich copy for the press, gave an impression of aristo-cratic decadence and corruption at the highest levels of British society.

7.32   Editorial, *The Times*, 11 June 1963.

■ Everyone has been so busy assuring the public that the affair is not one of morals, that it is time to assert that it is. Morals have been discounted too long ... No one would wish the security aspects of the matter to be ignored. There is no danger of this ... For the Conservative Party – and, it is to be hoped, for the nation – things can never be quite the same again.

The hope must be that they will become better. There is plenty of room for this. However multifarious and ingenious the causes to which the Conservative Central Office ascribe the desperate state of the Party's present fortunes as shown by the opinion polls, the overriding reason is that eleven years of Conservative rule have brought the nation psychologically and spiritually to a low ebb. The Conservatives came to power a few months before the present reign opened. They have been in office so far throughout the whole of it. The ardent hopes and eager expectations that attended its beginning have been belied.

They gibed at austerity, and in all truth the British people deserved some easement after their historic and heroic exertions, although history is never a nicely balanced business of rewards and penalties. They declared they had the right road for Britain. They would set the people free. Change, they declared, was their ally. Nothing else, they seemed later to think, mattered, compared with the assertion that the nation had never had it so good. Today they are faced with a flagging economy, an uncertain future, and the end of the illusion that Britain's greatness could be measured by the so-called independence of its so-called deterrent. All this may seem far from Mr Profumo, but his admissions could be the last straw. It remains strange that not a single member of the government resigned when the affair broke in March and he did not himself resign.

What the Conservatives need now, and what they have needed ever since Churchill was in his heyday, is courage. One of the paradoxes of modern war is that defeat is more likely to restore a nation's fibre than victory. There is no hiding place from the tidal wave of overthrow and disaster. All too dangerously comfortable is the slow, insidious, almost imperceptible but inexorable ebb tide. ■

Speculation over Macmillan's future continued throughout the summer of 1963. Although the government teetered, however, Lord Denning's official report on the Profumo Affair concluded that national security had not been breached and that the government had not behaved improperly. Macmillan himself, after several weeks of vacillation, had decided to soldier on when sudden illness in early October caused him to reverse this decision. The Conservative Party Conference in Blackpool, which convened in the midst of this crisis, was chaotic and troubled, as there was no clear successor to the Prime Minister. Lord Hailsham (Quintin Hogg) and R.A. Butler emerged as the principal contenders in a public feud most out of character with the normally staid Conservative conference atmosphere.

In the week that followed, however, Macmillan, from his hospital bed, decided with a small group of advisers that his successor should be Lord Home, the Foreign Secretary. The appointment of this low-public profile peer was thought to be so unsuitable that two prominent Conservatives, Enoch Powell and Iain Macleod, both refused to serve in a Home government. Macmillan tendered his resignation to the Queen on 18 October. Macleod subsequently explained his reaction in a sensational article in the Spectator *early in the New Year.*

7.33   Iain Macleod, 'The Tory leadership', *Spectator*, 17 January 1964, pp. 65–6.

■ ... The key day was Thursday, October 17, a day which for me began as an ordinary working day and ended with my firm decision that I could not serve in the Administration that I knew Lord Home was to be invited to form. The first indication that the day was going to be unusual came at breakfast. My wife came back from a long telephone conversation with one of our oldest friends ... to say that the succession was to be decided that afternoon ... I was surprised, but not disturbed. To me it seemed clear that if the situation was going to gell swiftly, the choice must be Butler; if there was deadlock, it would surely come back to the Cabinet. I had not, of course, appreciated then that it was in fact an essential part of the design that the Cabinet should have no such opportunity ...

... Alone in the Chancellor's room over a drink I told [Reginald Maudling] ... of my wife's telephone conversation. He had heard nothing ... A decision today, he thought, could only be for Butler. And with this he was more than content. He spoke on the telephone to Lord Dilhorne, and the Lord Chancellor confirmed that he and others were to present their collective views that afternoon. They had already been separately to see Macmillan that morning. To all suggestions that the Cabinet (or the Cabinet less the chief contenders) should meet, Dilhorne was deaf ...

Curiouser and curiouser it seemed ... It is some measure of the tightness of the magic circle on this occasion that neither the Chancellor of the Exchequer nor the Leader of the House of Commons had any inkling of what was happening.

After lunch I returned to the Central Office to clear some papers. In mid-afternoon the telephone rang. It was an important figure in Fleet Street. He told me the decision had been made, and that it was for Home. He himself found this incredible, but he was utterly sure of his source. I telephoned Maudling and Powell and arranged to meet as soon as we could at my flat ... as did another member of the Cabinet. Lord Aldington also came to my flat and joined in our discussions ...

From the beginning I was in no doubt that if, as Joint Chairman of the Party and Leader of the House of Commons, I felt strongly enough to tell Lord Home that I thought it wrong for him to accept an invitation to form an administration, I could not honourably serve with him in that administration ... So we spoke on the telephone.

... I told him that there was no one in the party for whom I had more admiration and respect; that if he had been in the House of Commons he could perhaps have been the first choice; but I felt that those giving advice had grossly underestimated the difficulties of presenting the situation in a convincing way to the modern Tory Party. Unlike Hailsham, he was not a reluctant peer, and we were now proposing to admit that after twelve years of Tory government no one amongst the 363 members of the party in the House of Commons was acceptable as Prime Minister ...

Before long it was established that Maudling and Hailsham were not only opposed to Lord Home but believed Butler to be the right and obvious successor and would be ready and indeed happy to serve under him. The rest of us felt this understanding between those hitherto the three principal contenders was of decisive importance: the succession was resolving itself in the right way. We telephoned the Chief Whip, who, rather than embark on a lengthy discussion over the line, decided to join us. He naturally did everything he could to persuade us to accept the situation as he saw it, but we finally asked him to report to the Prime Minister the fact of the understanding which had arisen between Butler, Maudling and Hailsham. He promised to do this.

... Next morning ... Macmillan ... sent his letter of resignation to the Palace, and the same morning tendered advice to the Queen in the form of a memorandum which we are told incorporated all the four reports which Macmillan had asked for ... The memorandum then purported to be not the advice of one man, but the collective view of a party. There is no criticism whatever that can be made of the part played by the Crown. Presented with such a document, it was unthinkable even to consider asking for a second opinion. Nevertheless, the procedure which had been adopted opens up big issues for decision in the future ...

When Lord Home was sent for by the Queen and began inquiries to see whether he could form a government if he accepted her commission, Maudling and Hailsham kept to their agreement with Butler and declined to serve unless Butler did. Butler himself reserved his position, intimating that he would not serve under Lord Home unless satisfied that it was 'the only way to unite the Party'. At this stage at least two members of the old Cabinet besides myself – Powell was one of them – who knew what the situation was, used their influence towards what they believed the right solution by answering Lord Home's inquiry in the negative. When, in the event, Butler decided to serve and Lord Home's government was formed, Powell thought it right to stand by the answer he had given. ∎

Labour's rising fortunes

In contrast to the shambolic character of the final months of the Macmillan administration, the Labour Party emerged from 1963 with a united and convincing platform under the leadership of Harold Wilson.

The right wing of the Labour Party, while defeated over Clause IV, had come to dominate Labour politics during the early 1960s. Moreover, the strength of the right at constituency level had grown through the development of the Campaign for Democratic Socialism [CDS] since 1959. By coming out against Britain's entry to the European Economic Community, Gaitskell had united the party and was well placed in what was likely to be an election year, when a sudden illness led to his untimely death in January 1963. Wilson's succession – given his history of activism on the party's left wing – was thus surprising. In document 7.34, former CDS members recall the events which led to his appointment.

7.34   Discussion on the succession of Harold Wilson, 1990 (from B. Brivati (ed.), 'Witness seminar: the Campaign for Democratic Socialism, 1960–64', *Contemporary Record*, 7, 2, Autumn 1993, pp. 381–2).

■ **Haseler** [*Professor Stephen Haseler, co-organiser of the CDS Youth Section*]: What happened during this leadership election in 1963? This is a very important aspect of Labour Party history. Here you have this successful campaign by the revisionists, Gaitskell unfortunately dies ... Then we come to a leadership election and there is a split between the two right-wing candidates Callaghan and Brown ... How did Wilson get elected?

Mayhew [*Lord Mayhew, the organiser of the Socialist Campaign for Multilateral Disarmament*]: I remember a meeting which might have been organised by CDS at Jack Diamond's flat.

Taverne [*Dick Taverne, treasurer of the CDS*]: There were two, an initial one in Jack Diamond's flat, but the elaborate analysis of who we should back was at Tony Crosland's flat in the Little Boltons. Those present also included Desmond Donnelly ... George Brown had certain weaknesses which could be regarded very seriously; it was felt that Jim Callaghan was inexperienced and some said shallow, that Harold Wilson would not put a foot wrong, would win us the next election but would then run the party into the ground. I remember somebody using those very words ...

Jay [*Lord Jay, leading Gaitskellite MP*]: The reason why Harold Wilson won was because George Brown was the alternative.

Mayhew: The meeting in Jack Diamond's flat was called against Wilson, we all went to decide how to stop Wilson. The trouble was that we only had Brown and Callaghan. I said, 'Well, I'm not going to vote either for a crook or a drunk so I'll vote for Jim', and I am afraid my vote was wasted.

Jay: How right you were.

Jones [*Professor George Jones, co-organiser of the CDS Youth Section*]: ... I can well recall my utter dismay ... We knew the Left was still there and Wilson was seen as our enemy. He was the one we had been fighting all along – he had stood against Gaitskell, and here it was all being thrown away. There was terrible disillusionment ...

Donoughue [*Lord Donoughue, CDS organiser*]: I met Bill very soon after that key meeting and he said that it seemed that our Campaign slogan would be: Better George drunk than Harold sober. Our dilemma was that CDS had been geared towards younger people and that we didn't have anybody at that level to succeed Gaitskell. Secondly we had always wanted to get back into power, that was not a dishonourable objective, and at that time Harold, to professional insiders, looked like somebody who would win elections and that wasn't a foolish judgement. He won four out of five. I think they were in the most terrible dilemma, with no candidate and although there were reservations about Harold, they could see that one of his pluses was as an election winner, that he was more likely to win it than George Brown ... ■

Wilson proved to be an extremely able leader, presenting a unified and progressive image to a public weary of the scandal-ridden and divided Conservative government. At the Labour Party Conference in Scarborough in October 1963 he outlined his vision for Britain's revival, a presentation which contrasted markedly with the mood of the Conservative conference of the same year.

7.35   Harold Wilson, speech to the party conference, Scarborough, 1963
(*Report of the Sixty-Second Annual Conference of the Labour Party,* London, Labour Party, 1963, pp. 134–40).

■ There is no more dangerous illusion than the comfortable doctrine that the world owes us a living. One of the dangers of the old-boy network approach to life is the thought that it is international, that whatever we do, whenever we run into trouble, we can always rely on a special relationship with someone or other to bail us out. From now on Britain will have just as much influence in the world as we can earn, as we can deserve. We have no accumulated reserves on which to live ...

It is, of course, a cliché that we are living at a time of such rapid scientific change that our children are accepting as part of their everyday life things which would have been dismissed as science fiction a few years ago. We are living perhaps in a more rapid revolution than some of us realise ...

The problem is this. Since technological progress left to the mechanism of private industry and private property can lead only to high profits for a few, a high rate of employment for a few, and to mass redundancies for the many, if there had never been a case for Socialism before, automation would have created it. Because only if technological progress becomes part of our national planning can that progress be directed to national ends ...

That is why we must, in the Labour Party, devote a lot more thought to providing facilities for the use of leisure, and this is why again ... we shall have to be a lot more imaginative about the provision for retraining the workers made redundant by the development of new skills and new techniques.

Now I come to what we must do, and it is a fourfold programme. First, we must produce more scientists. Secondly, having produced them we must be a great deal more successful in keeping them in this country. Thirdly, having trained them and kept them here, we must make more intelligent use of them when they are trained than we do with those we have got. Fourthly, we must organise British industry so that it applies the results of scientific research more purposely to our national production effort ...

... in all our plans for the future, we are re-defining and we are re-stating our socialism in terms of the scientific revolution. But that revolution cannot become a reality unless we are prepared to make far-reaching changes in economic and social attitudes which permeate our whole system of society.

The Britain that is going to be forged in the white heat of this revolution will be no place for restrictive practices or for outdated methods on either side of industry ... ■

The general election of 1964 returned the Labour Party to power for the first time in thirteen years, although with a majority of only four seats.

7.36   **General election results, October 1964 (Charts derived from D. Butler and G. Butler (eds),** *British Political Facts, 1900–1985,* **London, Macmillan, 7th edn, 1994, p.217).**

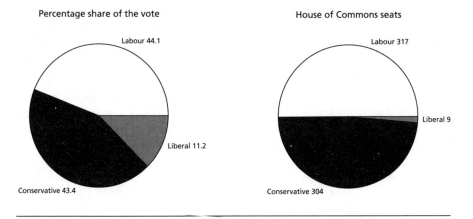

Percentage share of the vote

Labour 44.1

Liberal 11.2

Conservative 43.4

House of Commons seats

Labour 317

Liberal 9

Conservative 304

CHAPTER EIGHT

Responsibility without Power: Foreign and Imperial Policy, 1951–6

IN 1951 Britain could still claim to be the third-ranking world power. Although dwarfed by the United States and the Soviet Union, Britain retained global interests through its remaining colonial possessions and the developing Commonwealth. After the first British atomic bomb had been tested at Monte Bello Island in October 1952, the country's continuing prestige appeared to be confirmed through membership of an exclusive nuclear 'club'. In spite of the economic costs of the Second World War, the British economy remained much larger than that of any of Britain's European neighbours; and although the underlying problems of the economy continued to be expressed through the weakness of sterling, there was no reason to assume that economic recovery would not continue. When the Conservative Party returned to power, therefore, the major preoccupation was with the preservation of this world role.

But with hindsight the years leading up to the Suez Crisis in the autumn of 1956 have been seen as a period of rapid decline and missed opportunity. Continuing disturbances throughout the empire overstretched the country's limited resources. Even at points considered of vital strategic interest, the government could not always assert its authority, as the withdrawal of British troops from the Suez Canal Zone in 1954 demonstrated. Continuing economic vulnerability underscored Britain's reliance on the United States; as the Suez Crisis demonstrated all too plainly, the 'special relationship' was by no means a satisfactory one. Moreover, the relatively strong position of the country led its makers of foreign policy to hold back from participation in the movement for European integration, and many critics have argued that Britain unwisely 'missed the boat' by withdrawing from the Messina Conference in 1955, which led to the establishment of the European Economic Community.

The Burden of a World Role

The sterling crisis with which Winston Churchill's government was preoccupied during its first year after the 1951 general election emphasised the extent to which the country was overstretched in its defence and foreign policy commitments. But realistic assessments of the problem were not accompanied by a rapid paring down of Britain's commitments before 1957. Policy was guided instead by the determination not to destabilise confidence further by giving an impression of panic, or to abandon ties which could prove a future source of economic strength.

The charts shown as document 8.1 illustrate the extent to which foreign policy and defence commitments proved a continuing source of strain throughout the 1950s. While defence expenditure in Britain did not compare with the level of the United States or the Soviet Union, as a proportion of gross domestic product Britain was spending more than any other comparable country. Moreover, the determination to proceed as a nuclear power meant pouring a large proportion of the country's scientific and techno-logical research and development into defence programmes.

8.1   **The burden of British defence expenditure, 1950–7 (charts derived from Malcolm Chalmers, *Paying for Defence: Military Spending and British Decline*, London, Pluto Press, 1985, pp. 51, 68, 113).**

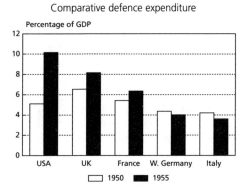

Comparative defence expenditure

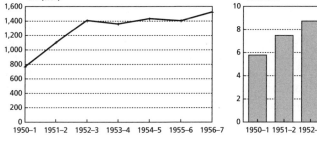

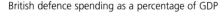

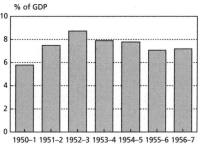

The government was well aware of these problems. By the summer of 1952, the mood was one of pessimism. Document 8.2, which comes from a Cabinet memorandum sub-mitted by the then Foreign Secretary Anthony Eden on Britain's overseas commitments, sets out the dilemma in clear terms.

8.2   Anthony Eden, Cabinet memorandum on overseas obligations, 15 June 1952 (PRO CAB 129/53, C(52)202).

■   CABINET

BRITISH OVERSEAS OBLIGATIONS

Memorandum by the Secretary of State for Foreign Affairs

The object of this paper is to consider the tasks to which the United Kingdom is committed overseas and to examine where if anywhere our responsibilities can be reduced so as to bring them more into line with our available resources …

4. The essence of a sound foreign policy is to ensure that a country's strength is equal to its obligations. If this is not the case, then either the obligations must be reduced to the level at which resources are available to maintain them, or a greater share of the country's resources must be devoted to their support. It is becoming clear that rigorous maintenance of the presently accepted policies of Her Majesty's Government at home and abroad is placing a burden on the country's economy which it is beyond the resources of the country to meet. A position has already been reached where there is no reserve and therefore no margin for unforeseen additional obligations …

6. There are very strong arguments against a complete abandonment of a major commitment. First, in the present state of world tension, unless arrangements have been made for the burden to be transferred to friendly shoulders, the Russians would be only too ready to fill any vacuum created by a British withdrawal, with a consequent shifting of the balance of power against the West. It is further obvious that when an area falls into Communist hands its economic and trading value to the Western world becomes greatly reduced while Western capital assets are liquidated with little or no compensation.

7. Secondly, withdrawal from a major commitment would affect the international status of the United Kingdom. By reducing the value of the United Kingdom as a partner and ally, it would undermine the cohesion of the Commonwealth and the special relationship of the United Kingdom with the United States and its European partners and other allies …

8. Thirdly, the British world position brings with it concurrent and beneficial results of an economic and financial nature. The abandonment of our position in any area of the world may well have similar concurrent and adverse effects on our economic and trading interests.

9. Finally, there is the general effect of loss of prestige … once the prestige of a country has started to slide there is no knowing where it will stop …

Conclusions

28. It is apparent from this review that there are few ways to effect any reductions in our overseas commitments which would provide immediate relief to our economic difficulties ...

29. If, on a longer view, it must be assumed that the maintenance of the present scale of overseas commitments will permanently overstrain our economy, clearly we ought to recognise that the United Kingdom is over-committed and must reduce the commitment. The only practical way of removing this permanent strain would be for the United Kingdom to shed or share the load of one or two major obligations, *e.g.* the defence of the Middle East, for which at present we bear the responsibility alone ... or the defence of South-East Asia, where we share responsibility with the French ... Our present policy is in fact directed towards the construction of international defence organisations for the Middle East and South-East Asia in which the United States and other Commonwealth countries would participate. Our aim should be to persuade the United States to assume the real burdens in such organisations, while retaining for our-selves as much political control – and hence prestige and world influence – as we can. As regards the defence of Western Europe, we should seek to induce the United States to assume a larger share of the common burden. A further substantial alleviation might be possible in 1954 and subsequent years if the build up of German contingents enables us to reduce British forces in Germany without endangering the common Western defence effort ...

30. The success of this policy will depend on a number of factors, some favourable, some unfavourable. The United States is the only single coun-try in the free world capable of assuming new and world-wide obligations; being heavily committed to the East–West struggle they would not readi-ly leave a power-vacuum in any part of the globe but would be disposed, however reluctantly, to fill it themselves if it was clear that the United Kingdom could no longer hold the position (as they did, for example, in Greece). On the other hand, the history of the Middle East command negotiations and the unwillingness of the United States Chiefs of Staff to commit forces to it illustrates the American reluctance to enter into new commitments in peace-time. In South-East Asia only the sketchiest form of co-operation exists. Moreover, distrust of the British and fear of becom-ing an instrument to prop up a declining British Empire are still strong. (This is truer among Republicans than Democrats, but we must clearly prepare ourselves to deal with either Government.) As regards the United Kingdom part, a policy of this kind will only be successful with the United States in so far as we are able to demonstrate that we are making the max-imum possible effort ourselves, and the more gradually and inconspicu-ously we can transfer the real burdens from our own to American shoulders, the less damage we shall do to our position and influence in the world. ∎

Britain's continuing economic problems had far-reaching implications for defence strategists. In particular, economic pressure heightened further the attractions of deterrence based on nuclear weapons. The paper on 'global strategy' submitted, at the Prime Minister's request, by the Chiefs of Staff to the Cabinet in July 1952 (document 8.3), was an important stage in this process. Conventional rearmament in Western Europe – labour intensive and expensive – on the scale envisaged by the United States' NSC-68 document of April 1950, was seen by the COS as impractical, given the economic difficulties facing most Western governments. Not only would nuclear weapons provide a cost-effective deterrent to potential aggressors, it was argued, but an independent British deterrent would make it far more likely that the USA would have to take British views into account when developing future North Atlantic Treaty Organisation defence strategy. It was on this basis that Britain continued to support an atomic programme, and proceeded with development of the hydrogen bomb.

8.3   Chiefs of Staff, 'Defence policy and global strategy', 17 June 1952 (PRO CAB 131/12, D(52)26).

■ 1. In this report we examine allied strategic policy. We suggest how the present policy should be modified to take into account factors which have arisen since it was established and the United Kingdom £4,700 million rearmament programme initiated. The chief of these factors are the notable increase in United States atomic power and the economic situation ...

6. Existing allied military policy is largely centred in the North Atlantic Treaty Organisation ... and this has the effect at present of making the United States reluctant to assume further responsibilities for defence in peace-time in other areas such as the Middle East and South-East Asia. In the background of NATO policy is the vague assumption that the Americans have built up a large stock of atom bombs which they are capable of dropping on Soviet key points from numerous bases about the world. Only America amongst the Allies has this formidable weapon, whose power is so closely guarded that, with the sole exception of the United Kingdom – and possibly Canada – other NATO countries have very little idea of the truth about it. They are unable to estimate for themselves its full potentialities and are therefore in no position to assess its possible strategic effects in war ...

10. We believe that, during the first few weeks following any Soviet aggression, Russia would be subjected to such a devastating attack upon so high a proportion of her vital centres that she would be unlikely to survive it as a Power capable of waging a full scale war. We consider that if this factor is judiciously publicised, and the necessary priorities accorded to its development, it is not only an effective deterrent but a war-winning factor of the first order ...

12. A new factor of fundamental importance, which has been the subject of some twelve months' intensive examination by the Air Defence Committee, is that it is now clear that there is in the foreseeable future no effective defence against atomic air attack ...

19. When the present strategic policy was established, it was still thought that Russia might be contemplating an early attack. But ... the Russian leaders are unlikely to embark on a war which could lead only to catastrophic devastation in Russia even though the Free World would receive fearful punishment too. The Russians are bound to fall back on attempts to gain their ends by other means ...

21. We conclude that war is unlikely provided that the Cold War is conducted by the Allies in a patient, levelheaded and determined manner. The United Kingdom must use its influence among the Allies to ensure that this is done. The implication is that the Allies must face the prospect of a prolonged period of Cold War waged by the Russians, their satellites and the Chinese, with great intensity and ingenuity ...

36. The first essential of allied policy must be to establish and maintain as long as may be necessary a really effective deterrent against war. It is only under cover of such a deterrent that the Allies will be able to carry out their Cold War policy ...

38. To ensure that this offensive will be immediately ready and completely effective, the Allies must give the necessary priority to the air striking forces, both where and when necessary. The world is passing out of the era when the number of atom bombs is the crux of the matter and is entering an era when the main problem will be to ensure by all means that the weapons can be delivered without prohibitive loss to the attacker ... This task will not be easy ... It will mean constant endeavour to keep a jump ahead in scientific development ...

39. There is a complementary deterrent which the Allies cannot afford to overlook. It must be made clear to the Russians that the Allies are able to make their advance across Europe both slow and difficult – a state of affairs which we are now approaching. This element of the deterrent must be provided by a sufficiency of land and air forces at a high state of readiness in Western Europe, supported by atomic air power. The Russians must be made to realise that the delay which will be imposed on them in Western Europe will be sufficient to enable the Allied air offensive to be effective before Europe has been over-run ...

41. ... The idea of outlawing atomic warfare naturally appeals to the best sentiments of all decent people, as well as to the unreasoning instinct of self-preservation. Therein lies its danger. The fact is that the Free World cannot hope, spread out as it is in an attenuated ring round the great mass of Russia and China, to contain the enemy by land forces deprived of support by atomic weapons. The Free World can maintain superior strength, and thus prevent the outbreak of war, only by matching science against man-power. We suggest that the existence of the great atomic deterrent is of vital importance to humanity and freedom to use it must be maintained. The Allies must keep their lead in this field, and the free peoples should be educated to see beyond emotion and to appreciate the reality ... ■

Britain and Europe

In the years before the Suez Crisis, British policy towards Europe reflected the country's traditional approach of attempting to secure a balance of power on the Continent which would keep the need for direct involvement to a minimum. It was well understood that a strong Franco-German alliance on the Continent, supported by Britain and the United States, could provide a sufficient deterrent to the Soviet Union without Britain having to risk its prestige as an independent power by becoming directly involved in new organisations such as the European Coal and Steel Community or the proposed European Defence Community (EDC). While the government would have much preferred to see integration continue along a looser, intergovernmental model under the aegis of the Organisation for European Economic Co-operation and NATO, federalist initiatives were tolerated, provided that the British could remain outside without jeopardising their national interests. By 1957, however, this policy was already coming unstuck. The failure of the EDC in August 1954 led to the pledge to station British forces permanently in Germany, albeit within the intergovernmental framework of the Western European Union; and Britain's failure to participate in the negotiations which led to the formation of the EEC in 1958 has been judged a missed opportunity to influence the structure and political culture of institutions which it would soon be compelled to join.

It might have been thought that a Churchill Cabinet would prove much more sympathetic to the federalist movement in Europe than had their predecessors under Clement Attlee. Churchill himself had been personally associated with proposals for integration since 1940, when he had proposed an Anglo-French union. But upon regaining office, he was careful to assert traditional British policy regarding Europe, an attitude which he outlined to the Cabinet shortly after taking office.

8.4   Winston Churchill, Cabinet memorandum on 'United Europe', 29 November 1951 (PRO CAB 129/48, C(51)32).

■ It may simplify discussion if I set forth briefly my own view and the line I have followed so far.

1. At Zürich in 1946 I appealed to France to take the lead in Europe by making friends with the Germans, 'burying the thousand-year quarrel', &c. This caused a shock at the time but progress has been continual. I always recognised that, as Germany is potentially so much stronger than France, militarily and economically, Britain and if possible the United States should be associated with United Europe, to make an even balance and to promote the United Europe Movement.

2. As year by year the project advanced, the Federal Movement in many European countries who participated became prominent. It has in the last two years lost much of its original force. The American mind jumps much too lightly over its many difficulties. I am not opposed to a European Federation including (eventually) the countries behind the Iron Curtain,

provided that this comes about naturally and gradually. But I never thought that Britain or the British Commonwealth should, whether individually or collectively, become an integral part of a European Federation, and have never given the slightest support to the idea. We should not, however, obstruct but rather favour the movement to closer European unity and try to get the United States' support in this work.

3. There can be no effective defence of Western Europe without the Germans. As things developed my idea has always been as follows: there is the NATO Army. Inside the NATO Army there is the European Army, and inside the European Army there is the German Army. The European Army should be formed by all the European parties to NATO plus Germany, 'dedicating' from their own national armies their quota of divisions to the army now under General Eisenhower's command. Originally at Strasbourg in 1950 the Germans did not press for a national army. On the contrary they declared themselves ready to join a European Army without having a national army. The opportunity was lost and there seems very little doubt that Germany will have to have a certain limited national army from which to 'dedicate'. The size and strength of this army, and its manufacture of weapons, would have to be agreed with the victorious Powers of the late war. In any case the recruiting arrangements for covering the German quota would have involved a considerable machinery.

4. In the European Army all dedicated quotas of participating nations would be treated with strict honourable military equality. The national characteristics should be preserved up to the divisional level, special arrangements being made about the 'tail', heavy weapons, &c. I should doubt very much the military spirit of a 'sludgy amalgam' of volunteers or conscripts to defend the EDC or other similar organisations. The national spirit must animate all troops up to and including the divisional level. On this basis and within these limits national pride may be made to promote and serve international strength.

5. France does not seem to be playing her proper part in these arrangements. France is not France without 'L'Armée Française'. I warned MM. Pleven and Monnet several times that a 'Pleven Army' would not go down in France. The French seem to be trying to get France defended by Europe. Their proposed contribution for 1952 of five, rising to ten, divisions is pitiful, even making allowances for the fact that they are still trying to hold their Oriental Empire …

6. On the economic side, I welcome the Schuman Coal and Steel Plan as a step in the reconciliation of France and Germany, and as probably rendering another Franco-German war physically impossible. I never contemplated Britain joining in this plan on the same terms as Continental partners. We should, however, have joined in all the discussions, and had we done so not only a better plan would probably have emerged, but our own interests would have been watched at every stage. Our attitude towards further economic developments on the Schuman lines resembles that which we adopt about the European Army. We help, we dedicate, we play a part, but we are not merged and do not forfeit our insular or Commonwealth-wide character. I should resist any American pressure to treat Britain as on the same footing as the European States, none of whom have the advantages of the Channel and who were consequently conquered.

7. Our first object is the unity and the consolidation of the British Commonwealth and what is left of the former British Empire. Our second, the 'fraternal association' of the European-speaking world; and third, United Europe, to which we are a separate closely – and specially – related ally and friend ... ■

German rearmament

By far the most controversial proposal of the early 1950s was for the rearmament of West Germany. Coming so soon after the end of the war, it was understandable that the French in particular, but many Germans as well, were firmly opposed to any such development. On the other hand, it did not make sense for Western Europe to defend itself *without* making use of German military potential. The economic burden alone had become intolerable, and the Americans were especially frustrated at Western Europe's seeming inability to defend itself effectively. The US solution was to encourage rearmament within the context of integration. As discussed in Chapter 5, the success of the European Coal and Steel Community had led to a proposed European Defence Community, towards which the Germans could contribute divisions without the need for a separate West German military command.

The plans for a European Defence Community fell through in August 1954, when the French Chamber of Deputies failed to ratify the treaty. The British, who had always been sceptical of the project, quickly stepped in to retrieve the situation. The diplomatic formula proposed by Anthony Eden permitted Germany and Italy to enter the Brussels Pact (to be known as the Western European Union) and NATO, in return for a British guarantee, to reassure France, in the form of four divisions and a tactical air force permanently stationed in West Germany. The German and Italian armed forces were additionally forbidden to produce or use atomic, biological or chemical weapons. In the following memorandum for the Cabinet, Eden outlines his proposals on the eve of the London Conference of Britain, Canada, the USA, France, Italy, Germany and the Benelux countries, on German rearmament, which approved his plan.

8.5   Anthony Eden, Cabinet memorandum on the London Conference, 27 September 1954 (PRO CAB 129/70, C(54)298, pp. 1–2).

■ The problem will be to reconcile –

(i) The German desire for rapid restoration of sovereignty and membership of the North Atlantic Treaty Organisation (NATO);

(ii) French reluctance to admit either, until elaborate safeguards have been agreed, notably a complicated and probably unworkable system for the control of armament manufacture on the Continent; and

(iii) American reluctance or inability to repeat the undertakings they gave in connection with the European Defence Community (EDC) about maintaining American military strength in Europe.

2. M. Mendès-France may press the Conference to agree to this or that unnecessary or dangerous proposal on the grounds that without it he will not get a favourable vote from the French Assembly. We cannot allow our discussions to be conducted on this basis. The task of the conference must be to produce a workable plan designed to meet legitimate French requirements but not to attempt tortuous gymnastics in order to get a majority for M. Mendès-France.

3. If we produce a workable plan the Americans are unlikely to allow it to fail through the lack of the essential American support. If, however, we are to do this it will be necessary for the French to face some unpleasant realities. They will have to accept German sovereignty and German membership of NATO and withdraw or drastically reduce their safeguard proposals. If they are to do this, they must be given some striking *quid pro quo*. The assurance most likely to strike French opinion is the continued presence of British troops in Europe …

4. In my opinion the key to the success of the Conference will be a new commitment by the United Kingdom to maintain our present forces on the Continent and not to withdraw them against the wishes of the majority of the enlarged Brussels Treaty Powers. This would not give France a veto, but we should no longer be able to withdraw forces at our sole discretion and would have to obtain the consent of the majority of the seven expanded Brussels Treaty partners, who should take their decision in knowledge of the Supreme Commander, Europe's (SACEUR's) views. Given our close ties with the three Benelux countries, I think we can always rely on obtaining this majority if we have a reasonable case. It would be necessary also to provide for certain exceptions to the general rule: an overseas emergency so acute that there was no time to go through the process of consultation, or balance of payments difficulties which made it financially impossible for us to maintain the strength of our forces on the Continent.

5. I realise that this would be an unprecedented commitment for the United Kingdom, but the hard fact is that it is impossible to organise an effective defence system in Western Europe, which in turn is essential for the security of the United Kingdom, without a major British contribution. This situation will persist for many years to come. By recognising this fact and giving the new commitment we may succeed in bringing the Germans and the French together and keeping the Americans in Europe. If we do not, the Conference may fail and the Atlantic Alliance fall to pieces.

6. I therefore seek the authority of my colleagues to give a new British undertaking at an appropriate stage during the Conference. It will be most important meantime to keep it secret. This undertaking would be –

(i) to maintain on the Continent the effective strength of the British forces now assigned to SACEUR, *i.e.*, our four divisions and the Tactical Air Force, or whatever SACEUR regards as equivalent fighting capacity; and

(ii) not to withdraw those forces against the wishes of a majority of the Brussels Treaty Powers, who should take their decision in knowledge of SACEUR's views.

7. This undertaking would be subject to the understanding that an acute overseas emergency might oblige us to short-circuit this procedure and that, if the maintenance of our forces on the continent of Europe throws at any time too heavy a strain on the external finances of the United Kingdom, it will be open to the United Kingdom to ask that the financial conditions on which the formations are maintained should be reviewed by the North Atlantic Council. ■

Missing the boat? Britain and the origins of the EEC

After the rapid progress of the early 1950s, the failure of the French to ratify the EDC treaty came as a heavy blow to the integration movement on the Continent. From a British perspective, however, Eden's triumph at the London Conference in December 1954 had succeeded in guiding the Europeans back firmly into an intergovernmental and Atlanticist model for integration. The government attached no particular importance to the meeting of the Six at Messina in June 1955. But the Messina Conference appointed a committee, under the chairmanship of the Belgian Foreign Minister, Paul Henri Spaak, to formulate proposals for a customs union. The withdrawal of the British observer from the Spaak Committee meant that the Six would continue independently to undertake negotiations which would culminate in the establishment of the European Economic Community and Euratom, the European Atomic Energy Authority, in 1958.

British attitudes towards the Messina proposals were sceptical. There was certainly no question at this stage that membership of the proposed new institutions should be contemplated in London. The following brief, prepared at the Foreign Office, summarises the position struck by Eden's government towards the prospect of a continental common market.

8.6   Foreign Office brief on the Messina Conference proposals, January 1956 (PRO FO 371/122022).

■ … A major objective of British post-war policy has been to promote the recovery and cohesion of Western Europe, with British participation and British leadership. Hence our share in the creation and activities of OEEC,

WEU and NATO, which provide more effective international cooperation than ever achieved before. The Messina powers want, however, to go further, and to achieve tighter European integration through the creation of European institutions with supranational powers, beginning in the economic field. As is explained in a more detailed brief, the Messina plans for a Common Market and EURATOM might, if certain conditions are fulfilled, produce long-term economic benefits. But the present indications are that those conditions will not be fulfilled and these plans are therefore likely to be economically harmful. The under-lying motive of the Six is, however, essentially political; to bind Germany to the West and prevent her gravitating to the East; and to stimulate and give concrete shape to the European idea, thus providing an effective rival appeal to Communism and the means of finally burying Franco-German rivalry ...

■ **3.** As against this, the political objections to the Messina plans are:

(*a*) That in their efforts to integrate themselves the Six will divide Europe into two camps and thus harm its unity and purpose;

(*b*) That the Germans will prove to be so much the strongest element that far from being controlled they would dominate;

(*c*) That a European third force might develop neutralist tendencies and seek to take up an independent position between the USA and the USSR, thus disrupting the Atlantic Alliance ...

While we should not hesitate to make known the objections of HM Government to joining these plans, we should show no open hostility to them and should seek to ensure that in so far as they are put into effect they avert the economic and political dangers.

4. We should do this by:

(*a*) persuading the Six to discuss their plans for a Common Market in the Council of OEEC with the view of reconciling their plans with the wider interests of OEEC as a whole and with GATT;

(*b*) persuading the Six to allow the Euratom plan to be modified and fitted into the looser and a more flexible framework now under discussion with OEEC;

(*c*) maintaining close relations with the Six and, if their plans come to fruition, establish, if necessary, an institutional arrangement with them, but within the framework of OEEC.

5. Simultaneously, having regard in particular to the German aspect ... we should endeavour

(*a*) to make the OEEC concept as positive and attractive to the imagination as we can, and

(*b*) to emphasise that in our view the narrower and the wider framework do not necessarily exclude each other; if the narrower one can be fitted into the wider one, we shall be quite happy, – so long as no one demands that we should go into the narrower one ourselves ... ■

Cold War or Détente?

While Winston Churchill was a staunch anti-Communist, he returned to office determined to pursue *détente* with the Soviet Union. In part, he seems to have been obsessed with playing the role of international peacemaker, a final dramatic gesture at the end of his remarkable career. But he had clearly become uneasy over the rigid ideological hostility which characterised US–Soviet relations in this period, and believed that the time had come to negotiate from a position of strength, now that NATO had been firmly established.

While Josef Stalin remained alive, and the United States remained gripped by the anti-Communist hysteria of Senator Joseph McCarthy, there was no diplomatic opening for Churchill to pursue. A combination of events convinced the Prime Minister that his opportunity had finally arrived in the spring of 1953. The election of Dwight D. Eisenhower, with whom Churchill had a good personal friendship from the war years, to the US presidency in November 1952; the signing of the EDC treaty in May of that year, which seemed to resolve the problem of German rearmament; and, above all, Stalin's death in March 1953 – all were factors in Churchill's reasoning. In May 1953, to the surprise of his own Cabinet, he announced in the House of Commons his intention to seek a meeting with the Soviets.

8.7   **Winston Churchill, speech to the House of Commons on foreign affairs, 11 May 1953 (*Hansard*, 5th ser., 515: 895–8).**

■ **The Prime Minister (Sir Winston Churchill):** … The supreme event which has occurred since we last had a debate on foreign affairs is, of course, the change of attitude and, as we all hope, of mood which has taken place in the Soviet domains and particularly in the Kremlin since the death of Stalin. We, on both sides of the House, have watched this with profound attention. It is the policy of Her Majesty's Government to avoid by every means in their power doing anything or saying anything which could check any favourable reaction that may be taking place and to welcome every sign of improvement in our relations with Russia …

… I think it would be a mistake to try to map things out too much in detail and expect that the grave, fundamental issues which divide the Communist and non-Communist parts of the world could be settled at a stroke by a single comprehensive agreement. Piecemeal solutions of individual problems should not be disdained or improvidently put aside. It certainly would do no harm if, for a while, each side looked about for things to do which would be agreeable instead of being disagreeable to each other.

Above all, it would be a pity if the natural desire to reach a general settlement of international policy were to impede any spontaneous and healthy evolution which may be taking place inside Russia. I have regarded some of the internal manifestations and the apparent change of mood as far more important and significant than what has happened outside. I am anxious that nothing in the presentation of foreign policy by the NATO Powers should, as it were, supersede or take the emphasis out of what may be a profound movement of Russian feeling.

... I must make it plain that, in spite of all the uncertainties and confusion in which world affairs are plunged, I believe that a conference on the highest level should take place between the leading Powers without long delay. This conference should not be overhung by a ponderous or rigid agenda, or led into mazes and jungles of technical details, zealously contested by hoards of experts and officials drawn up in vast cumbrous array. The conference should be confined to the smallest number of Powers and persons possible. It should meet with a measure of informality and a still greater measure of privacy and seclusion. It might well be that no hard-faced agreements would be reached, but there might be a general feeling among those gathered together that they might do something better than tear the human race, including themselves, into bits.

For instance, they might be attracted, as President Eisenhower has shown himself to be, and as 'Pravda' does not challenge, by the idea of letting the weary, toiling masses of mankind enter upon the best spell of good fortune, fair play, well-being, leisure and harmless happiness that has ever been within their reach or even within their dreams.

I only say that this might happen, and I do not see why anyone should be frightened at having a try for it. If there is not at the summit of the nations the will to win the greatest prize and the greatest honour ever offered to mankind, doom-laden responsibility will fall upon those who now possess the power to decide. At the worst the participants in the meeting would have established more intimate contacts. At the best we might have a generation of peace ... ■

Churchill's determination to arrange a summit meeting was at odds not only with Eisenhower's hard-line anti-Communist Secretary of State, John Foster Dulles, but with the Foreign Office and much of the Cabinet, including Eden and Lord Salisbury, foreign affairs spokesman in the House of Lords. The French and the Germans, in particular, feared that public support for détente, encouraged by so senior a figure as Churchill, would wreck ratification of the EDC. It was widely felt that the Soviets would use the opportunity to attempt to drive a wedge between the Western allies, and that a firm signal of Soviet good intentions should be a prelude to any joint meeting. At French prompting, a meeting of Britain, France and the United States was hastily arranged in Bermuda to forestall Churchill's plans, a meeting which did not actually take place until December. Thus, when it became known in July that the Prime Minister had sent a personal message to the Soviet Foreign Minister, V.M. Molotov, without consulting the Cabinet, the government was plunged into serious crisis. Document 8.8, an extract from the Cabinet minutes, demonstrates the extent to which the 1951–5 government suffered from divided leadership in foreign affairs.

8.8   Cabinet minutes, proposed meeting with M. Malenkov, 8 July 1954 (PRO CAB 128/27, part I, CC(54)48th, Conclusions, *Confidential Annex*).

■ ... THE PRIME MINISTER said that some of his colleagues might think that the Cabinet should have been consulted before he had sent to M. Molotov the personal and private message embodied in Foreign Office telegram to Moscow No. 873. It had been his practice as Prime Minister, both during the war and since the present Government took office, to exchange personal messages with Heads of Governments and more particularly with the President of the United States. Most of these messages had been seen before despatch by the Foreign Secretary, who could always suggest that reference should be made to the Cabinet if he thought this necessary. The Prime Minister hoped that he would continue to enjoy the confidence of his colleagues in continuing a practice which, in his opinion, had proved beneficial in the conduct of public affairs.

THE LORD PRESIDENT said that he was glad that this opportunity had been given to discuss the constitutional aspects of this matter. He did not contest the right of a Prime Minister to determine policy. But, if a Prime Minister took a decision of policy which involved the collective responsibility of the whole Government without prior consultation with his Cabinet colleaues, any of his colleagues who dissented from the decision might thereby be forced to the remedy of resignation. The message which the Prime Minister had sent to M. Molotov, though framed as a personal enquiry, was in his opinion an important act of foreign policy; and it would have been preferable that the Cabinet should have been given an opportunity to express their views on it before it was sent.

THE LORD PRIVY SEAL said that he also regarded this as an important act of policy, on which the Cabinet should have been consulted ... For his part, if his view had been sought, he would have been inclined to advise against making such an approach at the present time ...

THE LORD PRESIDENT said that the message had been despatched to Moscow on 4th July. The Prime Minister and the Foreign Secretary had arrived in London on 6th July and could then have held full consultation with their Cabinet colleagues. Was the message so urgent that its despatch could not have been delayed for three days?

THE PRIME MINISTER said that, in his anxiety to lose no opportunity of furthering the cause of world peace, he might have taken an exaggerated view of the urgency of the matter. There had seemed no reason to delay what he regarded as a personal and informal enquiry which could not commit his colleagues ...

THE LORD PRESIDENT said that in his opinion the Cabinet's freedom of action had to some extent been limited by the message which the Prime Minister had sent. When the Cabinet came to take a decision on the substance of the issue, they might wish to decide that it would be preferable not to go forward with this project for a meeting with M. Malenkov. But, if they so decided, and if the Russians then chose to give publicity to the messages exchanged between the Prime Minister and M. Molotov, the public would be left with the impression that the Prime Minister had wished to arrange such a meeting but had been deterred from doing so by his Cabinet colleagues. That consideration might now influence the Cabinet's eventual decision. ■

Imperial Policy

Decolonisation

British imperial policy in this postwar period is often favourably compared to the French, and it is indeed true that decolonisation never threatened the stability of the British state to any comparable extent. While the French colonial wars in Indochina and Algeria weakened national self-confidence, the latter leading to the collapse of the Fourth Republic in 1958, British emergencies in Malaya, Kenya or Cyprus – to take a few examples – made little political impact at home. France relied heavily upon continued direct influence in South-East Asia and North Africa in order to maintain a pretence of world power status, whereas British national prestige in these years derived from a number of factors: from victory in the Second World War, the special relationship with the USA and possession of nuclear weapons, as well as from her imperial and Commonwealth ties. Thus it was generally less painful for the British government to accede to nationalist demands in the colonies. Moreover, decolonisation was greatly accelerated by the enormous pressure to reduce foreign and defence expenditure.

Key to the decolonisation process was the continued success of the Commonwealth as an international organisation which projected an image of Britain as a mature and successful world power. Although allegiance to the Sterling Area gradually weakened as successive economic crises continued to put pressure on the pound, the Commonwealth was still viewed as an important component in Britain's economic revival. Commonwealth unity, however, was under threat at many points. The transition to multiracial membership proved particularly difficult. Britain faced censure from many members over its treatment of New Commonwealth immigrants, a factor which partly accounts for the initial reluctance to introduce immigration restrictions at home, as discussed in Chapter 7.

Abroad, decolonisation policy in southern and East Africa, where the interests of minority white settler populations had to be reconciled with black African nationalist movements, proved exceedingly difficult, as demonstrated clearly in the wake of the Mau Mau rebellion in Kenya in 1952. The Central African Federation of Northern and Southern Rhodesia and Nyasaland was launched in 1953, a rich region of the continent with vast potential for economic development. But while the CAF was presented as a model for multiracial decolonisation, the structure of its constitution overwhelmingly favoured the white minority, and the resultant tension would lead to its demise later in the decade, exacerbating the problems thrown up by the election of a racist Afrikaner Nationalist government to power in South Africa in 1948.

The following memorandum, prepared by the Commonwealth Relations Office in 1956, examines many of these issues.

8.9   Commonwealth Relations Office, memorandum on the probable development of the Commonwealth over the next ten or fifteen years, June 1956 (PRO CO 1032/51, no. 112).

■ ...

6. ... in considering the links that hold the Commonwealth together weight must be given ... to the facts that: –

(i) in recent years we have actually been drawing closer in understanding with the old Commonwealth countries. It is true that they are becoming stronger and are hence physically better able to pursue their own line where they wish. But, as they increasingly understand the reality of their independence they have fewer inhibitions in co-operating with us: there is less temptation for them to strike an independent line merely in order to demonstrate their independence. Our physical means of maintaining close consultation with them on all matters have greatly increased. Consequently they have an increased understanding of our problems, as we have of theirs. We may expect this tendency to increase during the next few years;

(ii) the economies of all Commonwealth countries which are members of the Sterling Area are very closely tied up with our economy. They are accustomed to trade with us, as we are with them. That is why it is in their interest that their currencies are tied to sterling and the fact that their currencies are tied to sterling increases the tendency for us to trade with each other. These bonds should continue independently whether some Commonwealth countries (particularly the emergent ones) become Republics or even leave the Commonwealth. These economic bonds with us inevitably affect the policies of the countries concerned, and will tend to keep them in the Commonwealth ...

South Africa

... 29. *Constitutionally* the Union is likely sooner or later to become a Republic. Her relations with India are likely to continue strained, but there is no present reason to expect that she will leave the Commonwealth. Her Government's reaction to the admission to Commonwealth Membership of African States, such as the Gold Coast or Nigeria, shows signs of mellowing.

30. But these States, when admitted, are reasonably certain to be active supporters of Indian criticism of South African native policy, and might join India in public denunciation of that policy in the United Nations and other international gatherings. The emergence within the Commonwealth of two groups with conflicting views on so important a matter (particularly as our

sympathies are opposed to South African policy) would place an increasing strain on the United Kingdom and possibly on other 'old' Members in trying to hold the balance, and might result in a situation in which the Union would leave the Commonwealth ...

33. *Economically* the Union has every prospect of marked industrial and economic development. At present the economy of the country is mainly in the hands of the English-speaking element and many British firms have established manufacturing subsidiaries in South Africa ...

34. Neither politically nor in business will sentiment count for anything: but economic development is likely to provide substantial scope for United Kingdom exports ...

The Central African Federation

50. *Economically* the Federation, with its great mineral and industrial potential, and its abundant supply of labour, has every prospect of a marked and progressive advance ...

51. Everything will depend first on the working out of the policy of partnership between European and African, and secondly upon a co-operative understanding between the Federation and the three territories of Northern Rhodesia, Southern Rhodesia, and Nyasaland. The Africans of the two Northern territories are suspicious of the Europeans of Southern Rhodesia and of the Federal Government whom the Europeans inevitably dominate at the present time ...

53. On the assumption that this can be achieved, a prosperous and strong new Commonwealth country, with close links with the United Kingdom, and offering a substantial and an assured market for British goods, can be looked for in Central Africa over the period now under review. Failure to secure it might not only set back the political advancement of the Federation, but might imperil the stability of the Federal structure ...

UK policy over the next 10 to 15 years

69. The United Kingdom will, on any reasonable expectation, continue itself to develop.

70. It will become progressively less a dominating feature in the *Commonwealth* as the 'old' Commonwealth countries expand industrially and in population, and with the emergence of large Afro-Asian groups of Commonwealth countries; and in the *world* as the USA, the Soviet Union and Germany expand.

71. The Commonwealth can hardly remain in being without the uniting bond of the United Kingdom and the Monarchy.

72. While it does so remain, the United Kingdom as its oldest member, occupies a world position far more important than she could claim solely in her own right; though that will increasingly cease to be the case as the major elements in the Colonial empire become self-governing.

73. Were the United Kingdom to stand by herself, her importance would still be great, but immensely less than it is while she remains the centre of the Commonwealth.

74. If that is so, it will be vital in decisions of policy to give the fullest weight to the necessity to keep the Commonwealth together, and to Commonwealth reactions.

... ■

Decolonisation proceeded with increasing urgency from 1954, not simply because of economic pressure to reduce overseas commitments, but also because of nationalist demands and unrest in many colonies. It became vital to strike a realistic balance between British economic and political interests and good relations with emerging nationalist leaders. In the Gold Coast, which became independent Ghana in 1957, the movement led by the popular nationalist Kwame Nkrumah was 'tamed' in the years leading to the transition of power, so that, while the new government was not considered to be particularly adept, the likely consequences of self-government were viewed as acceptable in Whitehall. In document 8.10 the Adviser on External Affairs to the Governor of the Gold Coast (Ghana), Francis Cummings-Bruce, outlines his views on the future of Anglo-Ghanaian relations for Sir Gilbert Laithwaite, the Permanent Under-Secretary of State for Commonwealth Relations.

8.10   F.E. Cummings-Bruce, memorandum to Sir Gilbert Laithwaite on the future of the Gold Coast, August 1955 (PRO PREM 11/1367).

■   NOTES ON THE FUTURE GOLD COAST SCENE
WITH SPECIAL REFERENCE TO EXTERNAL RELATIONS
AFTER INDEPENDENCE

A. LONG TERM PROSPECTS

...

3. Politically the country faces a period of instability. It will be within the power of government to keep the situation under control, if the party in power proves capable of exercising restraint towards its opponents and learns how to handle law and order, and if administration is maintained at a reasonable standard ...

4. The good record of African Ministers is largely due to the personal influence of the Governor, the unprecedented amount of money in the government's hands from the cocoa boom, and the absence of serious problems. Ministers have learned much, but there is not likely to be much statesmanship in Government policy after independence....

B. DOMESTIC PROSPECTS IN THE TRANSITIONAL PERIOD

....

8. So long as order is maintained, the effects of weak government need not be disastrous on account of the buoyancy of primary production. The basic economy of the country should remain sound, with continuation of production of foodstuffs and export of cocoa, gold and diamonds at present levels: and the Volta River Project would result in a great addition to resources ...

11. Delay of independence would bring great advantages in the field of future domestic administration. But unless delay was clearly the result of internal factors, postponement would have great dangers for future external relations, and these dangers outweigh domestic administrative considerations ...

12. A change of Government before independence at present seems to be unlikely. A non-CPP [Convention People's Party] government would probably be better informed and have a more responsible approach to external relations; but it would not necessarily handle administration any better than the CPP; and it remains to be seen whether the opponents of the CPP could ever muster and retain enough solidarity to work together as a Government.

C. EXTERNAL RELATIONS AFTER INDEPENDENCE

....

17. The Nkrumah Government, if in power after independence, will be inclined to assert its independence of British apron-strings in various ways, some of which may be embarrassing. It seems likely to indulge in active steps of anti-colonialism in West Africa and perhaps further afield ...

18. In commercial policy there is likely for a time to be some encouragement of domestic enterprise at the expense of overseas interests and some prejudice in favour of foreign countries at our expense. But if we are patient and accommodating, our strong position ought not to be seriously undermined ...

19. In seeking from a CPP Government any positive contribution in Commonwealth defence we should be swimming against the neutralist stream. But the Gold Coast Government seems likely to be prepared to cooperate over defence facilities if carefully handled.

D. GENERAL CONCLUSION

20. The Gold Coast is likely to settle down eventually at a comparatively low level of efficiency. The conditions for reasonable commercial relations with the UK seem likely to be satisfied. The first ten years after independence will be of disproportionate importance for the future and there is a serious

danger that during this period the country will lose overseas personnel to an extent that may undermine the administration beyond repair. ■

The road to Suez

Both the Churchill and the Eden government were determined to maintain and protect British bases overseas at a number of points considered to be vital to the country's national security interests. As Foreign Secretary, Eden set out where possible to achieve this through diplomatic negotiation. Experienced diplomatic leadership could not always provide the answer, however, in an increasingly complex international environment in which British room for manoeuvre was circumscribed by the reality of United States power. The rest of this chapter will focus on British policy on Egypt and the Suez Crisis, which marked a milestone in the development of the 'special relationship'.

Anglo-Egyptian relations deteriorated rapidly from the autumn of 1951. The outbreak of terrorist attacks on British camps stationed at Suez led to a British Army action in January 1952 to disarm the Egyptian Auxiliary Police, during which forty-one Egyptians were killed. Popular disaffection with the British led to a coup in July, which replaced King Farouk's regime with a military junta of army officers, led by General Muhammad Neguib and Colonel Gamal Abdel Nasser. Eden's decision to open negotiations with the new regime was opposed, not only by a die-hard 'Suez Group' of backbench Conservatives, but also by Churchill himself. The following passage, taken from the diary of the Foreign Office official in charge of Middle Eastern affairs, gives a flavour of the controversy which raged between the Foreign Office and No. 10 Downing Street.

8.11   Evelyn Shuckburgh, diary, 29–30 January 1953 (in Evelyn Shuckburgh, *Descent to Suez: Diaries 1951–56*, London, Weidenfeld & Nicolson, 1986, pp. 75–6).

■ *29 January*

... Jock Colville came round to see me in a great state of agitation. He said there was going to be a row. He had gone overnight to Southampton and travelled up with the PM. The latter was in a rage against A.E., speaking of 'appeasement' and saying he never knew before that Munich was situated on the Nile. He described A.E. as having been a failure as Foreign Secretary and being 'tired, sick and bound up in detail'. Jock said that the Prime Minister would never give way over Egypt. He positively desired the talks on the Sudan to fail, just as he positively hoped we should not succeed in getting into conversations with the Egyptians on defence which might lead to our abandonment of the Canal Zone. Jock, who has hitherto sided strongly with the PM over this Egypt question, seemed seriously concerned. He said, 'The only hope is that Neguib will behave so badly that our two masters will see eye to eye.' In other words, the hope is that the talks will fail, which is Winston's hope ...

30 January

A Cabinet in the afternoon on Egypt. Expectation of more fireworks, but none took place. I spent a very uncomfortable half-hour with the Private Secretaries at No. 10, during which Colville, Pitblado and Montague Browne all attacked A.E. and the Foreign Office for their policy on Egypt. They thought we should sit on the gippies and have a 'whiff of grapeshot'. If it meant letting the British communities in Alexandria and Cairo be massacred that could not be helped. Anyway, the soldiers were notoriously pessimistic and they thought it ridiculous that we should not be able to cope with the Egyptian Army with the eighty thousand men we have in the Zone. The Chiefs of Staff, they said (obviously quoting the Prime Minister), always say that the force available for any emergency is insufficient. You have to prove the contrary. If we go out of the Sudan and Egypt it will be another stage in the policy of scuttle which began in India and ended at Abadan. It will lead to the abandonment of our African colonies. The Prime Minister is trying to arrest history. People said at Munich that Britain was finished and that history was against us, but Winston had proved it wrong ... ■

Supported by the Chiefs of Staff, who doubted the value of the Suez base anyway, Eden proceeded to negotiate a settlement with the Egyptians over withdrawal from the Canal Zone. The terms of the 1954 Anglo-Egyptian Treaty are outlined in document 8.12, an initialled memorandum. Britain's subsequent entry into the Baghdad Pact in March 1955, joining Turkey, Iraq and Pakistan, was intended to bolster the prestige of Britain's loyal allies in the area, and to check the growing influence of the Egyptian regime. Eden's failure to persuade Jordan to participate in this anti-Egyptian regional alliance, however, signalled the bankruptcy of his Middle Eastern policy.

8.12   **Anglo-Egyptian Treaty memorandum, initialled at Cairo on 27 July 1954 (Cmd 9230, PP XXXIII 1953–4, pp. 2–3).**

■   HEADS OF AGREEMENT. ANGLO-EGYPTIAN
             DEFENCE NEGOTIATIONS
             REGARDING THE SUEZ CANAL BASE

It is agreed between the Egyptian and British Delegations that, with a view to establishing Anglo-Egyptian relations on a new basis of mutual understanding and firm friendship, and taking into account their obligations under the United Nations Charter, an agreement regarding the Suez Canal base should now be drafted on the following lines.

2. The agreement will last until the expiry of seven years from the date of signature. During the last twelve months of this period the two Governments will consult together to decide what arrangements are necessary upon the termination of the agreement.

3. Parts of the present Suez Canal base will be kept in efficient working order in accordance with the requirements set forth in Annex 1 and capable of immediate use in accordance with the following paragraph.

4. – (i) In the event of an armed attack by an outside Power on Egypt or any country which at the date of the signature of the present agreement is a party to the Treaty of Joint Defence between Arab League States or on Turkey, Egypt will afford to the United Kingdom such facilities as may be necessary in order to place the base on a war footing and to operate it effectively. These facilities will include the use of Egyptian ports within the limits of what is strictly indispensable for the above-mentioned purposes.

(ii) In the event of a threat of an attack on any of the above-mentioned countries, there shall be immediate consultation between the United Kingdom and Egypt.

5. The organisation of the base will be in accordance with Annex 1 attached.

6. The United Kingdom will be accorded the right to move any British material into or out of the base at its discretion. There will be no increase above the level of supplies to be agreed upon without the consent of the Egyptian Government.

7. Her Majesty's forces will be completely withdrawn from Egyptian territory according to a schedule to be established in due course within a period of twenty months from the date of signature of this agreement. The Egyptian Government will afford all necessary facilities for the movement of men and material in this connexion.

8. The agreement will recognise that the Suez Maritime Canal, which is an integral part of Egypt, is a waterway economically, commercially and strategically of international importance, and will express the determination of both parties to uphold the 1888 Convention guaranteeing the freedom of navigation of the Canal.

9. The Egyptian Government will afford overflying, landing and servicing facilities for notified flights of aircraft under RAF control. For the clearance of any flights the Egyptian Government will extend most-favoured-nation treatment.

10. There will be questions of detail to be covered in the drafting of the agreement including the storage of oil, the financial arrangements necessary, and other detailed matters of importance to both sides. These will be settled by friendly agreement in negotiations which will begin forthwith. ■

The Suez Crisis

By the time that Colonel Nasser announced his decision to nationalise the Suez Canal Company in order to compensate for the withdrawal of Western loans to finance the Aswan Dam project on 27 July 1956, Eden was already determined to consolidate his position as Conservative Party leader and Prime Minister by proving his anti-appeasement credentials and cutting Egypt down to size. Nasser's consolidation of power in Egypt and increasingly independent role in world affairs was seen by the British as deliberately provocative. Egyptian political development threatened the British because of the way Nasser attempted to encourage extreme nationalism in other colonies and former colonies.

But the decision to join France and Israel in a covert plan to seize the canal and bring down the Egyptian regime proved a disastrous and costly mistake. British withdrawal from Suez, at the insistence of the United States, effectively ended Eden's career, critically damaged Britain's international standing, and brought relations with both the USA and France to a postwar low point.

The minutes of the Cabinet meeting on the day following Nasser's nationalisation announcement suggest that the British government was prepared to resort to the use of force from the outset of the crisis.

8.13   **Cabinet minutes on Suez, 28 July 1956 (PRO CAB 128/30, part II).**

■ ....

The Prime Minister said that ... the Cabinet must decide what our policy must be. He fully agreed that the question was not a legal issue but must be treated as a matter of the widest international importance. It must now be our aim to place the Suez Canal under the control of the Powers interested in international shipping and trade by means of a new international Commission on which Egypt would be given suitable representation. Colonel Nasser's action had presented us with an opportunity to find a lasting settlement of this problem, and we should not hesitate to take advantage of it. An interim note of protest against the decision to nationalise the Canal should be sent forthwith to the Egyptian Government and this should be followed up, as soon as possible, by more considered representations concerted with the Americans and the French. We should also consider inviting other maritime and trading countries to support this diplomatic pressure. Commonwealth Governments might suggest that the matter should be referred to the Security Council. He did not favour this course, which would expose us to the risk of a Soviet veto. It would be necessary, however, to consider denouncing the Canal Base Agreement of 1954 in view of the fact that Egypt had given an undertaking in this Agreement not to interfere with the Canal. The fundamental question before the Cabinet, however, was whether they were prepared in the last resort to pursue their objective by the threat or even the use of force, and whether they were ready, in default of assistance from the United States and France, to take military action alone.

The Cabinet agreed that our essential interests in this area must, if necessary, be safeguarded by military action and that the necessary preparations to this end must be made. Failure to hold the Suez Canal would lead inevitably to the loss one by one of all our interests and assets in the Middle East and, even if we had to act alone, we could not stop short of using force to protect our position if all other means of protecting it proved unavailing ...

The Cabinet –

(1) Agreed that Her Majesty's Government should seek to secure, by the use of force if necessary, the reversal of the decision of the Egyptian Government to nationalise the Suez Canal Company.
(2) Invited the Prime Minister to inform Commonwealth High Commissioners in London of this decision later that day.
(3) Invited the Prime Minister to send a personal message to the President of ⁻the United States asking him to send a representative to London to discuss the situation with representatives of the Governments of the United Kingdom and France.
(4) Appointed a Committee of Ministers consisting of: –
Prime Minister (In the Chair)
Lord President
Chancellor of the Exchequer
Foreign Secretary
Commonwealth Secretary
Minister of Defence
to formulate further plans for putting our policy into effect.
(5) Instructed the Chiefs of Staff to prepare a plan and time-table for military operations against Egypt should they prove unavoidable.
(6) Invited the President of the Board of Trade to arrange for the further export of arms and military supplies to Egypt to be stopped ... ■

Over the following months, Eisenhower sought a diplomatic solution to the Suez Crisis, while Eden proceeded to collude with the French and Israelis on plans for military intervention. But the government had ample warning of the likely US response to direct intervention. Only days after the Cabinet meeting recorded above, Eisenhower wrote to the Prime Minister urging caution.

8.14   **Dwight D. Eisenhower, letter to Anthony Eden, 31 July 1956 (PRO PREM 11/1098).**

31 July 1956

TOP SECRET

Dear Anthony,

From the moment that Nasser announced nationalization of the Suez Canal Company, my thoughts have been constantly with you. Grave problems are placed before both our governments, although for each of us they naturally differ in type and character. Until this morning, I was happy to feel that we were approaching decisions as to applicable procedures somewhat along parallel lines, even though there were, as would be expected, important differences as to detail. But early this morning I received the messages, communicated to me through Murphy from you and Harold Macmillan, telling me on a most secret basis of your decision to employ force without delay or attempting any intermediate and less drastic steps.

We recognize the transcendent worth of the Canal to the free world and the possibility that eventually the use of force might become necessary in order to protect international rights. But we have been hopeful that through a Conference in which would be represented the signatories to the Convention of 1888, as well as other maritime nations, there would be brought about such pressures on the Egyptian government that the efficient operation of the Canal could be assured for the future ...

I realize that the messages from both you and Harold stressed that the decision taken was already approved by the government and was firm and irrevocable. But I personally feel sure that the American reaction would be severe and that the great areas of the world would share that reaction. On the other hand, I believe we can marshall that opinion in support of a reasonable and conciliatory, but absolutely firm, position. So I hope that you will consent to reviewing this matter once more in its broadest aspects. It is for this reason that I have asked Foster to leave this afternoon to meet with your people tomorrow in London.

I have given you here only a few highlights in the chain of reasoning that compels us to conclude that the step you contemplate should not be undertaken until every peaceful means of protecting the rights and the livelihood of great portions of the world had been thoroughly explored and exhausted. Should these means fail, and I think it is erroneous to assume in advance that they needs must fail, then world opinion would understand how earnestly all of us had attempted to be just, fair and considerate, but that we simply could not accept a situation that would in the long run prove disastrous to the prosperity and living standards of every nation whose economy depends directly or indirectly upon East–West shipping.

With warm personal regards – and with earnest assurances of my continuing respect and friendship,

As ever,

D.E. ■

Collusion with France and Israel was consistently denied by the British government. But today it is possible to piece together, from French and Israeli sources, the terms of the Sèvres Protocol of October 1956, which sealed plans for joint intervention.

8.15   The Sèvres Protocol, October 1956 (in K. Kyle, *Suez*, London, Weidenfield & Nicolson, 1991, pp. 565–6).

■ PROTOCOL

The results of the conversations which took place at Sèvres from 22–24 October 1956 between the representatives of the Governments of the United Kingdom, the State of Israel and of France are the following:

1   The Israeli forces launch in the evening of 29 October 1956 a large scale attack on the Egyptian forces with the aim of reaching the Canal Zone the following day.

2   On being apprised of these events, the British and French Governments during the day of 30 October 1956 respectively and simultaneously make two appeals to the Egyptian Government and the Israeli Government on the following lines:

A *To the Egyptian Government*
   (*a*) halt all acts of war.
   (*b*) withdraw all its troops ten miles from the Canal.
   (*c*) accept temporary occupation of key positions on the Canal by the Anglo-French forces to guarantee freedom of passage through the Canal by vessels of all nations until a final settlement.

B *To the Israeli Government*
   (*a*) halt all acts of war.
   (*b*) withdraw all its troops ten miles to the east of the Canal.

In addition, the Israeli Government will be notified that the French and the British Governments have demanded of the Egyptian Government to accept temporary occupation of key positions along the Canal by Anglo-French forces.

It is agreed that if one of the Governments refused, or did not give its consent within twelve hours, the Anglo-French forces would intervene with the means necessary to ensure that their demands are accepted.

C The representatives of the three Governments agree that the Israeli Government will not be required to meet the conditions in the appeal addressed to it, in the event that the Egyptian Government does not accept those in the appeal addressed to it for their part.

3   In the event that the Egyptian Government should fail to agree within the stipulated time to the conditions of the appeal addressed to it, the Anglo-French forces will launch military operations against the Egyptian forces in the early hours of the morning of 31 October.

4   The Israeli Government will send forces to occupy the western shore of the Gulf of Akaba and the group of islands Tirane and Sanafir to ensure freedom of navigation in the Gulf of Akaba.

5   Israel undertakes not to attack Jordan during the period of operations against Egypt.

But in the event that during the same period Jordan should attack Israel the British Government undertakes not to come to the aid of Jordan.

6   The arrangements of the present protocol must remain strictly secret.

7   They will enter into force after the agreement of the three Governments.

David Ben-Gurion   Patrick Dean   Christian Pineau ■

The Anglo-French assault upon Egypt, which began on 31 October 1956, elicited a furious response from the USA. Eisenhower, facing imminent elections, was incensed at being disregarded at such a sensitive time. Dulles's condemnation of the action in the United Nations on 2 November triggered a sterling crisis which forced the British government to withdraw its troops. No clearer message could have been delivered; the British economy was simply not strong enough to support an independent foreign policy. In the following record of Cabinet discussions, the inevitability of retreat is beyond doubt. Vicky's cartoon (document 8.17) depicts Dulles explaining to Eden how to handle the Eisenhower 'genie'.

8.16   Cabinet minutes, 29 November 1956 (in PRO CAB 128/30, part II, CM(56)90).

■ The Foreign Secretary said that the atmosphere in the United Nations had shown some improvement in the last few days. But it was clear that the Assembly would continue to debate the Suez situation at intervals and would maintain their pressure for the early withdrawal of the Anglo-French force ...

The Foreign Secretary said that in his judgment the economic considerations were now even more important than the political. We could probably sustain our position in the United Nations for three or four weeks; but, so far from gaining anything by deferring a withdrawal of the Anglo-French force, which we could, if we wished, complete in the next fortnight, we should thereby risk losing the good will of public opinion, which in all countries wished the clearance of the Canal to proceed as rapidly as possible. On the other hand, if we withdrew the Anglo-French force as rapidly as was practicable, we should regain the sympathy of the United States government; we should be better placed to ask for their support in any economic measures which we might need to take; and we should have removed, as far as lay within our power, all impediments to the further clearance of the Canal. But we could not properly maintain (and should not seek to do so) that our withdrawal of the Anglo-French force was dependent on a firm guarantee that clearance of the Canal would proceed forthwith. It was unlikely that the Secretary-General of the United Nations would be either able or willing to give such a guarantee; and it would be preferable that we should base our action on our previous undertaking that the Anglo-French force would be withdrawn as soon as its place was taken by an effective United Nations force, which was competent to carry out the functions assigned to it by the General Assembly. This point would shortly be reached, and it would therefore be possible for the Cabinet, if they agreed, to authorise the withdrawal of the Anglo-French force, while emphasising that this action was based on our confident expectation that rapid progress would now be made by the United Nations towards the clearance of the Canal, an agreement about its satisfactory administration thereafter, and a comprehensive settlement of the long-term problems of the Middle East.

The Chancellor of the Exchequer said that it would be necessary to announce, early in the following week, the losses of gold and dollars which we had sustained during November. This statement would reveal a very serious drain on the reserves and would be a considerable shock both to public opinion in this country and to international confidence in sterling. It was therefore important that we should be able to announce at the same time that we were taking action to reinforce the reserves both by recourse to the International Monetary Fund and in other ways. For this purpose the good will of the United States Government was necessary; and it was evident that this good will could not be obtained without an immediate and unconditional undertaking to withdraw the Anglo-French force from Port Said. He therefore favoured a prompt announcement of our intention to withdraw this force, justifying this action on the ground that we had now achieved the purpose for which we had originally launched the Anglo-French military operation against Egypt and that we were content to leave to the United Nations, backed by the United States, the responsibility, which the General Assembly could now be deemed to have accepted, for settling the problems of the Middle East ... ■

8.17   'Vicky', 'See, as soon as you stop rubbing it up the wrong way the genie appears and brings you every gift your heart desires', *New Statesman* cartoon, 22 December 1956.

CHAPTER NINE

Planning and Crisis:
Economic and Social Policy,
1964–70

WHEN the Labour Party entered office under the premiership of Harold Wilson in 1964, it did so in the context of widespread concern over the stagnation and relative decline of the British economy. Wilson had pitched his campaign around the promise to modernise the economy and to deliver the high rates of growth which the Conservatives had conspicuously failed to deliver after 1959. From the outset, however, there was a large disparity between those objectives and what was actually delivered. The economy was plagued in these years by a series of sterling crises which culminated in the devaluation of sterling in 1967. By the end of the decade the balance of trade had regained a healthy surplus as a result. But Labour's experiments with statism in this period – extending and developing Macmillan's flirtation with indicative planning – had a mixed record.

In particular, Wilson pinned his hopes on the success of an incomes policy to maintain stability in the economy, as an alternative to either the humiliation of devaluation or the social injustice of deflation. In practice, however, the goodwill of the trade unions was eroded, as incomes policy was used increasingly by the government as a deflationary tool rather than as an adjunct to growth. In the absence of a workable incomes policy, the government resorted both to traditional deflationary measures and, with reluctance, to devaluation.

The social policy record of the first Wilson governments was on balance more successful, rising to the challenge posed by the 'rediscovery of poverty' in the middle years of the decade. Public expenditure on the social services increased considerably between 1964 and 1970, and the rising value of benefits in real terms meant that the distribution of income in society was shifted towards the lowest income groups. Education policy was a further focus of policy-making; the encouragement of comprehensive schools, the introduction of the polytechnics, and the founding of the Open University were initiatives designed to extend access to higher education.

The Economic Record

Immediately on taking office, the Wilson government announced the creation of new administrative machinery to achieve its objectives. A Department of Economic Affairs (DEA) would develop a long-term national plan for growth,

250   BRITAIN IN THE TWENTIETH CENTURY 1939–1970

and provide a focus for economic policy-making outside of the Treasury; the Ministry of Technology would promote the co-ordination of research and development between the public and private sectors, ensuring the future competitiveness of industry.

British rates of economic growth lagged behind those of the country's competitors in the 1960s; productivity levels were also comparatively low. Many reasons were put forward for this disappointing performance: low levels of investment in modern production techniques, inadequate research and development, bad marketing and poor industrial relations.

9.1 **Comparative annual rates of economic growth, 1950–73 (chart derived from A. Graham and A. Seldon (eds),** *Government and Economies in the Postwar World,* **London, Routledge, 1990, p. 276).**

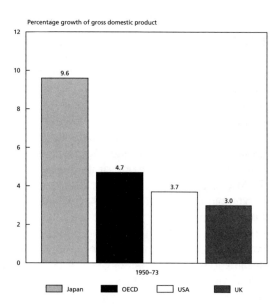

9.2 **Comparative level of real output per man-hour in 1965 (chart derived from Donovan** *Royal Commission on Trade Unions and Employer Organisations,* **London, HMSO, Cmnd 3623, PP 1967–8, XXXII, p. 74).**

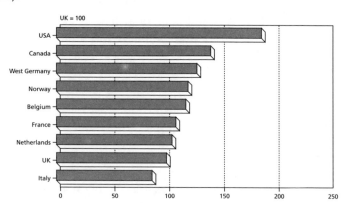

Labour believed that a turnabout in Britain's economic fortunes could be achieved through voluntary agreements with the trade unions and employers' organisations on the growth of incomes and productivity. One of the government's first acts was the signing of a tripartite declaration of intent in autumn 1964, intended to link income growth to productivity. In February, under George Brown's leadership at the DEA, a Prices and Incomes Board was established to monitor price and wage rises.

9.3   Joint statement of intent on productivity, prices and incomes, 16 December 1964 (reported in *The Times*, 17 December 1964).

■ ... 5. We, Government, management and unions, are resolved to take the following action in our respective spheres of responsibility.

6. The Government will prepare and implement a general plan for economic development, in consultation with both sides of industry through the National Economic Development Council. This will provide for higher investment; for improving our industrial skills; for modernization of industry; for balanced regional development; for higher exports; and for the largest possible sustained expansion of production and real incomes.

7. Much greater emphasis will be given to increasing productivity. The Government will encourage and develop policies designed to promote technological advance in industry, and to get rid of restrictive practices and prevent the abuse of monopoly power, and so improve efficiency, cut out waste, and reduce excessive prices. More vigorous policies will be pursued designed to facilitate mobility of labour and generally to make more effective use of scarce manpower resources, and to give workers a greater sense of security in the face of economic change. The Government also intend to introduce essential social improvements such as a system of earnings-related benefits, in addition to the improvements in national insurance benefits already announced.

8. The Government will set up machinery to keep a continuous watch on the general movement of prices and of money incomes of all kinds and to carry out the other functions described in paragraph 10 below. They will also use their fiscal powers or other appropriate means to correct any excessive growth in aggregate profits as compared with the growth of total wages and salaries, after allowing for short-term fluctuations.

9. We, the representatives of the Trades Union Congress, the Federation of British Industries, the British Employers' Confederation, the National Association of British Manufacturers, and the Association of British Chambers of Commerce, accept that major objectives of national policy must be:

to ensure that British industry is dynamic and that its prices are competitive;

to raise productivity and efficiency so that real national output can increase, and to keep increases in wages, salaries, and other forms of incomes in line with this increase;

to keep the general level of prices stable.

10. We therefore undertake, on behalf of our members: to encourage and lead a sustained attack on the obstacles to efficiency, whether on the part of management or of workers, and to strive for the adoption of more rigorous standards of performance at all levels; to cooperate with the Government, in endeavouring in the face of practical problems, to give effective shape to the machinery that the Government intend to establish for the following purposes:

(i) to keep under review the general movement of prices and of money incomes of all kinds;

(ii) to examine particular cases in order to advise whether or not the behaviour of prices or of wages, salaries, or other money incomes is in the national interest as defined by the Government after consultation with management and unions.

11. We stress that close attention must be paid to easing the difficulties of those affected by changed circumstances in their employment. We therefore support, in principle, the Government's proposals for earnings-related benefits and will examine sympathetically proposals for severance payments.

12. We, Government, management, and unions, are confident that by cooperating in a spirit of mutual confidence to give effect to the principles and policies described above, we and those whom we represent will be able to achieve a faster growth of real incomes and generally to promote the economic and social wellbeing of the country. ■

The ambitious plans embodied in the autumn 1964 statement of intent were threatened from the outset by economic instability. The 'dash for growth' pursued by the previous Chancellor of the Exchequer, the Conservative Reginald Maudling, had saddled the incoming administration with a balance of payments deficit of some £800 million, necessitating unwelcome deflationary measures and jeopardising the Cabinet's intention to raise spending on the social services. In spite of the crisis, the new Chancellor James Callaghan's first Budget did fulfil election pledges to abolish prescription charges and raise pensions. But international doubts over the government's ability to hold the fixed exchange rate of $2.80 to the pound was a constant strain.

9.4   **James Callaghan, *Time and Chance*, London, Collins, 1987, p. 167.**

We had been in office for only three weeks when the first large attack against sterling was launched from the Continent. It was in essence an attack by speculators which I had been half expecting and had believed I was mentally braced to overcome. But in all the offices I have held I have never experienced anything more frustrating than sitting at the Chancellor's desk watching our currency reserves gurgle down the plughole day by day and knowing that the drain could not be stopped. I could not even share the misery with others, because the market operators at the Bank of England insisted that the daily losses should be kept secret so that speculators would not know how much damage they were inflicting.

Each day turned into a game of bluff. It would begin with reports being placed on my desk in the early morning recording the amount of Continental sterling sales, since, with the time difference, their foreign exchanges opened an hour before London. There might follow a lull until lunchtime when up-to-date figures of the morning selling in London and further sales on the Continent would arrive. It was early afternoon in London before Wall Street got to work and early reports of their dealings would arrive at teatime. Finally, very late at night, there would come news from the Far East where they were already starting another day. The process never stopped.

It was like swimming in a heavy sea. As soon as we emerged from the buffeting of one wave, another would hit us before we could catch our breath. ▪

9.5 **Norman Mansbridge, 'I suppose you know you're doing that all wrong', *Punch* cartoon, 31 March 1965.**

Many members of the new Labour government had supported an early devaluation of sterling precisely because they believed that rational planning for growth could only be achieved once sterling had been stabilised at a realistic rate. But Wilson in particular was determined for political reasons not to associate Labour with the humiliation of devaluation. In the following passage, Susan Crosland, the wife of then Treasury Secretary Anthony Crosland, recalls how the subject of devaluation became the 'great unmentionable' in the days following the general election.

9.6   Susan Crosland, *Tony Crosland*, London, Cape, 1982, pp. 125–8.

■ ... That afternoon Nicky Kaldor and Robert Neild came to Hobury Street. The three men were in passionate agreement: whoever got at Callaghan or Brown first would say that the crucial thing was to devalue the pound immediately. They knew that if that was done, the onus would be placed where it belonged – on the previous Government. What they didn't know was that the decision had already been taken.

That evening, on our way to the Browns' flat, Tony said: 'It's essential I have a word alone with George. Harold's bound to feel the psychological need to announce policy on Day One next week. It's imperative to persuade George and Jim to hold the argument before deciding about devaluation.' ...

On our way home I learned of the ... serious, violent altercation that had occurred privately between the two men. George told Tony the decision had already been taken not to devalue the pound and the subject was never, never to be raised again. Tony was horrified and angry ...

As in other Labour households, that Sunday at Hobury Street was not a day of rest. The telephone refused to stop ringing. People came and went. Nicky Kaldor got through on the telephone, his voice melancholy. He'd just been stitched up in hospital following a motor accident. His car had overturned. His mind had been on devaluation instead of the fact that he was about to drive across a one-way thoroughfare. He'd been to see Callaghan the night before and learned the same thing that Tony had learned from Brown. Nicky had told Callaghan that such a decision shouldn't be taken after virtually no sleep. 'Tony and Robert Neild and I are in agreement that the whole Labour Party policy is jeopardised if we don't devalue now,' Nicky said to Callaghan.

'If you want to work for me, you must not argue against things that have already been decided,' Callaghan said to Kaldor.

So Nicky agreed to work for the Chancellor as a temporary civil servant – on taxation policy only. On Sunday Callaghan rang Robert Neild, who also agreed to go to the Treasury, though appalled that the three men at the top had taken the crucial decision in the excitability of three children at a birthday party. ■

Continuing international scepticism ensured that sterling failed to stabilise in the first half of 1965. Callaghan was forced to take a further series of deflationary measures in July. By the time that George Brown's National Plan *was finally published in September, the calculations on which it had been based were already out of date. As an instrument for guiding industry and business, it was never a credible document.*

9.7 *The National Plan* **(London, HMSO, Cmnd 2764, PP XXX, 1964–5).**

■ … 6. The Plan is designed to achieve a 25 per cent increase in national output between 1964 and 1970. This objective has been chosen in the light of past trends in national output and output per head and a realistic view of the scope for improving upon these trends. It involves achieving a 4 per cent annual growth rate of output well before 1970 and an annual average of 3.8 per cent between 1964 and 1970 …

The Nature and Purpose of Planning

10. Our economy, like most others in the modern world, is a mixed one. The Government element is important; public spending is a large part of total expenditure; for this reason the Government must raise large sums in taxation; a large part of the basic industry of the country is carried on by public corporations; the Government are able to exercise authority in many other fields. All this gives the Government great economic power and influence. They intend to use this to secure faster growth and national solvency.

11. Most manufacturing industry and commerce is, and will continue to be, largely governed by the market economy. But this does not necessarily, and without active Government influence, bring about the results which the nation needs …

12. Sometimes government action may be required to strengthen the forces of competition, for example, by reinforcing the legislation against restrictive practices or providing for more disclosure in company accounts. In other cases … important social costs arise which are not expressed in market prices; and positive Government action is required to supplement market forces. Each case must be judged on its merits. Care will be taken not to destroy the complex mechanisms on which the market economy is based …

13. Both Government and industry have to plan several years ahead and it is desirable to co-ordinate the forward estimates of both. Public expenditure cannot be planned realistically without some idea of the rate at which the economy can be expected to grow and of the size of other claims on resources …

The Industrial Inquiry

16. The first stage in making a plan is to find out the facts, not simply about the past but about future intentions, potentialities and problems. This is the main purpose of the Industrial Inquiry which has been carried out this year.

Building on the pioneering work of the National Economic Development Council the inquiry has been extended to cover most of the economy, both the public and the private sectors and the production of both goods and services. Industries were asked what 25 per cent national growth from 1964 to 1970 would mean for them. The co-operation received has been excellent.

17. Perhaps the most encouraging result of the inquiry was in the field of exports. The replies from industry suggested that these could grow by about $5\frac{1}{2}$ per cent a year in volume. This is substantially faster than the average of about 3 per cent a year over the past decade ...

18. The inquiry suggested that national productivity (output per head) could grow by 3.2 per cent a year between 1964 and 1970 ... In light of past trends ... it should be possible to improve on industry's forecast, and to do substantially better given new policies to raise industrial efficiency and economise manpower; but again fundamental changes in attitudes are required. ■

Many of the government's supporters believed that an incomes policy could be made to work on a voluntary basis – and linking wage rises to productivity growth would be vital to the success of the National Plan. But this illusion was shaken in the late spring of 1966, when the National Union of Seamen went on strike in pursuit of a 17 per cent wage rise, infuriating the Prime Minister, and severely damaging the economy. Wilson attacked the NUS openly, and the government introduced legislation over the summer to empower the Prices and Incomes Board to defer wage agreements, an important extension of state intervention in the collective bargaining process. The Bill occasioned the resignation from the Cabinet of the Transport and General Workers' Union leader Frank Cousins and marked the end of any honeymoon period between the government and the Trades Union Congress.

9.8   Harold Wilson, statement to the House of Commons on the seamen's strike, 20 June 1966 (*Hansard*, 5th ser., 730: 38–43).

■ **The Prime Minister (Mr Harold Wilson):** With permission, I should like to make a statement about the seamen's strike.

... I should like to indicate how the Government see the situation following last week's meetings. We have made clear to the Executive of the union the serious damage which the strike is inflicting and is capable of further inflicting on our economic position, even if, so far, the damage has been far less than was hoped by some of those who saw in the strike a means of crippling the economy and securing a reversal of essential Government policies.

Secondly, we have made it clear that, while we have done everything in our power to secure a satisfactory and honourable settlement, if the strike continues the Government must react to it with every measure necessary to protect the interests of the nation. This they fully understand, as public statements have shown. It is not our desire to see this union smashed or weakened. If this were to occur it would result from actions not of Government but of those exercising their powers within and upon the union.

The Executive can now be in no doubt that, although they started the strike against a background of considerable public support for the seamen's case, public sympathy has been progressively alienated, first by their brusque rejection of the Pearson Report, secondly by their continuing refusal to follow the course urged upon them by the Trades Union Congress and the Government, and thirdly – and I said this in clear terms to the Executive – by the public reaction to television films and Press reports of the action of certain militant individuals in individual ports against seamen seeking freedom to express their own point of view ...

It has been apparent for some time – and I do not say this without having good reason for saying it – that since the Court of Inquiry's Report a few individuals have brought pressure to bear on a select few on the Executive Council of the National Union of Seamen, who in turn have been able to dominate the majority of that otherwise sturdy union.

It is difficult for us to appreciate the pressures which are being put on men I know to be realistic and reasonable, not only in their executive capacity but in the highly organised strike committees in the individual ports, by this tightly knit group of politically motivated men who, as the last General Election showed, utterly failed to secure acceptance of their views by the British electorate, but who are now determined to exercise backstage pressures, forcing great hardship on the members of the union and their families, and endangering the security of the industry and the economic welfare of the nation ... ■

9.9   Frank Cousins, speech to the House of Commons on the Prices and Incomes Bill, 14 July 1966 (*Hansard*, 5th ser., 731: 1788–99).

■ ... Why did I have to take this step? I have a deep conviction that we are going the wrong way, that we are tackling the wrong problem. Therefore, we are bound to be using the wrong methods and finding the wrong solutions ...

We approached not only the last election, but the election in 1964, and the conferences of the party which determined the policy on which we went to the electorate, on the basis of a planned economy – the planned growth of the economy.

This included wages. We have gradually drifted unwittingly, and sometimes unknowingly, into an atmosphere in which we regard the possibility of a solution as being directly related to the ability to restrain wages. This is a wrong philosophy, and it has always been proved to be wrong ...

I do not know whether industrialists in the House will challenge this, but I think that it is clear to everyone that the cost per unit of production is the important thing, not the wage rate of the person doing it. If a man on a stamping machine steps up his output by 500 units an hour by a new process, and if those units are sold at 1d. apiece, he will have to be given £1 an hour increase so that he may have half the value of what he is doing. But we do not do this. We recognise that the whole spread of production levels among all manufacturing industries in the drive which ought to take place will improve our total standard of living.

Whether we like it or not, that is what the policy says. The policy says, 'We want a bigger cake and the way to get the bigger cake is to control wage levels so that everybody gets a fair share'. How nice it would be. We shall have a different division of the same kind of cake. But I do not want a different division of the same kind of cake. I want a division of a larger cake. I want a division of it created by the direct association of employers and employees at the negotiating table in improving the efficiency of output ...

Who creates efficiency of operation? Efficient management seeking higher productivity and being prepared to pay for it; good investment policies, being prepared to think ahead; good Government action to encourage in every direction possible the creation of production. Those are the things that matter, and I say to my colleagues that right hon. and hon. Gentlemen opposite do not know how to do it ...

I would ask my right hon. and hon. Friends not to fritter away the most valuable asset that they have, one that does not belong to right hon. and hon. Gentlemen opposite. I refer, of course, to the support of the men and women who make up the great British trade union movement, who helped to put them in and who will help maintain them. Given the chance, they will increase productivity. Let us encourage them to do so. ■

By the summer of 1966 speculators' pressure on the pound had grown untenable. Support for devaluation was growing inside the Cabinet, but Wilson and Callaghan remained opposed. In his memoirs, the then Home Secretary Roy Jenkins has recalled the tension which surrounded the decision not to devalue at that time. Wilson chose instead to support Callaghan's package of harsh deflationary measures, including a wage freeze which lasted until February 1967. In his announcement of these measures to the House of Commons, Wilson declared that the National Plan had been 'blown off course'.

9.10   **Roy Jenkins, *A Life at the Centre*, London, Macmillan, 1991, pp. 191–5.**

■ On the Saturday morning he departed for Moscow for a doubtfully necessary seventy-two hour visit to a British trade fair, buttressed by talks with Kosygin. This was the weekend of the 'July plot', which Harold Wilson came to believe had almost led to his replacement as Prime Minister ...

What was the reality of that weekend as I saw it? ...

As soon as I arrived at the House of Lords dinner [on Saturday evening] I received a message via David Dowler that Brown's office had said it was imperative I speak to him that evening, as he was on the verge of explosion and resignation ... The burden of what he had to say was that Wilson had decided on deflation not devaluation and that he (Brown) was going to resign rather than put up with this.

The next morning I had a briefer and less swirling but more fundamentally confused telephone conversation with Callaghan. I thought from my previous talks with him that he had moved in favour of devaluation, and my objective was to keep him and Brown in a solid front so that they could exercise the joint influence of the economic departments upon Wilson ...

It turned out that Callaghan was pursuing a different line from me ... He thought that inaction, that is the postponement of deflationary measures, was making devaluation inevitable. But once he had got deflation in the bag, he was against devaluation. I, on the other hand, was prepared to accept deflation only if an accompanying devaluation gave us a chance to *reculer pour mieux sauter*. (This was also Brown's position, except that he was more reluctant than I was to see the need for deflation even with devaluation.) ...

I went back to London on the Sunday afternoon, saw Tony Crosland and found that our views were very close. Then I telephoned George Brown and ... we arranged that he would dine with me at Brooks's Club on the following evening ... he was still resigning and believed that Crossman and Mrs Castle would do so with him ...

Later ... [on Monday night] Crossman saw me on his initiative, and made it clear that while he and Mrs Castle were solid on the merits he had no more intention of resigning than I had ...

The next day, Tuesday, 19 July, was sunk in a trough of physical dismalness, with leaden skies and pouring rain ...

The Cabinet met that afternoon at 5.00 and sat for four and a half hours. The ban was taken off the open discussion of devaluation but the majority, led by Wilson, did just as good a job against it in result if not in argument. Those in favour were six and no more: Brown, Crossman, Crosland, Castle, Benn and me, a curious mixture it may be thought. Of the others, those with the most open minds appeared to be Gardiner, Healey, Greenwood and possibly Marsh ...

The Cabinet met again for another four hours the following morning and agreed to the package of deflation and austerity. George Brown was present, but sat back taking no part so that it was impossible to tell whether he was resigning or not ... Late that night he decided not to resign. Two weeks later Wilson rescued him from the torpedoed Department of Economic Affairs and made him Foreign Secretary. ■

9.11   Harold Wilson, announcement to the House of Commons on economic measures, 20 July 1966 (*Hansard*, 5th ser., 732: 627–8).

■ **The Prime Minister (Mr. Harold Wilson):** With permission, Mr. Speaker, I wish to make a statement.

Sterling has been under pressure for the past two and a half weeks. After improvement in the early weeks of May we were blown off course by the seven-week seamen's strike and when the bill for that strike was presented in terms of the gold and convertible currency figures in June the foreign exchange market reacted adversely. But there were deeper and more fundamental causes. Many have been at home and of these I shall speak in a moment. Several have been overseas. For several weeks past there has been an increasing pressure on liquidity in the world's financial centres. Action taken by the United States' authorities to strengthen the American balance of payments has led to an acute shortage of dollars and Euro-dollars in world trade and this has led to a progressive rise in interest rates in most financial centres and to the selling of sterling to replenish dollar balances. Last Thursday, action was taken by the Bank of England to raise its discount rate and to double its call on the clearing banks for special deposits. On that day I informed the House that I would shortly be announcing further measures to deal not only with the short-run pressure on sterling, but also with the underlying economic situation.

Action is needed for the purpose of making a direct impact on our payments balance, and particularly on certain parts of our overseas expenditure which, in recent years, has been growing rapidly. Action is needed equally to deal with the problem of internal demand, public and private, and to redeploy resources, both manpower and capacity, according to national priorities, and check inflation.

Exports until the seamen's strike have been rising. By value, in the first five months of this year they were 9 per cent. higher than in the same period last year. By volume, the increase over the same period last year was 6 per cent., a rate of increase higher than that laid down in the National Plan. But abundant market opportunities abroad for British products – which are competitive enough in terms of quality, performance and price – are being lost owing to the shortage of labour. Order books are too long, and delivery dates excessively protracted. Hours of work have been reduced and incomes have been rising faster than productivity.

What is needed is a shake-out which will release the nation's manpower, skilled and unskilled, and lead to a more purposive use of labour for the sake of increasing exports and giving effect to other national priorities. This redeployment can be achieved only by cuts in the present inflated level of demand, both in the private and public sectors. Not until we can get this redeployment through an attack on the problem of demand can we confidently expect growth in industrial production which is needed to realise our economic and social policies. ■

The measures that Wilson announced in July 1966 failed to solve the sterling problem. The decision to devalue was finally taken in November 1967. The fixed rate of sterling was reduced from $2.80 to $2.40 to the pound. The announcement was accompanied, belatedly, by a further package of deflationary measures. In January 1968 prescription charges were reintroduced, and the raising of the school-leaving age to 16 had to be deferred. The decision to devalue represented an enormous defeat for the Chancellor, who had always believed that devaluation could be avoided by a strong incomes policy backed up by modernising reforms in Britain's economic infrastructure. Callaghan announced his resignation from the Treasury soon after the decision was taken.

9.12   James Callaghan, *Time and Chance*, London, Collins, 1987, pp. 217–19.

■ I was not ready until nearly the end to give up the struggle to find our salvation through these measures. Nor was I alone. The American Treasury and Federal Reserve held the view right up to the week of devaluation that the pound was not intrinsically overvalued, but in the end they did not back their opinion with their money. If they had taken up the question of a long-term loan more energetically, when it was discussed in the early summer of 1967, there would have been time to negotiate the arrangements before the storm hit us in October and November ...

One event followed another helter-skelter during November. Harold Wilson has recounted that on 1 November the Governor of the Bank of England told him that he did not intend to recommend devaluation, despite the effect of the apparently awful trade figures on sterling. But the very next day a personal and 'top secret' packet was placed on my desk from Sir Alec Cairncross, at that time the Head of the Government Economic Service and subsequently to become the Master of St Peter's College, Oxford. Alec had been one of the staunchest of the praetorian guard determined to maintain sterling's parity, so it had a profound effect on me when I opened the packet and found it contained a personal and pessimistic typed memorandum on the outlook, together with a covering, handwritten letter from him for my eyes alone. In this, he said that, having started with the conviction that I was right to try as hard as possible to solve our problems without devaluing, he had after long consideration changed his mind and was now a 'convert to devaluation' ...

I spent Friday 3 November wrestling with the problem in isolation: we had gone over the ground often enough; there were no new arguments to rehearse, no new facts to be discovered. No one else could take the decision except me. If those like Alec Cairncross who throughout the previous three years had not wavered were now privately reaching such conclusions, was I justified in continuing the struggle: or would I be serving only a wrong-headed stubbornness?

By Saturday morning my mind was clear. It would not be sensible to continue any longer to defend the existing parity of sterling against continual attacks if our only support was by means of short-term credits from other countries needing to be renewed every few months. This was living from hand to mouth. It left the currency without long-term adequate reserves ...

All this was in my mind as I walked from my study in 11 Downing Street through the communicating door to No. 10 on Saturday morning, and over a cup of coffee discussed with the Prime Minister our narrowing alternatives. The two of us sat alone in the quiet Cabinet Room looking out onto Horseguards Parade. Everything was peaceful. People were strolling through St James's Park on their Saturday pursuits. No one out there had any idea of the welter of emotions I felt. My mind went back to a similar Saturday morning three years before, when the three of us had held our first discussion and decided against devaluation. I felt the three years of struggle had been of no avail. ■

'In Place of Strife'

By the last years of the 1960s Britain had acquired a reputation for chaotic industrial relations. While the Labour Party could claim to be well placed to handle such matters, its record since 1964 was not good. The 1966 Prices and Incomes Act which had occasioned the resignation of Frank Cousins from the government had not improved the incidence of strikes. Furthermore, the Donovan Royal Commission on the trade unions which finally reported in 1968 was a disappointment, failing to provide any coherent strategy for dealing with the problem and coming down firmly against the introduction of legal sanctions to enforce industrial discipline. In response to mounting public concern, moreover, the Conservative Party had produced proposals for legislation. It was in these circumstances that Wilson decided to act, a decision which would prove a disastrous mistake.

Statistically, while the number of industrial disputes in Britain was relatively high, the more serious problem was the incidence of unofficial strike action. Unpredictable and volatile 'wildcat strikes' seemed to demonstrate the 'bloody-mindedness' of the British worker, with highly damaging effects on international confidence in the British economy.

9.13   Comparative number of stoppages per 100,000 employees, 1964–6 (chart derived from Donovan *Royal Commission on Trade Unions and Employers Organisations,* London, HMSO, Cmnd 3623, PP 1967–8, XXXII, p. 95).

Number of stoppages per 100,000 employees, 1964–66

9.14   Official and unofficial strikes in the UK, 1964–6 (chart derived from Donovan *Royal Commission on Trade Unions and Employers Organisations,* Cmnd 3623, PP 1967–8, XXXII, p. 97); figures for unofficial strikes include where a strike involving more than one union was not recognised by all unions involved and strikes by unorganised workers.

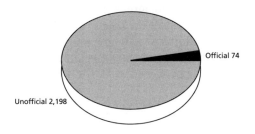

Official 74

Unofficial 2,198

Wilson seized on proposals put forward by Barbara Castle to modernise British industrial relations, appointing her to head the newly created Department of Employment and Productivity in April 1968. Castle's white paper, In Place of Strife, *was published at the beginning of 1969. A brave attempt to chart a new relationship between unions, employers and the state, it proved enormously controversial. The paper was popular with the public, as it represented a genuine attempt to reform industrial relations; but while the proposals included measures to strengthen the position of the unions, it also entailed legislation to prevent unofficial strike action, violating the principle of government non-intervention in the collective bargaining process. Many Cabinet ministers felt that to take on the unions so late in the life of the government was politically foolhardy. Rejected within Cabinet, by the party's National Executive Committee, and by the Trades Union Congress itself, In Place of Strife came close to splitting the labour movement irretrievably. In the end, Wilson was forced to compromise with the TUC, shelving legislation in return for a binding agreement from the unions to crack down on unofficial action. Castle's diary reveals the tension produced by the episode.*

9.15 *In Place of Strife: A Policy for Industrial Relations,* **January 1969 (London, HMSO, Cmnd 3888, PP 1968–9, LIII, pp. 5–35).**

■ 1. There are necessarily conflicts of interest in industry. The objective of our industrial relations system should be to direct the forces producing conflict towards constructive ends. This can be done by the right kind of action by management, unions and Government itself. This White Paper sets out what needs to be done ...

3. ...The Government places the following proposals before Parliament and the nation convinced that they are justified on two main grounds. First, they will help to contain the destructive expression of industrial conflict and to encourage a more equitable, ordered and efficient system, which will benefit both those involved and the community at large. Second, they are based on the belief that the efforts of employers, unions and employees to reform collective bargaining need the active support and intervention of Government ...

31. It is essential to provide rules and procedures for the rapid and effective settlement of grievances and other issues. When procedures are agreed which meet these criteria ... provision should be made for previous conditions to be maintained while any matter is being considered in accordance with the procedures. There should also be rules and procedures governing disciplinary matters, including dismissal, and agreed procedures for the handling of redundancies. Consideration should be given to the inclusion of provision for a quick recourse to arbitration in grievance procedures if agreement is not reached at the early stages of the procedure. There should be provision for important matters to be raised with the highest levels of management ...

33. The Government, too, through the work of the Department of Employment and Productivity, shares the responsibility of bringing about the necessary changes in our system of industrial relations. This has caused it to expand and extend its existing arrangements for conciliation and to create a Manpower and Productivity Service. But as the Donovan Report pointed out, and as both the T.U.C. and the C.B.I. recognise, there remains a major gap in the public apparatus for change. There is no institution primarily concerned with the reform of collective bargaining. This is why the Government proposes to establish a Commission on Industrial Relations ...

86. ... Britain's special problem in industrial relations arises not from official strikes and lock-outs, but from sudden industrial action taken before

adequate negotiation or discussion of the problems has taken place. Such strikes can cause serious damage, not only to other employees in the same firm but to employees elsewhere and above all to the country's economic development ...

93. It is for this reason that the government will seek to reinforce, through the Industrial Relations Bill, the machinery of conciliation which already exists. The method proposed would be to give the Secretary of State a discretionary reserve power to secure a 'conciliation pause' in unconstitutional strikes and in strikes where, because there is no agreed procedure or for other reasons, adequate joint discussions have not taken place. The power would only be used when, if the strike (or lock-out) continued, the effects were likely to be serious ...

98. It is ... a matter for concern that at present it is possible for a major official strike to be called when the support of those involved may be in doubt. A number of unions already have provisions in their rules making a ballot of their members obligatory before a strike. In other cases the holding of a ballot is discretionary; in others there are no provisions about ballots in the rules. Where a major official strike is threatened the Secretary of State will discuss with the unions concerned the desirability of holding a strike ballot and will seek to persuade them to consult their members unless there are valid reasons why they should not. Where no agreement is reached, the Industrial Relations Bill will give the Secretary of State discretionary power to require the union or unions involved to hold a ballot on the question of strike action ... ∎

9.16 Barbara Castle, diary, June 1969 (in Barbara Castle, *The Castle Diaries, 1964–70*, London, Weidenfeld & Nicolson, 1984, pp. 672–9).

∎ *Tuesday, 17 June*

The most traumatic day of my political life ...

Any hope that the TUC's intransigence would have hardened the attitude of the inner Cabinet soon disappeared. Dick said that he couldn't commit himself until soundings had been made with the TUC: if they objected, this wouldn't help us out with the PLP or with the Party in the country, which was adamantly opposed to any penal powers. Bob, who obviously hasn't done any serious counting of heads as John Silkin would have done, gave us an impressionistic sketch of Party morale: everyone was satisfied that there was going to be a compromise. 'My bet is that you won't get it through the House, or a guillotine, if the TUC rejects it.' To this Harold retorted irritably, 'It was you who told the PLP that, if they rejected the Bill, there would have to be a dissolution. I never thought that credible.' Roy was tentative. He said he didn't share Dick's view about the state of the Party in the country; nor did he underestimate the difficulties of just climbing down ...

By this time it was 11 am and we had to go into Cabinet disunited and unprepared. Harold went over the old ground: we had offered to drop penal clauses in return for an amendment to rule and been turned down; we now had to consider alternatives for legislation; we had examined the possibility of proceeding under the 1906 Act and rejected it; the First Secretary now had worked out a new version of the conciliation pause which he would ask me to explain to them. This I duly did. Harold then promptly called on the Foreign Secretary. Faithful as ever, Michael plunged into the deep end. If there was to be a legal sanction at all, my new form was preferable. Could the TUC really proceed by circular? Neither the wording nor the status of their document were good enough. Harold and I ought to be in a position to make that perfectly clear. It was a brave effort, but the wreckers were not interested in the merits or demerits of my proposals. All they wanted was a settlement: peace at any price ...

[Later] Harold hit back more convincingly than I have ever seen him in Cabinet. He pointed out that it was now nearly 7 pm, at which hour he was supposed to be addressing the trade union group. What was he to say to them? If Cabinet wanted peace at any price, they had better find someone else to go and negotiate. He wasn't prepared to do so on those terms ...

Finally in our desperation a solution evolved (strongly pressed by me) that Harold and I should go to the TUC tomorrow with an entirely free hand to get the outcome we thought was right on the understanding that Cabinet would have a free hand, too, to endorse or reject our action when we reported back ...

The trade union group meeting didn't exactly restore my faith in human nature. Almost to a man (except for John Hynd), the speakers were for prostrating themselves before the TUC. Harold, with nothing to say, said it too long-windedly. When we went over to No. 10 to meet Vic, Harold hadn't a card in his hand. ■

Labour and Social Policy

New challenges to the welfare state

Labour came to power at the same time that a new wave of research by academics and concerned social workers brought to an end more than a decade of complacency about the achievements of the postwar welfare state. The demographic statistics alone were worrying, showing a higher proportion of dependants to wage earners than at any previously recorded period. Even more disturbing was increasing evidence that poverty, particularly among children and the elderly was far more widespread than commonly assumed.

What was new about much of the social research of the mid-1960s was the way it redefined the concept of poverty, in a relative rather than an absolute sense. The publication of The Poor and the Poorest *by Brian Abel-Smith and Peter Townsend of the London School of Economics galvanised official thinking on this problem and led to the establishment of an important new campaigning organisation, the Child Poverty Action Group.*

9.17 Brian Abel-Smith and Peter Townsend, *The Poor and the Poorest,* London, G. Bell & Sons, 1965, Occasional Papers on Social Administration no. 17, pp. 62–6.

■ Poverty is a relative concept. Saying who is in poverty is to make a relative statement – rather like saying who is short or heavy. But it is also a statement of a much more complex kind than one referring to a unilineal scale of measurement. It refers to a variety of conditions involving differences in home environment, material possessions and educational and occupational resources as well as in financial resources – most of which are measurable, at least in principle. Income or expenditure as defined in this paper should be regarded as only one of the possible indicators. We need to develop other indicators of the command of individuals and families over resources ...

One conclusion that can be drawn from both surveys is that national assistance is inefficient. While it is impossible to give precise figures it is clear that substantial numbers in the population were not receiving national assistance in 1953–54 and 1960 and yet seemed, prima facie, to qualify for it. In the latter year, for example, there were nearly one million persons who had pensions or other state benefits and whose incomes fell below assistance rates plus rent ...

Possibly the most novel finding is the extent of poverty among children. For over a decade it has been generally assumed that such poverty as exists is found overwhelmingly among the aged. Unfortunately it has not been possible to estimate from the data used in this study exactly how many persons over minimum pensionable age were to be found among the $7\frac{1}{2}$ million persons with low income in 1960. However, such data as we have suggest that the number may be around 3 million. There were thus more people who were not aged than were aged among the poor households of 1960. We have estimated earlier that there were about $2\frac{1}{4}$ million children in low income households in 1960. Thus qualitatively the problem of poverty among children is more than two-thirds of the size of poverty among the aged. This fact has not been given due emphasis in the policies of the political parties. It is also worth observing that there were substantially more children in poverty than adults of working age ...

Between 1953 and 1960 the Ministry of Labour surveys suggest that the number of persons living at low levels increased from 7.8 per cent to 14.2 per cent ... some part of the apparent increase ... seems attributable to (a) the relative increase in the number of old people in the population, (b) a slight relative increase in the number of men in late middle age who are chronically sick, and (c) the relative increase in the number of families with four or more children, at a time when family allowances have increased much less than average industrial earnings and when the wages of some low-paid workers may not have increased as much as average industrial earnings. On the whole the data we have presented contradicts the commonly held view that a trend towards greater equality has accompanied the trend towards greater affluence. ■

The evidence on poverty indicated that William Beveridge's plan for the welfare state had misfired in a number of ways. Crucially, whereas it had been intended originally that National Assistance benefits would diminish in importance as the vast majority of people would be entitled to the more generous benefits of the insurance system, instead the numbers of people needing to claim extra help had increased steadily. Even more worrying, large numbers of pensioners eligible for assistance failed to claim it. In 1966 the government tackled these problems by merging the National Assistance Board – renamed the Supplementary Benefits Commission – with the Ministry of Pensions to form the Ministry of Social Security. The problem of low take-up of benefits nevertheless persisted in spite of the reform.

9.18   Ministry of Pensions and National Insurance, 'Ministry of Social Security Bill 1966: explanatory memorandum by the Minister of Pensions and National Insurance', May 1966 (Cmnd 2997, PP 1966–7, LIX, pp. 1–2).

■ 1. The Government propose to introduce a scheme of non-contributory benefits in place of national assistance which will, among other things, provide a form of guaranteed income for those who require such a benefit over a long period. The purpose of the changes is to eliminate those features of the existing scheme which are misunderstood or disliked, while preserving the humanity and efficiency of its administration. The Government believe this will ensure that the elderly will have no hesitation in claiming the new benefit to which they are entitled and which will be awarded with dignity.

2. They also propose to bring together in one new administration the existing National Insurance, War Pensions and Family Allowance schemes, now the responsibility of the Ministry of Pensions and National Insurance, and the new scheme of non-contributory benefits. In the future there will no longer be the sharp distinction which now exists in the administration of contributory and means-tested benefit.

3. The Ministry of Social Security Bill provides for the establishment of a Ministry of Social Security, which will have overall responsibility for the administration of social security cash benefits ... To preserve responsiveness to human needs there will be within the Ministry of Social Security a Supplementary Benefits Commission comprising persons chosen for their interest in, and knowledge of, social problems. Subject to Regulations made by the Minister, the Commission will be responsible for guiding the new scheme of non-contributory benefits. Responsibility for determining indi-

vidual awards of benefit will rest not with the Minister but with the Commission subject to appeal to an Appeal Tribunal. The Commission will also form a source of valuable advice on a wide range of problems in the field of social security outside those spheres covered by the bodies already set up to advise the Minister of Pensions and National Insurance which, except as mentioned in paragraph 19, will continue in existence ... ■

Education and opportunity

Considerable attention was paid in these years to the development of equal opportunities in education. The Robbins Report on higher education of 1963 had already led to the expansion of the university sector. Labour extended this in several ways.

In 1965 Anthony Crosland at the Department of Education and Science (1965–7) issued a controversial circular which requested local authorities to submit plans for the reorganisation of secondary education on the comprehensive model.

9.19 **Department of Education and Science, Circular 10/65,** *The Organisation of Secondary Education*, **12 July 1965, pp. 301–7.**

■   **I Introduction**

1. It is the Government's declared objective to end selection at eleven plus and to eliminate separatism in secondary education ...

The Secretary of State accordingly requests local education authorities, if they have not already done so, to prepare and submit to him plans for reorganising secondary education in their areas on comprehensive lines ...

26. It is for the authorities ... to devise the most satisfactory plans in relation to local circumstances. In doing so, they should appreciate that while the Secretary of State wishes progress to be as rapid as possible, he does not wish it to be achieved by the adoption of plans whose educational disadvantages more than off-set the benefits which will flow from the adoption of comprehensive schooling ...

36. A comprehensive school aims to establish a school community in which pupils over the whole ability range and with differing interests and backgrounds can be encouraged to mix with each other, gaining stimulus from the contacts and learning tolerance and understanding in the process. But particular comprehensive schools will reflect the characteristics of the neighbourhood in which they are situated; if their community is less varied and fewer of the pupils come from homes which encourage educational interests, schools may lack the stimulus and vitality which schools in other areas enjoy. The Secretary of State therefore urges authorities to ensure, when determining catchment areas, that schools are as socially and intellectually comprehensive as is practicable ...

44. Plans should be submitted within one year of the date of this Circular, although the Secretary of State may exceptionally agree an extension to this period in the case of any individual authority. Plans should be in two parts as follows:

(*a*) A general statement of the authority's long-term proposals ...

(*b*) A detailed statement of the authority's proposals, whether or not they have already been discussed with the Department, covering a period of three years starting not later than September 1967. ■

Other important initiatives concerned the expansion of opportunities in higher educa-tion. Crosland announced the consolidation of the non-university higher education sec-tor in 1965, with the establishment of thirty 'polytechnic' colleges. Another imaginative initiative was the decision to launch a 'university of the air', subsequently to be chris-tened the Open University, early in 1966.

9.20   *A University of the Air,* **February 1966 (London, HMSO, Cmnd 2922, PP 1965–6, XIII, p. 3).**

■ **1.** In the educational world, as elsewhere, technological discoveries are making a profound impact. Television and radio, programmed learning and a wide range of audio-visual aids have already brought about considerable changes. The most important, undoubtedly, is that the best of our teachers can now be made available to vastly wider audiences. A distinguished lec-ture that at one time might have been heard only by a handful of students, or a few hundreds at most, can now be broadcast to millions of listeners. It has, therefore, become possible for the first time to think in terms of a University of the Air.

2. A substantial network of educational institutions provide higher and further education for both full-time and part-time students. But opportun-ities can be still further enlarged to meet the needs of many not attracted by traditional institutions or unable, for a variety of reasons, to take advantage of them.

The Government believe that by an imaginative use of new teaching tech-niques and teacher/student relationships, an open university providing degree courses as rigorous and demanding as those in existing universities can be established.

3. Its purpose will be three-fold. It will contribute to the improvement of educational, cultural and professional standards generally, by making avail-able to all who care to look and listen, scholarship of a high order. Secondly, a minority of those showing general interest will want to accept the full disciplines of study and make use of all the facilities offered ...

Thirdly, it will have much to contribute to students in many other parts of the world as well as those studying in the United Kingdom. In the developing countries in particular, there is an urgent need not only for elementary education but for a highly trained corps of men and women, equipped to provide leadership in national life.

4. From the outset it must be made clear that there can be no question of offering to students a make-shift project inferior in quality to other universities. That would defeat its whole purpose, as its status will be determined by the quality of its teaching.

Its aim will be to provide, in addition to television and radio lectures, correspondence courses of a quality unsurpassed anywhere in the world. These will be reinforced by residential courses and tutorials. ■

Industry and Technology

The new Ministry of Technology was launched in 1964 with the objective of encouraging both the modernisation of industrial organisation and the reorientation of research and development away from the defence sector, towards the exploitation of new technological breakthroughs for British industry.

The 'Mintech', as the new department became known, was not a runaway success. In the following passage, key figures in the administration assess its record.

9.21 Witness seminar, the Ministry of Technology, February 1990 (Institute of Contemporary British History).

■ **Bray** [Jeremy Bray, Parliamentary Secretary, 1967–9]: On the question of the broader strategy I think the underlying problem was that there was no relationship between what the Ministry of Technology was doing and what the economic, and particularly macro-economic, policy of the government was. Patrick [Blackett] had a good OR [operational research] background but he had absolutely no grasp of economics at all, not even really of company management. He was a very good scientist, superb naval operational researcher, but really not the sort of hard headed research director of a company. Otto Clarke's attitude too was that what we were doing was great fun, worthwhile if it worked but nothing at all to do with the economy, the really serious stuff was being done at the Treasury ... We were in the Ministry of Technology, all philosophers and grand strategists, we were none of us managers ...

Benn [Tony Benn, Minister 1966–70]: ... Jeremy is very modest, he ... wrote a book called *Decision in Government* and Wilson said, 'If you publish it I'll sack you'. I went to Wilson and said, 'You're wrong', then went to Jeremy and said, 'Don't get sacked'. Jeremy published the book and was duly sacked but it was an attempt to integrate what we were doing with central economic policy-making ... But the fact was that Wilson did not want the Treasury challenged. He was quite happy to have a big industrial department but he didn't want the central functions of the Treasury challenged. Now Otto did enjoy it, he was probably more of a MINTECH man than I was because I was more interested in its impact on the environment and working people and survival and so on. But Otto was an economist and he was always keen that we should learn from Japan. He was the one who wanted me to go to Japan, which I did, and so on ...

Hennessy [Peter Hennessy, ICBH]: You get the sense, Ken, that the problems were really far greater than any department of state, to put it crudely.

Binning [Kenneth Binning, Assistant to Controller of Technology, Mintech, 1964]: Yes, they were inappropriate to government in fact. The problems were problems relating to all the economy. There was, to some extent and I don't know if Bruce Williams would agree, there was something of a sort of platonic fallacy around that if you could only get a grip on the problem and identify what it was and set it out clearly, everybody would behave rightly. This unfortunately is not true in this world and there was a lot of effort made to identify issues, both in terms of technology and in terms of the micro-economics of industry but it didn't make people behave differently, I'm afraid.

Williams [Sir Bruce Williams, Economic Adviser, Mintech]: For the job that MINTECH appeared to have, and it kept changing, I don't think the quality of the staff was ever adequate. It certainly wasn't in any fundamental sense full of technocrats. I think the experiment, if we can call it that, was doomed to failure from the beginning because of a failure to decide what the various departments ought to be doing and the way MINTECH was set up without considering what its relationship to the Board of Trade would be was a major fault. One reason why MINTECH kept on getting more things to do was that it realised if it was going to do this then it would need to be able to have a direct relationship with that industry or some other industry, which was the point that Ken was making ...

Hennessy: As Chief Scientific Adviser to the government as a whole, Lord Zuckerman, do you agree with that? You have an overview of all this and do you think that Bruce and Ken are right?

Zuckerman [Lord Zuckerman, former Chief Scientific Adviser, MoD]: Yes, I think they are ... At the end with the setting up of the British research and development corporation, Tony Benn appeared not once but twice before the central committee on science and technology which had industrialists on it, a minimum of scientists, and at which again I insisted that the civil service should also appear. Tony appeared twice, Otto Clarke appeared with a team to explain what they had in mind, so that on three separate occasions that I recall now, we discussed, interrogated, disagreed and the general consensus was that it was a bad idea. It was a bad idea because it was attempting to take over from British industry what British industry was not going to give. There was certainly not going to be any sharing of your best commercially secret technical secrets between the government department, which was mistrusted by the particular industries, etc. I had a feeling then it was biting off far more than it could chew ...

Jones [Peter Jones, Superintendent of Research, Aldermaston]: I would like to pick up the point about the non-clarity of objective and again I talk from the bottom end of this thing and that was certainly the sense that came through. The scientists and engineers were told to take technologies and see where these might be useful to industry. Immediately they said 'what's the problem?'. So we sent them out to industry and they went to talk to industry, to talk to government organisations, and said 'what are your problems?' ... The smaller industries who had almost no research effort at all ... didn't even know their problem and perhaps rather cruelly I have to come back to the point that the truth of the matter, we found, in almost every case was the people who ran such industries only regarded the technical man as somebody to help them out when they were up against it against a competitor. They were the last resort rather than something you put in the forefront for the long-term benefit of the company. They didn't want to know, so there was enormous difficulty there. Nevertheless, of the projects we undertook ... we went into the NHS – the implants which were used for hip implants came out of Aldermaston materials technology. Kidney dialysis machines also came out of our materials technology ... We'd done the development, we made it work and got it to a prototype stage where somewhere, somehow we found an industry, usually a small one, would pick it up and say 'We'll make that, and there's a profit in it too', and it went from there. But it was a very hit-and-miss business all the way. ∎

CHAPTER TEN

Protest and Reform: British Politics, 1964–70

WITH the Labour Party, led by Harold Wilson, taking up the reins of government in 1964, it seemed that a more progressive chapter in British political history was beginning. But the failure of his government to modernise and reform the country's institutions or to transform its economic performance led to widespread disillusionment with Labour by the end of the decade. The Wilson administration did, however, initiate a number of institutional reforms in these years, with some success, making a genuine attempt to revitalise the institutions of government.

The Conservative Party replaced Alec Douglas-Home as leader with Edward Heath in 1965; the contrast between the aristocrat and the self-made grammar-school boy was marked. Under Heath's leadership, the party undertook a wide-ranging policy review in 1965. In the years which followed, the Conservatives began to advocate a more aggressive return to free market strategies for prosperity and finally departed from the romance with indicative planning that had been a feature of Harold Macmillan's premiership.

Outside of Westminster, these years were marked by protest and discontent. Race and immigration continued to feature as an increasingly controversial subject. Youth protest at home centred on the universities and reached a high point in 1968 as indignation over the United States' war in Vietnam spilled over into the streets of London. Regionalism also revived during this time; both Plaid Cymru and the Scottish National Party experienced a surge in support from the middle of the decade. Most serious, however, were events in Northern Ireland, where Catholic protest over Protestant bias in the allocation of local services eventually led to civil disturbance on such a scale that British troops were sent in 1969.

1964–6: The Changing of the Guard

The general election of 1964 had returned Labour to power, but with an overall majority of only four seats. This placed a greater imperative than ever on the importance of unity between right and left, and Wilson was careful to balance the composition of the Cabinet. It was clear that a new election would have to take place before long, and this electioneering atmosphere contributed to the Prime Minister's stress on style and image.

Wilson had promised a 'first hundred days' of reform, in emulation of the popular Kennedy administration in the USA earlier in the decade. He also imported a personal political staff into Downing Street, a practice which caused some unease, among both civil servants and his colleagues in the party. The contrast in prime ministerial style with Alec Douglas-Home was profound. Under Wilson, the premiership became the hub of the administration's reforming zeal. Wilson's pipe-smoking, man-of-the-people image was rapidly taken up by contemporary cartoonists.

10.1 'Vicky' (Victor Weisz), 'A nation neglects its eggheads at its peril ...', *Evening Standard* cartoon, 30 October 1964.

The Conservatives in opposition

The Conservative Party had to come to terms with Labour's more dynamic programme and style under Wilson. Home at first resisted stepping down, but his lacklustre performances in the House of Commons and the increasing unrest of the 1922 Committee made his early resignation almost inevitable.

Cecil King, chairman of the International Publishing Corporation, which controlled the Daily Mirror, Sunday Mirror, Sun and People, recorded his view of the subsequent leadership struggle in his diary.

10.2 Cecil King, *The Cecil King Diary, 1965–1970*, London, Cape, 1972, pp. 23–6.

■ *Sunday, July 25th, 1965*

On Thursday afternoon rumours were rife around Fleet St (but not apparently equally rife around the H. of C.) that Home was resigning. And this he duly did in the evening. Home has always filled me with amazement. I suppose I met him first as Lord Dunglass in the 'thirties. I have never been able to detect anything in him at all. He is a pleasant country gentleman of a very familiar type. I agreed with those who greeted his appointment to the Foreign Office with derision, and his nomination to 10 Downing St with stupefaction …

Now the fight is on again – this time between Heath and Maudling. I know them both and like them both. Time was when Maudling had the leadership in his hand – and let it slip. This time he has another chance – mainly because Heath has enemies, though for the right reason. Heath really is a positive force – a leader – while dear Reggie, though very intelligent, does like a good lunch and parties that go on late into the night. There is no doubt in my mind that Heath is certainly the best available man to be Tory P.M., and probably the best potential P.M. in the House …

Mike [King, Cecil King's son] saw Heath on Friday morning. Heath told him that he had the support of the younger men, but was not popular with the Knights of the Shires. Tufton Beamish was doing his best with the latter, and Macleod, a Maudling man before, has swung round behind Heath. Later in the day Tufton Beamish told Mike he thought Heath was in. But later today it was announced that Enoch Powell was a candidate. This is presumably a move to get his rather Goldwaterish ideas better known, though it may be an attempt to weaken Heath. No one supposes he will score an appreciable number of votes.

Cromer rang me up from the Bank on Friday to say that the foreign bankers regard Maudling as the architect of our present financial misfortunes and that, therefore, if he is chosen as Leader the effect on the pound will be bad …

Sunday, August 1st, 1965

… On Tuesday the result was announced: Heath 150, Maudling 133, Powell 15. Maudling immediately conceded the victory to Heath. Maudling was surprised and upset by the result; and is said only to have conceded under pressure.

The change is of real importance as we now have an alternative government, as we had not before. I have been telling Heath for at least two years that he is the Tories' best bet, and more recently have conveyed both to Whitelaw (the Conservative Chief Whip) and to Bob Renwick the view that Alec Home just will not do, and that their most marketable personality was Ted Heath. ■

Under the leadership of Edward Heath, the Conservatives focused on overhauling their policy proposals to provide a stronger alternative to the Labour government. They were conscious that a new election could be called at short notice, so this process advanced rapidly; a new statement of policy was issued within months. Putting Britain Right

Ahead *signalled the beginnings of a renewed public emphasis on the free market, and away from state intervention in planning the economy.*

10.3　Conservative Party, *Putting Britain Right Ahead*, 1965 (Conservative Party Archives), pp. 7–21.

■ The Conservative Party believes in encouraging people to get on with the job. Too many tax burdens and restrictions bear down on the very people in this country upon whose vigour and initiative our prosperity and our export trade depend. It is high time that these burdens were reduced and that incentives to display talent and ability were increased. We need to see less tax falling on rising earnings and on success. We need more direct incentives to encourage savings ...

The Labour Government's Corporation and Capital Gains Taxes will also need drastic revision. A Conservative government would weed out those provisions which penalise personal initiative and small companies and make it unnecessarily hard for people to get started on their own.

We also believe that more of the cost of the social services would be transferred from the Exchequer to the employer. This would enable the levels of individual and company taxation to be reduced. It would also provide an incentive for the more efficient use of labour ...

As well as opening up personal opportunities and creating a new dynamic in business, Britain needs a completely new approach to the problems of employment. For as far ahead as we can see, Britain will be a country with increasing labour demands. The old idea of training for one job and sticking to it for life, which has been the lot of millions, will have to go out of the window ...

The fact is that pointless strikes, inter-union squabbling and, above all, restrictive labour practices and over-manning weaken our efficiency. The quicker we can re-organise on more efficient lines, the faster we will be able to fill all the new jobs that will be coming up ...

A Royal Commission on the subject of trade unions and employers' associations is now sitting ...

There is an urgent need for a new Act covering the whole of industrial relations.

Straightaway, therefore, on our return to office we would ask the Royal Commission to let us have their views urgently on a number of pressing issues – set out below – so that we could get on with early legislative action.

> ... Our suggestion is to establish a new and powerful Registrar of Trade Unions and Employers' Associations. He would see that the rules of both conformed to certain basic principles. This would be a condition of registration. The principles would govern such questions as admission of members, election and responsibility of officials, finance and

disciplinary powers. A trade union would then be redefined as an association of employees or employers with a written constitution approved by the new Registrar.

Where such unions are established, employers should accept the duty to recognise and negotiate with them if the majority of their employees desire this. ·

We also suggest that a range of new Industrial Courts are required. These would concentrate on the settlement of industrial disputes – including disputes arising out of dismissals, disputes between trade unions and their individual members and appeals against decisions of the Registrar ...

The present social security system was formed nearly twenty-five years ago. It must now be reshaped ...

We have therefore designed a new and coherent social policy. The aim is to help those in need effectively and, wherever possible, to set them on their own feet again ...

Nearly two-thirds of the adult male working population are already in occupational pension schemes. We believe that an arrangement should be made for all to be covered by occupational or similar pensions on top of the State basic pension ...

Under this new plan, the present State graduated pensions scheme would become a residual state scheme for those relatively few who would not otherwise be covered ...

Britain has become part of a close-knit commercial, financial, military and political world system. We cannot opt out of it and at the same time maintain our security and prosperity ...

In maintaining peace, in seeking disarmament, in promoting economic development, in safeguarding and expanding our commerce, in building up our strength to exert political influence in the world, we can best achieve our objectives in a wider grouping.

It was on these grounds that Britain sought suitable conditions for membership of the European Economic Community – a prospect unwelcome to the Labour Party. It is on these grounds that, when the present difficulties and uncertainties in Europe are resolved, we believe it would be right to take the first favourable opportunity to join the community and to assist others who wish, in the Commonwealth and in EFTA, to seek closer association with it. Until this becomes possible a future Conservative Government will co-operate with other European countries in joint policies in the common interest. ■

The general election of 1966

By the beginning of 1966 the political signs were good for Harold Wilson. The Labour Party unexpectedly crushed Conservative hopes in a by-election at Hull North on 27 January, recording a 4.5 per cent swing in the government's favour. The official announcement of a general election was widely expected when it came on 28 February.

Labour entered the 1966 election campaign with a 9 per cent lead in the polls, and few doubted that the party would be returned to power with an increased majority. In the event, Wilson obtained a 97-seat victory, the mandate he needed to tackle the twin issues of economic instability and modernisation. In the coming few months, Labour's popularity seemed unassailable, and Wilson's personal standing as Prime Minister was almost unprecedented.

10.4 **Public approval ratings for Harold Wilson and Edward Heath, October 1965 to October 1966 (chart derived from D. Butler and G. Butler (eds),** *British Political Facts, 1900–1985,* **London, Macmillan, 6th edn, 1986, p. 259).**

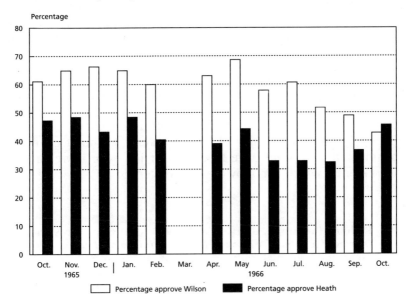

For all Wilson's public popularity after the 1966 election, the diaries of his colleagues have revealed deep unease over his premiership at this time. As Tony Benn's comments overleaf indicate, Wilson became increasingly obsessed with the opinion polls and lost sight of Labour's ideological agenda. In Cabinet, his style of management seemed dictatorial and manipulative. Richard Crossman's diary as a Cabinet minister has proved particularly critical in this regard.

10.5   **Tony Benn, diary, Tuesday 21 June 1966 (in Tony Benn, *Out of the Wilderness: Diaries 1963–67*, London, Hutchinson, 1987, pp. 436–7).**

■ ... To the Commons and this evening to Number 10 for a buffet supper that Harold had laid on. Among those who came were Peter Shore, Ron Brown [MP for Shoreditch and Finsbury], George Wallace [MP for Norwich North], Gerald Kaufman, Marcia, Percy Clark, and Dick's PPS, Geoffrey Rhodes, and members of the PLP permanent staff. Harold began by giving his usual analysis. The public 'are not interested in politics and want to play tennis and clean their cars and leave things to the Government. By contrast the party wants to do things and change things, and the main thing is to keep it on the move like a caravan so that it does not have time to stop and fight.'

The discussion roamed on for some time, so I plucked up my courage and said that if there was a conflict between what the public wanted and what the Party wanted, I was on the side of the Party. Anyway, I didn't agree that the public wasn't interested in politics. They may be sick of Party bickering but they are interested in a whole host of issues that are essentially political and it was the Party's job to show the connection between issues that concerned the public and the political ideology and decisions that we expressed. It was for us to propagandise and campaign, just as it was the job of the Labour pioneers to convince the people fifty years ago that unemployment had something to do with politics.

What worries me is that Harold may be going to preside over a period of decline just as serious as occurred under Macmillan and accept the same basic philosophy of 'never had it so good' affluence that Macmillan accepted. Consensus is no substitute for putting key issues and institutions deliberately into the crucible of controversy. If we don't change things fundamentally, we shall have failed in our job even if we survive as a Government – which is not by any means certain. ■

10.6   **Richard Crossman, diary, 24 July 1966 (in Richard Crossman, *The Diaries of a Cabinet Minister, Vol. One: Minister of Housing, 1964–66*, London, Hamish Hamilton and Cape, 1975, pp. 582–3).**

■ What is really wrong ... is that we have no real instrument of central decision-taking for the home front ... In its absence the P.M. has run the Government Prime Ministerially, arbitrating between George Brown and Callaghan, and in every other field retaining the right of final decision and, in this particular crisis, working direct with the Permanent Secretaries behind the backs of their Ministers. As for his own personal decisions, they've been taken in consultation with a very small inner private circle ...

This week we have had the beginnings of a collective Cabinet reaction against this Prime Ministerial method. The odd thing is that I, who wrote the introduction to Bagehot, am now busily trying to reassert collective Cabinet authority because I see how disastrous it is to allow Cabinet government to decline into mere Prime Ministerial government. It's better to get back to something much more like Cabinet responsibility; just as it is better to get back to effective Cabinet responsibility to Parliament, and the reassertion of parliamentary control over government – one of those bright ideas Harold announced during the election campaign and at the beginning of the Session but which has got entirely lost since then.

I think it is true after this week nobody in Cabinet will ever again believe that this triumvirate can safely be left in charge. If I achieved anything it was by asserting the right of Cabinet to take part in the making of economic strategy so that Harold conceded that we must be given that right. If we really have achieved an economic strategy committee parallel to the Defence Committee, it could produce a complete change in the relationship between the P.M., the First Secretary and the Chancellor on the one side and the rest of the Cabinet on the other. We shall have to wait and see whether this has been achieved, however, when Harold returns from his two days in Washington at the end of next week. ■

The Revolution Fails

The years of the first Wilson governments were marked by a number of attempts to reform the institutions of British government. Many of these initiatives failed; others proved more successful. The 1960s are remembered in particular as a decade of 'permissiveness', and many of the reforms for which the decade has been remembered, such as the Sexual Offences Act and the Abortion Act (both of 1967), were associated with Roy Jenkins's tenure at the Home Office. This chapter, however, will focus on examples of initiatives which affected the constitutional structure of the state and the workings of government.

Wilson had promised to reform the machinery of Whitehall before 1964, and in 1966 he appointed Lord Fulton, vice-chancellor of the new University of Sussex, chairman of a commission to study the recruitment practices and structure of the civil service. The Fulton Report of 1968 recommended a number of changes intended to make the civil service more efficient and professional. But although its findings were accepted by the government, reform of the service was ultimately blocked from within Whitehall. The administration's failure to modernise the machinery of government has been judged an important missed opportunity.

10.7 *The Civil Service* **(Fulton Report), June 1968 (London, HMSO, Cmnd 3638, PP 1967–8, XVIII, pp. 104–6).**

1. The Home Civil Service today is still fundamentally the product of the nineteenth-century philosophy of the Northcote–Trevelyan Report. The problems it faces are those of the second half of the twentieth century. In spite of its many strengths, it is inadequate ... for the most efficient discharge of the present and prospective responsibilities of government ... For these ... defects the central management of the Service, the Treasury, must accept its share of responsibility.

2. We propose a simple guiding principle for the future. The Service must continuously review the tasks it is called on to perform; it should then think out what new skills and kinds of men are needed and how these men can be found, trained and deployed.

3. A new Civil Service Department should be set up with wider functions than those now performed by the 'Pay and Management' group of the Treasury, which it should take over ...

4. The new department should be under the control of the Prime Minister. We hope that he will retain direct responsibility for senior appointments, machinery of government and questions of security ...

5. The Permanent Secretary of the Civil Service Department should be designated Head of the Home Civil Service.

6. All classes should be abolished and replaced by a single, unified grading structure covering all civil servants from top to bottom in the non-industrial part of the Service ...

7. The Service should develop greater professionalism both among specialists (e.g. scientists and engineers) and administrators (i.e. the new counterparts of the present Administrative and Executive Classes) ...

9. A Civil Service College should be set up. It should provide major training courses in administration and management and a wide range of shorter courses. It should also have important research functions ...

11. While the Civil Service should remain predominantly a career Service, there should be greater mobility between it and other employments ...

13. Management services units with highly qualified and experienced staff should be set up in all major departments.

14. Departments should establish Planning Units.

15. In addition to the Permanent Secretary, there should also be in most departments a Senior Policy Adviser to assist the Minister. The Senior Policy Adviser would normally be head of the Planning Unit. His prime job would be to look to and prepare for the future and to ensure that present policy decisions are taken with as full a recognition as possible of likely future developments ...

19. A Minister at the head of a department should be able to employ on a temporary basis such small numbers of experts as he personally considers he needs to help him ... ■

Local government reform met with a similar fate to attempts to revitalise Whitehall. The commission appointed under the chairmanship of Lord Redcliffe-Maud recommended far-reaching change which reflected a contemporary belief in the increased efficiency of large-scale organisation and comprehensiveness of provision. In the discussion reproduced below, some of the participants in the commission consider its record and the reasons for its failure.

10.8 **Witness seminar, the Redcliffe-Maud Report, February 1989 (Institute of Contemporary British History).**

■ **Kennet** [Lord Kennet, Parliamentary Secretary, Ministry of Housing and Local Government, 1966–70]: My memory of it is that Crossman wanted to have the Royal Commission for one great overriding reason and that was to settle the running warfare between the counties and county boroughs. His main demand of it, I think, was on the planning side and it has to be borne in mind that this Royal Commission took its existence from the minister responsible for planning. We certainly took it for granted then that you couldn't very effectively plan town and country planning in England, or parts of it, at the district level. That, I think, is what probably gave the initial impetus towards 'big is beautiful' ...

Pugh [Sir Idwal Pugh, Deputy Secretary, MHLG, 1966–9]: ... There had been the London government commission some years before which had done virtually the same sort of job in relation to London, it made much larger London boroughs and also created a strategic authority in the GLC [Greater London Council]. This was certainly a guide. The 1960s was very much a planning decade and certainly it was a basic concept then that you needed large self-sufficient planning authorities of the order of a quarter of a million people ...

Mursell [Sir Peter Mursell, member of the commission]: The dominant memory that I've got about all the evidence from the different departments was on the question of size, pushing it up and up and up. Instinctively I, and I think a lot of others, felt that it must be wrong but the weight of evidence was enormous on size – 'big is beautiful' – ... you must have size in order to have a sufficient economic base.

Sharpe [Jim Sharpe, assistant commissioner responsible for research]: I think the combination of this almost unanimity among certain professional groups of minimums of 500,000 population – especially some of the educational groups – combined with the geographer's squeeze on the other side arguing for a wider scale for a spread city made for a pretty formidable line-up. They weren't colluding, it was just two quite different sets of conventional opinion, plus the central government's desire, I think, just to reduce the total number of local authorities. They were fed up with dealing with the East Hams of this world, to be quite frank. The three forces were aligned in the same direction ...

Mursell: We were all convinced that it would be best if we could get single-tier authorities throughout the country. But when we began to look at what you could do with metropolitan authorities, these enormous conurbations, they didn't fit anything. They were of the scale where education, health and welfare simply didn't fit, the imagination couldn't take it in and we then said, 'you've got to have something in the metropolitan areas which looks at the whole and splits down the rest to a more reasonable size' ...

Pugh: I think the GLC boroughs must have had some impression on the report; if London was going to be that way who could say that Manchester and Birmingham and so forth should not go the same way? ...

Osborn [Derek Osborn, MHLG official]: ... By the time they did report in 1969 it was too late to implement it before the 1970 election. There was only time to produce a White Paper. My impression was that the report ran very well with the Labour government in that last year of their administration (1969–70). It was what Whitehall wanted – Whitehall had been dominant in thinking 'big is beautiful' and the report had more or less chimed in with that. Whitehall liked the look of the single unitary authorities in most places; and they were prepared to go along with the two-tier structure of the metropolitan areas. All the areas would have had the right size of population for what was then regarded as necessary for the effective administration of the major services; and they all looked good in terms of producing appropriate areas for planning purposes, which was regarded as of crucial importance at that time. I think also, Lord Kennet will correct me, that it chimed rather well with the government's political preferences in that what it meant in many areas were bigger county boroughs which in a good year would be Labour areas. It would also provide room for the cities to grow where they needed to. So it had the right sort of political flavour ... So the report came out, the official machine ground into action, committees started drafting White Papers and in February 1970 the Labour government White Paper came out broadly accepting the report. If the 1969 election had gone Labour's way it would have moved straight into action to legislate in the autumn of 1970 ... The Conservatives had a fairly clear political perception; in the main the existing counties were to remain as the main authorities in the areas outside the metropolitan areas. They attracted strong political loyalties, and the Conservatives were not persuaded of the case for the major carve up of these areas which Redcliffe-Maud had recommended. Keeping the counties meant in turn that a second level of districts had to be retained for the more local services, since the counties would have been too big as unitary authorities ... ■

One successful act of reform came in 1968, when the voting age was reduced from 21 to 18. The proposal to reduce the voting age to 18 was generally welcomed on both sides of the House of Commons, although there were some dissenters. The arguments put forward by the Conservative backbencher John Boyd-Carpenter during the second reading debate on the Representation of the People Bill summarise the majority view.

10.9 **John Boyd-Carpenter, speech to the House of Commons on the Representation of the People Bill, 18 November 1968 (*Hansard*, 5th ser., 773: 952–3).**

■ **Mr. Boyd-Carpenter:** ... I think the time has come to make this change ... First, if this country's policy leads it to war, young men of 18 are conscripted to serve – and many do serve without such conscription ... There is a sound argument for saying that if young men or girls of 18 are to be treated for serious civil purposes as mature people – as being able to own property and contract marriage – it is some indication that they are also ripe for the responsibility of exercising the franchise.

That is not to say that all of them will exercise the franchise sensibly. But that is true of any other age group ...

Incidentally, it is interesting to note that for many years the age of 18 has been the one at which a young person has been treated as fully mature for National Insurance purposes, and it is also of historical interest that the heir to the Throne can succeed without a Regency resulting if he is 18 on the demise of the sovereign ...

There is a deeper reason for reducing the age to 18 ... There is a great deal of unrest and confusion among many of the more intelligent members of this generation, and there is undoubtedly a feeling of frustration. The acceptance of this proposal would not cure it, but it would reduce the causes of frustration. If an intelligent young person thinks that he or she knows how the country should be run – and at that age most of us thought precisely that; it was only as the years passed that doubts began to creep into our minds – it is frustrating to know that he or she can do nothing except demonstrate in the streets.

If these young people know that they have the same rights as older people to influence the way in which the country is governed, through the ballot box, it may have the effect of giving them an added sense of responsibility. It is not a cure-all, but it has a certain advantage in this direction, and it is for that and the other reasons which I have mentioned that I shall support this proposal in Committee ... ■

The Revival of Celtic Nationalism

Although there had been signs of an increase in support for regional parties in by-elections earlier in the decade, a distinct upsurge in support for Celtic nationalism was first recorded in 1966. By the time of the 1970 general election, however, nationalist support in Wales and Scotland again appeared to be in decline. Although founded in 1925, Plaid Cymru had never met with success at a parliamentary level until the 1966 by-election in Carmarthen which returned the party's president, Gwynfor Evans. The cultural and linguistic roots of Welsh nationalism coincided with growing disaffection over the state of the Welsh economy, which was over-reliant on agriculture and mining. Like Plaid Cymru, the Scottish National Party had made little headway since its founding in 1928. In 1967, however, the SNP captured a seat in the Hamilton by-election and made impressive gains in subsequent local elections.

The Wilson government responded to the rise of Celtic sentiment in several ways. In 1964 a separate Welsh Office was established for the first time, with James Griffiths appointed its first secretary of state. In 1967 his successor, Cledwyn Hughes, promoted a number of measures, such as the 1967 Welsh Language Act.

10.10   Welsh Language Act 1967 (*Public General Acts*, 1967, Part 2, ch. 66, pp. 1305–6).

■ An Act to make further provision with respect to the Welsh language and references in Acts of Parliament to Wales [27th July 1967]

Whereas it is proper that the Welsh language should be freely used by those who so desire in the hearing of legal proceedings in Wales and Monmouthshire; that further provision should be made for the use of that language, with the like effect as English, in the conduct of other official or public business there; and that Wales should be distinguished from England in the interpretation of future Acts of Parliament:

Be it therefore enacted by the Queen's most Excellent majesty, by and with the advice and consent of the Lords Spiritual and Temporal, and Commons, in this present Parliament assembled, and by the authority of the same, as follows:–

1. – (1) In any legal proceeding in Wales or Monmouthshire the Welsh language may be spoken by any party, witness or other person who desires to use it, subject in the case of proceedings in a court other than a magistrates' court to such prior notice as may be required by rules of court; and any necessary provision for interpretation shall be made accordingly ...

2. – (1) Where any enactment passed either before or after this Act specifies the form of any document or any form of words which is to be or may be used for an official or public purpose, the appropriate Minister may by order prescribe a version of the document or words in Welsh, or partly in Welsh and partly in English, for use for that purpose in such circumstances and subject to such conditions as may be prescribed by the order ...

3. – (1) Subject to subsection (2) of this section, anything done in Welsh in

a version authorised by section 2 of this Act shall have the like effect as if done in English ...

4. – Section 3 of the Wales and Berwick Act 1746 (which provides that references in Acts of Parliament to England include references to Wales and Berwick) shall have effect in relation to any Act passed after this Act as if the words 'dominion of Wales and' were omitted ... ■

Great care was taken when the Queen's eldest son was invested as the Prince of Wales in 1969. Prince Charles read his address in both English and Welsh, although as a propaganda exercise it undoubtedly did more for Britain's image abroad than it did to persuade the Welsh that the metropolitan bias of British government was weakening.

10.11 **Prince Charles, response to investiture as Prince of Wales, 1 July 1969 (reported in *Daily Sketch*, 2 July 1969).**

■ ... It is with a certain sense of pride and emotion that I have received these symbols of office, here in this magnificent fortress, where no one could fail to be stirred by its atmosphere of time-worn grandeur, nor where I myself could be unaware of the long history of Wales in its determination to remain individual and to guard its own particular heritage – a heritage that dates back into the mists of ancient British history, that has produced many brave men, princes, poets, bards, scholars, and more recently great singers, a very memorable 'Goon' and eminent film stars. All these people have been inspired in some way by this heritage.

I hope and trust that in time I shall be able to offer my own contribution and to do that I seek your cooperation and understanding. Speaking for myself, as a result of my two-month stay in this country, I have come to see far more in the title I hold than hitherto. I am more than grateful to the people of this Principality for making my brief stay so immensely worthwhile and for giving me such encouragement in the learning of the language.

I know that social conditions have changed since 50 years ago, and, of course, are still changing. The demands on a Prince of Wales have altered, but I am determined to serve and to try as best I can to live up to those demands, whatever they might be in the rather uncertain future. One thing I am clear about and it is that Wales needs to look forward without forsaking the traditional and essential aspects of her past ... ■

Northern Ireland

Politics in Northern Ireland had remained relatively quiet since the signing of the Anglo-Irish Treaty in December 1921. By the 1960s, however, the entrenched rule of the Protestant majority in Ulster had come to be increasingly resented by the Catholic minority, which was in practice widely discriminated against in the allocation of jobs and housing. The 'Troubles' which began in 1968 in violent clashes between the Royal Ulster Constabulary and civil rights demonstrators had escalated alarmingly by 1970.

In 1963 the moderate Unionist leader Captain Terence O'Neill had become Prime Minister of Northern Ireland, promising to launch a series of cautious reforms, which he hoped would head off serious protest against Unionist rule. When the Wilson administration took power in 1964, although concern over civil rights in the province was expressed on the Labour backbenches, the government maintained a policy of minimum direct interference in Ulster.

10.12 Roy Jenkins, speech to the House of Commons on Northern Ireland, 25 October 1967 (*Hansard*, 5th ser., 751: 1681–7).

■ **The Secretary of State for the Home Department** (Mr. Roy Jenkins): ... I said earlier that a sustained attack on the economic difficulties of the region can make it much easier to solve the special social and political problems of Northern Ireland. People employed in a vigorous modern economy with a technological base which demands high management and other skills are less likely to be obsessed by old quarrels. There have been many criticisms of the administration of Northern Ireland. The general feeling of concern which underlies many, although not all, of those criticisms is something which my right hon. Friend the Prime Minister and I share but we cannot simply put aside the constitution of Northern Ireland or ignore the historical facts which underlie the present position and present policy.

The Prime Minister told the House last April that he did not think that a Royal Commission to inquire into the administration of Northern Ireland was the answer. Under the Northern Ireland constitution, certain powers and responsibilities are vested in the Parliament and Government of Northern Ireland. Successive Governments here have refused to take steps which would inevitably cut away not only the authority of the Northern Ireland Government but also the constitution of the province. Nevertheless, my right hon. Friend and I have not concealed from the Prime Minister of Northern Ireland, with whom we have had continuing discussions, the concern felt here. I must add that we have not concealed on occasion our admiration for the courageous stand Captain O'Neill has taken on certain issues and at certain times.

The process of bringing about some *rapprochement* between Northern Ireland and the Republic is bound to be accompanied by mistrust and suspicion in the minds of many people on both sides. But a start has been made, and no one should underrate this easing of relations in Northern Ireland itself. I believe that nearly everybody in the House – certainly everybody on this side, but also many hon. Members opposite – wants to see rapid progress in that direction. After all, Northern Ireland is part of the United Kingdom.

That is its *raison d'être* as an entity. It exists because of its desire to be part of the United Kingdom, but that unity can have little meaning unless we work towards common economic and social standards and common standards in political tolerance and non-discrimination on both sides of the Irish Sea.

There is room for argument – and we have heard a good deal this morning – about the pace which is practicable or desirable. But we must at least be satisfied about the direction. Provided we can be so satisfied, there is a great deal to be said for not trying to settle the affairs of Northern Ireland too directly from London ...

Few issues in the past have shown a greater capacity to divert and dissipate the reforming energy of left-wing British Governments than deep embroilment in Irish affairs. But all that is subordinate to the desire – indeed, determination – that most of us have to see the making of real economic, social and political progress. There are at present reasonable grounds for hope, and I trust that they will not be disappointed. ■

The Labour government's position of minimal intervention in Ulster was shaken in October 1968. A demonstration in Londonderry sponsored by the Northern Ireland Civil Rights Association (NICRA) ended in violent clashes with the Royal Ulster Constabulary (RUC), and rioting occurred throughout the following night in the Catholic Bogside area of the city. This signalled the beginning of a number of violent episodes. In her maiden speech in the House of Commons the following spring, the young NICRA leader Bernadette Devlin made a passionate plea on behalf of the victims of violence and Protestant rule.

10.13 **Bernadette Devlin, maiden speech in the House of Commons, 22 April 1969 (*Hansard*, 5th ser., 782: 281–8).**

■ **Miss Bernadette Devlin (Mid-Ulster):** I understand that in making my maiden speech on the day of my arrival in Parliament and in making it on a controversial issue I flaunt the unwritten traditions of the House, but I think that the situation of my people merits the flaunting of such traditions ...

I had never hoped to see the day when I might agree with someone who represents the bigoted and sectarian Unionist Party, which uses a deliberate policy of dividing the people in order to keep the ruling minority in power and to keep the oppressed people of Ulster oppressed ... but the hon. Gentleman summed up the situation 'to a t'. He referred to stark, human misery. That is what I saw in Bogside. It has not been there just for one night. It has been there for 50 years – and that same stark human misery is to be found in the Protestant Fountain area, which the hon. Gentleman would claim to represent ...

Captain O'Neill listed a number of reforms which came nowhere near satisfying the needs of the people. Had he even had the courage of his convictions – had he even convictions – to carry out the so-called reforms he promised, we might have got somewhere. But none of his so-called reforms was carried out ...

We come to the question of what can be done about incidents like that in Derry at the weekend. Captain O'Neill has thought of a bright idea – that tomorrow we shall be given one man, one vote. Does he think that, from 5th October until today, events have not driven it into the minds of the people that there are two ideals which are incompatible – the ideal of social justice and the ideal and existence of the Unionist Party? Both cannot exist in the same society. This has been proved time and again throughout Northern Ireland by the actions of the Unionist Party ...

What will it mean to the people? Why do the people ask for one man, one vote, with each vote of equal value to the next?

The Unionist policy has always been to divide the people who are dependent upon them. The question of voting is tied up mainly with the question of housing, and this is something which the House has failed to understand. The people of Northern Ireland want votes not for the sake of voting but for the sake of being able to exercise democratic rights over the controlling powers of their own areas. The present system operates in such a way that Unionist-controlled councils and even Nationalist-controlled councils discriminate against those in their areas who are in the minority. The policy of segregated housing is to be clearly seen in the smallest villages of Ulster ...

In Dungannon, the Catholic ward already has too many houses in it. There is no room to build any more in that ward. It would appear logical that houses should be built, therefore, in what is traditionally known as the Protestant ward ... where there is space. But this would give rise to the nasty situation of building new houses in the Unionist or Protestant ward and thus letting in a lot of Fenians who might out-vote the others.

I wish to make it clear that in an area such as Omagh the same corruption is carried on because Protestants need houses and the only place for them is in a Catholic area ...

I was in the Bogside on the same evening as the hon. Member for Londonderry. I assure you, Mr. Speaker – and I make no apology for the fact – that I was not strutting around with my hands behind my back examining the area and saying 'tut-tut' every time a policeman had his head scratched. I was going around building barricades because I knew that it was not safe for the police to come in.

... when a police force are acting under orders – presumably from the top, and the top invariably is the Unionist Party – and form themselves into military formation with the deliberate intention of terrorising the inhabitants of an area, I can have no sympathy for them as a body. So I organised the civilians in that area to make sure that they wasted not one solitary stone in anger. [*Laughter.*]

Hon. Members may find this amusing and in the comfortable surroundings of this honourable House it may seem amusing, but at two o'clock in the morning on the Bogside there was something horrifying about the fact that someone such as I, who believes in non-violence, had to settle for the least violent method, which was to build barricades and to say to the police, 'We can threaten you'. ■

While O'Neill initially attempted to meet Catholic unrest with a programme of reforms, his conciliatory attitude alienated large sections of the Unionist Party and caused the resignation of four of his cabinet ministers. In the Ulster general election of February 1969, O'Neill's majority was much reduced. The hardline Democratic Unionists, led by the evangelical cleric Ian Paisley, were unsuccessful that time but did well enough to provide a clear warning to the O'Neillites. When Paisley and his deputy were returned in by-elections several months later, the embattled Ulster Prime Minister resigned. The Garland cartoon reproduced here depicts O'Neill sliding down the snake of Protestant Unionism, with Paisley at its head.

10.14 **Garland cartoon,** *Daily Telegraph,* **26 February 1969.**

The RUC proved unable to control the spiral of violence in Ulster. Riots in Derry and Belfast in the summer of 1969 were marked by a series of bloody sectarian confrontations. Major James Chichester-Clark, who had replaced O'Neill as Prime Minister, had little choice but to request the British army to reinforce the local police. The stationing of troops in Northern Ireland, originally intended as a temporary measure to protect the Catholic community from Protestant attacks, was a critical milestone. The Home Secretary, James Callaghan, additionally ordered the reorganisation and disarming of the RUC and the abolition of the exclusively Protestant auxiliary force, the B-Specials. In the 'Downing Street Declaration' of 19 August, London reassured the Protestant community over the constitutional status of the province, while committing the Unionist government to speeding up reforms to satisfy Catholic grievances.

10.15 **The Downing Street Declaration, 19 August 1969 (Cmnd 4154, PP 1968–9, LIII, pp. 3–4).**

■ **1.** The United Kingdom government reaffirm that nothing which has happened in recent weeks in Northern Ireland derogates from the clear pledges made by successive United Kingdom Governments that Northern Ireland should not cease to be a part of the United Kingdom without the consent of the people of Northern Ireland or from the provision in Section I of the Ireland Act, 1949, that in no event will Northern Ireland or any part thereof cease to be part of the United Kingdom without the consent of the Parliament of Northern Ireland. The border is not an issue.

2. The United Kingdom government again affirm that responsibility for affairs in Northern Ireland is entirely a matter of domestic jurisdiction. The United Kingdom Government will take full responsibility for asserting this principle in all international relationships.

3. The United Kingdom Government have ultimate responsibility for the protection of those who live in Northern Ireland when, as in the past week, a breakdown of law and order has occurred. In this spirit, the United Kingdom Government responded to the requests of the Northern Ireland Government for military assistance in Londonderry and Belfast in order to restore law and order. They emphasise again that troops will be withdrawn when law and order has been restored.

4. The Northern Ireland Government have been informed that troops have been provided on a temporary basis in accordance with the United Kingdom's ultimate responsibility. In the context of the commitment of these troops, the Northern Ireland Government have reaffirmed their intention to take into the fullest account at all times the views of her Majesty's Government in the United Kingdom, especially in relation to matters affecting the status of citizens of that part of the United Kingdom and their equal rights and protection under the law.

5. The United Kingdom Government have welcomed the decisions of the Northern Ireland Government relating to local government franchise, the revision of local government areas, the allocation of houses, the creation of a Parliamentary Commissioner for Administration in Northern Ireland and machinery to consider citizens' grievances against other public authorities which the Prime Minister reported to the House of Commons at Westminster following his meeting with Northern Ireland Ministers on 21st May as demonstrating the determination of the Northern Ireland Government that there shall be full equality of treatment for all citizens. Both governments have agreed that it is vital that the momentum of internal reform should be maintained.

6. The two Governments at their meeting at 10 Downing Street today have reaffirmed that in all legislation and executive decisions of Government every citizen of Northern Ireland is entitled to the same equality of treatment and freedom from discrimination as obtains in the rest of the United Kingdom, irrespective of political views or religion. In their further meetings the two Governments will be guided by these mutually accepted principles.

7. Finally, both Governments are determined to take all possible steps to restore normality to the Northern Ireland community so that economic development can proceed at the faster rate which is vital for social stability.

■

The Politics of 'Race' and Immigration

In the 1960s Britain was still in the early stages of its political adjustment to multiculturalism. The arrival of non-white immigrants in significant numbers was clearly unpopular with large numbers of white voters. The defeat of Patrick Gordon-Walker by an overtly racist candidate at Smethwick in the 1964 general election drove that point home to the Labour leadership. With its small majority in the House of Commons, it was unsurprising that Labour's early uncompromising stance in opposition to immigration controls was reversed. The government's strategy under Wilson was to limit immigration but to condemn racial discrimination.

The issue revealed a brutish and ugly side to British politics and society. The existence of widespread discrimination found political expression in the resurgence of far-right politics for the first time since the 1930s. The founding of the National Front in 1967 was one sign of this phenomenon, although it would remain a marginalised and small group; more worrying were the series of speeches delivered by the prominent Conservative MP Enoch Powell from 1968. Edward Heath was careful to distance mainstream Conservatism from Powell's utterances, expelling him from the party's shadow Cabinet, although signs of public support for his views were depressingly apparent.

While one of the Wilson government's first pieces of legislation was the 1965 Race Relations Act, it was a rather weak instrument which completely ignored the crucial issues of housing and employment. Wilson was anxious for the Bill to win bi-partisan support, and the Conservative Party would not agree to back a stronger measure.

10.16 **Race Relations Act 1965** (*Public General Acts*, **1965, Part 2, ch. 73, p. 1615**).

■ 1. (1) It shall be unlawful for any person, being the proprietor or manager of or employed for the purposes of any place of public resort to which this section applies, to practise discrimination on the grounds of colour, race, or ethnic or national origins against persons seeking access to or facilities or services at that place ...

2. (1) For the purposes of securing compliance with the provisions of section 1 of this Act and the resolution of difficulties arising out of those provisions, there shall be constituted a board to be known as the Race Relations Board, consisting of a chairman and two other members appointed by the Secretary of state.

(2) The Board shall constitute committees, to be known as local conciliation committees ... and it shall be the duty of every such committee –

(*a*) to receive and consider any complaint of discrimination ...

(*b*) to make such inquiries as they think necessary with respect to the facts alleged in any such complaint; and

(*c*) where appropriate, to use their best endeavours by communication with the parties concerned or otherwise to secure a settlement ... and a satisfactory assurance against further discrimination ...

(3) In any case where the local conciliation committee are unable to secure such a settlement, or such a settlement and assurance ... the committee shall make a report to that effect to the Race Relations Board; and if it appears to the Board, in consequence of such reports –

(*a*) that there has taken place in any place of public resort ... a course of conduct in contravention of that section; and

(*b*) that the conduct is likely to continue

the Board shall report the matter to the Attorney General or the Lord Advocate, as the case may be.

(4) The local conciliation committee shall make to the Board such periodical reports with respect to the exercise of their functions as the Board may require, and the Board shall, at such times as the Secretary of State may direct, make annual reports to the Secretary of State with respect to the exercise of their functions; and the Secretary of State shall lay before Parliament any report made to him under this subsection ...

5. (1) In any case where the licence of consent of the landlord or of any other person is required for the disposal to any person of premises comprised in a tenancy, that licence or consent shall be treated as unreasonably withheld if and so far as it is withheld on the ground of colour, race or ethnic or national origins:

Provided that this subsection does not apply to a tenancy of premises forming part of a dwelling-house of which the remainder or part of the remainder is occupied by the person whose licence or consent is required as his own residence if the tenant is entitled in common with that person to the use of any accommodation other than accommodation required for the purposes of access to the premises ...

6. (1) A person shall be guilty of an offence under this section if, with intent to stir up hatred against any section of the public in Great Britain distinguished by colour, race, or ethnic or national origins –

(*a*) he publishes or distributes written matter which is threatening, abusive or insulting; or

(*b*) he uses in any public place or at any public meeting words which are threatening, abusive or insulting, being matter or words likely to stir up hatred against that section on grounds of colour, race, or ethnic or national origins ... ■

In April 1967 the independent research organisation Political and Economic Planning (PEP) published the report of a survey (subsequently issued by Penguin Books in 1968) on racial discrimination in Britain which had been undertaken over the previous year. One of the first surveys of its kind, it revealed widespread and entrenched prejudice against non-white citizens at all levels of society. The PEP report made it clear that stronger anti-discrimination legislation would be necessary. In 1968 the scope of the Race Relations Act was widened, although the focus remained on conciliation proce-dures as opposed to penal sanctions for discrimination.

10.17 W.W. Daniel, *Racial Discrimination in England*, Harmondsworth, Penguin, 1968, pp. 209–24.

■ In the sectors we studied – different aspects of employment, housing and the provision of services – there is racial discrimination varying in extent from the massive to the substantial. The experiences of white immigrants, such as Hungarians and Cypriots, compared to black or brown immigrants, such as West Indians and Asians, leave no doubt that the major component in the discrimination is colour.

It is moreover impossible to escape the conclusion that the more different a person is in his physical characteristics, in his features, in the texture of his hair and in the colour of his skin, the more discrimination he will face.

... The implication of this for the future is that the second-generation Asian, qualified and fully educated in Britain, would tend to meet less discrimina-tion than a second-generation West Indian with similar characteristics.

The general conclusion that racial discrimination prevails would have been reached on the basis of any one of the three types of research procedure used: interviews with immigrants themselves, interviews with people in a position to discriminate, or validating situation tests. The three sources of information, taken together, place this conclusion beyond any possibility of doubt ...

What [occurs] ... is the process of stereotyping in which a generalized image of the coloured person, based on the characteristics of the less able, is devel-oped and projected on to all coloured people, without taking proper account of individual differences among them. Thus the well qualified coloured person is heavily penalized compared to a white person who has similar or inferior characteristics.

This process was exemplified by our tests relating to motor insurance, where some of the companies refused to make a quotation to the West Indian tester without even first asking him about any of the relevant factors. Other companies appeared, in their quotations, to have little or no regard for the facts that he was a professional man who had been in Britain for over eight years and had driving experience here. Thus these companies, which offered the Hungarian much better terms, seemed to assume that coloured people in general are worse risks than white people ...

Whether, in any case, discrimination is ever justified even in the discriminators' own limited interests is not certain from the information they gave us ... In relation to employment, however, it is possible to see that the stereotyping of coloured people was very much a non-rational process involving sweeping generalizations based on the characteristics of at most a minority of coloured people.

This is best exemplified by the myth of high mobility. The conviction that coloured people were a drifting, rootless mass was almost universal among employers ... [while] our survey of immigrants showed that ... half of them had been in their present job for three years or more.

... in housing ... discrimination appears to be even more general and more massive than it is in employment. With regard to private rental, taking the small proportion of lettings that are advertised and do not specifically exclude coloured people, two thirds are found to exclude them in practice. Our West Indian testers experienced similar rates of refusal when they applied to accommodation bureaux and estate agents. If he wishes to buy, the coloured person will find that a large proportion of houses for sale are not available to him. When he finds one that is he will have great difficulty in obtaining a mortgage loan on anything like normal terms both because of the type of house it is likely to be and the type of person he is rated to be, by the estate agents if not by the building societies. Consequently, he will have to borrow at a higher interest rate, over a shorter repayment period or on the basis of a higher deposit – or all three. Council housing is not yet a real possibility for him in the large majority of cases, as less than 1 per cent are currently housed in this way ...

Inherent in this account is one of the two main reasons why our general conclusion must be a pessimistic one ...

The first is that as immigrants become more accustomed to English ways of life, as they acquire higher expectations and higher qualifications, so they experience more personal direct discrimination ...

[Secondly] ... awareness of discrimination, hostility and prejudice reinforces any tendency on the part of people to withdraw into their own closed communities where they can insulate themselves against its effects and regulate their lives to avoid its most overt manifestations ...

Thus, although there is substantial, direct, personal discrimination against coloured people here and now, perhaps the most important effects of this lie in the impetus it is giving to the creation in Britain of alienated groups of second-class citizens. ■

In theory the general election of 1966 put Labour in a much stronger position to assert a positive line on race and immigration issues. But then in the summer of 1967 publicity surrounding the arrival of Asians from Kenya caused panic over the prospect of a new wave of immigration. Two senior Conservative politicians, Enoch Powell and Duncan Sandys, spearheaded a campaign to control what they believed to be a potentially disastrous development. In particular, a series of extraordinary public speeches by Powell in the first half of 1968 inflamed public opinion. The most notorious of these, reproduced below, was delivered after the introduction of the Commonwealth Immigrants Bill and only days before the introduction of the new Race Relations Bill. Richard Crossman's diary provides an honest account of the dilemma in which the Cabinet was placed.

10.18 **J. Enoch Powell, speech to the West Midlands Area Conservative Political Centre at the Midland Hotel, Birmingham, 20 April 1968 (in B. Smithies and P. Fiddick (eds), *Enoch Powell on Immigration*, London, Sphere, 1969, pp. 35–43).**

■ A week or two ago I fell into conversation with a constituent, a middle-aged, quite ordinary working man employed in one of our nationalised industries. After a sentence or two about the weather, he suddenly said: 'If I had the money to go, I wouldn't stay in this country.' I made some deprecatory reply, to the effect that even this government wouldn't last for ever; but he took no notice, and continued: 'I have three children, all of them been through grammar school and two of them married now, with family. I shan't be satisfied till I have seen them all settled overseas. In this country in fifteen or twenty years time the black man will have the whip-hand over the white man.'

I can already hear the chorus of execration. How dare I say such a horrible thing? How dare I stir up trouble and inflame feelings by repeating such a conversation? The answer is that I do not have the right not to do so. Here is a decent, ordinary fellow-Englishman, who in broad daylight in my own town says to me, his Member of Parliament, that this country will not be worth living in for his children. I simply do not have the right to shrug my shoulders and think about something else ...

It almost passes belief that at this moment twenty or thirty additional immigrant children are arriving from overseas in Wolverhampton alone every week – and that means fifteen or twenty additional families of a decade or two hence. Those whom the gods wish to destroy, they first make mad. We must be mad, literally mad, as a nation to be permitting the annual inflow of some 50,000 dependants, who are for the most part the material of the future growth of the immigrant-descended population. It is like watching a nation busily engaged in heaping up its own funeral pyre ...

It can be no part of any policy that existing families should be kept divided; but there are two directions in which families can be reunited, and if our former and present immigration laws have brought about the division of families, albeit voluntary or semi-voluntarily, we ought to be prepared to arrange for them to be reunited in their countries of origin ...

There are among the Commonwealth immigrants who have come to live here in the last fifteen years or so, many thousands whose wish and purpose is to be integrated and whose every thought and endeavour is bent in that direction ...

We are on the verge here of a change ... Now we are seeing the growth of positive forces acting against integration, of vested interests in the preservation and sharpening of racial and religious differences, with a view to the exercise of actual domination, first over fellow-immigrants and then over the rest of the population ...

For these dangerous and divisive elements the legislation proposed in the Race Relations Bill is the very pabulum they need to flourish. Here is the means of showing that the immigrant communities can organise to consolidate their numbers, to agitate and campaign against their fellow-citizens, and to overawe and dominate the rest with the legal weapons which the ignorant and the ill-informed have provided. As I look ahead, I am filled with foreboding. Like the Roman, I seem to see 'the River Tiber foaming with much blood'. That tragic and intractable phenomenon which we watch with horror on the other side of the Atlantic but which there is interwoven with the history and existence of the States itself, is coming upon us here by our own volition and our own neglect. Indeed, it has all but come. In numerical terms, it will be of American proportions long before the end of the century. Only resolute and urgent action will avert it even now. Whether there will be the public will to demand and obtain that action, I do not know. All I know is that to see, and not to speak, would be the great betrayal. ■

10.19 **Richard Crossman, diary, 13 February 1968 (in Richard Crossman,** *The Diaries of a Cabinet Minister, Vol. Two: 1966–68,* **London, Hamish Hamilton and Cape, 1976, pp. 678–9).**

■ The big news in the morning press was Duncan Sandys's call for action against the Kenya Asians. This of course is despite the fact that it was Duncan Sandys who signed the Kenya Independence Treaty in 1964 and gave special assurances to the Kenya Indians that they would remain British nationals. Our first Cabinet Committee was that on Commonwealth Immigration with our friend Jim Callaghan in the chair ... Jim arrived with the air of a man whose mind was made up. He wasn't going to tolerate this bloody liberalism. He was going to stop this nonsense as the public was demanding and as the Party was demanding. He would do it come what may and anybody who opposed him was a sentimental jackass. This was the tone in which he conducted this Cabinet Committee and it was extremely interesting to see the attitude of the members round the table. Whitehall had lined up the D.E.A., the Ministry of Labour, the Ministry of Education, all the Departments concerned, including even the Foreign Office, behind the Home Office demand that law must be changed. Only the Commonwealth Department stood out against this pressure and George Thomas, the Minister of State, made a most passionate objection to the Bill in strictly rational form, saying this was being railroaded through and Jim was getting backing from all the Departments. A few years ago everyone there would have regarded the denial of entry to British nationals with British passports as the most appalling violation of our deepest principles. Now they were quite happily reading aloud their departmental briefs in favour of doing just that. Mainly because I'm an M.P. for a constituency in the Midlands, where racialism is a powerful force, I was on the side of Jim Callaghan and said that we had a sharp choice. We had either to take the risk of announcing in advance that there would be no ban on immigration in the hope that this would stem a panic rush, or we had to announce the Bill. The one thing not to do was to hesitate and be indecisive. Between these two courses I felt that a country such as France might possibly choose in favour of the first but the British people wouldn't. There was virtually no opposition to this view except from George Thomas and Elwyn Jones. ■

The General Election of 1970

After the period of austerity which followed the devaluation of November 1967, Britain's balance of payments was once more in surplus at the end of 1969. The economy seemed to have stabilised, and the local elections of May 1970 recorded a swing back to Labour. With these factors in mind, Wilson called a general election for June 1970. Initial indications suggested that Labour would be returned for the third time.

While Wilson conducted a low-key campaign, the Conservatives ran on a controversial platform which was launched during what was essentially a publicity exercise at the Selsdon Park Hotel on the outskirts of London in January 1970, which reiterated the policies outlined in Putting Britain Right Ahead. *While Wilson sneered at 'Selsdon Man' and the pundits believed that such a marked difference of emphasis in Conservative policy had seriously damaged the party's chances, in the event there was a swing of 5 per cent in the Tories' favour, and Heath was returned as Prime Minister. The victory owed as much to the dullness of the Labour campaign as it did to the Conservative manifesto.*

10.20 **Report on the Conservatives' general election campaign,** *The Times*, **2 February 1970.**

■ By last night Mr Heath and the Tory Shadow Cabinet had settled their broad strategy for the approach to the next general election and had drafted the outline of the first Queen's Speech they will lay before Parliament if they come back to power. This was the outcome of 15 hours of intense discussion at a council of war held in the Selsdon Park hotel, near Croydon.

The following are to be the legislative priorities:–

1. The Budget and the Finance Bill that flows out of it. There would be an immediate attack on the burden of direct taxation and a calculated switch of emphasis to indirect taxation.

2. The carrying of the Industrial Relations Bill based on the party publication *Fair Deal at Work*.

3. Pensions for those over 80 excluded by postwar legislation from equitable pension entitlement.

4. Bills to enforce the law by changing the law of trespass to cover unruly demonstrations, accompanied by the enlargement of the police force as a deterrent to crime and violent behaviour, and the reform of the processes of law to make prompter justice attainable.

5. A Bill to put Commonwealth Immigrants and aliens on the same footing and to carry out published Conservative policy on immigration. There would no longer be an automatic right to British citizenship.

A set of administrative priorities has also been decided:–

1. Action would be taken administratively to bring immigration under tighter control while the immigrants and aliens Bill was passing through Parliament.

2. Tory finance and trade Ministers would discuss with industry and others proposals for changes in the tax structure.

3. Parliamentary procedures would be studied and discussed, and the specialized committee system developed.

4. Discussions would be opened with local authorities for the renegotiation of housing subsidies so that Exchequer support was given mainly for slum clearance and housing the very old and the disabled.

No important change was made during the weekend discussions in any established party policy announced since Mr Heath became leader in July 1965.

Selective employment tax would be abolished, the regional employment premium be tapered off, and the tax system reformed and simplified as a matter of urgency, but there is no commitment yet to value-added tax as a substitute for purchase tax and s.e.t... .

Whoever the Tory Chancellor may prove to be, there is no doubt what his instructions are. He has to set Britain free, as Lord Butler of Saffron Walden, as Chancellor, set the people free in 1951! ■

10.21 **General election campaign posters, 1970 (Conservative Party Archives).**

CHAPTER ELEVEN

From World Power to European Power: Foreign Policy and Decolonisation, 1957–70

ALTHOUGH the Suez Crisis of 1956 proved to be a costly error of judgement, it did not result immediately in any fundamental rethinking of Britain's overseas position. Instead, Harold Macmillan spent his first years as Prime Minister scrambling to find a new formula for the preservation of Britain's international role. While the economic consequences of the crisis underscored the need to pare down defence spending, the defence white paper of 1957 proposed to cut the services without reducing commitments east of Suez. At the time it was believed that this trick could be accomplished by promoting the role of an independent nuclear deterrent. But by 1963 it was apparent that this strategy had failed; Britain could not afford to stay in the nuclear arms race without the patronage of the United States, and the 'special relationship' with the latter compromised Britain's claim to independence, upon which its position ultimately depended.

The cost of this approach was Britain's increasing isolation in relation to the Six founder members of the European Economic Community. While the prospect of acting as a bridge in the Western Alliance between the United States and the continental countries certainly appeared attractive to the Prime Minister, who announced that Britain would seek EEC membership in 1961, it did not appeal to French President de Gaulle, who vetoed the application in 1963. Moreover, the fast pace of decolonisation in Africa, as well as increasing fragmentation within the Commonwealth over thorny issues such as white rule in southern Africa, made the future of that organisation seem increasingly uncertain.

By the time that Harold Wilson became Prime Minister in 1964, therefore, British foreign policy had reached an important crossroads. The Labour government was initially determined to maintain the east-of-Suez strategy pursued under its Conservative predecessors. It was only repeated economic crises, culminating in the November 1967 devaluation of the pound, which forced the abandonment of Britain's world role. Although the country's second EEC application was vetoed in 1967, by the end of the decade the combination of economic pressure, the estrangement of Anglo-American relations over Vietnam and tension in the Commonwealth underscored the logic behind British entry into the Community.

Defence Policy after Suez

Upon taking office, Macmillan's short-term priority was to stabilise the economy, as sterling continued to flow out of the country's reserves throughout 1957. It was in this context that Macmillan's new Minister of Defence, Duncan Sandys, was briefed to review defence expenditure and to reduce the size of the armed forces.

The Sandys white paper of April 1957 was seen at the time as a bold attempt to achieve the government's objectives. His ability to force through sizeable cuts in service personnel was due in part to the strong support of the Prime Minister, and in part to recent administrative changes which weakened the power of the Chiefs of Staff. But most importantly, the white paper fully endorsed the adoption of a strategy of massive retaliation, and gave the development of an independent nuclear deterrent the central role in British defence policy. It was hoped that an independent deterrent would solve a number of problems without necessitating a retreat from a world role. Diplomatically, it would deter future aggressors such as President Nasser of Egypt, and firmly cement the Anglo-American relationship; politically, it would enable the government to end conscription and soothe the right wing of the Conservative party in the humiliating aftermath of Suez; economically, it was assumed that heavier reliance on the deterrent would permit conventional force reductions on a scale large enough to reduce the defence burden substantially, as had indeed happened following a similar US decision in 1953.

11.1   **HM Government,** *Defence: Outline of Future Policy* **(Sandys white paper), April 1957 (London, HMSO, Cmnd 124, PP 1956–7, XXIII, pp. 1–10).**

■   ...

4. In recent years military technology has been making dramatic strides. New and ever more formidable weapons have been succeeding one another at an increasing rate. In less than a decade, the atom bomb dropped at Hiroshima has been overtaken by the far more powerful hydrogen or megaton bomb. Parallel with this, the evolution of rocket weapons of all kinds, both offensive and defensive, has been proceeding apace ...

10. The growth in the power of weapons of mass destruction has emphasised the fact that no country can any longer protect itself in isolation. The defence of Britain is possible only as part of the collective defence of the free world. This conception of collective defence is the basis of the North Atlantic, South-East Asia and Baghdad alliances.

11. The trend is towards the creation of integrated allied forces. Therefore, provided each member nation plays its fair part in the joint effort, it is not necessarily desirable that each should seek to contribute national forces which are by themselves self-sufficient and balanced in all respects ...

15. The free world is to-day mainly dependent for its protection upon the nuclear capacity of the United States. While Britain cannot by comparison make more than a modest contribution, there is a wide measure of agreement that she must possess an appreciable element of nuclear deterrent power of her own. British atomic bombs are already in steady production and the weapon has now been developed. This will shortly be tested and thereafter a stock will be manufactured.

16. The means of delivering these weapons is provided at present by medium bombers of the V-class, whose performance in speed and altitude is comparable to that of any bomber aircraft now in service in any other country. It is the intention that these should be supplemented by ballistic rockets. Agreement in principle has recently been reached with the United States Government for the supply of some medium-range missiles of this type ...

20. The possession of nuclear air power is not by itself a complete deterrent. The frontiers of the free world, particularly in Europe, must be firmly defended on the ground. For only in this way can it be made clear that aggression will be resisted.

21. Britain must provide her fair share of the armed forces needed for this purpose. However, she cannot any longer continue to make a disproportionately large contribution.

22. Accordingly, Her Majesty's Government, after consultation with the Allied Governments in the North Atlantic Council and in the Council of the Western European Union, have felt it necessary to make reductions in the British land and air forces on the continent. The strength of the British Army of the Rhine will be reduced from about 77,000 to about 64,000 during the next twelve months; and, subject to consultation with the Allied Governments in the autumn, further reductions will be made thereafter. The force will be reorganised in such a way as to increase the proportion of the fighting units; and atomic rocket artillery will be introduced which will greatly augment their fire-power.

23. The aircraft of the Second Tactical Air Force in Germany will be reduced to about half their present number by the end of March, 1958. This reduction will be offset by the fact that some of the squadrons will be provided with atomic bombs. A similar reduction will be made in the light bomber force in England, which is assigned to NATO ...

34. With the reduction in the size of garrisons and other British forces overseas, it is more than ever essential to be able to despatch reinforcements at short notice. With this object, a Central Reserve will be maintained in the British Isles.

35. To be effective, the Central Reserve must possess the means of rapid mobility. For this purpose, a substantial fleet of transport aircraft is being built up in RAF Transport Command ...

37. On account of its mobility the Royal Navy, together with the Royal Marines, provides another effective means of bringing power rapidly to bear in peacetime emergencies or limited hostilities. In modern conditions the role of the aircraft carrier, which is in effect a mobile air station, becomes increasingly significant ...

39. It is the Government's intention to maintain British naval strength East of Suez at about its present level. One carrier group will normally be stationed in the Indian Ocean.

40. Provided that the Services are reshaped and redistributed on the lines indicated above and that commitments are curtailed in the manner proposed, the Government are satisfied that Britain could discharge her overseas responsibilities and make an effective contribution to the defence of the free world with armed forces much smaller than at present ...

47. The Government have accordingly decided to plan on the basis that there will be no further call-up under the National Service Acts after the end of 1960 ... ■

In practice, the Sandys white paper was to have disappointing consequences. Continuing emergencies in Africa and east of Suez required a high level of conventional support, and anticipated cuts were at times moderated. In addition, the costs of developing and manufacturing an effective nuclear arsenal soon proved to be much higher than anticipated; defence spending was not reduced significantly after 1957.

11.2 **British defence expenditure, 1957–70 (chart derived from M. Dockrill, *British Defence since 1945*, Oxford, Blackwell, 1988, pp. 151–2).**

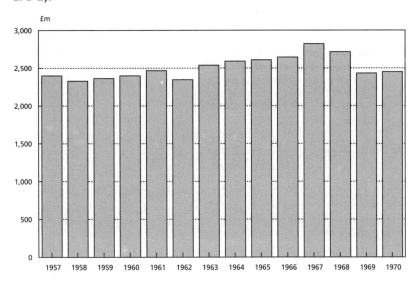

11.3   Size of the armed forces, 1957–70 (chart derived from M. Dockrill, *British Defence since 1945*, Oxford, Blackwell, 1988, pp. 151–2).

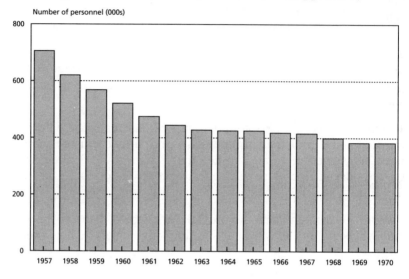

Number of personnel (000s)

The most important consequence of the Sandys white paper was its impact on Anglo-American relations. Over the following year, the 'special relationship' – which had been strained almost to breaking point over Suez – was resuscitated through a renewed nuclear partnership. In return for the stationing of sixty US Thor intermediate-range ballistic missiles in Britain, President Eisenhower agreed in the autumn of 1957 to the full restoration of nuclear information exchanges with Britain. This agreement, extracted in document 11.4, was thought essential to enable British nuclear scientists to keep up with the superpowers. The agreement, moreover, seemed to confirm a unique relationship with the United States.

11.4   *Amendment to the Agreement between the Government of the United Kingdom of Great Britain and Northern Ireland and the Government of the United States of America for Co-operation on the Uses of Atomic Energy for Mutual Defence Purposes of July 3, 1958,* 7 May 1959 (London, HMSO, Cmnd 733, PP 1958–9, XXXIV, p. 3).

■ The Government of the United States of America and the Government of the United Kingdom of Great Britain and Northern Ireland on its own behalf and on behalf of the United Kingdom Atomic Energy Authority;

Desiring to amend in certain respects the Agreement for Cooperation on the Uses of Atomic Energy for Mutual Defense Purposes (hereinafter referred to as the Agreement for Cooperation) signed at Washington on the Third day of July, 1958;

Have agreed as follows:

ARTICLE I

The following new Article shall be inserted after Article III of the Agreement for Cooperation:

...

A. the Government of the United States shall transfer to the Government of the United Kingdom the following in such quantities, at such times prior to December 31, 1969, and on such terms and conditions as may be agreed:

1. non-nuclear parts of atomic weapons which parts are for the purpose of improving the United Kingdom's state of training and operational readiness;

2. other non-nuclear parts of atomic weapons systems involving Restricted Data which parts are for the purpose of improving the United Kingdom's state of training and operational readiness when in accordance with appropriate requirements of applicable laws;

3. special nuclear material for research on, development of, production of, or use in utilisation facilities for military applications; and

4. source, by-product and special nuclear material, and other material, for research on, development of, or use in atomic weapons when, after consultation with the Government of the United Kingdom, the Government of the United States determines that the transfer of such material is necessary to improve the United Kingdom's atomic weapon design, development or fabrication capability ... ■

CND and the disarmers

The continued pursuit of an independent nuclear deterrent was widely approved at home. Possession of the hydrogen bomb undoubtedly helped to assuage the sense of national humiliation engendered over Suez, and the Labour Party leader, Hugh Gaitskell, argued that the British deterrent would help to ensure the country's independence from the United States. But a large minority, both within the Labour Party and on the left in general, rejected such lines of reasoning.

In 1958 the Campaign for Nuclear Disarmament was founded by a distinguished group of intellectuals and activists, to lobby for unilateral nuclear disarmament. By 1960 CND had won enough support to persuade the Labour Party conference to vote in favour of unilateralism, although Gaitskell campaigned successfully to reverse the policy the following year.

11.5   The Aldermaston march, 1958 (Mary Evans Picture Library).

11.6   **Michael Foot, speech on unilateralism, October 1960** (*Report of the Fifty-Ninth Annual Conference*, **London, Labour Party, 1960, pp. 189–90).**

■ I have never had the slightest doubt that Sam Watson, George Brown, and others who think like them, are as passionately eager to avoid a war as I am. I have never had the slightest doubt about that. Our difference is that we see differently where the real danger of war comes from. We in this country have undertaken enormous risks for reasons which the Executive thinks are good. We supply the Americans with nuclear bases and missile sites. We have in this country the principal base from which a counter-attack or an attack would be made on the Soviet Union if a war came. And if a war did come, this country would be utterly obliterated, partly because of the existence of the bases in this country. Nobody can deny this. We have undertaken enormous, almost incalculable risks. Nobody can deny it.

Why do we do so: Why do the Executive say that we should have to undertake those risks? I hope I will put the answer fairly. They say that if we do not supply the Americans with nuclear bases; if we do not maintain our suppport for the nuclear strategy, then we can have no effective influence in the Western alliance, and particularly with the Americans. I would say that is their case. Even with the bases we are not having a great influence on the Americans now …

If you tie up the whole of your military machine with that of a much greater military power and become dependent on them for the supply of essential weapons, then you lose a part of your independence and you lose a great deal of your influence …

I say that we are taking these enormous risks without any fair exchange. But fortunately for the peace of the world it is not true that you can only have effective influence if you have an H-bomb of your own or supply bases to your allies. If that were true, as Frank Cousins says, it would be a reason for every country having these bombs, including the Germans. If it were true that in order to have effective influence you must supply your allies with nuclear bases, then the neutral nations would be demanding these bases. But open your eyes and see what is happening in the world. The opposite is true. The neutral nations are getting much stronger … ■

The Skybolt crisis

It was not domestic protest which ultimately undermined Britain's nuclear strategy; for it soon became apparent that Britain could not develop a deterrent without relying heavily on the United States. The Sandys white paper had envisaged that in the short term the British deterrent would consist of Vulcan bombers armed with British Blue Steel short-range missiles. Hopes for the future were placed on the development of the Blue Streak surface-to-surface missile, but poor performance and high costs forced its cancellation in February 1960. Macmillan subsequently placed his hopes on plans to purchase US Skybolt missiles, which could be fired from Vulcans at a long range. Superficially, this appeared to be a satisfactory arrangement, allowing Britain to buy its nuclear deterrent at a much cheaper cost than that involved in developing a similar weapon at home. But the dangers of such heavy reliance on the US defence programme were brought home in November 1962, when Skybolt was cancelled by President J.F. Kennedy's Secretary of Defense, Robert McNamara.

In mid-December 1962 the Skybolt crisis was resolved at a conference in Nassau, the Bahamas, between Macmillan and the President. Against the advice of many US strategists, anxious above all to limit the proliferation of nuclear weapons, Kennedy agreed to allow Britain to purchase Polaris missiles, which could be fitted to British submarines and armed with British nuclear warheads. Under the terms of the agreement, British Polaris submarines had to be assigned to the North Atlantic Treaty Organisation. Although Macmillan secured the right to use Polaris independently in a national emergency, it was extremely unlikely that this would happen. Through NATO, the United States essentially retained control over the deployment of British submarines, and the 'independence' of the British deterrent thus looked increasingly fictional. The terms of the Polaris agreement were argued uneasily within the Cabinet, as the following passage shows.

11.7   **Cabinet minutes, discussion of the Nassau decisions, 21 December 1962 (PRO CAB 128/36, part 2, CC(62)76).**

■ *The First Secretary of State* drew attention to the principal differences between the United States draft in telegram No. Codel 16 and the subsequent joint draft in telegram No. Codel 18 which had been elaborated in further discussion on 20th December and on which the advice of the Cabinet was now sought. It was clear that a great deal had been achieved by the Prime Minister and his colleagues in Nassau in persuading the President to move away from the original United States position. Whereas the United States draft would have committed the United Kingdom Government to 'an agreement to meet their NATO non-nuclear force goals at the agreed NATO standards', the latest draft referred only to 'agreement on the importance of increasing the effectiveness of their conventional forces'. Again the latest draft included a new provision that our strategic nuclear forces would be used for 'the integrated defence of the Western Alliance in all circumstances except where Her Majesty's Government may decide that the supreme national interests are at stake'. The Prime Minister had particularly directed attention ... to these words, which had the effect of giving us the sole right of decision on the use of our strategic nuclear forces, and had asked whether the Cabinet endorsed the view, which he shared with the Foreign Secretary, the Commonwealth Secretary, and the Minister of Defence, that these words could be publicly defended as maintaining an independent United Kingdom contribution to the nuclear deterrent.

The Cabinet accordingly considered first the wording of this passage in the statement. There was some doubt whether, as it stood, the exception would be generally interpreted as allowing Her Majesty's Government to use United Kingdom strategic forces in circumstances not involving the defence of the Western Alliance, or where it would be taken to mean only that the Government could decline to use those forces in particular circumstances involving the interests of the Alliance ... We might easily suffer from the growth of a suspicion that our military independence was, or might be, less secure than, for example, that of the French ... An alternative form of words was suggested, emphasising first the right of Her Majesty's Government to act in accordance with the supranational interest, subject to which United Kingdom strategic nuclear forces would only be used in defence of the Alliance.

While Ministers were agreed upon the value to this country of an arrangement by which we should eventually have within our own control a virtually indestructible second strike deterrent weapon of proven capability, and with prospects of a long life, it was recognised that the conditions which the United States Government were stipulating represented a heavy price in money and otherwise.

The Chief Secretary, Treasury, ... [suggested that] while the wording of the passage about conventional forces in telegram No. Codel 18 represented a very great improvement on the wording earlier proposed ... it could be further improved if the idea were introduced that the effectiveness of our conventional forces ought to be increased 'on a world-wide basis': without some such addition it would be widely misunderstood as necessarily implying an increase in the strength of the British Army of the Rhine, which would be very difficult to achieve. This passage of the proposed joint statement was also unsatisfactory in that it gave currency to a new (and probably unsound) United States strategic doctrine of a 'nuclear shield' and a 'non-nuclear sword'.

Summing up the discussion *the First Secretary of State* said that there seemed to be general agreement in the Cabinet that the Prime Minister and his colleagues deserved their full support for the largely successful efforts that they had made to evolve a satisfactory agreement with the United States Government. In conveying their sense of this feeling to the Prime Minister it would however be right to emphasise their view that the Government were being asked to pay a heavy price and that for this reason the independent role of Her Majesty's Government in the use of nuclear forces must be clearly and unambiguously expressed ... ■

Macmillan's Grand Design

In March 1957, while Macmillan was busily patching up relations with President Eisenhower, the Treaties of Rome were signed by the Six founder members of the EEC and Euratom (France, West Germany, Italy, Belgium, Luxemburg and the Netherlands). As discussed in Chapter 8, the British government had adopted an aloof scepticism towards these negotiations since the Messina Conference of 1955. In November 1956 the government, led by Anthony Eden, had attempted to avoid the threat of a protectionist bloc on the Continent by proposing the formation of a wider free-trade area of European states, linking the EEC countries to non-member European states through a free market in industrial products. But British attempts to dilute the EEC were unsuccessful, resented by the Six even before the return of Charles de Gaulle to power in France in May 1958. De Gaulle's domination of an increasingly powerful EEC was viewed over the following months with mounting unease across the Channel.

In November 1959 the Stockholm Agreement established the European Free Trade Area of seven states: Britain, Denmark, Norway, Sweden, Switzerland, Austria and Portugal. EFTA itself was only a limited free-trade agreement not comparable to the EEC, and Macmillan's hopes that negotiations between the Six and the Seven could help to keep doors open to markets within the EEC showed few signs of success. Frustration was compounded by increasing signs that Britain was being excluded from the high table of cold war diplomacy. The first US–Soviet bipolar summit took place at the end of 1959; the following May, Macmillan's attempts to promote *détente* were ruined when the Paris summit of Britain, the United States and the Soviet Union was cut short by the capture of an American U-2 spy plane and its pilot over Soviet territory. Moreover, the accelerating pace of decolonisation in this period, discussed below, made the future of Britain's international markets seem increasingly uncertain. This combination of circumstances led many officials and politicians in Britain to advocate an application to join the EEC.

By the end of 1960 Macmillan began to pursue the idea of British membership of the EEC. It was apparent that de Gaulle would not be persuaded to share leadership of the Community without a clear 'quid pro quo'. On the other hand, the United States showed growing enthusiasm for British membership. In the weeks following the election of the young President Kennedy, Macmillan formulated a new diplomatic initiative which he dubbed 'the grand design', hoping to attract the attention and approval of the new US leader.

11.8   Harold Macmillan, 'Grand design', December 1960 (PRO PREM 11/3325).

■ …

25. What do we want?

What does de Gaulle want?

How far can we agree to help him if he will help us?

(a) *We want Sixes and Sevens settled*

We must make it clear to the French that we mean what we say – that if it is not settled, Europe will be divided politically and militarily …

It is obvious that the conditions which led to WEU have disappeared, and the basis on which we undertook these obligations has radically changed. Then France did not discriminate against British trade. Then France wanted British support against the danger of a renascent Germany. The first condition has gone. We assume that the French are happy about the second. Or are they? The French must judge.

(b) *De Gaulle wants the recognition of France as a Great Power, at least equal to Britain.*

He suspects the Anglo-Saxons.

So long as the 'Anglo-Saxon domination' continues, he will not treat Britain as European, but as American – a junior partner of America, but a partner …

De Gaulle feels that he is *excluded* from this club or partnership …

26. Can what we want and what *de Gaulle* wants be brought into harmony? Is there a basis for a deal?

Britain wants to join the European concern; France wants to join the Anglo-American concern. Can terms be arranged? Would de Gaulle be ready to withdraw the French veto which alone prevents a settlement of Europe's economic problem in return for politico-military arrangements which he would accept as a recognition of France as a first-class world Power? What he would want is something on Tripartitism and something on the nuclear. Are there offers which we could afford to make: And could we persuade the Americans to agree?

27. *Tripartitism*

We and the Americans have already accepted in principle de Gaulle's proposal for tripartite consultation covering all the main strategy and tactics of the anti-Communist struggle ...

The Standing Group is, after all, a Tripartite body for NATO – accepted because it is traditional. Why should we not use it to build a wider and more effective system of consultation? The first step would be to strengthen our military representation on it. But could we not go further and arrange for civil representation too – the British and French Ambassadors and an American of equal rank ... the Standing Group could then become the instrument for close co-operation between the President of the United States, the British Prime Minister and the President of France in the struggle against Communism in all fields ...

29. The objections usually raised to Tripartitism are (i) that it would upset the other members of NATO, and (ii) that it would impair our own special relationship with the Americans.

My plan would be the less likely to upset the other Allies because it builds, unobtrusively, on an existing organisation which they have accepted.

It need not injure our *special* position with the United States, which we should certainly seek to preserve .... What de Gaulle would want would be something much *more formal*, more *organised*, more *institutionalised*. But just for this reason, it would be less *intimate*. It would therefore *not* necessarily impinge upon the wider and more special relations between us and the Americans in many spheres.

30. *Nuclear*

De Gaulle's second – and to him vital – ambition is the nuclear weapon.

Can we give him our techniques, or our bombs, or any share of our nuclear power on any terms which

  i) are prudent and publicly defensible for us, at home, in the
     Commonwealth, and generally;
  ii) the United States will agree to?

At first this seems hopeless. But since I think it is the one thing which will persuade de Gaulle to accept a European settlement ... I think it is worth serious examination ... ■

In July 1961 the Cabinet agreed to apply for EEC membership, influenced in particular by the arguments of the Cabinet committee chaired by Cabinet Secretary Sir Frank Lee, which came down in favour of membership.

11.9   Sir Frank Lee, 'Association with the European Community', Cabinet memorandum, 6 July 1960 (PRO CAB 129/102 Part I, C(60)107).

■ On 27th May the European Economic Association Committee agreed that the broad choice for the United Kingdom was either to seek a close association with the European Economic Community or to continue to remain aloof from it while doing all we could to mitigate the economic and political dangers of the division in Europe. The Prime Minister subsequently circulated a list of questions about the future of the Community, and about the broad political and economic considerations which should determine the choice of policy, and asked that these should be studied by officials of the Departments concerned. These studies have now been carried out, under the auspices of the Economic Steering (Europe) Committee. A report by that Committee is circulated herewith by direction of the Prime Minister ...

FOREIGN POLITICAL QUESTIONS

QUESTION 2

If it is going to succeed, is it desirable that the United Kingdom should be associated with it so that we can influence its policies?

ANSWER

(*a*) Yes. If the Community succeeds in becoming a really effective political and economic force, it will become the dominating influence in Europe and the only Western *bloc* approaching in influence the big Two – the USSR and the United States. The influence of the United Kingdom in Europe, if left outside, will correspondingly decrease. Though we may hope to retain something of a special position *vis-à-vis* the United States, the latter will inevitably tend to attach more and more weight to the views and interests of the Six ...

(*b*) ... if we were to be effectively associated with the Community, we should not only be able to benefit from its political and economic influence, but would have the opportunity to influence its policies ...

TRADE AND ECONOMIC QUESTIONS

QUESTION 10

What direct trade and economic advantages do we expect to gain from joining the Six?

ANSWER

(*a*) The industrial policy of the Six, in contrast to their agricultural policy, is competitive and expansionist. Joining the Six would give large potential trade and economic advantages for British industry. We should be joining an area which is economically the most rapidly expanding in the world and we can reasonably hope that our commerce and industry would be invigorated by this ...

(b) But it should be emphasised that all the above advantages are potentialities that joining the Six might enable us to realise, not inevitable consequences of joining. If our economy and our exports are to grow faster in the future the main changes must come from within the United Kingdom. Even before union the exports of the Six were growing faster than ours. If we are to prosper, we shall have to be fully competitive with them – whether we are in the Common Market or not – and the removal of tariff barriers against the Six would force greater competitiveness on our industries ...

(c) Whether we join the Six or not we shall have to reduce the proportion of our output devoted to consumption, and increase the proportion which is invested or exported. If we join the Six and seek to secure the benefits of association with the Community, we shall have to be fully competitive with them and this may involve changes in our industrial structure which may be both more rapid and of a different character than would be the case if we stayed outside. While these changes were taking place, there would be greater need for mobility of labour in the United Kingdom, and some social hardship might be involved. In this connexion, however, we must remember that changes in the pattern of industry are taking place all the time, and that in an expanding economy they can be accomplished without undue difficulty, Moreover, we were ready to face industrial changes when we originally proposed a free trade area, although the changes required for the Common Market may be a little greater than those which a free trade area would have involved. If, on the other hand, we decide to stay out of the Common Market, we shall not be faced with these particular, short-term problems, at any rate in the same form. But neither will United Kingdom industry have the advantages of our association with the Six, and this may lead to stagnation and the country as a whole being the poorer for it ...

SOVEREIGNTY QUESTIONS

QUESTION 19

To what extent would joining the Six require us to give up sovereignty, i.e., to give up such control as we still have over our domestic economic policies including agriculture and our social policies?

ANSWER

Between now and 1970 there would be some progressive loss of sovereignty in a number of matters affecting domestic policy, of which agriculture is likely to be an important example. It is difficult to say how much would be involved in any single field. The terms of application of the generally imprecise provisions of the Rome Treaty affecting the issues other than tariffs have still to be agreed between the Six in many cases. If we were to join the EEC at an early date we could take part in the formulation of these provisions, and influence the extent to which they affected freedom in domestic policy. The effects of any eventual loss of sovereignty would be mitigated:

(i) by our participation in majority voting in the Council of Ministers and by our being able to influence the Commission's preparatory work;

(ii) if resistance to Federalism on the part of some of the Governments continues, which our membership might be expected to encourage ... ■

It is not known at what stage de Gaulle made up his mind to veto the British application for EEC membership. The immediate pretext was the announcement of the Polaris agreement reached at Nassau between Kennedy and Macmillan in December 1962, discussed above. De Gaulle rejected the invitation to partipate in a multilateral nuclear force held out at Nassau on the grounds that it would jeopardise France's sovereignty over its defence policy. In January 1963 he announced at a press conference his intention to veto British entry to the Community. Macmillan's 'grand design' had not persuaded the General, who over the following years pursued an increasingly independent course in foreign policy.

11.10 'Summary of General de Gaulle's press conference of January 14', January 1963 (PRO PREM 11/4413).

■ 1.   *France's position towards Britain's entry into the Common Market and the political evolution of Europe.*

...

Britain applied to join the Common Market after refusing to participate earlier, creating a Free Trade Association, and 'putting some pressure on the Six to prevent a real beginning being made in the application of the Common Market'.

... 'the nature, the structure, the very situation' of England 'differed profoundly from the countries of the Six'. She is insular, maritime, linked to distant countries, essentially industrial and commercial and with slight agricultural interest.

The whole question is whether Britain can place herself 'inside a tariff which is genuinely common', renounce all Commonwealth preference, give up agricultural privileges, and 'more than that' regard her EFTA engagements as 'null and void'. Only England can answer this question ...

2.   *The French position towards President Kennedy's proposals for a multilateral force – that is towards the Bahamas Agreement.*

... For a long time Europe was protected by the American deterrent. Now there is the 'new and gigantic fact' that the Russians can directly threaten America. In such circumstances the defence of Europe has become of secondary importance to the United States. Cuba illustrated this. No one can now say 'where, when, how and in what measure American nuclear weapons would be used to defend Europe'. This has led to the French determination to equip themselves with their own atomic force. This may be combined with those of their allies but integration with them cannot be imagined ...

The Polaris offer is of 'no apparent interest to France' at present because she has neither the submarines to launch them nor the nuclear warheads to fit to them ... In any event the Agreement was contrary to the principle of national independent defence. A multilateral force was a possibility, theoretically, but in practice was unworkable, due to the tangle of liaison and communications difficulties at the moment of 'atomic apocalypse' ... ■

The Wind of Change

Decolonisation accelerated after Suez, both because the value of attempting to maintain colonial possessions was increasingly questioned in this period, and because of the pressure for independence originating among nationalists in the dependent territories. Macmillan's modernising Colonial Secretary, Iain Macleod, oversaw the transition to independence and Commonwealth membership of Nigeria, Cyprus, Sierra Leone, Tanganyika, Jamaica, Trinidad, Uganda, Kenya, Zambia, Zanzibar, Malawi and Malta.

The relationship between Suez and decolonisation would seem to be confirmed by Macmillan's early encouragement of pragmatic thinking about the future of the empire and development of the Commonwealth. Soon after taking office, he sent the following minute to the chairman of the Cabinet Colonial Policy Committee.

11.11 Harold Macmillan, 'The balance sheet of empire', minute to the Lord President of the Council, 28 January 1957 (PRO CAB 134/1555).

■ It would be helpful if the Colonial Policy Committee could submit to the Cabinet their estimate of the probable course of constitutional development in the Colonies over the years ahead.

It would be good if Ministers could know more clearly which territories are likely to become ripe for independence over the next few years – or, even if they are not ready for it, will demand it so insistently that their claims cannot be denied – and at what date that stage is likely to be reached in each case.

It would also be helpful if this study would distinguish those Colonies which would qualify for full membership of the Commonwealth, and would indicate what constitutional future there is for the others which may attain independence but cannot aspire to full Commonwealth membership.

I should also like to see something like a profit and loss account for each of our Colonial possessions, so that we may be better able to gauge whether, from the financial and economic point of view, we are likely to gain or lose by its departure. This would need, of course, to be weighed against the political and strategic considerations involved in each case. And it might perhaps be better to attempt an estimate of the balance of advantage, taking all these considerations into account, of losing or keeping each particular territory. There are presumably places where it is of vital interest to us that we should maintain our influence, and others where there is no United Kingdom interest in resisting constitutional change even if it seems likely to lead eventually to secession from the Commonwealth ... ■

Pragmatic thinking was encouraged by the increasing record of failure of complex plans for federation elaborated in London. In particular, the Central African Federation, discussed in Chapter 8, reached the point of crisis at the beginning of 1959, when the federal government, dominated by Southern Rhodesia, began a campaign of repression aimed against the Congress movement led by Dr Hastings Banda. The official inquiry into the crisis, chaired by Lord Devlin, produced a report highly critical of these actions. The CAF was eventually dissolved in 1963.

11.12 *Report of the Nyasaland Commission of Inquiry,* July 1959 (London, HMSO, Cmnd 814, PP 1958–9, X, pp. 1, 21–3, 74).

■ ...

1. By the warrant given by you on 6th April, 1959 under the powers conferred upon you on the same day by the Nyasaland (Commissions of Inquiry) Order in Council, 1959, you appointed us to be a Commission of Inquiry for the purpose of enquiring into the recent disturbances in Nyasaland and the events leading up to them and to report thereon ...

2. All our hearings took place in private ... The protection of privacy, essential to the Government, was needed just as much by many of the individuals who gave evidence before us. Nyasaland is – no doubt only temporarily – a police state, where it is not safe for anyone to express approval of the policies of the Congress party, to which before 3rd March, 1959 the vast majority of politically-minded Africans belonged, and where it is unwise to express any but the most restrained criticism of government policy ...

42. ... conflict of thought and feeling between a Government that is still paternal in outlook and an opposition that is not yet as mature as it believes itself to be is no doubt a common feature in the emergence of democracy all over the world. What is peculiar to Nyasaland is that the feelings of anger and bitterness and frustration which this sort of conflict commonly engenders were largely concentrated on one point, namely the controversy over Federation ... The advantages of Federation were thoroughly, and we believe disinterestedly, examined in the two conferences in 1951 to which we have referred and they are fully set out in the reports of those bodies. Briefly, the conclusion which was arrived at was that the economies of the three territories had become so inter-dependent that closer association

between them in the field of economic planning was essential. This closer association would inevitably lead, it was felt, not only to greater prosperity but to the provision of better facilities for education, health services and social services generally ...

43. Little if any of this is disputed by those who oppose Federation. Their answer is that nothing matters except political freedom. They want above all else self-government for the black people in Nyasaland such as they have seen happening in other parts of Africa. They think that under the British Government they may eventually get it and that under Federation they never will ... The Government's view is that these nationalist aspirations are the thoughts of only a small minority of political Africans, mainly of self-seekers who think that their prospects of office will be worse under Federation; and that the great majority of the people are indifferent to the issue. We have not found this to be so ... Federation means the domination of southern Rhodesia; the domination of Southern Rhodesia means the domination of the settler; the domination of the settler means the perpetuation of racial inferiority and of the threat to the Africans' land: that is the argument ... Even amongst the chiefs, many of whom are loyal to the Government and dislike Congress methods, we have not heard of a single one who is in favour of Federation. Witness after witness appeared before us for the sole purpose of stating that the cause of all the troubles we were investigating was Federation. We heard of course criticism of government action during the disturbances based on the belief that the Government had shot people without cause; but instead of this creating a feeling against the British connection, it was all put down to Federation; very little was said against imperialism. One critic of the Government was so little anti-imperialist in his sentiments that he wound up a denunciation by saying that the Governor was a disgrace to the British Empire. Always Federation was the cause of all the trouble ...

149. We are not, under our terms of reference, concerned with the underlying causes of the emergency. We have heard many opinions about where the responsibility for it should ultimately lie; it is not part of our task to choose between them. We apprehend, however, that it will be generally agreed that on the facts we have found and in the situation that existed on 3rd March, however it was caused, the Government had either to act or to abdicate; and since with the forces at its disposal the maintenance of order could not be achieved within the ordinary framework of the law, it had to resort to emergency powers. Everyone may not agree about the extent to which it exercised them and the manner in which it did so. It exercised its powers with the object of stamping out Congress wherever it could be found and in the later parts of this report we shall describe the means which were taken to that end ... you will have observed that in some important respects our findings do not confirm the appreciation of the facts set out by the Government in the White Paper. In particular we have not found any detailed plan for massacre and assassination ... ∎

The racial policies of southern African states continued to provide the biggest source of tension within the Commonwealth. During his tour of Africa at the beginning of 1960, Macmillan delivered a stern warning to the South African government, which aroused considerable interest throughout the Commonwealth. But the speech served only to widen the gulf between Britain and the apartheid regime. Only a month later, police firing on a crowd of demonstrators killed dozens of Africans in what became known as the Sharpeville Massacre. Increasing international concern over the violence of the regime continued to strain relations with London until 1961, when South Africa became a republic and withdrew from the Commonwealth. Subsequent ambivalence in the attitude of the British government towards a regime which was coming to be seen as an international leper would continue to provide a source of tension within the Commonwealth for many years.

11.13 Harold Macmillan, speech to both Houses of the Parliament of the Union of South Africa, Cape Town, 3 February 1960 (quoted in A.N. Porter and A.J. Stockwell, *British Imperial Policy and Decolonization, 1938–64. Vol. 2: 1951–64*, Basingstoke, Macmillan, 1989, pp. 524–8).

■ ...

Sir, as I have travelled round the Union I have found everywhere, as I expected, a deep preoccupation with what is happening in the rest of the African continent. I understand and sympathise with your interest in these events, and your anxiety about them. Ever since the break-up of the Roman Empire one of the constant facts of political life in Europe has been the emergence of independent nations. They have come into existence over the centuries in different forms, with different kinds of Government, but all have been inspired by a deep, keen feeling of nationalism which has grown as the nations have grown.

In the twentieth century and especially since the end of the war, the processes which gave birth to the nation states of Europe have been repeated all over the world. We have seen the awakening of national consciousness in peoples who have for centuries lived in dependence upon some other power. Fifteen years ago this movement spread through Asia. Many countries there of different races and civilisations pressed their claim to an independent national life. Today the same thing is happening in Africa and the most striking of all the impressions I have formed since I left London a month ago is of the strength of this African national consciousness. In different places it takes different forms but it is happening everywhere. The wind of change is blowing through this continent and, whether we like it or not, this growth of national consciousness is a political fact. We must all accept it as a fact, and our national policies must take account of it.

... I sincerely believe that if we cannot do so we may imperil the precarious balance between the East and West on which the peace of the world depends ... As I see it the great issue in this second half of the twentieth century is whether the uncommitted peoples of Asia and Africa will swing to the East or to the West. Will they be drawn into the Communist camp? Or will the great experiments of self-government that are now being made in Asia and Africa, especially within the Commonwealth, prove so successful, and by their example so compelling, that the balance will come down in favour of freedom and order and justice? ...

As a fellow member of the Commonwealth it is our earnest desire to give South Africa our support and encouragement, but I hope you will not mind my saying frankly that there are some aspects of your policies which make it impossible for us to do this without being false to our own deep convictions about the political destinies of free men to which in our own territories we are trying to give effect. I think we ought, as friends, to face together, without seeking to apportion credit or blame the fact that in the world of today this difference of outlook lies between us ... ∎

Foreign Policy under Labour

Given the Labour Party's determination to effect reform in domestic policy, it is perhaps surprising that foreign policy under the Wilson premiership of 1964–70 was cautious, with few indications of fresh thinking on Britain's overseas role. In spite of enthusiasm on the left for a more radical foreign policy agenda, Wilson's government proceeded cautiously.

Wilson's first major speech on foreign affairs in the House of Commons after the election was careful to stress his government's determination to preserve the east-of-Suez policy pursued under Macmillan, and confirmed the continued centrality of the Atlantic Alliance.

11.14 **Harold Wilson, speech to the House of Commons on foreign affairs, 16 December 1964 (*Hansard*, 5th ser., 704: 417–43).**

∎ ...

The House will agree that recent developments in world affairs require all of us to re-examine the lines of policy on which we and our allies have been working, to restate our objectives, to determine our priorities and chart the course which may well determine our policy for the next 10 years not only in Britain or in the Alliance, but in the world ...

There has been an evolution in Soviet thinking on war and co-existence, which we have debated in past debates. The Chinese have exploded a nuclear device. The United Nations has more than doubled in size as the Colonial empires have passed into history. We now have a situation in which Africa has more votes in the General Assembly than any other Continent ...

I think that the objectives for which we are all working in world affairs are clear, and I do not believe there will be much controversy about them. We have to find means of strengthening our relations with our Allies and with our Commonwealth partners, reconciling the divisive trends that have recently developed ...

In our policies within the Alliance and outside it we must do everything in our power to enable us to take advantage of the opportunities which I believe now present themselves for reducing tension between East and West ...

We must ensure that the most effective machinery is created for stopping small wars from escalating into big ones, for quarantining small outbreaks of militarism or subversion, and we must be prepared to bring new thinking to the strengthening of the United Nations peace-keeping machinery. Because of Britain's world role we have to examine and, wherever necessary, strengthen our own ability to contribute to this task, whether by our own contributions to peace keeping within the United Nations or by our own direct actions ...

The problem we are facing derives from the fact that alone in the world – apart from the United States and the USSR – we are trying to maintain three roles. There is the strategic nuclear role. There is our conventional role within NATO, our commitment to the defence of Europe, to which we are committed by interest and by treaty. And there is our world role, one which no one in this House or indeed in the country, will wish us to give up or call in question ...

We should be abdicating from what I regard as our duty to the Commonwealth and to world peace and we should be abdicating from any hope of real influence in the world, if we were to think that this role could be abandoned. Indeed, in its fulfilment it may well be necessary, in certain respects, to develop our strength, but in the way we do it and in the detailed control of expenditure, we have to apply imaginatively and ruthlessly the principles of cost-effectiveness and value for money ...

I want to make it quite clear that whatever we may do in the field of cost-effectiveness, value for money and a stringent review of expenditure, we cannot afford to relinquish our world role – our role which, for shorthand purposes, is sometimes called our 'east of Suez' role, though this particular phrase, however convenient, lacks geographical accuracy ...

So when we argue about our right to a central place, whether in the Alliance, whether in the United Nations, whether in world affairs generally, about our influence, about our presence at the top table and all the rest of it, let us recognise that our rights depend on this worldwide role, that it is a distinctive role and that no one else can do it ...

Defence is taking too big a share of our real resources in terms of foreign exchange, scarce types of manpower and load on the most advanced industries ...

Every one of us realise, facing the kind of economic problems we have been facing, the need to redeploy some of this into the civil field – above all, into export industries ...

... that is why we have pressed for acceptance of the idea of joint R and D projects between Britain and the United States ... Some joint research projects of this kind could be extremely beneficial, and could not only save us money but save the Americans money as well ...

... Our approach to these issues at a time of great fluidity in foreign affairs and in defence will, as I have said, govern the pattern of world affairs for a decade and perhaps more than a decade ahead. I think the House will agree that we find the nature of these problems challenging, presenting all the nations of the world with an unrivalled opportunity to move in security to disarmament and peace. I do not believe that at any time since the war Britain has been presented by the conjuncture of world events with such a great opportunity to play her full part in this most important of all tasks. It is the firm intention of Her Majesty's Government, as I am sure it will be of the whole House, to see that we seize this opportunity and in so doing exercise an influence – an influence for good and an influence for peace greater even than at any time in our history. ■

The withdrawal from a world role was, therefore, not planned by the Labour government, but rather forced upon the Cabinet by continuing economic pressure. In Labour's first two years of office Denis Healey, Minister of Defence, attempted to save money through rationalisation and the cancellation of weapons programmes such as the TSR-2 low-level bomber; but these changes were not accompanied by a reduction of commitments abroad until the July 1966 sterling crisis, which finally began the process of review which would lead to a withdrawal from east of Suez. The supplementary defence white paper of 1967 was the first public admission that Britain's retreat from a world role had now become inevitable.

11.15 *Supplementary Statement on Defence Policy 1967*, **July 1967 (London: HMSO, Cmnd 3357, PP 1966–7, LIII, pp. 2–5).**

■   EUROPE

1. The security of Britain still depends above all on the prevention of war in Europe. We, therefore, regard it as essential to maintain both the military and the political solidarity of the North Atlantic Treaty Organisation. For this purpose, we must continue to make a substantial contribution to NATO's forces in order to play our part in the defence of Europe and to maintain the necessary balance within the Western alliance. This contribution will become even more important as we develop closer political and economic ties between Britain and her European neighbours ...

4. For some time we have argued that, since a Soviet attack in Europe is unlikely in present circumstances and we should probably receive ample warning of any change in those circumstances, some of the forces required

in Germany in an emergency could be held elsewhere in peacetime, provided that they could be returned promptly if a crisis occurred. We have therefore proposed to our allies in NATO and WEU that we should redeploy to the United Kingdom early in 1968 one brigade of BAOR and one squadron of RAF, Germany ...

OUTSIDE EUROPE

...

3. We explained in the Statement on the Defence Estimates 1966 (Cmnd 2901) that we would not undertake major operations of war, except in co-operation with allies, and would make our commitments to our friends dependent on the provision in time of whatever facilities we needed on the spot ... While the visible presence of even small forces – not necessarily dependent on large and expensive base facilities – may be a good deterrent, it will be more economical to rely mainly on sending forces from Britain in a crisis.

4. We have therefore revised our plans for deployment outside Europe so as to enable major reductions to be made in the size and cost of our forces as a whole ...

5. We have already announced, and gone some way to implement, plans to reduce forces in the Mediterranean, the South Atlantic and the Caribbean. We have also declared our intention to withdraw from South Arabia and the Aden base in January 1968 ...

6. In the Far East, we have decided to reach a reduction of about half the forces deployed in Singapore and Malaysia during 1970–71. The total number of men and women now working in or for the Services in Singapore and Malaysia is roughly 80,000 ... We estimate that by April 1968 the total will fall to about 70,000 ... We expect that, between April 1968 and 1970–71, the numbers in Singapore and Malaysia will drop by a further 30,000. This will leave a total of about 40,000, of which about half will be civilians ...

7. In parallel with these reductions, we intend to change our Far East commitments. We shall continue to honour our obligations under SEATO, but the forces assigned to specific SEATO plans will be progressively altered in nature and size ...

8. We cannot plan the period beyond 1970–71 in the same detail. The reductions over the next few years will be considerable: we are determined that they will take place in an orderly manner, which will enable our Commonwealth partners to adjust their plans, and will allow Singapore and Malaysia to make the necessary economic transition as smoothly as possible. We plan to withdraw altogether from our bases in Singapore and Malaysia in the middle 1970s; the precise timing of our eventual withdrawal will depend on progress made in achieving a new basis for stability in South East Asia and in resolving other problems in the Far East ... ∎

The devaluation crisis of November 1967 made the process of retrenchment even more urgent, as the government was pledged to impose further sharp reductions in public expenditure. This led to a speeding up of the timetable for withdrawal; in January 1968 Wilson announced these further defence cuts to the House of Commons.

11.16 Harold Wilson, statement to the House of Commons on withdrawal east of Suez, 16 January 1968 (*Hansard*, 5th ser., 756: 1577–85).

■ **The Prime Minister (Mr Harold Wilson):** With permission, Mr Speaker, I should like to make a statement.

1. On 18th December I informed the House that the government were engaged in a major review of every field of public expenditure as one of the measures necessary to achieve a progressive and massive shift of resources from home consumption, public and private, to the requirements of exports, import replacement and productive investment …

11. I begin with defence expenditure, the whole of which has been reviewed against the background of our commitments and alliances. Our decisions have been based on two main principles. First, the House will recognise that it is not only in our own interests but in those of our friends and allies for this country to strengthen its economic base quickly and decisively. There is no military strength whether for Britain or for our alliances except on the basis of economic strength; and it is on this basis that we best ensure the security of this country. We therefore intend to make to the alliances of which we are members a contribution related to our economic capability while recognising that our security lies fundamentally in Europe and must be based on the North Atlantic alliance. Second, reductions in capability, whether in terms of manpower or equipment, must follow and be based on a review of the commitments the Services are required to undertake. Defence must be related to the requirements of foreign policy, but it must not be asked in the name of foreign policy to undertake commitments beyond its capability. Major foreign policy decisions, therefore, are a prior requirement of economies in defence expenditure; and in taking these decisions we have to come to terms with our role in the world. It is not only at home that, these past years, we have been living beyond our means. Given the right decisions, above all given the full assertion of our economic strength, our real influence and power for peace will be strengthened by realistic priorities.

12. We have accordingly decided to accelerate the withdrawal of our forces from their stations in the Far East … and to withdraw them by the end of 1971. We have also decided to withdraw our forces from the Persian Gulf by the same date. The broad effect is that, apart from our remaining Dependencies and certain other necessary exceptions, we shall by that date not be maintaining military bases outside Europe and the Mediterranean.

13. Again, by that date, we shall have withdrawn our forces from Malaysia

and Singapore. We have told both Governments that we do not thereafter plan to retain a special military capability for use in the area. But we have assured them both, and our other Commonwealth partners and allies concerned, that we shall retain a general capability based in Europe – including the United Kingdom – which can be deployed overseas as, in our judgment, circumstances demand, including support for United Nations operations … Meanwhile, if our Commonwealth partners so desire and mutually satisfactory arrangements can be made, we would be prepared to assist them in establishing a future joint air defence system for Malaysia and Singapore and in training personnel to operate it …

14. We shall make an early reduction in the number of aircraft based in Cyprus while maintaining our membership of CENTO.

15. On the Gulf, we have indicated to the Governments concerned that our basic interest in the prosperity and security of the area remains; and, as I have said, the capability we shall be maintaining here will be available for deployment wherever, in our judgment, this is right having regard to the forces available …

18. These decisions will entail major changes in the role, size and shape of the forces, in the nature and scale of the equipment which they will require, and in the supporting facilities which are necessary …

20. *The Navy.* The aircraft carrier force will be phased out as soon as our withdrawal from Malaysia, Singapore and the Gulf has been completed. There will also be reductions in the rate of new naval construction, for example in the nuclear-powered Hunter/Killer submarines.

21. *The Army.* There will be a considerable increase in the rate of rundown of the Army and in the disbandment or amalgamation of major units …

22. *The Royal Air Force.* We have decided to cancel the order for 50 F111 aircraft. Further study is being given to the consequences of this decision on the future equipment of the Royal Air Force. Leaving out of account the results of this study, the cancellation of the F111 is estimated to yield total savings on the Defence budget of about £400 million between now and 1977–78 … ■

The Western Alliance

Wilson placed as much emphasis on the continuation of good Anglo-American relations as he did on the maintenance of Britain's world role. But escalating US involvement in the Vietnam War made smooth relations between the two countries difficult. While few members of the government approved of US policy in South-East Asia, it was vital for the future of the 'special relationship' to at least give the appearance of support.

Politically, it remained out of the question for the British government to send troops to fight alongside the Americans in Vietnam, given the level of domestic protest about even the diplomatic support on offer. The following cartoon, by Garland, illustrates the irony of an alliance between the right-wing Conservative MP Enoch Powell – long opposed to the Atlantic partnership – and student protest.

11.17 N. Garland, 'Excuse me – have I come to the right place?', *Daily Telegraph* **cartoon, 29 March 1966 (University of Kent Cartoon Archives).**

The retreat from east of Suez meant that in future British defence policy would be cen-tred on NATO and the defence of Western Europe. The second bid for EEC membership, discussed below, underlined Britain's transition from world power to European power. Moreover, de Gaulle's decision of 1966 to withdraw French military forces from NATO, and the United States' need to maximise its fighting forces in Vietnam, gave Wilson's Minister of Defence, Denis Healey, the opportunity to take a leading role in the reshap-ing of NATO strategy which occurred in the years following the Cuban missile crisis of 1962. In his memoirs, Healey explains the importance of those changes.

11.18 Denis Healey, *The Time of My Life*, **London, Penguin, 1989, pp. 307–10.**

■ … Despite our differences of temperament and experience, McNamara and I worked well together and became friends for life …

We were both anxious to find some way of organising more effective consultation between America and her allies on nuclear policy, and finally established a Nuclear Planning Group. McNamara was determined that the defence ministers themselves should understand the problems, rather than leave them to their officials; he insisted on designing a table just large enough for the ministers to sit around elbow to elbow, with no more than two officials behind each. It worked well enough so long as at least one European minister was prepared to take on the American on equal terms. Unfortunately ... most Continental governments regarded the defence ministry as unworthy of an able politician, and tended to appoint figures of little political influence. So I had to carry a disproportionate share of the European burden ...

For most of the Europeans, NATO was worthless unless it could prevent another war; they were not interested in fighting one. They thought that for Europe, at least, a conventional conflict would be as bad as a nuclear one; they also believed that nuclear weapons could deter any sort of war, while conventional weapons could not, at least in Europe. They could scarcely fail to be aware that as the Soviet Union approached nuclear parity with the United States, America's readiness to use nuclear weapons on their behalf would become less certain ...

The Americans were equally convinced that they could no longer accept an unlimited liability for the nuclear defence of Europe, and that nuclear deterrence was no protection against a conflict which might start by accident – as could have happened over Cuba or Berlin. So the stage was set for a period of transatlantic bargaining, in which Washington would implicitly threaten to remove its nuclear umbrella, perhaps by withdrawing some of its troops so as to reduce its stake in Europe's security, while Europe would increase its conventional contribution to the alliance, so as to raise the nuclear threshold and thus reduce America's nuclear liability ...

In any case, I had never believed that the Soviet Union was bent on the military conquest of Western Europe since it had failed to challenge the NATO airlift to West Berlin in 1950. And I was impressed by the fact that Russia became more, not less, cautious in challenging the West as its own nuclear forces increased. On the other hand, the risings in East Berlin and Hungary, like that which was to come in Czechoslovakia, showed that Russia might use force to maintain its control of Eastern Europe; once fighting started there, it might conceivably slop over the Iron Curtain and involve the West. So NATO did need conventional forces at least large enough to control such incidents ...

On March 7th, 1966 de Gaulle took France out of NATO and expelled all NATO's forces and headquarters from France, while remaining a member of the alliance for political purposes. From this moment on, I saw it as my role to act as a bridge between McNamara, who, as he now admits, really wanted NATO to abandon the first use of nuclear weapons altogether, and the Germans, who really wanted to go back to the strategy of massive nuclear retaliation, triggered by a tripwire on their Eastern frontier. We reached the necessary compromise on May 9th, 1967; on January 16th, 1968 NATO formally replaced the strategy of Massive Retaliation with the strategy of Flexible Response ... ▪

The second bid for Europe

The Labour Party had shown little enthusiasm for the Common Market since 1958; indeed, Hugh Gaitskell had opposed the first application for membership. Wilson seemed to pursue a similar line in the first two years of his premiership, although he did not rule out entry provided problems such as Commonwealth imports could be negotiated satisfactorily.

The combination of Britain's poor economic performance, strains with the United States over Vietnam, division in the Commonwealth, and increasing support for the idea of EEC membership among the public and the business community gradually persuaded Wilson to review his policy on Europe. After he undertook a tour of the European capitals at the beginning of 1967, the Cabinet agreed, with a sizeable minority against, to make a second application to the Community. This was announced at the beginning of May. De Gaulle quickly made clear his intention to use his veto for a second time. The British application was not withdrawn, however, and after the President's resignation in 1969 the way was open for a new round of negotiations. In document 11.19 Richard Crossman describes the shift of Cabinet opinion which preceded the decision to apply.

11.19 **Richard Crossman, diary, 30 April 1967 (in Richard Crossman, *The Diaries of a Cabinet Minister. Vol. 2: Lord President of the Council and Leader of the House of Commons, 1966–68*, London, Hamish Hamilton and Cape, 1976, pp. 334–6).**

▪ ... [John Silkin, the Chief Whip, and I] drove up to London together and had an excellent dinner in Chelsea to discuss our impressions [of the Cabinet meeting at Chequers which had taken place earlier in the day]. First of all what changes had occurred since last November? Certainly the biggest change was the attitude of the Prime Minister. After the last Chequers conference he had told me that he would be going round Europe with George Brown to make sure that he didn't commit us to anything and to make sure that the tour was nothing more than a probe. Well, he certainly converted himself during those visits to the six capitals and at Chequers this time he was as enthusiastic as George Brown. Indeed, apart from Wedgy Benn he's the only convert.

But although there have been very few conversions there's been a very big shift in opinion in two respects. In the first place the economic advantages which Common Marketeers used to point out are now seen to be acute economic difficulties in the short run. Not even the most ardent marketeer now denies that entry in our present economic plight will expose the pound to the gravest dangers and that there'll have to be one devaluation if not two. It would also expose us to even greater deflationary pressure unless we can get growth going before we go in. So we all see now that the Common Market in the short run is far less economically attractive and even Roy Jenkins admits that in the first three or four years we shall lose but not gain – it's only after we're in, after our economy has been reorganized, that there's a chance of profiting from membership.

The other shift in opinion relates to our own economy. Those who are in charge – Michael Stewart, George Brown, Harold Wilson, Jim Callaghan – all now feel that the attempt to have a socialist national plan for the British Isles keeps us balanced on such a terribly tight rope that it really has got to be abandoned and that of course is the main reason why they favour entry into the Market. Today Barbara made a tremendous speech saying that entry would transform our socialism and make us abandon all our plans. In a sense she's completely right. If anybody wanted, apart from myself, Britain to be a socialist offshore island, entry to the Market would mean the abandonment of that ideal. Up to the July freeze it was still possible to believe that we in the Wilson Government would strip ourselves of the sterling area, withdraw from east of Suez, and take the Swedish line of socialism. We could have done that a year ago but now it is felt by almost everyone that it's too late ...

I'm afraid John Silkin didn't say very much at dinner that evening – it consisted mostly of me dashing off my impressions. But there's one of his impressions which I mustn't forget. In the discussion he had given a carefully considered calculation of the amount of resistance Harold would have to expect in the Parliamentary Party which he didn't think would exceed more than fifty or so. At dinner he told me that he was convinced that Harold had learnt everything he needed from the meeting. He knew that he now had an overwhelming majority ready to permit him not merely to seek to enter the Market but to make a genuine bid to get in as soon as possible. ■

The problem of southern Africa

In Commonwealth affairs the most intractable difficulties of the Wilson years were those regarding southern Africa. The problem was to reconcile moral objections within Britain and the Commonwealth to segregationist policies and white domination, with the economic imperative of good relations with regimes in Rhodesia and South Africa, which were important markets for British exports.

White Rhodesian opinion became increasingly extreme with the collapse of the Central African Federation. After several years of speculation it had become clear by the beginning of 1965 that a unilateral declaration of independence was imminent. Wilson's attempts to find a compromise solution, involving power sharing between white Rhodesians and black African nationalists, met with little interest on the part of Ian Smith's government. When Smith proceeded with his 'UDI' in November 1965 the British government determined not to intervene with force but to impose gradual economic sanctions, with continued efforts to find a negotiated solution. However, Wilson's confidence that the dispute could be settled quickly was unfounded. By the end of the decade, a solution appeared remote.

11.20 Harold Wilson, speech to the House of Commons on Rhodesia, 11 November 1965 (*Hansard*, 5th ser., 720: 349–61).

■ ... The House will have heard with deep sadness of the illegal declaration of independence by the men who until that declaration constituted the Government of Rhodesia.

The House is aware from statements made in this Chamber by the previous British Government and the present one of the long record of discussions aimed at agreement on independence to be conferred by the only legal authority capable of granting independence, by this Parliament acting on legislation introduced by the British Government. I do not intend to retrace the course of those negotiations which have now continued over a period of three years, but I must repeat that at every point over those three years successive British Governments have warned the Rhodesians in the strongest terms ...

The British Government are in close touch with all other Commonwealth Governments about the consequences of this illegal act and about the measures we should take. The British Government will, of course, have no dealings with the rebel regime. The British High Commissioner is being withdrawn and the Southern Rhodesian High Commissioner in London has been asked to leave. Exports of arms, including spares, have, of course, been stopped. All British aid will cease. Rhodesia has been removed from the sterling area. Special exchange control restrictions will be applied. Exports of United Kingdom capital to Rhodesia will not be allowed. Rhodesia will no longer be allowed access to the London capital market.

Our Export Credits Guarantee Department will give no further cover for exports to Rhodesia. The Ottawa Agreement of 1932 which governs our trading relations with Rhodesia is suspended. Rhodesia will be suspended forthwith from the Commonwealth Preference Area and her goods will no longer receive preferential treatment on entering the United Kingdom. There will be a ban on further purchases of tobacco from Southern Rhodesia. We propose to suspend the Commonwealth Sugar Agreement in its relation to Rhodesia and to ban further purchases of Rhodesian sugar. We shall not recognise passports issued or renewed by the illegal Southern Rhodesian regime. A further statement will be made on citizenship questions.

We shall bring before Parliament on Monday a general Enabling bill to deal with this situation. It will, first of all, declare that Rhodesia remains part of Her Majesty's Dominions and that the Government and Parliament of the United Kingdom continue to have responsibility for it. It will go on to give power to make Orders in Council, to enable us to carry through the policy I have stated ...

I think that the solution of this problem is not one to be dealt with by military intervention unless, of course, our troops are asked for to preserve law and order and to avert a tragic action, subversion, murder and so on. But we do not contemplate, as I have made very clear, any national action, and may I say any international action, for the purpose of coercing even [*sic*] the illegal Government of Rhodesia into a Constitutional posture ... ■

South Africa proved to be, if anything, an even greater source of tension than Rhodesia within the Cabinet. When in 1967 several ministers became convinced of the advantages of selling arms to South Africa in view of the need to secure large export orders at home, the resulting dispute was hard fought. In document 11.21 Barbara Castle records the week in which Labour's left wing was able, with difficulty, to maintain the principle of no arms sales to the apartheid regime.

11.21 **Barbara Castle, diary, December 1967 (in Barbara Castle, *The Castle Diaries, 1964–70*, London, Weidenfeld & Nicolson, 1984, pp. 336–427).**

■ *Tuesday, 12 December*

... On my return home I found the arms for South Africa issue had blown up to enormous heights. Apparently Jim [Callaghan] dined at the House last night privately with the Under 40 group of Labour MPs and let his hair down about what he thought we needed to do to put the economy right. An interesting list: 1) drop the Industrial Expansion Bill ...; 2) freeze wages for eighteen months; and 3) reconsider our policy on arms for South Africa. All those present, whether from left or right, streamed out in consternation and went straight to see John Silkin to say they wanted to table a Motion. Since this merely endorsed the Government's present policy of an arms embargo, John gave it the OK. Seventy names were down in no time. We really shall have a row about this in Cabinet ...

Wednesday, 13 December

... In the middle of the afternoon I received an urgent message to go and see the PM. Wondering whatever could be in the air, I arrived at his room at the House. 'Ah, little Barbara,' said Harold genially ... 'I know you never leak but perhaps you can be persuaded to in a good cause. Barbara, I'm in a real spot over South Africa ... At OPD last Friday George [Brown] and Denis [Healey] fought for lifting the embargo and they got a hell of a lot of support ... So we agreed it should go to Cabinet, but not until a month's time. But the Party is in a terrific state and I intend to force a decision tomorrow.' ...

Friday, 15 December

… victory overall seemed certain. During the discussion a number of people had assumed that, in view of the alarm that had been aroused in the Party, it would now be impossible to go ahead with lifting the embargo: Dick [Crossman] himself deplored that our 'options' had been closed. But we reckoned without George. He proceeded to argue his case for accepting the South African request as though there had never been a murmur of protest from the Party. We had in front of us the paper that had been in front of OPD, pointing out that South Africa mainly wanted naval equipment (they wanted helicopters, too, but the paper reluctantly concluded that public opinion wouldn't stand for that). George argued passionately that the order would be worth £100m without spares, and if we did not accept it our civil trade would be at risk. In our present economic situation we couldn't afford to turn the order down and he was sure the Party would accept that if it was explained to them. This wasn't a moral issue: he hated apartheid as much as anyone, but these were not weapons of suppression and if we didn't deliver them someone else would, etc. Healey backed him up to the hilt. Anyway, why were we being hypocrites? We had not been applying the embargo for some time: we had sold His Excellency ammunition, Wasp helicopters and replacement aeroplanes since 1964.

One Minister after another weighed in in support …

Monday, 18 December

To my delight we were all suddenly summoned to an unexpected Cabinet meeting at 11 am – only item: arms for South Africa. So Harold is going to fight! … At the meeting Harold lost no time in coming to the point – and I have never seen him so grim and white, whether from fear or deliberate anger it was difficult to tell. For twenty minutes he dilated on the press stories … clearly coming from within the Cabinet. But he must point out that it was not just his position that was at stake, but the position of the government. He had a right to demand that Cabinet issue a statement repudiating the reports … Jim, I suppose, can't see Harold being deposed to make him king, so he was the first to say he had changed his mind: the events of the weekend convinced him that a holding statement could not now be made this afternoon, that we must reach a decision this morning and that the only possible decision now was to stick to the embargo. He was backed by Patrick [Gordon Walker] and, while George and Denis sat utterly silent, one person after another said that the only issue now was the position of the Prime Minister. The credibility of the Government depended on his credibility and the Cabinet must be ready to restore it. And so it was agreed. The statement that afternoon should include a categoric decision: no arms for South Africa …

Great moment for Harold in the House when he reached the crucial paragraph on South Africa. Our boys are utterly delighted and relieved. ■

List of Documents

4.8　　Stafford Cripps, memorandum on the dollar situation, 22 June 1949.
4.9　　Chart: Britain's balance of payments, 1945–51.
4.10　Herbert Morrison, speech to the House of Commons, 19 November 1945.
4.11　Walter Citrine on public ownership, in *Two Careers*, 1967.
4.12　Harold Wilson, speech to the House of Commons, 5 November 1948.
4.13　Sir Edwin Plowden on economic planning, in *An Industrialist in the Treasury: The Postwar Years*, 1989.
4.14　George Isaacs, *Statement on Economic Considerations Affecting Relations between Employers and Workers*, January 1947.
4.15　Charts: Living standards and industrial relations, 1939–51.
4.16　Cartoon: L.G. Illingworth, 'No visible means of support', *Punch*, 14 March 1951.
4.17　Michael Stewart, recollections of the National Insurance Act, in *Life and Labour: An Autobiography*, 1980.
4.18　Aneurin Bevan, speech to the House of Commons, 9 February 1948.
4.19　Chart: Gross expenditure on the National Health Service, 1948–51.
4.20　Sir Cyril Jones, report on the finances of the National Health Service, 15 July 1950.

5.1　　Clement Attlee, letter to Winston Churchill, 1 August 1945.
5.2　　Sir Frank Roberts, dispatch to the Foreign Office, 14 March 1946.
5.3　　Winston Churchill, 'Iron Curtain speech', 5 March 1946.
5.4　　Clement Attlee, minute to Ernest Bevin, 5 January 1947.
5.5　　Meeting of ministers to decide on construction of British atom bomb, 8 January 1947.
5.6　　Ernest Bevin, memorandum, 'The threat to Western civilisation', 3 March 1948.
5.7　　Cabinet discussion on India, 10 December 1946.
5.8　　Ernest Bevin, memorandum on withdrawal from Palestine, 18 September 1947.
5.9　　Arthur Creech Jones, 'British colonial policy with particular reference to Africa', 1951.
5.10　Ernest Bevin, memorandum on European policy, 18 October 1949.
5.11　Cabinet discussion on the Schuman Plan, 2 June 1950.
5.12　Chiefs of Staff report, 'Defence policy and global strategy', 7 June 1950.
5.13　Sir Pierson Dixon, memorandum, 9 April 1951.
5.14　Cabinet discussion on defence spending, 18 December 1950.
5.15　Chart: Defence spending, 1945–51.
5.16　Sir Roger Makins, memorandum, 'Some notes on British foreign policy', 11 August 1951.

6.1　　R.A. Butler, Cabinet memorandum on the economic position, 31 October 1951.
6.2　　R.A. Butler, draft memorandum on the 'ROBOT' scheme, 26 February 1952.
6.3　　Henry Channon, diary, March 1952.
6.4　　Cartoon: Giles, 'I suppose you realise that now they can get steaks like foreigners, British sportsmen have no excuse for not winning everything', *Daily Express*, 6 July 1954.
6.5　　Chart: Housing provision, 1951–64.
6.6　　*Report of the Committee of Enquiry into the Cost of the National Health Service* (Guillebaud Report), January 1956.
6.7　　R.A. Butler, speech to the party conference, Blackpool, 7 October 1954.
6.8　　Chart: The growth of consumerism, 1952–63.
6.9　　Harold Macmillan, speech at Bedford, 20 July 1957.
6.10　C.A.R. Crosland, *The Future of Socialism*, 1956.
6.11　Labour Party, *Industry and Society*, 1957.
6.12　Stuart Hall, 'Crosland territory', *New Left Review*, January and February 1960.
6.13　Cartoon: Philip Zec, *Daily Herald*, 8 April 1959.
6.14　R.A. Butler, *The Art of Memory*, 1982.

10.5   Tony Benn, diary, Tuesday 21 June 1966.
10.6   Richard Crossman, diary, 24 July 1966.
10.7   *The Civil Service* (Fulton Report), June 1968.
10.8   Witness seminar, the Redcliffe-Maud Report, February 1989.
10.9   John Boyd-Carpenter, speech to the House of Commons on the Representation of the People Bill, 18 November 1968.
10.10   Welsh Language Act, 1967.
10.11   Prince Charles, response to investiture as Prince of Wales, 1 July 1969.
10.12   Roy Jenkins, speech to the House of Commons on Northern Ireland, 25 October 1967.
10.13   Bernadette Devlin, maiden speech in the House of Commons, 22 April 1969.
10.14   Cartoon: Garland, *Daily Telegraph*, 26 February 1969.
10.15   The Downing Street Declaration, 19 August 1969.
10.16   Race Relations Act 1965.
10.17   W.W. Daniel, *Racial Discrimination in England*, 1968.
10.18   J. Enoch Powell, speech to the West Midlands Area Conservative Political Centre at the Midland Hotel, Birmingham, 20 April 1968.
10.19   Richard Crossman, diary, 13 February 1968.
10.20   Report on the Conservatives' general election campaign, *The Times*, 2 February 1970.
10.21   Posters: general election campaign, 1970.

11.1   HM Government, *Defence: Outline of Future Policy*, April 1957.
11.2   Chart: British defence expenditure, 1957–70.
11.3   Chart: Size of armed forces, 1957–70.
11.4   *Amendment to the Agreement between the Government of the United Kingdom of Great Britain and Northern Ireland and the Government of the United States of America for Co-operation on the Uses of Atomic Energy for Mutual Defence Purposes of July 3, 1958*, 7 May 1959.
11.5   Photograph: The Aldermaston march, 1958.
11.6   Michael Foot, speech on unilateralism, October 1960.
11.7   Cabinet minutes, discussion of the Nassau decisions, 21 December 1962.
11.8   Harold Macmillan, 'Grand design' December 1960.
11.9   Sir Frank Lee, 'Association with the European Community', Cabinet memorandum, 6 July 1960.
11.10   'Summary of General de Gaulle's press conference of January 14', January 1963.
11.11   Harold Macmillan, 'The balance sheet of empire', minute to the Lord President of the Council, 28 January 1957.
11.12   *Report of the Nyasaland Commission of Inquiry*, July 1959.
11.13   Harold Macmillan, speech to both Houses of the Parliament of the Union of South Africa, Cape Town, 3 February 1960.
11.14   Harold Wilson, speech to the House of Commons on foreign affairs, 16 December 1964.
11.15   *Supplementary Statement on Defence Policy 1967*, July 1967.
11.16   Harold Wilson, statement to the House of Commons on withdrawal east of Suez, 16 January 1968.
11.17   Cartoon: N. Garland, 'Excuse me – have I come to the right place?', *Daily Telegraph* 29 March 1966.
11.18   Denis Healey, *The Time of My Life*, 1989.
11.19   Richard Crossman, diary, 30 April 1967.
11.20   Harold Wilson, speech to the House of Commons on Rhodesia, 11 November 1965.
11.21   Barbara Castle, diary, December 1967.

Index